MW00738009

Ukraine's Quest
for Identity

Ukraine's Quest for Identity

Embracing Cultural Hybridity in Literary Imagination, 1991–2011

Maria G. Rewakowicz

LEXINGTON BOOKS
Lanham • Boulder • New York • London

Published by Lexington Books

An imprint of The Rowman & Littlefield Publishing Group, Inc.
4501 Forbes Boulevard, Suite 200, Lanham, Maryland 20706
www.rowman.com

Unit A, Whitacre Mews, 26-34 Stannary Street, London SE11 4AB

British Library Cataloguing in Publication Information Available

Library of Congress Cataloging-in-Publication Data

ISBN: 978-1-4985-3881-7 (cloth: alk. paper)
ISBN: 978-1-4985-3882-4 (Electronic)

♾™ The paper used in this publication meets the minimum requirements of American National Standard for Information Sciences—Permanence of Paper for Printed Library Materials, ANSI/NISO Z39.48-1992.

Printed in the United States of America

Contents

Preface

This study's pathway from an initial project proposal for a research scholarship at the Kennan Institute in Washington, DC, back in 2003, to its final realization as a published monograph has been unusually long but nonetheless gratifying. Current affairs, be it of political or cultural nature, demand as a rule an immediate reaction if one's goal is having a contemporaneous critical impact. For a scholar of any contemporary literature, sooner or later there comes a moment of deciding at what point to stop and how to provide a meaningful framework for literary phenomena continuously unfolding. For me that moment came with the celebration of Ukraine's twentieth anniversary of independence in 2011. However, as I embarked on writing, I soon realized that the first two decades after independence in fact constituted a qualitatively different period as compared to what followed, a period that could be characterized as transitional, hybrid, post-Soviet, or even, in some sense, soul-searching. While working on the book I witnessed an enormous political transformation in Ukraine. In 2012, the Ukrainian Parliament's adoption of a controversial law on the principles of state language policy, giving Russian the status of a "regional" language, triggered a wave of protests among the Ukrainian-speaking intelligentsia; and then, in the following year, the government's refusal to sign the Association Agreement with the European Union led to the Revolution of Dignity and war with Russia. To talk about identity formation in this context is qualitatively different from what transpired in this respect during the first two decades after the collapse of the Soviet Union. By the time I finished writing *Ukraine's Quest for Identity: Embracing Cultural Hybridity in Literary Imagination, 1991–2011*, Ukraine managed to celebrate its 25th anniversary of independence despite facing many challenges, and the political situation in the country could not have been more different than when I started writing it back in 2012. Then, the Yanukovych regime increasingly acted as if its rule were to last in perpetuity, and the ensuing politicization of the cultural sphere invariably contributed to the polarization among intellectual elites, causing rifts, growing unease and making everyone feel on edge.

Who could foresee back then that the eruption of the Euromaidan protests in November 2013 would halt Ukraine's straight path toward an authoritarian rule? But the tragic events in early 2014, with so many lives sacrificed in the name of democracy, did just that. The subsequent collapse of the Yanukovych government brought a considerable degree of relief among the democratically minded protesters, but their sense of victory was extremely short-lived. Russia's annexation of Crimea on March 18, 2014, followed by its aggression in the southeast provinces of Ukraine, proved the country's resistance and struggle for national dignity to be extraordinarily costly. And yet, amid all those tragedies, there is arguably a silver lining. Never before the sense of national belonging and pride in one's national identity were as distinctly delineated among Ukrainians as in the aftermath of the Russian Federation's invasion. Two decades of slow, if not occasionally conflicted, muddling through in terms of national soul-searching gave rise, literally overnight, to a strongly felt distinct national identity. The issue of Ukrainian and Russian language usage in Ukraine somewhat receded, because those willing to die for Ukraine's sovereignty represented both Russian- and Ukrainian-speaking fighters—government troops and volunteers alike.

When a country is at war, it might be tempting to dismiss the importance of various manifestations of the arts, including works of literature. However, oftentimes, the opposite is true. The cultural distinctiveness not only helps in alleviating colonial syndromes but also constitutes a rallying cry to coalesce around the cause. And while reflecting and comprehending the impact of new post-2014 realities on creative processes are timely and no doubt needed, this study is limited, as the title so explicitly points out, to the phase of "muddling through," or to the phase of distinctly post-Soviet and transitional dynamics of the first two decades of independence. And even though Ukrainian writers frequently took up the issues of national identity construction during that time, their overall social import was confined to rather narrow segments of Ukrainian society.

The premise of this book is twofold: first, that it is possible to identify the range and nature of post-independence literary texts according to their place within a grid of specific identities; and second, that those texts invariably represent value in the body of a new national literature, impacting the politics of canon formation. This monograph concentrates on major works of literature produced during the first two decades of independence and places them against the background of clearly identifiable contexts such as regionalism, gender issues, language politics, social ills, and popular culture. It also shows that Ukrainian literary politics of that period privileges the plurality and hybridity of national and cultural identities. I explore the reasons behind the tendency toward cultural hybridity and plural identities in the literary imagination by engaging postcolonial discourse and relying on the sociological method, as championed by Pierre Bourdieu, whereby literary production is viewed as socially instituted. Hence, cultural hybridity, identity negotiation, language politics and canon formation, viewed relationally and as constitutive of Ukrainian national literature, are the major themes addressed in the present study.

In many ways, in its quest for identity Ukraine has followed a path similar to other postcolonial societies, the main characteristics of which include a slow transition, hybridity and identities negotiated on the center-periphery axis. It is less evident if a more coherent and/or aggressive governmental cultural policy early on would make any difference. After all, any affirmative action endeavors on the part of the ruling elites beg for compromises and cooperation with the political opposition. And that was in short supply at the time. However, it is also true that producers of Ukrainian cultural goods faced limited opportunities because of institutional weaknesses, namely the fact that those with authority to grant literary value were constantly undermined by the old inefficient system or, even, by their own ideological bias, not to mention that they themselves often held subordinate positions vis-à-vis the field of power (i.e., the government).

Ukraine's Quest for Identity: Embracing Cultural Hybridity in Literary Imagination, 1991–2011 is the first study that looks at the literary process in post-independence Ukraine comprehensively and attempts to draw the connection between literary production and identity construction. The first chapter provides a theoretical framework, focusing especially on the concepts of cultural hybridity and identity. It also examines major premises of postcolonial theory and its proponents, and, at the same time, offers a critique of the most important approaches and schools in Ukrainian literary criticism since independence. Chapter 2 foregrounds the topos of location and a strong sense of territorial identity, demonstrated by a number of contemporary authors from various regions of Ukraine. I argue that the geography of belonging has played a crucial role in Ukrainian literature since 1991, mainly expressed through a tendency among writers to heighten regional differences in their texts, colored by a specific historical conditioning. This chapter, subdivided into three sections, deals respectively with the city as protagonist, the region as protagonist, and with cultural geographies as mapped out by one of the most important authors in contemporary Ukraine: Yuri Andrukhovych.

Chapter 3 offers a panorama of Ukrainian female voices of the post-independence period until 2011, focusing equally on feminist, postfeminist and non-feminist approaches, and elucidating major trends in women's literary discourse in the process. I discuss key works of women authors, grappling with gender and national identity issues, and claim that female literary voices in the post-independence period form an important group, simply because of the sheer amount of talent and preponderance of books published. The fourth chapter provides insights into language issues as reflected in literary practice both in terms of language choice and in terms of attitudes toward language, understood not just as a means of communication but also as a carrier of culture. It concentrates on two opposing ends of the language spectrum as applied in contemporary belles-lettres: on the one hand, works produced by Ukrainian Russophone writers; on the other—authors for whom the Ukrainian language constitutes the essence of their artistic identity and itself becomes a hero of sorts. I insist that the issue of language choice seriously challenges the conceptualization of national literature and invariably affects the politics of canon formation.

It comes as no surprise that social marginalization and social ills during the transitional period after independence become intensely reflected in post-independence belles-lettres. The collapse of the Soviet Union caused a massive paradigm shift in economy, politics and culture, and adjustments to a new reality often entailed people of various social strata turning to crime and substance abuse, at times resulting in illness and/or death. Chapter 5 zeroes in on the issues of social concerns and class distinction, as depicted in the fiction of such authors as Oles Ulianenko, Volodymyr Dibrova, and Yuri Izdryk, among others. These writers turn to the dreary realities of Ukrainian life after independence, including the growing criminal world and people living on the margins of society, in order to underscore the verisimilitude of their oeuvre. The strategies for depicting social fringes vary depending on which literary generation a given writer represents. For example, substance abuse is widespread among the urban youth and is especially thematized in the works of Liubko Deresh, Svitlana Povaliaieva, and Serhiy Zhadan, authors who study the youth counterculture of Lviv, Kyiv and Kharkiv, respectively. Still others, in order to differentiate their protagonists' class and ideology, often turn to language and irony, or parody and pastiche.

Chapter 6 explores the connection between popular literature and national identity construction and argues that popular genres, such as detective stories, thrillers, romances and science fiction, implicitly promote an all-Ukrainian identity, especially since they are trying to appeal to a wider audience, one not necessarily keen on reading works of "highbrow" literature. The power to promote a Ukrainian perspective on historical events, including national traumas, through works of popular literature has been exploited by a number of contemporary authors; arguably, most successfully by Vasyl Shkliar, Mariia Matios and Lina Kostenko. Popular literature written by female writers also advocates the empowerment of women, often by placing them in positions of power. Hence, there is a plethora of texts with professional women playing roles of chief protagonists. All in all, one must admit that the function of Ukrainian popular literature goes well beyond being merely entertaining; it constitutes an important tool to nurture a new sense of national belonging. Finally, the concluding chapter examines major trends and Ukrainian institutions, responsible for literary studies, artistic production and the maintenance of literary value. It attempts to provide a roadmap for the building of a consensus as to what a new national literature should encompass and represent.

This book reflects more than a decade of research into many aspects of Ukrainian post-independence literary production. It would not have been possible without the assistance of various individuals and institutions. My thanks go out to Marian J. Rubchak, Maxim Tarnawsky, Myroslava Tomorug Znayenko, Larissa M.L. Zaleska Onyshkevych, Tamara Hundorova, Halyna Hryn, George G. Grabowicz, Galya Diment, Katarzyna Dziwirek, Vasyl Makhno, Vasyl Lopukh, Ostap Kin, Lorraine Oades, Ana Rewakowicz, Anthony Seaberg, Serhy Yekelchyk and Tania Snihur for their support, advice and interest in my work. Parts of my research were generously supported by a scholarship grant from the Kennan Institute of the Woodrow Wilson International Center for Scholars, Washington, DC (2003–2004); Neporany Fellowship from the Canadian Foundation of Ukrainian Studies, Toronto, ON (2004–2005); Fulbright Research Grant, held at the Taras Shevchenko Institute of Literature, National Academy of Sciences of Ukraine, Kyiv, Ukraine (2009–2010); and three grants from the Shevchenko Scientific Society, New York, NY (2011, 2016–17), drawn from the John and Elizabeth Khlopetsky and Ksenia Kalmuk Funds, respectively. I am grateful to all of the above institutions for providing me with necessary means to conceptualize and develop the project's major themes and approaches. Finally, I want to thank Brian Hill at Lexington Books for embracing my book proposal and bringing it to realization, as well as Eric Kuntzman, his assistant, for patiently answering all my questions and being my guide on the road to its publication.

The present monograph incorporates portions of previously published articles, namely "Women's Literary Discourse and National Identity in Post-Soviet Ukraine," *Harvard Ukrainian Studies* 27 (2004–2005): 195–216 (Chapters 1 and 3). Reprinted with permission. © 2008 by the President and Fellows of Harvard College; "Geography Matters: Regionalism and Identities in Contemporary Ukrainian Prose," *Canadian American Slavic Studies* 44: 1–2 (2010): 82–101 (Chapter 2); and "Difficult Journey: Literature, Literary Canons, and Identities in Post-Soviet Ukraine," *Harvard Ukrainian Studies* 32–33 (2011–2014): 599–610 (Conclusion). Reprinted with permission, © 2015 by the President and Fellows of Harvard College. I am indebted to the editors of Harvard Ukrainian Research Institute and Koninklijke Brill NV, for their reprint permissions.

Finally, unless otherwise indicated, all translations are my own, as are any errors and misinterpretations.

Note on Transliteration

For the most part I use the Library of Congress system of transliteration in the body of this book, however with a few exceptions. The initial IA, IE and IU are rendered as Ya, Ye and Yu, respectively. The soft sign (ь) is omitted in all proper names and Ukrainian surnames with the adjectival endings "s'kyi" or "yi" become correspondingly "sky" and "y." Hence, I use Pashkovsky instead of Pashkovs'kyi, and Dnistrovy instead of Dnistrovyi. There might be a few inconsistencies in the spelling of some male authors' first names, stemming mostly from the way they themselves choose to have it spelled out in English. Therefore, I use Serhiy Zhadan rather than Serhii Zhadan, because this is how this writer is known in his English language publications but in some other cases first names with the similar endings will be spelled Andrii, Anatolii, Valerii, etc. However, I do preserve the Library of Congress system of transliteration without any modification in the notes and bibliography.

Chapter 1

Literature on Edge

Cultural Hybridity, Identities and Reading Strategies

The first two decades of Ukraine's independence can be imagined both in celebratory and faultfinding terms. It depends, of course, on one's positioning and angle of viewing. The Soviet (Russian) Empire, still nostalgically yearned for in some quarters, is invoked as a colonizer and oppressor by those who endured its rule. Elleke Boehmer put it succinctly: "After empire, [...] the history of the colonized needed repair."[1] Achieving national and cultural emancipation lies at the heart of the decolonization process. Moreover, as aptly captured by Jan Pieterse Nederveen and Bhikhu Parekh, it "requires not the restoration of a historically continuous and allegedly pure precolonial heritage, but an imaginative creation of a new form of consciousness and way of life."[2] However, this process for Ukrainians has been anything but smooth and balanced. The issue of national identity construction, contested and reshaped by secular, religious, progressive or reactionary biases, resulted on the one hand in a precarious and unstable political system, and, on the other, in a relatively free interconfessional practice.[3] Politically speaking, post-independence Ukraine has wavered between democratic and authoritarian regimes; culturally and linguistically, it floats on the East-West continuum, alternating between native Ukrainian and metropolitan Russian.

This book represents an attempt to thematize issues emerging from colonial relations and their aftermath, especially as they relate to culture in general, and literature in particular. It examines literary works through the prism of identity construction and relies on the notion of hybridity as conceptualized in postcolonial studies, but also goes beyond that, pointing to numerous theoretical possibilities that this concept might yield when applied to the

1

realities of post-independence Ukraine. A theory of hybridity allures because it is contextual; without considering in which context hybridity functions we will not be able to grasp the social change that occurred after independence. Thus, taking into account a colonial heritage, Ukrainian literary politics of the first two decades appears to privilege the plurality and hybridity of national and cultural identities. In the aftermath of the fall of the Soviet Empire, the issue of the social role of the literary work and its creators has reemerged, primarily in the context of a newly earned freedom and the state's seeming attempts at nationalizing agenda,[4] forcing writers and intellectuals alike to negotiate cultural positions.

While national identity construction is relevant to the project of nation and state building in post-Soviet Ukraine and is at times highlighted in literary works, I also want to analyze the construction and representation of other identities, namely territorial, ethnic, linguistic, class and gender. Using Pierre Bourdieu's theory of the cultural field, perceived as a radical contextualization, and situating it within a framework of postcolonial premises, this book explores implications and reasons behind the tendency toward plural kinds of identity. I am interested in what happens when a studied cultural field is affected by colonialism and/or imperialism. Hence my inquiry conceptualizes the post-independence period as "the space of possibles," using Bourdieu's term,[5] dependent on change in power relations, whereby literary production is viewed as socially instituted and entails both the material production (writer plus text) and the symbolic production (the work's value as determined by social agents—publishers, critics, teachers and readers).[6]

Examining cultural hybridity in its theoretical and practical configurations, I rely on major works of literature produced during the post-independence period and use them as testing sites for identity formation. I contend that it is possible to identify the range and nature of literary texts according to their place within a grid of specific identities and gauge them according to their impact on the politics of canon formation, that is, what should constitute the body of literary texts that can act as a measure of taste and value in a new national literature. In other words, I intend to connect a poetics of hybridity to a politics of identity construction. Literary texts must also be presented against the background of a struggle between those who dominate the literary field economically and politically and those who are endowed with a limited symbolic capital (or, to put it differently, the so-called literary establishment, on the one hand, and emerging authors, on the other).

Both historically and at present, the language question constitutes one of the most complicated factors in Ukraine. Despite the official status of Ukrainian, the Russian language retains its privileged position in certain spheres (for example, entertainment and the media), and its usage prevails, especially in the southeastern and eastern regions of the country. The issue facing literary critics (which till now has not been adequately addressed) is to decide how to arrive at the body of texts that form a national literature: is it a literature written only in Ukrainian or a literature written by Ukrainian citizens regardless of which language is being used. These questions still await resolution, although the overall tendency strives to embrace all cultural production regardless of language involved. For some, cultural hybridity along with identity negotiation facilitate answers to such questions; for others, it only muddles the project of national emancipation. One thing is clear—however one approaches or interrogates postcoloniality, the discourses of cultural hybridity, identity negotiation and language politics seem to figure prominently as strategies for reconfiguring a national continuity. How these discourses affect the constitution of Ukrainian national literature is precisely what I propose to do in this book.

Ukraine in its quest for identity follows a path that in many respects resembles other postcolonial societies, the main characteristics of which are decolonization, hybridity and identities negotiated on the center-periphery axis. And while in the 1990s the importance of a new literary generation for restoring a sense of national belonging was in no doubt, by the end of the second decade of independence, due to the lack of a long-standing coherent governmental cultural policy and the inauspicious political realities of Viktor Yanukovych's regime,[7] Ukrainian literature had displayed unmistakable signs of fatigue—those writers already established had slowed down publishing or did not produce anything particularly outstanding;[8] those still aspiring faced limited opportunities to make a name for themselves mostly because those social agents and institutions with power to consecrate were relatively weak and in a subordinate position within the field of power. As a result, it is fair to assert that Ukrainian writers exerted an uneven influence upon identity formation, yet, invariably, reflected these processes in their works.

CULTURAL HYBRIDITY

When viewed from a historical perspective, one can easily argue that hybridity is not a new concept. Cross-cultural encounters leading to the hybridizing processes were as common in the ancient world as they are today in the era of globalization. Amar Acheraïou rightly observes: "whenever cultures come into contact with each other, whether through trade, marriage alliances, or war, they are inevitably transformed by their proximity with cultural and racial otherness."[9] Yet he also points out that hybridity has always been closely connected to power and domination, especially in colonial contexts. In other words, inherent in such cultural encounters are seeds of inequality. Hence hybridity in its current theoretical incarnation often refers to situations of stark difference but there is no agreement, it seems, whether or not the concept itself offers a discursive remedy to transcend such profound inequalities engendered by colonialism, or it only exacerbates them.

Hybridity acquired a special saliency in cultural and postcolonial studies. In theoretical discourse on hybridity, there is a decisive shift away from the focus on race and bio-politics to the questions of culture and the very notion of identity. Homi Bhabha's version of cultural hybridity, for instance, underscores its textual, subversive and even celebratory possibilities. It also provides a way out of binary thinking, which is dismissed outright as essentializing by a majority of postcolonial critics. Bhabha views culture and identity as inherently ambivalent and links the notion of hybridity to the spatial metaphor of the "Third Space." This space, being the site of enunciation, subversion, displacement and heterogeneity, equips the colonized or subaltern subjects with an emancipatory potential:

> It is only when we understand that all cultural statements and systems are constructed in this contradictory and ambivalent space of enunciation, that we begin to understand why hierarchical claims to the inherent originality or "purity" of cultures are untenable, even before we resort to empirical historical instances that demonstrate their hybridity. Fanon's vision of revolutionary cultural and political change as a "fluctuating movement" of occult instability could not be articulated as cultural *practice* without acknowledgement of this indeterminate space of the subject(s) of enunciation. It is that Third Space, though unrepresentable in itself, which constitutes the discursive conditions of enunciation that ensure no primordial unity or fixity; that even the same signs can be appropriated, translated, rehistoricized and read anew.[10]

Bhabha's conceptualization of the "Third Space," even if promoted by him as a subversive practice of resistance or as an anti-imperialist agency, is often criticized for being overly abstract, too dependent on linguistic and Lacanian theories of signification, oblivious to the geopolitical context, and totally devoid of materiality, that is, disconnected from any concrete socio-political reality of the former colonies. Aijaz Ahmad, for example, highlights Bhabha's detachment from the daily post-independence realities of formerly colonized people by saying that he dispenses "with the idea that a sense of place, of belonging, of some stable commitment to one's class or gender or nation may be useful for defining one's politics."[11] Benita Parry, on the other hand, criticizes Bhabha's approach to hybridity as too textual: "As I read it, Bhabha's 'hybridity' is a twin-term for the 'catachrestic reinscription' of 'cultural difference' in the disjunctive postcolonial discursive space—that is, it is descriptive of the textual processes and effects held to constitute social forms and conditions, and not of those forms and conditions as articulated in social practices."[12] Jan Pieterse Nederveen in his article "Globalisation as Hybridisation" proposes yet another take on Homi Bhabha, pointing out that the critic "refers to hybrids as intercultural brokers in the interstices between nation and empire, producing counter-narratives from the nation's margins to the 'totalizing boundaries' of the nation."[13]

In the past decade, critics of postcolonialism, in general, and hybridity, in particular, underscore the elitist attitudes of migrant intellectuals who are necessarily of double or mixed cultural identity. In her 2007 book on hybridity, Anjali Prabhu identifies, for instance, three distinct positions this concept entails: hybridity as an all-encompassing phenomenon, enabling the subaltern to face or even triumph over the hegemonic (the position favored by Bhabha); hybridity as referring only to "metropolitan elite émigrés and far less to migrant diasporas and even less to those who have 'stayed behind' in the (ex)colony;"[14] and, finally, hybridity as "material reality" that reveals itself first and foremost in race. She herself makes a clear distinction between hybridity as a theoretical concept and hybridity as a social reality and leaves no doubt as to her own position vis-à-vis these two domains: according to her, they need to be colluded.[15] It seems to me that these positions, as outlined by Prabhu, do not exhaust all the possibilities inherent in the concept; however, one should keep in mind that she does not dismiss the importance of social reality in the conceptualization of theoretical premises of hybridity.

But the most unrelenting critique of postcolonialism as practiced by Bhabha and his ideological proponents comes from Amar Acheraïou:

> If evidence of non-elite attitudes towards the colonial project of assimilation or métissage is scant, non-elite responses to hybridity in contemporary discourses are entirely absent from academic discussions. This absence is hardly surprising, considering that today's debates on hybridity are mostly taken in charge by elites who are addressing other elites. As a result of these missing links in postcolonial debates, hybridity discourse is more fittingly conceptualized as a minor narrative with a hegemonic status and reach. Minor because it is produced by a migrant elite living in the West. Hegemonic because, first, this diaspora-centred narrative of postcoloniality narrates the condition of the diaspora as if it were emblematic of the global postcolonial condition; and second, it marginalizes or excludes vernacular and non-Anglophone literatures and scholarship published in the non-Western world.[16]

Acheraïou strongly believes that the hybridity discourse needs rethinking along the lines of "a wider historical, cultural, and ideological perspective"[17] and advances the idea of "a global hybridity of dissent and resistance" or "dissident planetary hybridity"[18] as a way of aspiring "to a more humane, equitable form of globalization."[19] He concludes his 2011 book by, again, implicitly criticizing Bhabha's take on hybridity and reiterating his own vision of hybridity whose basis is materialist and ethical:

> ... unlike mainstream postcolonial hybridity, the hybridity projected in this discussion is not articulated from the third space; in so far as this space is, as we have demonstrated, co-opted by global neoliberal and neocolonial structures of power, it cannot serve the resistive planetary hybridity I suggest. In other words, it is a hybridity whose foundation is not abstractly spatial, but concretely materialist and profoundly ethical; it is a hybridity with as many centers of consciousness as geographical points of origin; all these converge in the same defining, ever-expanding moment of global resistance, solidarity, and articulation of an alternative ethics of doing and being on a larger planetary scale.[20]

Acheraïou's relatively recent rethinking of hybridity prompts me to present my own conceptualization of the term in order to apply its framework to the concrete context of the Ukrainian cultural situation since independence. While I agree with Acheraïou's insistence on dispensing with a hybridity that accommodates neoliberal and neocolonial power relations, I do not reject its spatial character. However, for me this spatiality must not be abstract and indeterminate but site-specific (or contextual) and it must, by definition, allow for the coexistence of heterogeneous cultural elements.[21] Hence, hybridity, as I use it, refers first and foremost to culture but it also entails the issues of language use and ethnicity. It is a space encompassing both cultural artifacts and processes underlying their production. Cultural goods thus produced could be of mixed (hybrid) nature but this is not a necessary prerequisite because the space of hybridity in a specifically Ukrainian context signifies the coexistence of diverse cultural objects, be it Ukrainian, Russian or, indeed, mixed. And this space, when observed from a bird's-eye view, invariably displays a very hybrid quality despite the fact that its individual elements or reifications can be and are, in many instances, relatively homogeneous. The coexistence of parallel cultural entities—native, metropolitan and/or hybrid, which sometimes crisscross or even fuse, but often do not—makes the overall space of hybridity heterogeneous but not necessarily subversive or resistive. I do not exclude these two latter qualities but argue that they are relevant only in some cases,[22] and not universally, as implied in Bhabha's conceptualization. In other words, hybridity as a subversion of political and cultural domination is but just one of many possible configurations.

That being said, I view hybridity in its contemporary Ukrainian variant as a highly unstable though still strongly entrenched circumstance. It might, at best, eventually evolve into a coherent multicultural governmental policy, and at worst, might lead to a marginalization of either Ukrainian indigenous (native) or metropolitan (colonizer's) culture. It could also morph into what

Marwan M. Kraidy calls transculturalism (a mixture of several cultures) that he contrasts with multiculturalism. According to him, the latter "establishes boundaries of recognition and institutionalization between cultures," and the former "underscores the fluidity of these boundaries."[23] Within the context of transculturalism, hybridity for Kraidy becomes "the cultural logic of globalization,"[24] which strongly reverberates with Nederveen's arguments in his "Globalisation as Hybridisation." With the considerable global pressures in the media industry, for instance, it is indeed possible to discern the examples of such transcultural tendencies in Ukrainian TV programs, especially when it comes to reality shows,[25] most of which are of Western provenance. Suffice to say here that there are many conceptual layers in the universe of cultural hybridity and I intend to uncover them while focusing on individual cases.

When we apply the concept of cultural hybridity within the context of Ukrainian literature, then invariably we think of literature written in Russian but belonging to the Ukrainian cultural space. Some authors consciously see themselves as Ukrainian writers even though they express themselves in the metropolitan language. Andrey Kurkov is the best example of such a paradigm. But it is also possible to talk about hybridity in terms of style, genre and even worldview. One of the stylistic devices, used by some writers, is the utilization of a mixed language, the so-called *surzhyk*.[26] This substandard mixture of Russian and Ukrainian plays a specific role in prose narratives, and it is often used for purposes of verisimilitude or to underscore a protagonist's socioeconomic status. Students of processes of hybridity sometimes invoke Mikhail Bakhtin's distinction between intentional and organic hybridity in language and point out to a similar correlation in culture.[27] As a stylistic literary device, *surzhyk*, indeed, presents an example of intentional hybridity. Used unconsciously, because of specific historical circumstances, it exemplifies a case of organic hybridity and merely reflects the contact between two languages of an uneven social status, inherited from the colonial past.

Finally, in my conceptualization of cultural hybridity, I want to acknowledge the usefulness of a contrapuntal approach, advocated by Edward Said:

> As we look back at the cultural archive, we begin to reread it not univocally but contrapuntally, with a simultaneous awareness both of the metropolitan history that is narrated and those of other histories against which (and together with which) the dominating discourse acts. In the counterpoint of Western classical music, various themes play off one another, with only a provisional privilege being given to any particular one; yet in the resulting polyphony there is concert and order, an organized interplay that derives from the themes, not from a rigorous melodic or formal principle outside the work. In the same way, I believe, we can read and interpret English novels, for example, whose engagement (usually suppressed for the most part) with the West Indies or India, say, is shaped and

perhaps even determined by the specific history of colonization, resistance, and finally native nationalism. At this point alternative or new narratives emerge, and they become institutionalized or discursively stable entities.[28]

Said underscores the importance of an interplay and simultaneous awareness of various themes and cultural elements (metropolitan and indigenous) which lead to alternative outcomes and might eventually result in "discursively stable entities," as he puts it. Employing the concept of hybridity as a unifying framework for my discussion of post-independence literary production, I too refer to its spatial, contrapuntal and discursive potential to delineate the underlying nexus of identity formation.

IDENTITIES

In Ukraine, where the nation and state-building project is still underway, the issues surrounding national identity necessarily come to the forefront. However, other identities, namely territorial, ethnolinguistic, class and gender, also play an important role and are reflected in contemporary literature. In fact, as Jonathan Culler aptly observed, literature constitutes an ideal platform to test questions concerning identity:

> Is the self something given or something made, and should it be conceived in individual or in social terms? Literature has always been concerned with such questions, and literary works offer a range of implicit models of how identity is formed. There are narratives where identity is essentially determined by birth: the son of a king raised by shepherds is still fundamentally a king and rightfully becomes king when his identity is discovered. In other narratives characters change according to the changes in their fortunes; they acquire identity through identifications, which may go away but have powerful effects; or else identity is based on personal qualities that are revealed during the tribulations of a life.[29]

Culler apparently undermines theoretical treatments of identity, coming especially from postmodernists who question essentialist approaches. However, by underscoring the literary work's inherent exemplarity, he insists that in the realm of literature identity could be both given and constructed: "Not only are both options amply represented in literature, but the complications or entanglements are frequently laid out for us, as in the common plot where characters, we say, 'discover' who they are, not by learning something about their past but by acting in such a way that they become what then turns out, in some sense, to have been their 'nature.'"[30] Culler's inclusive approach to identity opens up many interpretative possibilities. Whether the self is or becomes someone appears to be less of an issue here. What is more important

is that the process of self-identification has roots in concreteness and historical specificity.

In many ways, identities are defined by social interactions. A person's
identity depends on his/her understanding of particular relationships, institutions or situations. And since relationships and situations often change,
individual identities too can be fluid and multiple at any given moment. This
is indeed in accordance with the postmodern understanding of what it takes
for the self to emerge. Stuart Hall famously remarked: "What is identity? It's
not inside of you. It's affected by how you have to retrace your connection.
And connections are not just going back to a single set of roots, but by the
pathways—the routes—through which those roots had been transformed."[31]
But because the process of national identity formation is invariably a collective and political activity, informed by concrete historical thinking about
ethnicity, empire, linguistic and cultural difference, it necessarily entails a
certain consensus, at least at some point of its evolution. It also needs the contrast with (or dependence on) relevant Others.[32] And, I argue, this relational
interdependence in self-identification processes (or "othering") is relatively
stable. Yet, despite the need for a collective effort, national identity formation
constitutes first and foremost a socially constructed undertaking promoted by
concrete persons in specifiable contexts.[33]

Three fundamental questions arise in discussing identity at its most basic
level: who I am, where I have come from, and where I am heading. And if
the answer to the first question, according to postmodernists, is very much
situational and fluid, the second one necessarily points to a concrete place and
a concrete historical time. In other words, to address the question of origin,
it is impossible to avoid a reference to a certain territory and a specific past.
Maurice Halbwachs, known for his work on collective memory, claims that
at the center of cultural identity formation lies memory, which can also be
defined as the active or subjective past, which differs from the remembered
past, that is, history: "Collective memory differs from history in at least two
respects. It is a current of continuous thought whose continuity is not at all
artificial, for it retains from the past only what still lives or is capable of living
in the consciousness of the groups keeping the memory alive. By definition it
does not exceed the boundaries of this group."[34]

Halbwachs maintains that the individual memory is too fragmented and/
or incomplete and that is why one must seek unity beyond the individual and
rely on group contexts. Hence what emerges in individual memory needs to
be "sanctioned" by collective memory.[35] Recalling events of the past, we are
always interpreting them, invariably bringing them to the present, and that
is why, memory is necessarily the function of now. Halbwachs's distinction
between history and collective memory posited not as one between public
and private but as one based on the relevance of the past to the present has

its application in nation-building projects. No wonder politics plays such a great role in the realm of the so-called national memory. National memory is often reified in monuments, museums, parks and for ruling political elites it is important to affect which events of the past are worthy of such reification.

The last question in the identification process concerns the future. Having imagined the past, the individual or the collective sooner or later will also be forced to imagine the future. This activity cannot be separated from the social circumstances imposed by the political reality of any given country. For a young state such as Ukraine, it is crucial to consolidate a collective "I," to build a consensus around common values, and to define national interests. National identity is a powerful tool that helps to consolidate the nation-state building project, and yet, as Anthony Smith pointed out, regardless of which model of national identity one follows (civic or ethnic), it is impossible to build a new nation without such consolidating factors as a national language, common laws or national culture. Post-independence Ukraine adheres to a civic model of national identity construction and emphasizes its openness to the free cultural development of all ethnic groups on its territory. The colonial heritage, however, makes this apparent tolerance somewhat muddled in the sense that, culturally speaking, things Ukrainian have not always occupied a privileged position.

How does identity politics play out in the works of literature in post-independence Ukraine? I contend that self-identification processes are very much reflected in contemporary literary production. For example, to speak of territorial identity, as reflected in literary texts, is to speak above all about authors and works that originate in Galicia, the most Western part of Ukraine, although other regions and cities are also represented, even if less prominently. But Galicia no doubt is in the advantageous position in the sense that this is the region that yields a substantial pool of readers still inclined to follow what is happening in Ukrainian literature, and the region from which some of the best-known and talented writers in present-day Ukraine come. The most representative figure of this group is, of course, Yuri Andruk-hovych, who at some point, especially in his early essays, toyed with the idea of Galicia being an integral part of Central Europe, although without outright calls for separation from the rest of Ukraine.[36] Other writers from Western Ukraine for whom geography matters are Yuri Vynnychuk, Taras Prokhasko and Viktor Neborak. However, the connection between a strong territorial affinity to a particular region or city and the issues of national identity can also be found in the writings of authors from central, southern and eastern regions of Ukraine; among them the most conspicuous are Andrey Kurkov, Serhiy Zhadan, Pavlo Volvach and Vasyl Kozhelianko, to name just a few.

Gender matters too in contemporary Ukrainian literature and the emergence and assertion of powerful women's voices comprises one of the most noticeable trends in literary discourses of post-independence Ukraine. In the realm of belles-lettres this female voice has found its niche and can easily compete with male writings both in prose and poetry. The construction of a new image for an independent female intellectual subject is often juxtaposed with the construction of a new vision for an independent Ukraine. This link is especially pronounced in Oksana Zabuzhko's novel *Fieldwork in Ukrai nian Sex* (*Pol'ovi doslidzhennia z ukrains'koho seksu*, 1996), in which the protagonist interweaves her personal failures with that of her nation. Zabu zhko, however, is but one of many voices among a very strong contingent of talented female poets and writers who assert their presence on the literary scene as forcefully as male counterparts. Natalka Bilotserkivets, Liudmyla Taran, Yevheniia Kononenko; the still younger Mariana Savka, Marianna Kiianovska, Svitlana Pyrkalo; and the youngest Irena Karpa, Sofiia Andruk hovych and Tania Maliarchuk do not foreground the issues of national iden tity to the same degree but all underscore gender relations.

In terms of ethnolinguistic identities, I contrast a group of writers for whom the Ukrainian language becomes a protagonist of sorts, such as Yevhen Pash kovsky or Viacheslav Medvid, with those writers who express themselves exclusively in Russian. The former group cannot count on a wide readership; their works are clearly for the select few. Both Medvid and Pashkovsky have a strong sense of national identification in ethnic rather than political terms. This comes in stark contrast to Andrey Kurkov who promotes an identity that is based on citizenship rather than blood ties and native land, and thus pro vides a good example of someone with a hybrid cultural identity.

Other authors such as Oles Ulianenko and Bohdan Zholdak depict in their fiction the dreary realities of Ukrainian everyday life, including the grow ing strata of the criminal world and people living on the margins of society. Zholdak, for example, employs *surzhyk*—the street-language admixture of Ukrainian and Russian—as a marker of class distinction and in order to underscore the verisimilitude of the social belonging of his protagonists. Yuri Izdryk, on the other hand, approaches the issue of social marginalization more abstractly and dwells on illness and even pathology as a path to the rec ognition of the self and its identity formation. Whereas Izdryk is preoccupied with self-identity of the individual, Serhiy Zhadan prefers to consider the intricacies of collective identity, especially among the youth of the generation who came of age in the early post-independence years.

Lastly, exploring the connection between popular literature and national identity construction can shed light on the social role of the literary work. By turning to popular genres such as detective stories, thrillers, romances and science fiction writers have an opportunity to considerably expand their readership and to promote an all-Ukrainian identity at the same time. Hence, the role of popular literature goes well beyond being just merely entertaining.

Ihab Hassan once remarked: "the postcolonial condition is not a happy condition"[37] and, indeed, colonial contact makes issues of identity and cultural identity in particular doubly problematic. And while belles-lettres texts provide more freedom and possibilities to play on the intricacies of indigenous versus metropolitan entanglements, in the realm of literary criticism and scholarship the arrival of new methodological paradigms is always slower and more complex. Before I embark on my own interpretive journey of the most representative post-independence works, I must first review reading strategies offered by critics studying Ukrainian literature both in the West and in Ukraine, and evaluate their efforts to transcend highly ideologized and outdated approaches inherited from the Soviet past.

POST-INDEPENDENCE READING STRATEGIES

The Postcolonial Turn

The pioneering efforts to read Ukrainian literature from the angle of postmodernism and postcolonial theory belong to Marko Pavlyshyn, an Australian scholar of Ukrainian descent. As early as 1992, he wrote an influential article titled "Post-colonial Features in Contemporary Ukrainian Culture" published in *Australian Slavonic and East European Studies*.[38] In this study Pavlyshyn makes a sharp distinction between the terms "postcolonial" and "anticolonial": "The cultural configurations of anticolonialism are regarded here as an echo and a mirroring of their colonial predecessors. The postcolonial, on the other hand, is understood as the fruit of a deconstruction of colonialism: as the unmasking and taking apart, and simultaneously the productive re-use, of the cultural structures of colonialism."[39] Pavlyshyn's narrow understanding of "postcoloniality" as a momentum transcending both colonial and anticolonial power relations and as a phenomenon akin to postmodernism, mainly of the deconstructive kind, invites many questions. His ascription of mimicry to anticolonial attitudes is also somewhat reductive. In fact, if the "postcolonial moment" "closes off the hegemony of various pasts,"[40] or constitutes "a leap from romanticism into postmodernity,"[41] that is, prescribes or promotes a specific mode of aesthetic practice, then it also faces the danger of becoming monological and rigid in the process, the very qualities Pavlyshyn attaches to the anticolonial. From the perspective of two decades of independence, his assertion that "however central for Ukrainian culture the idea of emancipation was in the past, today, when independence has been achieved, the project of liberation lost its logic of existence"[42] appears overly optimistic and somewhat premature. Moreover, it seems that Pavlyshyn's paradigm of postcoloniality as applied to Ukraine accommodates but a specific discourse, which is "less reactive" and "aware that the affirmation of an anticolonial credo inevitably relies upon, and preserves, the memory and structure of the opposite ideology."[43] In other words, anticolonialism, according to Pavlyshyn, uses the same rhetoric and tactics as colonialism does but with a negative charge. However, the postcolonial actuality is more complicated than that, as postcolonial critics rightly pointed out on numerous occasions. Elleke Boehmer, for example, contends that "postcolonial literature is that which critically scrutinizes the colonial relationship" and further states:

> It is writing that sets out in one way or another to resist colonialist perspectives. As well as a change in power, decolonization demanded symbolic overhaul, a reshaping of dominant meanings. Postcolonial literature formed part of that process of overhaul. To give expression to colonized experience, postcolonial writers sought to undercut thematically and formally the discourses, which supported colonization—the myths of power, the race classifications, the imagery of subordination. Postcolonial literature, therefore, is deeply marked by experiences of cultural exclusion and division under empire. Especially in its early stages it can also be a nationalist writing. Building on this, postcoloniality is defined as that condition in which colonized people seek to take their place, forcibly, or otherwise, as historical subjects.[44]

As it is clear from the above statement, the distinction between anticolonial and postcolonial, so central to Pavlyshyn, is non-existent here. Boehmer even allows for the inclusion of "a nationalist writing" in postcolonial literature, which, again, is a kind of practice that Pavlyshyn designates as anticolonial rather than postcolonial. These two descriptors in postcolonial criticism are rarely placed in such a sharp opposition, as Pavlyshyn deems necessary.[45] Gayatri Spivak's characterization of postcoloniality as "the heritage of imperialism"[46] is so broad and inclusive, for instance, that it assumes a diversity of various discourses, colonial, anticolonial, postcolonial or even transnational. Hence, it is safe to assert that the postcolonial represents a considerably more prevalent phenomenon in the aftermath of colonial emancipation than Pavlyshyn suggests. Vitaly Chernetsky also somewhat undermines Pavlyshyn's categorical typology:

> This double project of resistance and reparative critique, not merely overcoming anticolonialism, guides the best of postcolonial writing, including the work of the writers whom Pavlyshyn identifies as postcolonial—for example, Valery Shevchuk and the Bu-Ba-Bu group. In my opinion, we can clearly grant their work anticolonial status, for these writers do strive for a critical evaluation of the colonial past and the traces of this past that still form a prominent part of the psyche of the contemporary postcolonial subject.[47]

Clearly, he underscores the fact that those literary texts that Pavlyshyn considers postcolonial can easily be taken as anticolonial.

In many ways, the genealogy of Pavlyshyn's conceptualization of postcolonialism will become better understood if we examine his deep involvement in studying the literature of the 1960s, both of the dissident extraction and of the socialist realism canon.[48] Many representatives of this literary generation became politically active in the period of glasnost and perestroika (1985–1991), working hard to support cultural re-Ukrainianization and paving the way for independence. For writers such as Ivan Drach, Dmytro Pavlychko, Pavlo Movchan and Volodymyr Yavorivsky, to name just a few, literature and politics became inextricably linked. As Pavlyshyn rightly points out in one of his essays, the primary duty for these writers "is to promote Ukrainian state-and-nation building"[49] and thus, being mainstream and part of the Writers' Union, they "do not imagine themselves otherwise than as agents within a literary politics."[50] No wonder Pavlyshyn concludes that these literary figures in their anticolonial struggle emulate and perpetuate the structures inherited from the imperial past. To contrast such objectives and methods with those of the younger generation, he foregrounds the latter's transgressive, parodic, playful and skeptical qualities. The Bu-Ba-Bu group,[51] for example, is postcolonial, according to Pavlyshyn, because first, it does not concern itself with such grand projects as state-and-nation-building and second, because it undermines not only official Soviet culture but also "the Great Tradition of Ukrainian literature as a weapon in the struggle for national liberation."[52] However, when one looks closely at Bu-Ba-Bu's rhetoric of parody and subversion, in its essence it is also anticolonial because, deep down, its members yearn for a national space to express themselves freely and without any impediments. Pavlyshyn tends to neglect these features.[53] However, admittedly, his understanding of the postcolonial evolved with time and later softened to a degree.

Whereas in his 1993 essay "Ukrainian Literature and the Erotics of Postcolonialism: Some Modest Propositions" Pavlyshyn still insists on a well-defined difference between the postcolonial and the anticolonial (though acknowledging the "unstable, critical use" of the former), in his 2001 essay "Literary Politics vs. Literature: Ukrainian Debates in the 1990s" this distinction loses its categorical nature. He concurs that the anticolonial and postcolonial are more intertwined than he initially thought and the national issue cannot be completely absent from the new literature. Moreover, he also acknowledges that in the post-independence period it is virtually impossible to separate literary politics from literary production: "Wherever we have looked so far, we have encountered literary politics, even in places where at first glance literary politics was disdained. It seems that the end of the 1990s is still a time for a Ukrainian literature oriented toward solving problems and making suggestions in the non-literary world."[54] As Pavlyshyn has it,

Zabuzhko's novel *Fieldwork in Ukrainian Sex,* and especially Andruk-hovych's trilogy *Recreations (Rekreatsii,* 1992), *The Moscoviad (Moskoviada,* 1993) and *Perverzion (Perverziia,* 1996) are the best examples of the problematization of the colonial/anticolonial and postcolonial dynamics:

> The trilogy, for all its ambiguities and complexities, invited monological interpretation in one respect: it argued that what one needs after colonialism was post-colonialism. That is to say, anti-colonialism, the simple negation of colonial values and postulates, was not enough: one needed both distance from, and continuing awareness of, the colonial heritage and the tradition of opposition to it.[55]

Interestingly, in his 2012 contribution to the *Journal of Postcolonial Writing* titled "Andrukhovych's *Secret:* The return of colonial resignation," Pavlyshyn reiterates his early definitions of "colonial," "anticolonial" and "postcolonial," admitting, however, their unstable terminological distinctions.

In more recent writings on postcolonialism it is the dynamic between the postcolonial and the global that attracts more attention than the one, which preoccupied Pavlyshyn some two decades ago, namely his clear-cut distinction between the anticolonial and the postcolonial. Increasingly, there is also a recognition that the latter term is inherently ambiguous and could refer to a Eurocentric colonial past, including subaltern responses to Western domination on the one hand,[56] and on the other, to a very specific kind of theory, as represented, for example, by Homi Bhabha and his concepts of hybridity, difference, deterritorialization, migrancy and cosmopolitanism.[57] But in the context of globalization theory, it is the dynamic between post- and neocolonialism that comes to the forefront. Jonathan Friedman, for example, points out that initially the discourse on globalization referred to "the hierarchical nature of imperialism, that is, the increasing hegemony of particular central cultures, the diffusion of American values, consumer goods and lifestyles,"[58] in other words, a phenomenon that can be labeled as "cultural imperialism." However, he also brings to our attention an alternative approach, "which has focused on globalization as a recognition of what is conceived as increasing worldwide interconnections, interchanges and movements of people, images and commodities."[59] To further refine the framework of globalization Roland Robertson introduces the concept of "glocalization" as a way to counteract globalization's tendency toward cultural homogenization. He argues that the local does not need to be opposed to the global; on the contrary, "globalisation has involved the reconstruction, in a sense the production, of 'home,' 'community,' and 'locality.' To that extent the local is not best seen, at least as an analytic premise, as a counterpoint to the global."[60] Robertson's stand is also interesting because it claims that "the national society has been a central component of modern globalisation."[61] In that remark he clearly contradicts the idea that the forces of globalization necessarily undermine the nation-state.[62]

Vitaly Chernetsky, an American literary scholar originally from Ukraine, exemplifies the gradual transition from the postcolonial problematic to globalization theory. His early essays on Ukrainian contemporary literature clearly engage a postcolonial approach and show that he thoroughly studied Pavlyshyn's contribution. They dwell on the connection between the postmodern and the postcolonial,[63] but Chernetsky's more recent work has decisively moved toward a reading from a cultural globalization perspective.[64] However, while the title of his monograph *Mapping Postcommunist Cultures: Russia and Ukraine in the Context of Globalization* invokes globalization as a term of some substance, three chapters in the book, devoted specifically to Ukrainian literature, analyze the most representative texts of the post-independence period from a rather narrow perspective of Fredric Jameson's concept of a "national allegory," as related in the latter's well-known article "Third-World Literature in the Era of Multinational Capitalism," published in 1986. Chernetsky's seemingly uncritical embrace of Jameson's somewhat controversial "Three Worlds theory" yields some contradictions. First, by applying the concept of national allegories to post-independence Ukrainian texts, Chernetsky, perhaps quite unintentionally, suggests their third-world status. And second, those Ukrainian texts that he designates as examples of national allegories, he also considers as postmodern, and that in itself does not entirely conform to Jameson's conceptualization, whereby a distinction between postmodernism of the First World and nationalism of the Third World are contrasted and especially underscored. These incongruities do not seem to discourage the critic. On the contrary, he praises Jameson's overly generalizing approach: "What I think distinguishes Jameson's model in an important way is his emphasis on the necessity of reading any postcolonial text as national allegory, even those texts that do not overtly display allegorical properties."[65] Moreover, while acknowledging the existence of various paradigms in postmodern Ukrainian literature, from the magical, transgressive to corporeal, and performative practices, Chernetsky still insists on the relevance of Jameson's totalizing approach: "All of these paradigms, however, are infused with the signally postcolonial persistence of national allegory."[66]

Jameson wrote his controversial essay on national allegories in 1986, well before the collapse of the Soviet Union and at a time when the term "Third World" was beginning to lose its currency.[67] Aware of existing objections to the use of the "Third World" concept, he nonetheless insists on the applicability of the term in the descriptive sense, as well as continues to dwell on "the fundamental breaks between the capitalist first world, the socialist bloc of the second world, and a range of other countries which have suffered the experience of colonialism and imperialism."[68] Obviously, the first complication to Jameson's theory of three worlds occurred in 1991 when after the disappearance of the Soviet Union a number of new states emerged that could also claim "the experience of colonialism and imperialism" as their own, at the same time belonging to the second rather than the third-world paradigm. Another problematic assertion made by Jameson hovers around the question of a radical split between the private and the public as "one of the determinants of capitalist culture."[69] He argues that third-world texts lack this separation and the relations between public and private spheres are necessarily thrust into the political and that particular characteristic makes them somewhat alien to the reading audiences of the First World. He notes:

Third-world texts, even those which are seemingly private and invested with a properly libidinal dynamic—necessarily project a political dimension in the form of national allegory: *the story of the private individual destiny is always an allegory of the embattled situation of the public third-world culture and society.* Need I add that it is precisely this very different ration of the political to the personal which makes such texts alien to us at first approach, and consequently, resistant to our conventional western habits of reading?[70]

Jameson's somewhat patronizing attitude toward third-world literatures, displayed in the above passage, comes to the forefront even more so in his initial ruminations on the aspirations of non-canonical third-world texts to be deemed important as well as on their relationship to the canon:[71]

The way in which all this affects the reading process seems to be as follows: as western readers whose tastes (and much else) have been formed by our own modernisms, a popular or socially realistic third-world novel tends to come before us, not immediately, but as though already-read. We sense, between ourselves and this alien text, the presence of another reader, of the Other reader, for whom a narrative, which strikes us as conventional or naïve, has a freshness of information and a social interest that we cannot share.[72]

Jameson's totalizing approach and constant reminders of a radical difference between first-world texts and attitudes and those of the Third World invite a number of criticisms, which I discuss below. Interestingly, however, perhaps mindful of too a categorical distinction, Jameson concedes at one point that allegorical structures are not completely absent from first-world cultural texts but they are "unconscious" and "must be deciphered by interpretive mechanisms that necessarily entail a whole social and historical critique of our current first-world situation.[73]" Third-world national allegories, on the other hand, Jameson contends, "are conscious and overt: they imply a radically different and objective relationship of politics and libidinal dynamics."[74]

At the end of the essay the critic once more underscores the differences in allegorization between the first and third-world cultures and concludes that in the latter "the telling of the individual story and the individual experience cannot but ultimately involve the whole laborious telling of the experience of the collectivity itself."[75]

The most thorough and relentless critique of Jameson's concept of national allegory comes from a Marxist literary scholar, Aijaz Ahmad. In his book *In Theory: Classes, Nations, Literatures*, he devotes an entire chapter to the analysis of Jameson's controversial text. Ahmad questions the premises of the famed essay, and especially disapproves Jameson's use of "the Third World" as a theoretical category, pointing out that "a presumably pre- or non-capitalist Third World is empirically ungrounded in any facts."[76] Ahmad also doubts Jameson's insistence on the binary opposition nationalism vs. postmodernism (the former being ascribed to the third-world situation, whereas the latter to the Western one), saying: "There is neither theoretical ground nor empirical evidence to support the notion that bourgeois nationalisms of the so-called Third World will have any difficulty with postmodernism; they want it."[77] Ahmad then proceeds to propose the premise of the one world rather than three, clarifying further that "this world includes the experience of colonialism and imperialism on both sides of Jameson's global divide."[78] Finally, to debunk Jameson's theory of three worlds completely, he concludes:

> To say that all Third World texts are necessarily this or that is to say, in effect, that any text originating within that social space which is not this or that is not a "true" narrative. It is the site of this operation, with the "national allegory" as its metatext as well as the mark of its constitution and difference, is, to my mind, epistemologically an impossible category.[79]

However, Ahmad also has a problem with Jameson's usage of the category "nation" because the latter critic on many occasions replaces it with such wider categories as "collectivity," "societies" or "culture." And these inconsistencies allow Ahmad to deconstruct Jameson's contention that allegorization as such is characteristic of third-world texts only. In fact, Ahmad sees it quite possible that the difference between the First- and the Third World, on which Jameson insists over and over, is not as compelling as might originally appear.

Vitaly Chernetsky, in his monograph on Russia and Ukraine from the perspective of globalization, overlooks many of the above contradictions, pointed out so diligently by Ahmad, and applies, nonetheless, Jameson's concept of "national allegory" to the Ukrainian post-independence literary process. At the same time, however, without acknowledging it, he makes necessary adjustments to preserve the coherence of his arguments. First,

Chernetsky dispenses with the term "Third World" and consistently uses the term "postcolonial" in its stead. Second, when discussing Ukrainian texts, he only marginally dwells on the split between private and public spheres, the opposition so central to Jameson's thesis, and third, contrary to the latter's position, he does not perceive as contradictory or impossible for a text to be simultaneously a national allegory and postmodern, which is exactly the stand promoted by Ahmad.

Of the three chapters devoted to Ukrainian literature in *Mapping Postcommunist Cultures*, the first one even bears an explicit allusion to allegory in its title: "Allegorical Journeys, or The Metamorphoses of Magic Realism." But there is hardly any reference to Jameson's concept of "national allegory" in this chapter. Instead, focusing on magic realism and its specific Ukrainian variant, and analyzing mostly the fictional works of Valerii Shevchuk, Chernetsky refers here to another of Jameson's studies, "On Magic Realism in Film," one that, as the title suggests, engages the problematic of magic realism. The only passing reference to a national allegory comes at the very end of the chapter when Chernetsky discusses the oeuvre of Oles Ulianenko, and claims that his novel *Stalinka* (1994) "emerges as a clear instance of Jamesonian national allegory,"[80] without, however, any more elaborate explanation why it is the case. It is fair to say that the most apt examples of national allegories in Jamesonian understanding come in the chapter devoted to the poetics of the Bu-Ba-Bu group. One could indeed argue that carnivalesque and subversive qualities displayed in the texts by the members of the group, Yuri Andrukhovych, Viktor Neborak, and Oleksandr Irvanets, do conform to the definition of national allegory as proposed by Jameson, in the sense that the private and the public become inextricably intertwined. That is to say, Chernetsky rightly concludes that:

> The private, personal experiences of displacement emerge here as an allegory of the collective experience of the Ukrainian people during this time of paradigmatic change, thereby evidencing a profound affinity of Andrukhovych's writing with Jameson's model of "national allegory," one of the influential, if frequently criticized, attempts at constructing a theoretical model of postcolonial writing.[81]

What needs to be emphasized is that both Andrukhovych's oeuvre, and even more so Oksana Zabuzhko's, especially her novel *Fieldwork in Ukrainian Sex* (1996), which Chernetsky discusses in the chapter "Confronting Traumas, The Gendered/Nationed Body as Narrative and Spectacle," do not exhaust all the paradigmatic possibilities in Ukrainian literature of the post-independence period. Chernetsky is, of course, aware of this[82] but, nevertheless, does not underscore a clear exemplariness of the texts chosen by him for analysis. In

other words, Chernetsky dwells on only those works that implicitly or explicitly fit Jameson's model, however, he fails to observe that the existence of other
literary paradigms somewhat undermines Jameson's claim that "all third-world
texts are necessarily, ... allegorical,"[83] and that this very claim of universal
applicability of the national allegory makes it a theoretically untenable concept.

Yet, putting aside such incongruities, Chernetsky's analysis of Ukrainian
women's contribution in the final chapter is particularly rewarding. He begins
his discussion with a theoretical introduction based on his reading of Anne
McClintock's essay "No Longer in a Future Heaven: Nationalism, Gender
and Race." He agrees with McClintock's gendered approach to nationalism
as well as her take on the gender dynamic as found in the writings of such
leading theorists of liberational nationalism as Frantz Fanon, even though,
arguably, her insistence that "there is no single narrative of the nation"[84]
seems to contradict Jameson's model of a national allegory. The importance of women's national agency in any nation-building project, stressed
by McClintock's, finds its manifestation, according to Chernetsky, in the
Ukrainian post-Soviet context. He focuses not only on women authors, but
also on women literary scholars, and their preoccupation with issues of sexuality and corporeality from a feminist perspective, especially as related to
the transformation of national culture after independence. What Chernetsky
brings forth in the chapter on "the gendered/nationed body" constitutes in fact
another important reading strategy that will be addressed below. Suffice to
say here is that despite the author's aspiration to read texts from a globalization angle, his monograph is still very much rooted in the postcolonial rather
than global rhetoric and problematic. However, in Chernetsky's more recent
article, "From Anarchy to Connectivity to Cognitive Mapping: Contemporary
Ukrainian Writers of the Younger Generation Engage with Globalization"
(2010), as the title itself indicates, he wholeheartedly embraces globalization
as a theoretical category conducive to interpretation of new Ukrainian writing. Invoking Néstor García Canclini's study *Hybrid Cultures: Strategies
for Entering and Leaving Modernity* (1995), Chernetsky sees new Ukrainian
literary production as conforming with Canclini's vision of "contemporary
global culture as constituted by eclectic multidirectional contacts and borrowings that encourage the proliferation of new cultural forms."[85] A number
of authors discussed by Chernetsky, each in his/her own unique way, engage
heterogeneous global cultural influences while, at the same time, participate in the localizing process of building a new national post-independence
literature. In other words, without making a specific reference to the term,
Chernetsky advances the idea of "glocalization," as introduced by Roland
Robertson, whereby the forces of globalization do not need to undermine the
nation-state formations, and the local becomes a counterpoint for a global
tendency toward homogenization.

The Feminist Turn

The fall of the Soviet Empire and a collapse of the communist ideology brought about enormous opportunities for open-minded scholars to reassess their understanding of the social role of the literary work and to revisit the established canon of Ukrainian literature. While Pavlyshyn and Chernetsky represent the Western reading strategies, Solomiia Pavlychko and her female scholar colleagues constitute a group determined to overhaul ideologized ways of interpretation from within Ukrainian literary scholarship. Pavlychko's article "Does Ukrainian Literary Scholarship Need a Feminist School?" ("Chy potribna ukrains'komu literaturoznavstvu feministychna shkola?"), published in 1991,[86] signaled a turn to feminism as a viable reading strategy and initiated a very productive critical paradigm, which subsequently was eagerly taken up by other women scholars, namely, Tamara Hundorova, Vira Aheieva and Nila Zborovska. In fact, their propositions constitute the most interesting reading strategies in the post-independence period, especially for Ukrainian modernism and women authors. In addition to analyzing Ukrainian classics, they turn their attention to new literature, which scholars of more conservative proclivity rarely consider.

In many ways the attractiveness of feminist theory and gender studies for women scholars in Ukraine stems from a profound need to find new ways of interpreting literary texts after many years of stagnation and ideological constraints under the Soviet regime. The growing intellectual exchange between Ukrainian female scholars and their Western counterparts following the collapse of the Soviet Union spurred an increased awareness about the problems women face in independent Ukraine. This dialogue, including support from the West in the form of grants and fellowships, presented Ukrainian feminists with an opportunity to pursue not only their own scholarly projects but also a new social agenda for women in post-Soviet Ukraine. The latter is true especially for Pavlychko, whose interest in feminist discourse, as attested by her book *Feminism* (*Feminizm*, 2002), goes well beyond the confines of literary criticism.

Pavlychko's pioneering efforts to introduce feminist theory into Ukrainian literary scholarship as one of many possible methodological strategies cannot be overstated. Her contribution in this regard has never been questioned and since her untimely death in 1999 it has become an object of intense veneration among her feminist colleagues.[87] And even though Ukraine has its own quite strong feminist tradition going back to the second half of the nineteenth century,[88] the acceptance and advancement of the contemporary Western feminist project has been a fairly new phenomenon, which has its beginnings indeed in the early 1990s. In the article "Does Ukrainian Literary Scholarship Need a Feminist School?," Pavlychko briefly outlines the main theoretical accomplishments of Western feminism and strongly advocates its applicability to the Ukrainian context, especially since, according to her, despite an official rhetoric privileging women, in practice, they are not provided with equal opportunities. One example she gives, which speaks for itself, is the fact that only 13 out of 450 members of the Ukrainian Parliament are women.[89]

The greatest achievement of feminist literary scholars in Ukraine has to do with their calling into question the established canon, not only because it was ideologically biased, that is, promoting communist propaganda (in this respect they were not alone), but also because it clearly reflected a patriarchal mode of thinking. Their interpretative return to classic male authors such as Taras Shevchenko (1814–1861) and Ivan Franko (1856–1916) stemmed from the desire to remove the clichés attached to them (for instance, Shevchenko as a revolutionary democrat and Franko as a tireless worker for the good of common folk—"kameniar" [stonecutter]) and to read them through the prism of psychoanalysis or pure aestheticism.[90] Those women writers already recognized as firmly belonging to the canon were given a new look. Marko Vovchok (1833–1907), Olha Kobylianska (1863–1942), and especially Lesia Ukrainka (1871–1913), were praised not for their call for social justice, as was often the case under the Soviet regime, but for their feminist agenda and stand as new women in Ukrainian letters. For example, Vovchok (the pen name of Mariia Vilinska,) was never portrayed in Soviet literary histories as the Ukrainian equivalent of George Sand; she was instead praised for her depiction of hardship suffered by peasant women. Vovchok's almost laser-like concentration on women's fates and their underlying desire to be independent was frequently overlooked. Not to mention that the writer's own turbulent biography, which included numerous romantic affairs and financial independence owing to her literary work, was hardly emphasized.[91] It is also worth mentioning that a special friendship between Kobylianska and Ukrainka, as I will indicate below, was a particularly fascinating area of study both for Pavlychko and Hundorova.

In addition to classic authors, feminist critics turned their attention to figures often perceived as marginal in the established canon. Aheieva in her *Women's Space: The Feminist Discourse of Ukrainian Modernism* (*Zhinochyi prostir: Feministychnyi dyskurs ukrains'koho modernizmu*, 2003) quite purposely discusses a number of women authors who are not widely known but who, according to the critic, played a very important role in the development of modernist premises in Ukrainian literature. It is an important statement in the sense that it widens the focus of feminist modernist credentials beyond the standard icons of Kobylianska and Ukrainka. In the same category I would place Pavlychko's study on Ahatanhel Krymsky (1871–1942), a poet, writer and scholar of Middle East languages whose fin de siècle prose work *Andrii Lahovsky* touches on issues of homosexuality.

Revisiting the canon was by far the most important task faced by female critics, but there were other innovations as well. For example, Nila Zborovska's experimentation with the genre of literary criticism itself deserves attention and I will discuss it separately. On the organizational level, these feminists were quite successful in founding a new Center of Gender Studies in Kyiv and published, however briefly, an electronic journal *Vydnokola*. Pavlychko, as co-owner of the Osnovy publishing house, made sure that important works of Western feminism, such as Simone de Beauvoir's monumental book *The Second Sex*, were translated and published in Ukrainian.

While the feminist discourse in Ukrainian literary scholarship reveals itself most conspicuously in the area of canon reexamination, the issue of identity construction, especially in its national dimension, comes to the forefront only insofar as the Kyiv Center of Gender Studies[92] is compared with the Kharkiv Center of Gender Studies. Both centers were founded in the mid-1990s and both enjoyed prominence because of the efforts of their leading personalities. In the case of Kharkiv, they were mainly Irina Zherebkina and her husband Sergei Zherebkin, and in Kyiv, Solomiia Pavlychko, together with Vira Aheieva, Nila Zborovska and Tamara Hundorova. The differences between these two schools stem not only from the distinct interpretations of Ukraine's post-Soviet realities and its national agenda, but also from their contrastive applications of feminist theory. The Kharkiv Center foregrounds the philosophical and sociological aspects of feminism and only occasionally ventures into the literary sphere, whereas the Kyiv Center concerns itself predominantly with literary criticism and the development of new feminist methodologies in order to reinterpret Ukrainian classics. One should also bear in mind the fact (and it is not without significance) that the Kharkiv investigations are overwhelmingly in Russian, whereas the Kyiv contributions are largely in Ukrainian.

However, I do not want to leave the impression that national identity is determined by language alone. In fact, on other occasions I argue that national self-identification process goes well beyond the issues of language.[93] But as far as the Kharkiv Center is concerned, the use of the Russian language goes hand in hand with a very specific cultural identification, which is clearly divorced from the project of state- and nation-building endeavors in Ukraine. When one closely examines the writings of Irina Zherebkina and Sergei Zherebkin, one is struck by the absence of connectedness (territorial or linguistic) to things Ukrainian. Although they do take up Ukrainian subjects, they do so from without rather than from within. The fact that Kharkiv is territorially part of Ukraine seems to be intentionally overlooked. Their perspective on the women's movement in Ukraine and the related gender problematic is clearly an outside perspective. Thus, one can conclude that even the civic model of nationalism (which marginalizes ethnic "blood-and-soil" claims) is too much for them to bear. Vitaly Chernetsky puts it forthrightly:

> In the work of the Kharkiv school, one finds a curious slippage between a sustained feminist analytical project and the strategic use of feminist terminology for invectives against the Ukrainian state and the national culture, which the school apparently views as coextensive (even though through most of the postindependence era the Ukrainian government has shown little interest in promoting or supporting Ukrainian culture). Similarly to many other ex-Soviet russophones, the Kharkiv authors of the gender-studies school seem not to have done the work of mourning for the disintegrated Russian empire and find themselves arrested in melancholic longing for the unified russophone cultural space. They refuse to approach the Ukrainian language as a means of communication and regard its use as an aggressive imposition of *external* power [...] Indeed, by way of refusing to subscribe to a Ukrainian identity, apparently not only linguistically but of any kind, members of the Kharkiv school offer a bizarre latter-day confirmation of Fanon's insight: a colonial subject comes to experience the metropoly as the norm and *him/herself* as the Other.[94]

Irina Zherebkina's first contribution to Ukrainian feminist scholarship appeared in 1996 as a monograph entitled: *Women's Political Unconscious: The Problem of Gender and the Women's Movement in Ukraine* (*Zhenskoe politicheskoe bessoznatel'noe: Problema gendera i zhenskoe dvizhenie v Ukraine*). It is hard not to see this work as a response to the work published a year earlier by Martha Bohachevsky-Chomiak, *Bilym po bilomu: Zhinky v hromadians'komu zhytti Ukrainy, 1884–1939*, which constituted the author's Ukrainian version of the previously published *Feminists Despite Themselves: Women in Ukrainian Community Life, 1884–1939*. Zherebkina's project, thematically and theoretically much wider in scope than Bohachevsky-Chomiak's undertaking, strikes us as a hodgepodge of contemporary feminist theory, literary criticism, and historical and sociopolitical ruminations all woven together in a rather disjointed manner. She clearly benefits from Bohachevsky-Chomiak's meticulous research (judging by the number of endnotes) but disagrees with the latter with respect to the efficacy of presenting the women's movement in Ukraine as simultaneously feminist and nationalist. Zherebkina underscores the fact that women's organizations in contemporary Ukraine are in most part neo-conservative and by and large hostile to the feminist agenda. She also ascribes to them a preoccupation with nationalist ideology and an attempt to construe the Other (in this case: Russia) as the enemy. To Zherebkina, feminism and nationalism exclude each other, even though, as Kumari Jayawardena indicated in her book on feminism and nationalism in the Third World, these two ideologies go hand in hand when it comes to communities with colonial and semicolonial status.[95] In other words, combining the struggles for national and women's liberation is not a Ukrainian invention but a paradigm for all those subjected to imperialist powers.

However, Zherebkina's contention that an overall hostility to feminist discourse in Ukraine comes not just from male quarters but women's organizations as well has some validity. Solomiia Pavlychko also underscored the fact that in order to be accepted by society many leaders of women's organizations in Ukraine emphatically insist that they are "not feminists."[96] This reality often forces women scholars to take up defensive postures whenever debates about the efficacy of feminism and/or gender studies arise. I am referring here especially to a series of publications in the journal *Krytyka* in 1999[97] and in 2001.[98] Nevertheless, despite the struggle to maintain its authority in literary and cultural scholarship, the feminist voice in Ukraine is heard and increasingly finds its way to the pages of numerous periodicals, both scholarly as well as popular.[99]

To sum up the differences between these two feminist schools in the post-independence period one has to emphasize that the entire discourse on feminism coming out of the Kharkiv Center is considered by its adherents to be neutral and unmarked, even though its main proponents do not particularly mask their partiality with regard to the issues of nationalism in contemporary Ukraine. The Kyiv Center, on the other hand, is implicitly marked by supporters of the Kharkiv Center as nationalistic, or at least as nationally inclined.[100] The problem with such marking, however, is that it legitimizes itself only in the presence of the Other. To put it differently, the Kyiv school appears to have a national bias only because the Kharkiv school so completely lacks it. Under normal circumstances, that is to say, without postcolonial impediments, all one could say about the Kyiv feminist school is that it functions the way it should, namely, producing interesting works of literary scholarship, experimenting with new methodologies and theories. In other words, the connection between feminist discourse and identity formation within the bounds of Ukrainian literary scholarship is contextual rather than inherent.[101]

The actual critical texts put forth by the literary scholars of the Kyiv Center are striking for their breadth of feminist approaches, from feminist critique to psychoanalytical studies of female subjectivity, at the heart of which lies a desire to shake up the conservatism of the academy by introducing controversial topics. Solomiia Pavlychko's talent in that respect was unprecedented.[102] Her monograph *Discourse of Modernism in Ukrainian Literature* (*Dyskurs modernizmu v ukrains'kii literaturi*), which came out in 1997 (followed by a second edition in 1999), signaled an unorthodox approach to defining this movement in Ukrainian literature. First, she excluded the actual literary texts from her consideration, focusing instead on literary discourse around those texts. Second, she placed the special relationship between Olha Kobylianska

and Lesia Ukrainka at the center of Ukrainian modernist discourse, underscoring the lesbian subtext of their correspondence (considered quite shocking and unconventional at the time, even though this particular point had been
made earlier by Ihor Kostetsky in his lengthy introduction to the Ukrainian
rendition of Stefan George's oeuvre).[103]

Another important work by Pavlychko, her previously mentioned study
on Krymsky, *Nationalism, Sexuality and Orientalism: Ahatanhel Krymsky's
Complex World (Natsionalizm, seksual'nist', oriientalizm: Skladnyi svit Ahatanhela Kryms'koho*, 2000) also foregrounds issues of sexuality in general and
homosexuality in particular. This work is striking for the critic's attempt to
view Krymsky's oeuvre in its totality. He is presented not just as a poet and
writer but also as a scholar and political thinker. In fact, the most fascinating part of her study (chapter 3) deals with Krymsky's views on nationalism
and issues of identity. Her detailed description of the writer's evolution as he
came to terms with his own national identity found resonance in post-Soviet
realities. In this context Krymsky's orientalism also lends itself to an intriguing scrutiny. Pavlychko shows in great detail all the inconsistencies and
contradictions inherently present in the scholar's approach to studies of the
East. He was under a considerable influence of the Western perception of the
Orient as advocated by such scholars as Silvestre de Sacy and Ernest Renan,
so well deconstructed by Said in his *Orientalism* (1978), and viewed nations
of the Middle East, with colonial status at the time, as inferior despite the
fact that he loved and scrupulously studied classical texts belonging to their
cultures. One would assume that someone with so keen a sense of Ukraine's
colonial status vis-à-vis imperial Russia would display more understanding
for such countries as Lebanon, Syria or Egypt, but, as the record shows, with
regard to these nations his position during his two-year stay in the Middle
East was quite in line with those of the West as well as Russia.[104] Although,
unlike Western scholars, Krymsky did not display any anti-Semitic tendencies, as Pavlychko attests,[105] but he too was not free of biases, especially
when it concerned people of Turkic origin.[106] All three aspects of Krymsky's
oeuvre that Pavlychko presents in her investigation—nationalism, sexuality
and orientalism—constitute new reading strategies and confirm a special
place she earned in the field of Ukrainian literary scholarship. By studying
Krymsky's output in such a new comprehensive way, Pavlychko redefined
the Ukrainian fin de siècle, mainly in terms of who the major players were in
that particular period.

Pavlychko's direct contribution to feminism consists of a number of
articles published at various times and in various periodical and book publications, collected posthumously in the already-mentioned *Feminism*. This
anthology sketches Pavlychko's interest in feminism both as a methodological tool to be applied in studying literary works and as an intellectual space,

indispensable for discussing the social and national concerns of Ukrainian women. For example, her 1995–1996 article "Progress on Hold: The Conservative Faces of Women in Ukraine" indicates that the critic readily ventured outside literary quarters in order to voice her alarm about job discrimination and the marginal role women play in Ukrainian politics.[107]

Less socially active than Pavlychko, Tamara Hundorova's critical oeuvre is not solely defined by feminism. As her publications attest, Hundorova's scholarly interests have a much wider scope.[108] But her *Femina Melancholica: Sex and Culture in Olha Kobylianska's Gender Utopia (Femina Melancholica: Stat' i kul'tura v gendernii utopii Ol'hy Kobylians'koi,* 2002) constitutes an exception. In it the critic returns to and further elaborates Pavlychko's argument about the centrality of discourse on sexuality and gender in early Ukrainian modernism and the role Kobylianska and Ukrainka played in introducing these subjects into Ukrainian letters. Yet she insists on a constructed nature of their quasi-lesbian correspondence and places it in a Platonic context, a marked difference from Pavlychko's approach.

Hundorova selects the most important events and relationships in Kobylianska's life and juxtaposes them against the writer's output according to a carefully designed thematic framework. Nationalism, feminism, sexuality, androgyny and gender are all foregrounded not only because Kobylianska herself takes up these issues, but also because her personal drama unfolds along the same fault lines. As a result *Femina Melancholica* is not so much a literary biography as it is a contemplation on Kobylianska's multiple identities: a Ukrainian with a German upbringing, a feminist, an accomplished writer, a new woman who nonetheless longs to marry. All these identities, Hundorova argues, are rooted in liminality and each displays its own rites de passage. She argues, moreover, that Kobylianska's main contribution lies in the creation of a new cultural paradigm in Ukrainian literature, a paradigm that uniquely blends feminism, nationalism and modernism. Placing Kobylianska's oeuvre in the context of a European modernist paradigm, Hundorova reveals to what extent the issues taken up by the writer were on a par with other modernists of the fin de siècle era, regardless of their nationality.

Another scholar of the Kyiv gender school, Vira Aheieva, has published a number of important works of criticism,[109] but I would like to focus on her achievements as an editor, a role not always eagerly sought by other feminist critics. She used to be the editor, at the publishing house Fakt, of the series *Text plus Context*, which published Ukrainian classics and provided a contextual background for them in the form of little known or entirely new critical essays. Thus, she edited a book on Marko Vovchok—*Three Fates (Try doli,* 2002)—which presented not only Vovchok's short stories written in Ukrainian, but also the writer's texts written originally in Russian. *Three Fates* examines the role Vovchok played in Ukrainian, Russian and French literary circles through a number of essays by Pavlychko, Ksenya Kiebuzinski, Mykola Zerov, Viktor Petrov-Domontovych and Aheieva herself. In a similar fashion she prepared an edition of Lesia Ukrainka's *Lisova pisnia* in a volume entitled *My Soul Will Talk to Them: Lesia Ukrainka's "Forest Song" and Its Interpretations* (*Im promovliaty dusha moia bude: "Lisova pisnia" Lesi Ukrainky ta ii interpretatsii*, 2002).[110] These critical editions of Ukrainian classics play an important role in school curricula, invariably affecting the understanding of the changing nature of literary canons and indirectly influencing the formation of national identity among students. Presenting them with new readings of old classics can foster a new appreciation of national culture. Aheieva is also responsible for editing two collections of essays on feminism and gender studies: *Gender and Culture* (*Gender i kul'tura*, 2001) and *Gender Perspectives* (*Genderna perspektyva*, 2004). These collections provide a variety of interpretations from a feminist and gender perspective and include contributions both from the West and Ukraine.

The most intriguing contribution to the feminist literary discourse in post-Soviet Ukraine comes from Nila Zborovska.[111] She experiments with various genres and presents herself as both a literary critic and a writer. For example, her *Feminist Reflections: At the Carnival of Dead Kisses* (*Feministychni rozdumy: na karnavali mertvykh potsilunkiv*, 1999) is an interesting hybrid comprised of literary criticism and something that could be labeled "fictionalized memoirs." It is not an attempt on her part to emulate what the French feminists coined *as écriture feminine* or *parler femme*. Rather, it is a conscious effort to break the conventions and the horizon of expectation when it comes to literary criticism. As Rita Felski succinctly put it, genre "provides the cultural matrix against which the significance of the individual text can be measured."[112]

Feminist Reflections is neatly divided into two parts: the first is devoted to literary criticism and the second constitutes a hodgepodge of letters, literary rumors and reflections, a novella, and short stories, all making up a narrative that most closely resembles the genre of memoirs. Zborovska's memoirs, however, are anything but straightforward. They are fragmented, fictionalized and clearly dispense with chronology. She even creates a separate persona for her idiosyncratic narrative, Mariia Ilnytska, in order to emphasize yet another approach to literary and feminist issues. But despite the intentional bifurcation of the authorial self, Zborovska wants her reader to regard this particular work as an indissoluble whole.

Zborovska the critic practices what Elaine Showalter labels "feminist critique" and "gynocritics." In other words, she gives feminist readings of works by male authors and critiques works written by women. The former practice prevails. She deals with novels by such contemporary male writers as Yuri Andrukhovych, Yevhen Pashkovsky and Oles Ulianenko. She also presents interesting interpretations of Ivan Nechui-Levytsky and Todos Osmachka as well as explicates misogynist tendencies in Yuriy Tarnawsky's dramatic works.[113] As for "gynocritics," Zborovska concentrates for the most part on Oksana Zabuzhko's texts. Two other women she pays some attention to are Milena Rudnytska[114] and Lesia Ukrainka. Zborovska the writer delivers examples of well-constructed feminist writings. I use the word "constructed" in the sense that these narratives are to a large extent programmatic and evince issues typically problematized by feminists: mother-daughter relations, career versus motherhood, equality, relationships and even dealing with breast cancer. Undoubtedly, the hybridization of genre has allowed Zborovska to open up new territories for feminist explorations.

In *Feminist Reflections*, moreover, Zborovska brings a new dimension to literary criticism, namely a personal touch, her own individual self, which interacts and implicitly engages in polemics with the objects of her criticism. She continues to embed the elements from her personal life in her subsequent psychoanalytical study of Lesia Ukrainka. It is not a coincidence that this work is entitled *My Lesia Ukrainka* (*Moia Lesia Ukrainka*, 2002). It begins by telling the critic's own personal story, which mysteriously connects her with Ukrainka through the fact that her grandmother was born on the day Lesia Ukrainka died. Unlike her colleague, Aheieva, Zborovska devotes as much space to the analysis of Ukrainka's biography as she does to the readings of the latter's works. In a way, *My Lesia Ukrainka* challenges the premises of Ukrainian literary scholarship by expanding the boundaries of analysis to include the personal and the subjective.

Psychoanalysis and The Post-Chornobyl Library

In the second edition of *Discourse of Modernism in Ukrainian Literature* (1999) Pavlychko augments her study by adding two chapters, one on the psychoanalytic discourse and the influence of Sigmund Freud on Ukrainian letters in the first three decades of the twentieth century, and another one on the émigré poetic phenomenon of the New York Group. Her analysis of Ukrainian modernist discourses impacted by psychoanalysis is novel but still rather sketchy. Pavlychko first aims at tracing Freud's impact on literary production in fin de siècle Ukraine and after the revolution in the 1920s, and second, she also aims at presenting readings of literary works from that period by critics who fully incorporated Freud's theoretical premises in their interpretation. She concentrates mainly on the writings by Stepan Balei, especially his psychoanalytic analysis of Taras Shevchenko's works in *On Psychology of Shevchenko's Oeuvre* (*Z psykhologii tvorchosty Shevchenka*, 1916), and later on the critics active in the 1920s such as Stepan Haievsky, A. Khaletsky, Mykola Perlin, Valerian Pidmohylny and others. She further points out that these critics attempted to combine psychoanalysis with Marxism and comes to the conclusion that in the realm of literature the most interesting examples of Freudian postulates occur in fiction rather than in literary criticism, citing two biographical novels by Viktor Petrov, *Alina and Kostomarov* (*Alina i Kostomarov*, 1929) and *Kulish's Love Affairs* (*Romany Kulisha*, 1930) as the most representative works incorporating Freudian discourse.

Pavlychko's inroads into the history of psychoanalysis in Ukrainian modernism constitutes but an historical outline of its beginnings. It was never her goal to conceptualize Ukrainian literature from a psychoanalytical perspective, although, as her articles attest, she was quite supportive of this approach as one of many possible new productive interpretative methodologies.[115] Engaging psychoanalysis as a reading strategy was taken up most consistently by Nila Zborovska in her monumental study of modern Ukrainian literature titled *The Code of Ukrainian Literature: The Project of the Psychohistory of Modern Ukrainian Literature* (*Kod ukrains'koi literatury: Proekt psykhoistorii novitn'oi ukrains'koi literatury*, 2006).

In her monograph, Zborovska contends that in the space of postcoloniality, Ukrainian modern anticolonial literature[116] lends itself especially well to investigations from a psychohistorical point of view. She further elaborates that while a standard history of literature focuses on textual manifestations of national character as it evolves through various epochs, psychohistory, on the other hand, takes as its main task the problematization of such an evolution by underscoring the psychological motivation behind historical events, including creative endeavors. And since her whole conceptualization of Ukrainian literature hovers around its anticolonial premises, her main goal is to grapple with the issue of colonial corruption in the development of national character. Zborovska also agrees with the Indian scholar M. Ramamurti that only by scrupulously studying the past, one can be cleansed of conscious and unconscious complexes that hinder the development of national spirit.[117]

Methodologically, the critic relies on the motivational analysis of historical events as developed by the American social thinker Lloyd deMause. However, whereas deMause in his psychohistorical studies concentrates on the impact of child-rearing practices (or child abuse to be more precise) in the formation of the human psyche and subsequently nations,[118] Zborovska applies this model to the birth of Ukrainian modern literature. In addition to an intense concentration on motivational analysis, she also utilizes ideas developed by the psychoanalyst Melanie Klein, especially the latter's insistence on the importance of the maternal function in the development of subjectivity and access to culture and language. Zborovska contrasts Klein's vision of the significance of the maternal in the constitution of subjectivity with that of Freud, in which it is the paternal function that becomes a predominant force as far as the entrance into the social realm is concerned. At the heart of Zborovska's conceptualization of the psychohistory of Ukrainian literature lies the distinction between maternal (which takes form of the permissive and the supportive) and paternal (which is characterized by the aggressive and the authoritarian) modes of domination in literary production. She differentiates three distinct periods in its development: classical, modern and postmodern. In the classical period she includes works of Ivan Kotliarevsky who introduced the vernacular language into Ukrainian letters, as well as both romantic and realist authors of the nineteenth century. The second period comprises works of modernist writers and the third period, the postmodern one, is made up of works and activity of two literary generations, that of the 1960s and that of the 1980s. The inclusion of the so-called *shistdesiatnyky* (the generation of the 1960s) in the postmodern period comes as a surprise but because her classificatory criteria go beyond aesthetic concerns and concentrate instead on the psychological motivation, such a slippage appears to be justified within the proposed model.

Zborovska compares Russian and Ukrainian literatures and comes to the conclusion that the paternal mode of development prevails in the former, whereas in the latter dominates the maternal pathos. In fact, it almost seems that the whole project of the decolonization of Ukrainian literature should consist of recapturing the lost code of the paternal bravery, which in its ultimate manifestation should lead to the establishment of statehood. The critic contends that because the male (paternal) component was often corrupted due to the colonial status of Ukraine, no wonder women invariably were forced to be the carriers of male bravery. In literatures of healthy nation-states maternal and paternal components are balanced; in nations with the colonial past this balance is disturbed.

In many ways Zborovska's turn to psychohistory is not surprising considering that already in her feminist writings she displayed a penchant for the subjective and the personal. For one of the distinctive features of psychohistorical approach is the reliance on the emotional and subjective sensibility of the observer. DeMause put it quite explicitly:

> Like all sciences, psychohistory stands and falls on the clarity and testability of its concepts, the breadth and parsimony of its theories, the extent of its empirical evidence, and so on. What psychohistory does have which is different is a certain methodology of discovery, a methodology which attempts to solve problems of historical motivation with a unique blend of historical documentation, clinical experience and the use of the researcher's own emotions as the crucial research tool for discovery.[119]

The Code of Ukrainian Literature represents the critic's very personal take on the development of Ukrainian literature from the late eighteenth century to the present, a development in which the dynamics between the national and the imperial is constantly invoked and framed in psychoanalytical terms. What is clear from Zborovska's final and major work is that her position becomes increasingly more conservative and quite critical of contemporary attempts at postmodern experimentation. The importance of national self-awareness and self-identification and the emphasis on the aristocratic (in the spiritual sense) aspirations of a new national literature make Zborovska's stand somewhat at odds with her contemporary literary scholars. As a feminist critic she used to analyze postmodern texts in positive terms,[120] often underscoring their innovative qualities, but as a psychoanalytic and psychohistorical critic she dismissed postmodernist experiments as unproductive, imitative and supporting the imperial dominance.[121] Volodymyr Danylenko aptly observes that in *The Code of Ukrainian Literature*, Zborovska "turns away from postmodernism toward the inner world of man, foregrounding such categories as conscience, morality, responsibility, feelings of empathy and civic duty."[122] Moreover, he also intimates that the critic questions current parameters of the literary process and alludes to the necessity of looking for new critical paradigms.

In contrast to Zborovska, Tamara Hundorova embraces the Ukrainian literary postmodern, even though she also points out its weaknesses and inconsistencies.[123] In *The Post-Chornobyl Library: Ukrainian Literary Postmodernism (Pisliachornobyl's'ka biblioteka: Ukrains'kyi literaturnyi postmodern*, 2005),[124] she presents her own assessment of contemporary literature in the form of essays on the most representative texts, trends and discourses from the mid-1980s to the mid-2000s, foregrounding the issue of chronology. Her innovative reading strategy is rooted in the fact that she uses the Chornobyl catastrophe of 1986 rather than independence of 1991 as a starting point for a conversation on Ukrainian new literature and the new literary epoch. Chornobyl in Hundorova's text becomes a powerful metaphor for a postmodern, apocalyptic and hybrid culture that emerged in the 1990s from the ashes of the catastrophic event, manifesting itself in a series of various transformations—social, environmental and national. In this context, the post-Chornobyl library refers to that cultural production, which simultaneously entails existential threat brought about by the nuclear age and survival, or, to put it differently, a production that exists in the interstices of the past and the present, the imaginary and the real, the playful and the apocalyptic. But the critic also underscores positive moments of the catastrophic event— Chornobyl, after all, has become a civilizational symbol that helped instigating the birth of a new postmodern consciousness in Ukraine, which reveals itself most conspicuously in the re-reading of national culture, stressing its polyphonic, multilingual and intertextual attributes.

Inscribing Chornobyl as a classificatory marker and a period divider within a critical discourse allows Hundorova to view Ukrainian literary postmodernism in broader rather than narrower terms.[125] Hence, according to her, the post-Chornobyl library refers not only to the postmodernism of the Bu-Ba-Bu group in its carnivalesque edition, but it also includes works of authors belonging to the so-called Kyiv "ironic underground" (Volodymyr Dibrova, Bohdan Zholdak and Les Poderviansky), authors representing neo-modernism and neo-populism (Yevhen Pashkovsky and Viacheslav Medvid), and authors representing gendered voices (Zabuzhko, Halyna Pahutiak). In other words, all Ukrainian literature of the 1990s, according to Hundorova, belongs to the postmodern, post-Chornobyl epoch, even though some of its singular manifestations display other than postmodern characteristics. She also recognizes that whereas in the first half of the 1990s the main literary discourse hovered around the issue of artistic freedom, in the second half, the focus shifted to the diversity of aesthetic positions and to various understandings of the role literature should play in a society.

Hundorova's new approach to chronology led her to a new conceptualization of contemporary Ukrainian literature, but some old practices, like relying on literary generations as markers of periodization, remained intact. In fact, in her concluding English-language chapter, she intimates that "the self-consciousness of literary generations has played a significant role in the literary process of the 1990s."[126] This is the period, according to the critic, in which three literary generations co-existed, each competing for attention. The older writers of the "sixties" generation (Ivan Drach, Lina Kostenko, Dmytro Pavlychko, Valerii Shevchuk, Yuri Mushketyk and Volodymyr Yavorivsky), by and large politically engaged, were politely dismissed by the younger generation of the 1980s (Ihor Rymaruk, Vasyl Herasymiuk, Yuri Andrukhovych, Oksana Zabuzhko, Liudmyla Taran and Natalka Bilotserkivets). The latter generation reached its maturity in the second half of the 1980s, espousing high literary genres, and, in principle, rejecting political engagement. And finally, the generation of the 1990s, with Serhiy Zhadan as its most conspicuous leader, is the literary community championing aesthetic pluralism and ironic approach, at the same time being the most consistent in rejecting populist premises. All these groupings, at least rhetorically, were against the previously imposed Soviet ideology (*sovietchyna*), but, for the generation of the sixties, it was not so easy to dispense with populist premises.

In addition to introducing a different approach to chronology, Hundorova's reading of the new literature stands uniquely apart for two other reasons. First, she rightly observes that the post-independence literature is not only by necessity pluralistic but also bilingual; and second, she convincingly explains the 1990s politics of canon formation, pointing out the existence of its multiple varieties, official and unofficial. The critic also brings to attention the fact that popular literary genres have increasingly become more and more important and eventually will need to be recognized and accommodated in the canon:

The reverse canon of the 1990s embraced not only Ukrainian-language but also Russian-language mass literature. The preceding literary canon was monocultural and excluded works by Ukrainian authors written in Russian. In the 1990s Russian mass literature swamped the Ukrainian book market. By the end of the decade new printing houses and publishers had launched several fiction series, including Ukrainian detective stories, thrillers, science fiction, and romances. Some Russian-language authors, such as Andrei Kurkov and Marina and Sergei Diachenko, live and work in Ukraine and call themselves Ukrainian writers.[127]

The critic invokes the institutions such as the Writers' Union of Ukraine and the Taras Shevchenko Institute of Literature of the National Academy of Sciences and identifies them as those responsible for the creation of a new official national canon; however, she does not evaluate their effectiveness in this regard. The fact is that many authors, who came to prominence in the early 1990s, have not been readily acknowledged and initially embraced by academic literary scholars, especially by those of the older generation. Yet, Hundorova looks on a bright side and sees progress nonetheless: "the process of decanonization has become increasingly evident and has been accompanied by the emergence of new canons—every anthology that came out in the 1990s represented a distinctive canon of contemporary literature."[128] Interestingly, her proposition of the post-Chornobyl library as an apt lens for viewing contemporary Ukrainian literature has not received sufficient academic support but was embraced by younger critics.[129]

The Academic (Ir)Relevance

The formation of canons is a measure of strength or weakness of the institutions responsible for literary studies and artistic production. Following the collapse of the Soviet Union, there was understandably a need to revisit old presuppositions as far as the literary canon was concerned. Many female literary scholars who turned to feminist theory and at least initially were affiliated with the T. H. Shevchenko Institute of Literature,[130] took upon themselves precisely that task. Yet George G. Grabowicz in his polemical article "Literary Historiography and its Contexts" ("Literaturne istoriopysannia ta ioho konteksty"), mainly directed at the Ukrainian academic establishment, argues that not enough has been done in terms of reevaluating the past by such prominent institutions as the Academy of Sciences of Ukraine and especially its Institute of Literature.[131] He most forcefully criticizes those literary scholars who are affiliated with the Institute and who have failed to find new approaches when it comes to reading strategies, particularly when presenting new authoritative histories of literary periods. However, this process of reevaluation already started in the glasnost' period. One of the most characteristic traits of those years was to restore the names of writers previously forbidden, as well as to introduce the output of Ukrainian émigré literary figures. Moreover, Ukraine's independence brought about the necessity to reexamine contributions and significance of those writers who gained prominence under the Soviet regime. Judging by *A History of 20th Century Ukrainian Literature* (*Istoriia ukrains'koi literatury 20 stolittia*), a collective work under the general editorship of Vitalii Donchyk, published first in 1993 and reissued with some revisions in 1998, as far as the second half of the twentieth century is concerned, more attention is devoted to Soviet Ukrainian writers than to those debuting in the glasnost and post-independence periods. And this is precisely what Grabowicz sharply criticized in the previously mentioned article, ascribing to Donchyk a somewhat incomplete, if not biased, treatment of the new literature. In his 2011 critique of Ukrainian literary scholarship, Taras Koznarsky characterizes this history of twentieth-century Ukrainian literature as a product that is "transitional, hybrid [...], where the contours of the Soviet literary canon glare through new ideological scaffolding."[132]

The Taras Shevchenko Institute of Literature at the Academy of Sciences came up with a grand project of publishing the authoritative academic edition of the "History of Ukrainian Literature" in twelve volumes by 2008. Presumably, such a comprehensive approach would alleviate any imbalances or partiality displayed in already published histories, focusing on specific periods, like the one by Donchyk mentioned above. However, this twelve-volume edition still awaits its full realization,[133] and taking into account that the person responsible for the overall publication is again Donchyk, one might have some doubts whether or not a truly new approach would be adopted. While it is impossible to evaluate a publication still in progress, we might get a glimpse into its inner workings from what has been already published on the subject.

In 2005 the Institute released two ancillary publications, one on various theoretical and methodological aspects of the new history of Ukrainian literature in the form of a collection of essays, previously published in the scholarly journal *Slovo i chas*, titled *A New History of Ukrainian Literature* (*Nova istoriia ukrains'koi literatury*), and another one compiled by Ya. Tsymbal, *The Academic History of Ukrainian Literature in 10 Volumes* (*Akademichna istoriia ukrains'koi literatury v 10 tomakh*),[134] comprising the proceedings of several roundtables devoted to the academic history of Ukrainian literature in 10 volumes, which took place from 2002 to 2004. These two publications shed light on the intentions, approaches and various conceptualizations with regard to the planned history, expressed by participants of the roundtables and invited authors of *A New History of Ukrainian Literature*. The general concept of the history, as explicated by Donchyk in the opening chapter of *The Academic History* foresees a comprehensive treatment of the literary process and allows a methodological plurality as long as the national dimension of the literature is adequately expressed. But one is struck how little otherwise this approach differs from the one utilized in the Soviet eight-volume history, published by the Institute back in 1967–1971. The new twelve-volume history also relies on a collective authorship (with the exception of volume four, devoted entirely to Shevchenko, written by Ivan Dziuba) and is guided by chronology (often chopped into decades, an approach, which on occasions denies the coherence of aesthetic trends characteristic of a given period) rather than by such criteria as style, genre or even aesthetic and/or philosophical ideas. Each volume represents a mixture of articles on the historiography, outlines of a literary process, most important authors and general genres, such as poetry, prose and drama.

Notwithstanding considerable debates on the need to present a new vision, evident in both A New History of Ukrainian Literature and in The Academic History, the reported plan of work does not indicate an adoption of any innovative methodology. Despite the wishes of the history's chief editor, Vitalii Donchyk, to come up with a brand new product ("the history not yet seen"), the planned publication betrays old entrenched academic practices, though, admittedly, freed from the communist ideology but replaced by a pronounced national bias. The only gain, it seems, is the inclusion of the previously forbidden authors, works, and issues, especially those connected to the cause of national liberation. The general impression one receives from the proposed outline of the new history of Ukrainian literature is that of hesitancy, hybridity and inconsistency in the application of classificatory criteria. While the Institute's desire to involve in this project as many scholars as deemed necessary is understandable, the more individual approach, like inviting a single author per volume, would probably yield better results if not more coherent results. One thing is certain—these conservative academic historical and canonical propositions no doubt have some bearing on what is being eventually taught in schools; on the other hand, they are counterbalanced by the alternative propositions coming out mostly from the writers themselves.[135]

The factors that I have recognized as the most influential (or potentially influential) in the construction of literary canon(s) in post-independence Ukraine are language choice, ideology and institutions responsible for literary production, its evaluation and dissemination. As things stood by the end of 2011, all three areas displayed considerable weaknesses and uncertainties. One consolation might be that as a new generation of literary scholars matures, the old Soviet ideology will simply disappear. By the same token, the institutions, which contribute to the production and maintenance of literary value, as they grow younger, will also gradually shed the remnants of the ideologized past and entrenched traditions of Soviet ways.

Yet it is not always a given that youth necessarily entails progress and innovation. Ivan Dziuba, a leading *shistdesiatnyk*, dissident author, public intellectual, and now also an academician and scholar very much involved in the project of the twelfth-volume *History of Ukrainian Literature* discussed above, proposes interesting concepts of cultural paradigms relevant to the Ukrainian context. His three-volume publication, entitled *From the Well of Years* (*Z krynytsi lit*, 2006–2007), comprising his contributions from various sources (published and unpublished), is the case in point. In the second volume there are two articles, written just five years apart, which underscore the need to conceptualize the national culture comprehensively and holistically. In the 1987 essay, titled "Do We Conceive of National Culture as a Whole?" ("Chy usvidomliuiemo natsional'nu kul'turu iak tsilist'?"), Dziuba expresses the need to understand culture as a system of integrated and interdependent interactions in which one can discern several hierarchical levels of such reciprocal interplay. At the very bottom of these interactions lies the need for personal contacts and openness to various cultural products. The next level concerns the nature of cultural stimuli, which each artist or writer supplies for his/her own creative consumption. The subsequent two levels underscore the need for cultural syncretism, including hybridization of genres and various demonstrations of artistic symbiosis as generated, for example, by theatrical productions or motion pictures. The fifth level marries all cultural manifestations to specific aesthetic and stylistic tendencies at any given time, and, finally, the sixth level of interactions entails a thoroughly functioning national culture. In other words, the interrelationship of all the above levels constitutes a coherent whole of what Dziuba conceives of as a national culture, that is, not just high art and literature but culture that also reveals itself in everyday life with all its interactions. He readily admits that Ukrainian culture of the 1980s lacks such a functional fullness. He laments the neglect of the Ukrainian language and emphasizes the importance of its utilization in all spheres of social life, although warns against "purists" who advocate "Ukrainian approach only" and comprehend national culture in exclusionary rather than inclusive terms. However, it is clear from his narrative that the main task that awaits all those responsible for cultural production and its reception is to restore a systemic wholeness for Ukrainian national culture, previously undermined by Soviet totalitarianism and colonialism.

Dziuba's second essay on the subject, "Toward a Conception of the Development of Ukrainian Culture" ("Do kontseptsii rozvytku ukrains'koi kul'tury"), written in 1992, which coincided with his tenure as Minister of Culture (1992–1994), continues the critic's deliberations about the importance of achieving completeness in a newly liberated cultural sphere. But he also envisions for it a specific role—that of a consolidating factor in the nation-building process. Developing a new conception of national culture, according to Dziuba, assumes taking into account theoretical and contextual aspects. In the latter sphere the critic differentiates the problems as they relate to cultural phenomena at the world level, then specifically at the level of the post-Soviet space and, finally, at the level of one of post-Soviet states, that is, Ukraine. He understands that the Ukrainian postcolonial cultural situation offers new opportunities to incorporate the cultural experience from many different sources, at the same time he insists on developing its own national approach. Dziuba believes that culture not only plays an important consolidating role in the nation-building process, but is also the site of historical memory and national self-awareness. Cultural politics should therefore facilitate the development and self-realization of each individual as well as advance the well-being of a democratic state. Only a state with a full-fledged democracy can secure the free development of a national culture and aid in the promotion of its achievements around the world. The critic also debates the question whether or not cultural politics should take as its base an ethnic or civic principle. Without hesitation he stresses and chooses the latter.

The above postulates argue in favor of the active engagement of the state in helping to promote the development of national culture because, in the final analysis, this secures and consolidates its newly achieved independence. In other words, such a policy is in the state's own self-interest. Yet, however attractive and even commonsensical Dziuba's vision has been, especially to those nationally inclined, he was unable to advance his cultural policies far when he was still part of the Ukrainian government in the early years of independence. His later writings, particularly those dealing with the language issue, were not overly optimistic, as they reflected facts on the ground, including the situation in which the Ukrainian language had been increasingly squeezed out from the cultural space, mainly by mass products coming via Russian TV programs, or popular Russian books in the form of cheap pulp fiction. Viewing Ukrainian not only as a communicative tool but, more importantly, as a differentiating factor working for the strengthening of Ukrainian cultural distinctiveness, Dziuba's initial focus on the completeness of culture shifted eventually toward the questions of identity. He realized that national culture, as he envisioned it, is unachievable as long as the sense of national belonging or national identity is so poorly developed. But for all practical purposes culture and national identity, according to Dziuba, are inextricably linked: "a national culture emerges as a fundamental condition for national self-realization."[136] Later on in the same book he becomes even more explicit about this connection: "Culture becomes a means for expressing national identity and for providing raison d'être for a nation's existence."[137] This holistic approach to culture in which the fates of the nation and the individual are fused is also evident in Dziuba's approach to literary scholarship, especially in his studies on Shevchenko. It is necessary, the critic believes, to provide not only a broad context for the poet's creative activities but also to present him in such a way that his oeuvre acquires an utmost relevance for the post-independence situation. Marko Pavlyshyn in his insightful essay on Dziuba sums it up beautifully:

> In his book on Shevchenko Dziuba brought into play the two devices that had always served him well: the broad presentation of context, based on profound erudition and research; and detailed attention to the words of texts. At the same time, Dziuba avoided giving rise to the impression that his treatise belongs to the narrow field of literary scholarship. The implied reader is the ordinary person, armed with common sense and a curiosity about things of contemporary importance. Likewise, the implied author does not for a moment conceal his political engagement behind a mask of scholarly objectivity. He writes about Shevchenko because, from his perspective, the narrative of the maker of a unifying Ukrainian national identity is a narrative of the twenty-first century no less than of the nineteenth.[138]

Examining a literary phenomenon, in this case the work of Taras Shevchenko, from the perspective of its future cultural implications is one of the strategies that Dziuba pursues most vigorously. Ideally, for him, cultural goods that bear a national significance and constitute an integral part of a fully developed national culture should also become inscribed in the memory of world culture. Dziuba's longing for completeness and wider relevance for his own cultural heritage betrays defensive mechanisms against prolonged colonial oppression and imperial hegemony. It seems that his initial optimism was gradually replaced by a stoical resignation. Yet his belief in the need to advocate policies strengthening national identity at the state level has remained unchanged.

LITERATURE ON EDGE

One could argue that ways of interpreting literature do not necessarily impact literary production at any given time. Yet, if there has been one continuous thread of complaints within contemporary Ukrainian literary quarters, it refers to a lack of professional critics or commentators of the literary process in the post-independence period. Iryna Slavinska, summing up literary trends in 2011, provided, for example, an interesting statistic for Ukrainian book industry. According to her, Ukrainian-language book production increased 8 percent in 2011, and the trade in belles-lettres and translations conspicuously rose (50–70 percent) when compared to the previous year. However, these rather positive indicators had been eclipsed by other not so encouraging trends. First, the journalist concluded that an anemic literary life, resulting by and large in publishing pedestrian texts, had been animated only by a number

of literary scandals such as, for instance, an open feud between two of
Ukraine's best-known authors, Oksana Zabuzhko and Yuri Andrukhovych,[139]
or a refusal to continue a book tour by Lina Kostenko because of a perceived
negative reception and criticism of her novel *Notes of a Ukrainian Madman*
(2010).[140] Second, Slavinska predicted that a politicization and involvement
in current affairs by a majority of authors would further intensify in 2012. The
political situation in Ukraine under the Yanukovych regime was not particularly conducive to creative activities. Whether or not authors voiced their dis-
content publicly, in most cases they did not influence opinions of the masses,
and, as Slavinska indicated in her article, they did not have easy access to the
mass media. However distanced from political encroachments they wished
they could be, the reality was such that it made them captive of the gradual
decline in democratic values and increase in authoritarian practices, hence
detachment was hardly an option. No wonder, Slavinska asserted that in 2012
any artistic endeavor would be looked at from a political perspective, and it
would be impossible for any writer or artist to extract himself/herself from a
political context.

Instances of éngagé moments on the part of writers were already amply
manifest in 2011. Vasyl Shkliar and Mariia Matios, two celebrated authors
of popular literature, each in his/her own way declared war on the governing
regime. Shkliar refused to accept the Shevchenko Prize, the highest literary
award, bestowed on a writer by the Ukrainian government, unless Dmytro
Tabachnyk, a Russophone Minister of Education, was fired from his post.
Mariia Matios, on the other hand, protested in an open letter to the Attorney
General of Ukraine with a complaint of political persecution after his officers
entered the Piramida publishing house in Lviv and attempted to stop the distribution of one of her books.[141] Yuri Andrukhovych and Lina Kostenko also
became politically involved when the Ukrainian opposition forces attempted
to recruit them to participate in the upcoming parliamentary elections. It is
telling that neither agreed to such a direct political engagement.[142] These few
examples of the clear politicization of the literary process by the end of 2011
pointed to a radical paradigm shift among contemporary literati, underscoring
the fact that freedom of expression, seemingly achieved painlessly with the
declaration of independence, could not be taken for granted.

The uncertainty and mismanagement in political quarters, so conspicuous
in the post-independence period, invariably affects the cultural sphere. But
despite the absence of any coherent cultural policy on the governmental
level since independence, there have been a few interesting initiatives that
have alleviated a feeling of dispersion and isolation among producers of
literary goods as well as their consumers. Two such initiatives deserve mentioning. One is the establishment of a new chain of Ukrainian bookstores
"Ye," which opened first in Kyiv in 2007 and then in several other major

cities, providing easy access to Ukrainian books and serving as facilitators of numerous literary readings and book presentations. And another one is the creation of a website devoted to all things related to contemporary Ukrainian literature called "Litaktsent." Both these initiatives heavily promote not just Ukrainian literature but all things Ukrainian. Following the presidential elections in 2010 they also constituted important institutions that resisted neocolonizing efforts of the authoritarian Yanukovych regime. They have been augmented by a number of publishing houses that specialize in Ukrainian belles-lettres and have been building partnerships with already established as well as aspiring authors. All these institutions have been acting as independent nurturing niches for Ukrainian cultural growth. Moreover, the existence of a number of well-established literary festivals in Lviv, Kyiv and Chernivtsi, to name a few, of book fairs and publishers' forums (the most famous one taking place in Lviv each year in mid-September), provide a necessary space for the continuation and development of imaginative writing in contemporary Ukraine.

Two decades of national sovereign existence have produced literature, which reflects not only social change that has taken place since 1991, but also depicts a range of identities and how they have been formed. What follows is my story of how the most representative post-independence literary texts deal with the issue of identity formation, based on geography, gender, language and class, and how all these various identities are interwoven to bring about a sense of belonging to a nation, which manifests itself most conspicuously in the form of a fully crystallized national identity.

NOTES

1. Elleke Boehmer, *Colonial and Postcolonial Literature: Migrant Metaphors* (Oxford: Oxford University Press, 1995), 194.

2. Jan Pieterse Nederveen and Bhikhu Parekh, eds. *The Decolonization of Imagination: Culture, Knowledge and Power* (London: Atlantic Highlands, 1995), 3.

3. See especially Catherine Wanner, *Communities of the Converted: Ukrainians and Global Evangelism* (Ithaca and London: Cornell University Press, 2007). See also her article "Missionaries and Pluralism: How the Law Changed the Religious Landscape in Ukraine," in *Contemporary Ukraine on the Cultural Map of Europe*, ed. Larissa M.L. Zaleska Onyshkevych and Maria G. Rewakowicz (Armonk, NY: M.E. Sharpe, 2009), 89–100, and Andrew Sorokowski, "The Status of Religion in Ukraine in Relation to European Standards" (ibid., 69–88).

4. Accepting the national symbols from the period of the Ukrainian National Republic (1917–1921) was one of the ways to ascertain a newly won statehood but the government was less forceful in pushing the policy of Ukrainization in all spheres of social and political conduct, as was the case back in the 1920s under Soviet rule.

5. Pierre Bourdieu, *The Field of Cultural Production* (New York: Columbia University Press, 1993), 30.

6. Ibid., 37.

7. See Kateryna Pan'o, "Knyzhkove zahostrennia: Chomu vlada voiuie z pys'mennykamy," *Druh chytacha*, January 29, 2011, accessed May 30, 2017, http://vsiknygy.net.ua/neformat/9026.

8. See Iryna Slavins'ka, "2011: literaturni pidsumky," *Ukrains'ka pravda*, December 21, 2011, accessed December 22, 2011, http://www.life.pravda.com.ua/culture/2011/12/21/91726/.

9. Amar Acheraïou, *Questioning Hybridity, Postcolonialism and Globalization* (Houndmills: Palgrave Macmillan, 2011), 17.

10. Homi Bhabha, *The Location of Culture* (London: Routledge, 2004), 54–55.

11. Aijaz Ahmad, "The Politics of Literary Postcoloniality," in *Contemporary Postcolonial Theory: A Reader*, ed. Padmini Mongia (London: Arnold, 1996), 287.

12. Benita Parry, "Signs of Our Times: A Discussion of Homi Bhabha's *The Location of Culture*," in *The Third Text Reader on Art, Culture and Theory*, ed. Rasheed Araeen, Sean Cubitt and Ziauddin Sardar (London: Continuum, 2002), 248.

13. Jan Pieterse Nederveen, "Globalisation as Hybridisation," *International Sociology* 9 (1994): 172.

14. Anjali Prabhu, *Hybridity: Limits, Transformations, Prospects* (Albany: SUNY Press, 2007), 12.

15. Ibid., 2.

16. Acheraïou, *Questioning Hybridity*, 115.

17. Ibid., 107.

18. Ibid., 196.

19. Ibid.

20. Ibid., 197.

21. In a way, there is some affinity here with the Bakhtinian understanding of hybridization, as it also refers to sites, such as parish feasts and fairs, where fools become kings, the comic mixes with the serious, and the social class becomes irrelevant. See M.M. Bakhtin, *Rabelais and His World* (Cambridge, MA: MIT Press, 1968), 5. See also Nederveen Pieterse, "Globalisation as Hybridisation," 171.

22. One such case is the phenomenon of Verka Serduchka (the stage name of an actor/singer Andrii Danylko) in Ukrainian pop culture. Danylko stirred a real controversy at the Eurovision Song Contest in 2007 when in the presented song s/he sang what sounded like "I want to see Russia good-bye," and which s/he claimed was really "I want to see lasha tumbai." See Serhy Yekelchyk, "What Is Ukrainian about Ukraine's Pop Culture?: The Strange Case of Verka Serduchka," *Canadian American Slavic Studies* 44 (2010): 228–30.

23. Marwan M. Kraidy, *Hybridity, or the Cultural Logic of Globalization* (Philadelphia: Temple University Press, 2005), 150.

24. Ibid., 161.

25. Many Ukrainian TV media programs can be labeled as "hybrid genres," that is, shows, which are national "domesticated" versions of successful U.S. and

European originals. This category includes shows such as "X Factor" or "So You Think You Can Dance," etc.

26. For more on *surzhyk*, see Laada Bilaniuk, *Contested Tongues: Language Politics and Cultural Correction in Ukraine* (Ithaca: Cornell University Press, 2005), 103–41.

27. Cf. M.M. Bakhtin, *The Dialogic Imagination: Four Essays*, ed. Michael Holquist (Austin: University of Texas Press, 1981), 358–60.

28. Edward Said, *Culture and Imperialism* (New York: Vintage Books, 1994), 51.

29. Jonathan Culler, *The Literary in Theory* (Stanford: Stanford University Press, 2007), 34.

30. Ibid.

31. Colin MacCabe, "An Interview with Stuart Hall, December 2007," *Critical Quarterly* 50 (2007): 33–34. To be exact, Hall does not dismiss roots altogether but views them alone as insufficient.

32. For Ukraine such relevant Others are, of course, Russia, and, to a lesser degree, Europe.

33. The constructed or "imagined" nature of any nation has been especially advocated by Benedict Anderson in his classic book *Imagined Communities: Reflections on the Origins and Spread of Nationalism*, Rev. ed. (London: Verso, 1991).

34. Maurice Halbwachs, *The Collective Memory*, trans. Francis J. Ditter, Jr. and Vida Yazdi Ditter (New York: Harper, 1980), 80.

35. Ibid., 24.

36. This view is especially advocated in Andrukhovych's essays, namely in his *Dezorientatsiia na mistsevosti* (1999). To some extent his novels also reflect this preoccupation with geography.

37. Ihab Hassan, "Queries for Postcolonial Studies," in *The Third Text Reader*, 239.

38. This essay was later reprinted in Ukrainian translation under the title: "Kozaky v Iamaitsi: Postkoloniial'ni rysy v suchasnii ukrains'kii kul'turi," *Slovo i chas* 4–5 (1994): 65–71, and in his book *Kanon ta ikonostas* (Kyiv: Chas, 1997), 223–36.

39. Marko Pavlyshyn, "Post-colonial Features in Contemporary Ukrainian Culture," *Australian Slavonic and East European Studies* 6.2 (1992): 41.

40. Ibid., 42.

41. Ibid., 48.

42. *Kanon ta ikonostas*, 216.

43. "Post-colonial Features," 45.

44. Elleke Boehmer, *Colonial and Postcolonial Literature: Migrant Metaphors* (Oxford: Oxford University Press, 1995), 3.

45. However, I do need to point out that Ella Shohat's definition of the term "post-colonial," comes close to Pavlyshyn's conceptualization: "The term 'post-colonial' would be more precise, therefore, if articulated as 'post-First/Third Worlds theory,' or 'post-anti-colonial critique,' as a movement beyond a relatively binaristic, fixed and stable mapping of power relations between 'colonizer/colonized' and 'center/periphery.' Such rearticulations suggest a more nuanced discourse, which allows for

movement, mobility and fluidity." See her "Notes on the Post-colonial, *Social Text* 10.2–3 (1992): 108.

46. Chakravorty Gayatri Spivak, *Outside of the Teaching Machine* (New York: Routledge, 1993), 280.

47. Vitaly Chernetsky, *Mapping Postcommunist Cultures: Russia and Ukraine in the Context of Globalization* (Montreal: McGill-Queen's University Press, 2007), 53.

48. See especially his "Aspects of the Literary Process in the USSR: The Politics of Re-Canonisation in Ukraine after 1985," *Southern Review* 24 (1991): 12–25, reprinted in Ukrainian as "Kanon ta ikonostas," *Svito-vyd* 3 (1992): 69–81.

49. "Literary Politics vs. Literature: Ukrainian Debates in the 1990s," *The Soviet and Post-Soviet Review* 28 (2001): 148.

50. Ibid., 149.

51. The group consists of authors Yuri Andrukhovych, Oleksandr Irvanets, and Viktor Neborak, and its name stands for the first syllables of *burlesk* (burlesque), *balagan* (mess), and *bufonada* (buffoonery).

52. Pavlyshyn, "Demystifying High Culture? Young Ukrainian Poetry and Prose in the 1990s," in *Perspectives on Modern Central and East European Literature: Quests for Identity*, ed. Todd Patrick Armstrong (Houndmills: Palgrave, 2001), 13.

53. Myroslav Shkandrij echoes Pavlyshyn's reasoning in this respect. See his *Russia and Ukraine* 259–68.

54. Pavlyshyn, "Literary Politics vs. Literature," 153–54.

55. Ibid., 154.

56. See, for example, Revathi Krishnaswamy, "The Criticism of Culture and the Culture of Criticism: At the Intersection of Postcolonialism and Globalization Theory," *Diacritics* 32.2 (2002): 106.

57. See Neil Larsen, "Imperialism, Colonialism, Postcolonialism," in *A Companion to Postcolonial Studies*, ed. Henry Schwarz and Sangeeta Ray (Oxford: Blackwell, 2000), 25.

58. See his *Cultural Identity and Global Process* (London: Sage Publications, 1994), 195.

59. Ibid.

60. Roland Robertson, "Globalization or Glocalization," *Journal of International Communication* 1 (1994): 38.

61. Ibid., 48.

62. Timothy Brennan makes it explicit: "The underlying logic linking globalization theory and postcolonial studies has, in at least one respect, a perverse cast. The mutual hostility of both to the nation form (particularly as nation-*state*) is projected as an irrepressible ultramodernism." See his "Postcolonial Studies and Globalization Theory," in *The Postcolonial and the Global*, ed. Revathi Krishnaswamy and John C. Hawley (Minneapolis: University of Minnesota Press, 2008), 49.

63. See especially his "The New Ukrainian Literature: Between the Postmodern and the Postcolonial" and "The Trope of Displacement in Post-Colonial Ukrainian Fiction" both published in 2002.

64. I have in mind especially his 2010 article "From Anarchy to Connectivity to Cognitive Mapping: Contemporary Ukrainian Writers of the Younger Generation Engage with Globalization."

65. *Mapping Postcommunist Cultures*, 54.

66. Ibid., 55.

67. This was pointed out by Neil Larsen in his essay "Imperialism, Colonialism, Postcolonialism:" "... small but significant class of intellectuals that had learned in the 1960s to say 'third world' become more hesitant about saying it. 'Postcolonial,' a term with far more ambiguous political resonances, fit this hesitation much better and, beginning in the early 1980s, gradually replaced 'third world,' at least in some contexts." Ibid., 41.

68. Fredric Jameson, "Third World Literature in the Era of Multinational Capital," *Social Text* 15 (1986): 67.

69. Ibid., 69.

70. Ibid.

71. Although it is also true that Jameson sees the current situation as a perfect moment to rethink humanities curriculum, "to re-examine the shambles and ruins of all older 'great books,' 'humanities,' 'freshman-introductory' and 'core course' type traditions" (Ibid., 67).

72. Ibid., 66.

73. Ibid., 79.

74. Ibid., 80.

75. Ibid., 84–85.

76. Aijaz Ahmad, *In Theory: Classes, Nations, Literature* (London: Verso, 1992), 101.

77. Ibid., 102. Chernetsky himself, as I already indicated, even though he advances Jameson's concept of national allegory, at the same time does not see any contradiction in the fact that Ukrainian literary texts he studies are by and large examples of postmodern literature.

78. Ibid., 103.

79. Ibid., 105.

80. *Mapping Postcommunist Cultures*, 204.

81. Ibid., 226.

82. In fact, he admits that the three paradigms he chose to focus on "do not, of course, exhaust the entire field of contemporary Ukrainian cultural production" (Ibid., 185) but, again, does not admit that this contradicts Jameson's claim to universality as far as his national allegory concept is concerned.

83. "Third World Literature," 69.

84. Anne McClintock, "No Longer in a Future Heaven: Nationalism, Gender and Race," in *Imperial Leather: Race, Gender and Sexuality in the Colonial Context* (New York: Routledge, 1995), 360.

85. Chernetsky, "From Anarchy to Connectivity to Cognitive Mapping: Contemporary Ukrainian Writers of the Younger Generation Engage with Globalization," *Canadian American Slavic Studies* 44 (2001): 104.

86. This article appeared in the preeminent literary scholarly journal *Slovo i chas* (formerly known as *Radians'ke literaturoznavstvo*), no. 6 (1991): 10–15, as part of a "Feminist Seminar," in which two other scholars participated besides Pavlychko, namely Tamara Hundorova and Vira Aheieva. Pavlychko's article was later posthumously reprinted in her book *Feminizm* (Kyiv: Osnovy, 2002), 19–27. *Feminizm* is a

compilation of Pavlychko's articles written on feminism between 1991 and 1999. It also compiles all the interviews and talks she gave to various newspapers, journals, and other media. Unfortunately, the editor of this anthology, Vira Aheieva, limits the bibliographical information to publication dates and does not provide the original sources of the reprinted material.

87. See, for example, Vira Aheieva, "Intelektual'na biohrafiia Solomii Pavlychko," *Dukh i litera* 7–8 (2001): 248–61, which was later reprinted as an introduction to Pavlychko's *Feminizm*, 5–16. See also Oksana Zabuzhko, *Inshyi format* (Ivano-Frankivsk: Lileia-NV, 2003), 25.

88. See Martha Bohachevsky-Chomiak, *Feminists Despite Themselves: Women in Ukrainian Community Life, 1884–1939* (Edmonton: Canadian Institute of Ukrainian Studies, 1988).

89. See her *Feminizm*, 25. Since this article was written in 1991, Pavlychko must have in mind the twelfth convocation of the Supreme Soviet of the Ukrainian SSR (later renamed the Verkhovna Rada Ukrainy), which came about as a result of the partially free elections held in March 1990. This convocation issued the Declaration of State Sovereignty of Ukraine on July 16, 1990, and declared Ukrainian independence on August 24, 1991. Retroactively, this convocation was later proclaimed as the first one in independent Ukraine.

90. See Oksana Zabuzhko, *Shevchenkiv mif Ukrainy: Sproba filosofs'koho analizu* (Kyiv: Abrys, 1997) and Tamara Hundorova, *Franko—ne Kameniar* (Melbourne: Monash University, 1996). A decade later Hundorova reprinted this study and added additional material in a book titled: *Franko ne Kameniar. Franko i Kameniar* (Kyiv: Krytyka, 2006).

91. A fresh look at Vovchok's literary contribution was presented in a volume edited by Vira Aheieva, *Try doli: Marko Vovchok v ukrains'kii, rosiis'kii ta frantsuz'kii literaturi* (Kyiv: Fakt, 2002).

92. It must be noted that the Kyiv Center did not survive for long after Pavlychko's untimely passing. Moreover, Nila Zborovska, who later became more preoccupied with psychoanalysis than feminism, also denounced her association with feminism. But, the sheer number of works produced by the Center during its existence makes this endeavor enduring.

93. See my article "Language Choice and the Notion of National Literature in Post-Soviet Ukraine: The Case of Andrey Kurkov," *Tilts/Mist/Tiltas* 1 (2007): 6–14.

94. Chernetsky, *Mapping Postcommunist Cultures*, 240.

95. See her *Feminism and Nationalism in the Third World* (London: Zed Books, 1986), 1–3.

96. *Feminizm*, 189.

97. See Liudmyla Taran, "Pryvyd povstaloho zhinochoho dukhu," *Krytyka* 1–2 (1999): 18–21; Nila Zborovs'ka, "Shevchenko v 'zhinochykh studiiakh'," *Krytyka* 3 (1999): 25–28 and "Chomu v ukrains'kii literaturi nemaie liubovnykh romaniv," *Krytyka* 7–8 (1999): 27–31; Vira Aheieva, "Khto boit'sia pryvydu matriarkhatu?," *Krytyka* 5 (1999): 22–23.

98. The September issue of *Krytyka* (2001) includes a series of articles biased against feminism and gender studies in Ukrainian scholarship, namely Mar'ian

Shkorba, "Genderni dity liberalizmu," 20–23; Larysa Berezovchuk, "Pryshestia dyskursu," 24–29; Inna Bulkina, "Zhinocha dohma," 30–31. The November issue includes a response by Vira Aheieva, "Na storozhi starozhytnostei," 28–29.

99. For example, such major journals and magazines as *Slovo i chas*, no. 8–9 (1996), and no. 11 (1997); *Art-Line* (March 1998), and *Ï*, no. 17 (2000) and no. 23 (2003) devoted special issues to feminism.

100. I am referring here to a seminar lecture "(Anti)national Feminisms: Women's Voices of Transition and Nation Building in Ukraine," presented by Tatiana Zhurzhenko at the Munk Centre for International Studies, University of Toronto, March 18, 2002.

101. It is interesting to note that whereas Chernetsky contemplated the output of the Kharkiv Center as part of a Ukrainian discourse on feminism, two years later Stefaniia Andrusiv excluded it completely from consideration on the grounds that the Center does not view itself as belonging to the Ukrainian intellectual space. See her "Suchasne ukrains'ke literaturoznavstvo: teksty i konteksty," *Slovo i chas* 5 (2004): 53.

102. For example, her elucidation of queer aspects in Ukrainian literature stands out in the context of post-Soviet literary criticism.

103. See Ihor Kostets'kyi, "Stefan George: Osobystist', doba, spadshchyna. Peredmova," in *Vybranyi Stefan George*, ed. Ihor Kostets'kyi, vol. 1 (Stuttgart: Na hori, 1968–71), 149.

104. See Pavlychko, *Natsionalizm, seksual'nist', oriientalizm: Skladnyi svit Ahatanhela Kryms'koho* (Kyiv: Osnovy, 2002), 192.

105. Ibid., 176.

106. Ibid., 189.

107. Originally published in Mary Buckley, ed., *Post-Soviet Women: From the Baltic to Central Asia* (Cambridge: Cambridge University Press, 1997), 219–34.

108. See especially her *Proiavlennia slova: Dyskursiia rann'oho modernizmu* (Lviv: Litopys, 1997), *Pisliachornobyl's'ka biblioteka: Ukrains'kyi literaturnyi postmodern* (Kyiv: Krytyka, 2005) and *Kitch i literatura* (Kyiv: Fakt, 2008).

109. For example, *Ukrains'ka impresionistychna proza* (1994) and *Poetesa zlamu stolit'. Tvorchist' Lesi Ukrainky v postmodernii interpretatsii* (1999).

110. Some other important works in this series edited by Aheieva are: *Don Zhuan u svitovomu konteksti* (2002) and *Proza pro zhyttia inshkykh: Iurii Kosach—teksty, interpretatsii, komentari* (2003).

111. The critic died in August 2011, after a long battle with cancer.

112. Rita Felski, *Beyond Feminist Aesthetics: Feminist Literature and Social Change* (Cambridge, MA: Harvard University Press, 1989), 83.

113. Yuri Tarnawsky (b. 1934) is a bilingual émigré poet and writer and a founding member of the New York Group of Ukrainian poets that was active especially in the late 1950s and in the decade of the 1960s.

114. Milena Rudnytska (1892–1976), journalist, politician, and civic activist, became the most vocal leader of the women's movement in Western Ukraine during the interwar period. She authored a book titled *Ukrains'ka diisnist' i zavdannia zhinochoho rukhu* (The Ukrainian Reality and the Tasks of the Women's Movement, 1934).

115. See her articles "Feminizm iak mozhlyvyi pidkhid do analizu ukrains'koi kul'tury," in *Feminizm*, 32 and "Metodolohichna sytuatsiia v suchasnomu ukrains'komu literaturoznavstvi," in *Teoriia literatury* (Kyiv: Osnovy, 2002), 487.

116. It is understandable from the context that Zborovska considers all Ukrainian modern literature as anticolonial, that is, the literature that has as its starting point the publication of the epic poem *Eneida* in the vernacular by Ivan Kotliarevsky in 1798 and continues up to the present.

117. Zborovs'ka, *Kod ukrains'koi literatury* (Kyiv: Akademvydav, 2006), 10–11.

118. See especially his *The Emotional Life of Nations* (New York: Karnac, 2002).

119. Lloyd DeMause, *Foundations of Psychohistory* (New York: Creative Roots, 1982), 90.

120. See especially her essays on Andrukhovych in *Feministychni rozdumy: Na karnavali mertvykh potsilunkiv*.

121. *Kod ukrains'koi literatury*, 496–97.

122. Volodymyr Danylenko, "Variatsii na temu kolonial'noi psykhohistorii," *Slovo i chas* 2 (2007): 84.

123. The critic especially underscores the kitsch qualities and tendencies in the activity of the Bu-Ba-Bu group. See her *Kitch i literatura: Travestii* (Kyiv: Fakt, 2008), 235–48.

124. The second revised edition was published by Krytyka in 2013.

125. In fact, in her Foreword the critic presents a rather surprising chronology, in which she sees the beginnings of Ukrainian postmodern experiments as early as in 1946 when the first almanac of the Artistic Ukrainian Movement was published.

126. Hundorova, *Pisliachornobyl's'ka biblioteka: Ukrains'kyi literaturnyi postmodern* (Kyiv: Krytyka, 2005), 239.

127. Ibid., 257.

128. Ibid.

129. See especially Bohdana Matiiash, "Serioznyi postmodern, abo 'literaturoznavstvo bez bromu'," *Znak* 10 (2005): 4 and R.B. Kharchuk, "Khranytel'ka pisliachornobyl's'koi biblioteky," *Kur'ier Kryvbasu* 4 (2006): 186.

130. Tamara Hundorova is the only one who still works at the Institute and heads its Department of Literary Theory.

131. This article was originally published in *Krytyka* 12 (2001) and later reprinted as "Pisliamova" to his *Do istorii ukrains'koi literatury: Doslidzhennia, esei, polemika* (Kyiv: Krytyka, 2003), 591–607. I am referring to the latter edition.

132. Taras Koznarsky, "Ukrainian Literary Scholarship in Ukraine Since Independence," *Canadian Slavonic Papers* 53 (2011): 442.

133. As of this writing, the first four volumes have been published: Vols. 1 (2013), 2 (2014), 3 (2016), and 4 (2014). The first two volumes are devoted to the old literature, from the period of Kyivan Rus' through the end of the eighteenth century, the third volume covers the period from the end of the eighteenth century through the 1830s, and the fourth volume is fully devoted to the life and oeuvre of Taras Shevchenko, authored in its entirety by Ivan Dziuba.

134. Originally, this authoritative history was conceived as a ten-volume publication but has since then expanded to become a twelve-volume edition.

135. One such proposition is the publication of *Mala entsyklopediia aktual'noi literatury* (1998), edited by Volodymyr Yeshkiliev and Yuri Andrukhovych. But publications of this kind do not play a prominent role in establishing school curricula.

136. Ivan Dziuba, *Spraha* (Kyiv: Ukrains'kyi svit, 2001), 113.

137. Ibid., 224.

138. Marko Pavlyshyn, "Defending the Cultural Nation before and after 1991: Ivan Dziuba," *Canadian-American Slavic Studies* 44 (2010): 42–43.

139. It appears that it is coming more aggresively from Zabuzhko's side. See "Oksana Zabuzhko pro Andrukhovycha: Iuryn psykholohichnyi vik—18 rokiv," http://life.pravda.com.ua/society/2011/08/9/83127/view_comments/, accessed June 15, 2017.

140. See Chapter 6 for more details on this.

141. See her interview on the site of BBC Ukrainian: http://www.bbc.co.uk.ukrainian/news/2011/01/110113_matios_ie_is.shtml?print=1, accessed March 31, 2012.

142. However, by contrast both Matios and Shkliar did participate in the 2012 elections, with Matios winning a seat from the UDAR Party of Vitaly Klychko, and Shkliar losing.

.

Chapter 2

Cultural Geographies

Regionalism and Territorial Identities in Literature

Since independence, the geography of belonging has played a crucial role in Ukrainian literature.[1] In fact, a decentralization of the literary process on the one hand, and a tendency by a number of writers to heighten regional differences in their texts (along with attendant cultural identities), on the other, emerge as some of the chief characteristics of the post-Soviet period. One could even say that this literary trend toward regionalism and decentralization echoes similar discourses in the political and economic spheres of post-independence nation-building activities. Yet, behind this seeming espousal of geographic and cultural difference in works of imaginative writing, there is, it appears, a larger concern among authors. Often colored by their specific historical conditioning, it is mainly a concern for the well-being of Ukraine as one unified country. It is somewhat reflective of what Jim Wayne Miller contemplates about a similar process in America:

> With a better understanding of the role writing has played in creating our national identity, it should be possible to take a different view of regional writing today. We should be able to understand that, contrary to the conventional belief that regions belong to the past and are forever passing away, our various regions in America are still forming. Their parameters may shift, but they endure—and they may become even more distinct, rather than less so, as time passes. It should be possible, then, to view regional writing (and the life such writing is concerned with) not as a remnant of a colorful past, nor as disquieting alien life within the national boundaries, nor as a quaint refuge from the rest of the country (or from the wider world), but rather as indicative of the process by which the country continues to become a land and a people.[2]

51

Miller further elaborates the point that regions and regionalism do not need to be viewed as divisive or opposing national unity, but, to the contrary, can be contributive to the centralization process precisely by allowing the exploration of cultural and regional diversity. Similarly, David Jordan in his "Introduction" to *Regionalism Reconsidered: New Approaches to the Field* states that "regionalism is more than just nostalgic 'local color,' [...] it comprises a dynamic interplay of political, cultural, and psychological forces"[3] and references critics who suggest that "a harmonious interaction between a human community and the environment it inhabits need not be an anachronism, even in developed industrial societies."[4]

Miller's apologetic tone and defensive posture also stem from his willingness to refute the perception of regionalism as reactionary, or "associated with backwardness and limitation."[5] But the latter viewpoint, it seems, is already dated and largely dismissed by the postmodernists. Roberto M. Dainotto, for example, invoking Homi Bhabha's "location of culture" as the new episteme of place and Edward Said's call for "concrete geographical identity" as a mechanism against the imposition of cultural unity, contends that "regional literature is a most illustrious protagonist of this *fin de siècle* project of localizing the aesthetic."[6] Furthermore, for Dainotto, regionalism is "an attempt to find a *new* place from which to study literature, and from which to engender a different, "changed ecology" of cultural production."[7] While Dainotto's foregrounding of regional difference in literature as a positive development coincides with that of Miller's, they differ in their understanding of the role regionalism plays in forming the cultural unity of national literature. In Dainotto's approach regionalism "depicts itself as some kind of liberation front busy to set marginal and vernacular cultures free from an all-equalizing nation."[8] In Miller's approach regionalism, while appreciative of local life and traditions, does not dispense with its relationship to the national life. Miller believes that "the local and global, regional and national, the particular and the universal, are not antithetical concepts; rather, they complement each other."[9]

How do these theoretical considerations apply to the decentralized contemporary Ukrainian literature within the first two decades after independence? As I already implied in the beginning of this chapter, Miller's approach fits the Ukrainian paradigm better than Dainotto's in the sense that it does not dispense with the relation between the local and the national. The literary production in post-Soviet Ukraine provides ample examples of regional perspectives. In fact, the two main schools of prose writing in the 1990s bear the names of two Ukrainian cities, namely the Zhytomyr School, and the Stanyslaviv or Stanislav (also called Galician) School.[10] Yet, contrary to Dainotto's premise, the preoccupation with the local life and culture by the members of each of the respective schools has not neutralized the need for cultural unity of the national literature. It seems that rather than deny such a need, both schools strived to construct and impose their own particular under-standing of what the national literature should constitute.

Another divergence from Dainotto's theoretical proposition worth mentioning is the reliance among Ukrainian writers on history, or, to be more precise, on local branches of national history. Dainotto views regionalism as "the figure of an otherness that is, essentially, otherness *from*, and against, history."[11] Moreover, he promotes the turn from history to geography as "a true reevaluation of all values" and believes that "the goal posited by the literature of place is therefore an ethical one: to replace the 'insufficient' historical remedy with the geographical cure."[12] I argue that the literature of place and region, as represented by a number of contemporary Ukrainian writers and poets, does not have to exclude history from its consideration. On the contrary, history very often becomes inextricably linked to a particular place, and the consideration of that place is presented through a specific historical lens.[13] And, strikingly, Ukrainian urban fiction in particular provides interesting examples where spatial and temporal parameters do not clash, but rather complement each other.

THE CITY AS PROTAGONIST

While the discussion of regionalism in Ukrainian literature since 1991 is no doubt warranted, especially when one looks at the totality of works by Yuri Andrukhovych (b. 1960), Taras Prokhasko (b. 1968) or Yuri Vynnychuk (b. 1952), all three coming from the Halychyna (Galicia) region in Western Ukraine, as well as at the existence of numerous literary groups in various Ukrainian cities in the 1990s,[14] here I want to narrow my focus to the representation of a few concrete cities in a few selected fictional and poetic accounts. Each of these cities represents not just concrete urban settings but also provides a certain set of beliefs, myths and historical narratives that emanate beyond their boundaries to impact the adjacent surrounding territories. These Ukrainian geographical entities, from the most cosmopolitan city of Kyiv, through the provincial outposts of Rivne and Chernivtsi, to the arguably most European city among them all, Lviv, become symbolic *loci* of sorts, caught up in some myth, and through which, nonetheless, a specific historical reality unfolds, often with a considerable dose of fantasy, utopia and/or dystopia. All four cities emerge in the works discussed below as sites of historical memory, originating either in the more recent or more distant past. The interplay of place and time constitutes an important element of these belletristic accounts and becomes an effective tool through which to channel the question of identity. To underscore the nature of territorial self-identification among selected Ukrainian authors, I will contrast their imaginative writings about specific places with that of the Ukrainian poet Vasyl Makhno (b. 1964), who left Ukraine in 2000, settling in New York City, and who began to write poems about this megalopolis soon thereafter. His diasporic poetic vision about the most cosmopolitan city in the United States adds a new dimension to the discussion on identity.

Similarly, I will also present the story about the city of Lviv as told by the poet Viktor Neborak (b. 1961). First, however, let us consider a few selected fictional narratives by Andrey Kurkov (b. 1961), Oleksandr Irvanets (b. 1961), Vasyl Kozhelianko (1957–2008) and Yuri Vynnychuk. They all construct visions of the city, in which the relationship between people and their places is explored against the background of "the wider world," as Miller puts it. The sense of belonging to the local territory is underscored, yet the sense of belonging to the nation and the world is not dismissed. Perhaps the most fascinating element in the writings of the above authors is their uncanny way of presenting the city as a space facilitating a contiguous coexistence of differences inscribed on the template of a distinct historical period, with numerous references to the contemporaneous political and social situation. Their use of history does not prevent their celebrating the city as a generator and site of authentic identity, simultaneously regional and national.

The city depicted in Kurkov's novels, Kyiv, is the city of the post-Soviet period and thus the most contemporary of all the places discussed. Arguably, it yields the most realistically construed picture of Ukraine's capital, but it is often the city of the invisible criminal underground network of the first half of the 1990s and its actual urban places are introduced and displayed through consistently dark lenses. Irvanets, on the other hand, uses his hometown of Rivne to invoke the relatively recent Soviet past and the title of his 2002 novel *Rivne/Rovno* (giving both Ukrainian and Russian pronunciations) comes as a warning of sorts. His vision of the city is a divided, dystopian place where totalitarian rule coexists literally behind the wall but can in no time encroach on and destroy the Western democratic half. Kozhelianko's hometown of Chernivtsi brings yet another historical reality into the forefront, namely the period of World War II. There is a clear attempt on Kozhelianko's part to instill a new sense of gravitas for Chernivtsi by shedding its periphery and transforming the city into the center of Ukrainian nationalism. Finally, Vynnychuk presents Lviv as a mythologized place nostalgically rooted in the Austro-Hungarian past. His city comes across more as a point of reference rather than a topographical entity. It is a center somewhere out there, but not here, yet its presence stimulates and engenders a strong sense of local (regional) identity. All four writers use the idea of place (here: the urban place) in conjunction with history in order to assert the uniqueness of a concrete geographical territory and, at the same time, in order to put forth the idea of a regional identity, which, in their judgment, is compatible with the idea of a national identity being formed in independent Ukraine. If there is a common thread that connects the writings of these authors it is the element of journey, which is present in most of their fiction. The narrative of a journeying hero provides ample opportunities for exploring various places. These places are sometimes geographically accurate and sometimes not; sometimes convey urban settings in all their verisimilitude, and at other times they are merely products of a writer's imagination. Whatever preference any given writer cherishes, one thing is clear: the attachment to a particular place invariably triggers questions of identity.

Kurkov's Kyiv

It would be a mistake to imply that the city of Kyiv, its landscapes and people, figure prominently only in Andrey Kurkov's fiction. In fact, there is a considerable corpus of fictional works whose story line unfolds in the capital city. Such references could be historical or contemporary, pertaining to specific neighborhoods or providing a general urban ambience, yet what unites them all is that they play a decisively subordinate role to the overall plot. For example, in Oles Ulianenko's novels Kyiv becomes the place in which his protagonists are entangled in the struggle between evil and good; in Oles Ilchenko's novel *The City with Chimeras* (*Misto z khymeramy*, 2009) we view Kyiv through the prism of its architectural landmarks, left to posterity by a famous fin-de-siècle architect Vladyslav Horodetsky; Yevheniia Kononenko's protagonists live and work almost exclusively in Kyiv, and in her book of essays *Heroines and Heroes* (*Heroini ta heroi*, 2010) there is a whole section devoted to the capital city, incidentally, the place she was born; Volodymyr Dibrova's novel *Andriivsky Uzviz* (2007; 2nd ed. 2008) begins with the description of one of Kyiv's most famous streets that connects the upper and lower levels of the capital city, and its name provides the title for the whole novel but this fictional work has very little to do with Kyiv's urban landscapes other than Andriivsky Uzviz in the novel's Prologue; and in Oksana Zabuzhko's novel *The Museum of Abandoned Secrets* (*Muzei pokynutykh sekretiv*, 2009) there are numerous passages that dwell on the beauty of specific streets and places, especially in the city's downtown area. Yet, none of the above writers attempts to ascribe to Kyiv a role other than auxiliary. Andrey Kurkov's attitude in this respect is different. In his works, Ukraine's capital city becomes for him a hero of sorts. In fact, in one of his interviews Kurkov admitted that he made a conscious decision to resurrect Kyiv on the world literary map:

> When it comes to Kyiv, seven years ago I decided to put it back as a place of action on the world literary map, or at least on Europe's map. And I believe that

thanks in large measure to "Picnic on Ice"[15] and "A Friend of the Deceased"[16] I succeeded. There were quite a few funny situations connected to this. For example, when a former ambassador of Belgium came here, I got a phone call, a meeting was arranged, and then he told me that before leaving for Kyiv, he was advised by the Belgian Foreign Service people to see the film "A Friend of the Deceased."[17] Not to mention the fact that for the last three or four years quite a few tourists from Germany and Switzerland come here and use my books as guides around Kyiv (on some occasions I accompany them).[18]

Kurkov, born in Leningrad but a resident of Kyiv since he was two years old, introduces a unique dimension into Ukrainian letters. Kyiv is his hometown, and even though he writes in Russian, he considers himself a Ukrainian writer. And this is not without significance considering his commercial success in the West. One can even argue that no other contemporary Ukrainian author writes about Kyiv with such fealty and devotion as Kurkov does, especially in those novels that have been translated into English to date. The strong sense of belonging to a concrete place (Kyiv) that permeates Kurkov's works cannot but affect his overall national affinity and self-identification. Clearly, he rejects a narrow, ethnic ('blood-and-soil') type of national identity in favor of a civic type, which promotes the idea of national identity as a rational association of citizens bound by common laws and a shared territory.[19] That, however, does not mean that issues of cultural identity, including the language question, are not close to his heart. For example, despite using Russian as a medium of artistic expression, he is against the introduction of Russian as a second state official language, a position strongly advocated by those politicians concerned with election votes in the southeastern region of Ukraine. Moreover, he is fluent in Ukrainian, uses the language in interviews with Ukrainian journalists, and is well versed in contemporary Ukrainian literature produced by his Ukrainian-language colleagues.[20] In an interview with a BBC correspondent, Bohdan Tsiupyn, Kurkov even stated that he considers himself Ukrainian because his mentality is Ukrainian.[21] In the same interview Kurkov promoted the idea of national literature that transcends confines of the language factor. He believes that everything created on Ukraine's territory belongs to Ukrainian culture:

Most importantly, I believe that all that is being done on Ukraine's territory belongs to Ukrainian culture. For example, a literature written in Tartar, Hungarian, or Yiddish, the latter being used by Joseph Burg, the oldest writer who still writes in Yiddish and lives in Chernivtsi—all this belongs to Ukrainian culture. Of course, one can be an ethnocentrist and state that only Ukrainian-language literature is truly Ukrainian, but this is beyond logic because every ethnicity that is active, every nationality produces its own cultural product, which belongs to Ukraine.[22]

It would be hard to deny a Ukrainian character to Kurkov's fiction. Most of his works, at least thematically, hover around issues and situations, whether political or social, that arose in post-Soviet Ukraine after 1991. Another common thread is that regardless of where plots take their protagonists—East, West or Antarctica, all action originates and ends in Kyiv, a place beloved by Kurkov and his heroes alike. This is especially true for the novels *Death and the Penguin* and *A Matter of Death and Life*, both originally published in 1996. These works concentrate on economic and social absurdities, created by the collapse of the Soviet Union. The protagonists in both novels, males in their early thirties, face isolation, lack of a social network and difficulties in adapting to new economic realities, and sooner or later find themselves implicated in criminal enterprises.

In a typically Kurkov manner there is always an element of surprise in the otherwise straightforward suspense stories. For example, in *Death and the Penguin* it is the hero's unusual pet (a penguin named Misha) that seems to act with more dignity than humans themselves, not to mention that in the end it is the penguin's owner, Viktor, who, after arranging for Misha to be taken back to Antarctica, "becomes" the bird, fleeing to the icy continent to escape the mafia and possible assassination. ("The penguin," said Viktor bleakly, "is me."[23]) In the novel *A Matter of Death and Life*, the main character, who at first wants to die because of personal failures and hires an assassin, by a strange twist of fate changes his mind and hires another assassin to kill the first one. In the end, wracked by guilt, he marries the murdered man's widow. Unlike Kurkov's later works, these stories unfold entirely in Kyiv. The writer's attention to the city itself, naming streets and familiar places, turning Kyiv into an implicit character, is what foreign readers seem to notice and like in Kurkov's oeuvre. The two other novels translated into English, *Penguin Lost* (2004) and *The Case of the General's Thumb* (2003),[24] expand geographically beyond the confines of Kyiv. In the sequel to *Death and the Penguin* we find the main protagonist in Antarctica where he ended up fleeing the mafia. Determined to find Misha at all cost, Viktor returns to Kyiv but is forced to travel first to Moscow and then Chechnya, all in an effort to trace his penguin. Only now, beyond the borders of Ukraine, the issue of national identity comes into play. While in Chechnya, the hero does not forget to emphasize that he is from Kyiv, Ukraine, not from Moscow, in order to secure better treatment for himself among the Chechen fighters.

Marko Pavlyshyn rightly observes that while giving "symbolic weight to an unexpected spatial nexus between Ukraine and Antarctica, it [*Death and the Penguin*] does not confer any special meaning upon the familiar connection between Ukraine and Russia, thereby decoupling the Russian language from its colonizing role."[25] However, Kurkov's *Penguin Lost* and *The Case of the General's Thumb* do, in fact, bring Russia into consideration. While the former novel constitutes (among other things) an implicit commentary on the cruelty and absurdity of the war in Chechnya, the latter highlights competing interests between the Russian and Ukrainian secret services. But, again, Pavlyshyn correctly contends that Kurkov writes in Russian "in a way that does not claim Ukraine as part of a Russian cultural space."[26] Ukraine's relationship with Russia is not portrayed by this author as anything other than one between equal international partners.

Kurkov's focus on contemporary issues and his ruminations on the difficulties in the economic transition in post-Soviet Ukraine shortly after independence through the prism of his observations of the local life in the capital city give his fiction some deserved esteem. The author not only faithfully reflects the city of the 1990s but also avoids mythologizing or stepping into the fantastic.[27] Kyiv emerges here as a tangible place, one that actually attracts with its simplicity and "everydayness," however gloomy and uncertain it might be at the time. In its significance, Kurkov's Kyiv seems to overflow its urban boundaries and to become larger than just the central metropolis of Ukraine. In a way, Kurkov depicts the capital city as if it were some kind of a macro-region synonymous with Ukraine itself. Whatever transpires in Kyiv, Kurkov asserts, it also reverberates on its near and far edges.

Irvanets's *Rivne/Rovno*

Oleksandr Irvanets, a member of the famed Bu-Ba-Bu group, is perhaps better known as a poet and playwright rather than a fiction writer. But in 2002 he published his first novel *Rivne/Rovno*, which received some attention, thanks in part to its explicit commentary on competing identities in a newly independent Ukraine. *Rivne/Rovno* reads like a warning against the reestablishment of Soviet authoritarian rule, yet does not offer too much comfort and confidence in the supposedly democratic and pro-Western regime. The scenario Irvanets imposes on his hometown Rivne, the provincial capital of the Rivne oblast, bears a striking resemblance to the one that existed in the divided Berlin during the Cold War era. Just as in the case of Berlin, the wall erected between the two different ideological halves of the city plays a crucial role and in the end prompts the main character to act seemingly against his convictions.

Paradoxically, it is not an ideological chasm of the divided Rivne that dominates the plot of the novel. The dystopian framework of the narrative merely offers its author a pretext to tell the story of his city, the city he remembers mostly from his childhood and youth. In that respect Irvanets's Rivne is mapped out considerably more rationally than Kurkov's Kyiv. To start with, Irvanets provides his readers with a detailed map of Rivne's downtown, showing all the main streets and the precise contour of the wall. The text of

Rivne/Rovno is also interspersed with a dozen or so photographs, highlighting places captured not randomly but according to the story line. There is a correspondence between the selected images and the protagonist's whereabouts. All of this points to the fact that there are only two main characters in the novel, the playwright Shloima Etsirvan and the city of Rivne.

It is probably no coincidence that the name of the hero is not a Ukrainian one. The writer seems to promote the idea that attachment to locality transcends ethnic descent (quite in line with what we find in Kurkov). After all, local patriotism is largely blind to ethnic difference. And even though one can easily see in Etsirvan an anagram of Irvanets, it is not possible to follow the same route as Shloima. One can only speculate whether this is just a playful postmodernist device on Irvanets's part, or there are other subtle intimations with regard to this name.[28] Judging by some further remarks in the novel, this device could be a way for the author to underscore the ethnic diversity of the city, past and/or present.

We are introduced to Shloima Etsirvan as he prepares for the premiere of his play in the western part of Rivne. We also learn at the outset that the main protagonist ended up in the democratic half of the city by coincidence. He just happened to be visiting a friend when the war that divided the city into the separate eastern and western sections first began, thus preventing him from returning home. On the day of Etsirvan's premiere he receives an invitation and the necessary permit allowing him to cross the wall and visit his relatives. He does not want to pass up this opportunity and makes a journey to the eastern part of his hometown. What happens after that is rather predictable to all those familiar with Soviet totalitarian practices. The hero is under constant supervision, his movements are restricted, and even when he manages to escape for a brief moment and visits his mother and sister, he ends up being beaten in a park and returned to the custody of his guards. As it turns out, his subsequent stay in the hospital and forced participation in a meeting, arranged earlier by his former colleagues from the Union of Writers, leads to some unwelcome consequences. Shloima is instructed to help the authorities to unify the divided city by opening the door to the underground sewage system located under the wall, so that the military can enter the Western section. The protagonist, eager to return to West Rivne in order not to miss his premiere, agrees to the plan. After his initial hesitation about carrying out the imposed mission, together with manifestation of some strange circumstances indicating that resistance is futile, the hero of *Rivne/Rovno* completes his mission.

This plot, however, does not adequately convey the interaction between Etsirvan and the city. His journey/flight through the streets, parks, schools and hospitals of the Soviet section of Rivne elicits memories of his childhood and adolescence. Passing the House of Ideological Work, he recalls at what cost this building was erected (the destruction of the Jewish cemetery);

crossing the central Lenin Square, he contemplates the fact that an entire section of the city had to be leveled to allow for the realization of the new Soviet vision in urban planning; sitting in the park he remembers walking with his friends through its alleys, using them as shortcuts to downtown; or, finally, seeing the building in which his high-school sweetheart used to live, he loses himself in memories, daydreaming of his first love.

These reveries about Ertsivan's past, which is inextricably linked to the places, streets and buildings of his hometown, underscore the hero's deep attachment to the local ambience regardless of its ideological and/or political line. It virtually prepares the reader to accept the unthinkable in the end, that is, a loss of freedom and democracy in exchange for having this city, Rivne, as one undivided entity. At the same time, the author devotes quite a bit of energy to parodying the Soviet way of life, including laughing at the empty and pompous statements of Soviet writers, Ertsivan's former colleagues, whenever they are given an opportunity to speak. This also gives Irvanets a chance to incorporate into the text real literary characters, writers and groups that are being overly criticized by the Soviet functionaries of East Rivne. But the final chapter reads like a hymn to the beauty of the city. The hero's joy when he sees Rivne as one undivided whole seems to justify the act of his earlier betrayal.

As the author has it, the goal of unification takes precedence over the nature of a political regime. This fictional dystopia invokes the real historical event that also resulted in the unification of most of the Ukrainian lands. I am referring here to the 1939 Molotov-Ribbentrop Pact between Germany and the Soviet Union, which made it possible for Stalin to annex Halychyna (Eastern Galicia) and make it part of Soviet Ukraine. This was not an event greeted by Western Ukrainians at the time. In fact, many perished during the Soviet secret police—the NKVD's reign of terror, but for the first time in a long while Ukraine was unified as a political entity (even if not quite sovereign).

The novel is mostly devoted to the character's journey through East Rivne, but we also get a glimpse into the life of the western part of the city. Here life could not be more dynamic and prosperous, but it becomes evident quite early on that this part of the city has foreign forces stationed in it. Moreover, we learn that Ertsivan's play, the premiere of which is staged by a German director, with a German actress in the main role, imitates life, but through the presence of foreign guests it unfolds as an event of transnational significance. It almost seems as though the sense of national identity is deliberately muddled. In *Rivne/Rovno* Irvanets skillfully maneuvers through layers of hypothetical situations and in the process avoids straight answers. The ambivalent character of his dystopia disturbs rather than placates, but this is precisely what might be expected from a gifted writer.

Irvanets's Rivne, first divided and then unified, while topographically accurate, represents a dystopian and consciously constructed place, which comes both as a cautionary symbol against the return of Soviet-like rule and a metaphor against a divisive mindset among his compatriots (e.g., the discourse of two Ukraines).[29] Clearly, Irvanets seems to convey the idea that the sense of national unity should trump its ideological divisions.

Kozhelianko's Chernivtsi

Vasyl Kozhelianko published nine novels, but made his reputation mainly thanks to *A Parade in Moscow* (*Defiliada v Moskvi*). It came out in 2001 as a separate volume, after first being serialized in the journal *Suchasnist'* in the second half of the 1990s. Kozhelianko is also known as a writer who uses a device in his texts that he calls "alternative history." By mixing real events with products of his imagination, the writer creates a new historical reality—the sole purpose of which is to underscore the significance and power of the Ukrainian state. Here we are dealing with an interesting reversal: it is Ukraine rather than Russia that becomes the new center. Foregrounding nationalism and transforming Ukraine into a new empire (an underlying theme in Kozhelianko's prose) can be read as both a psychological compensation for the colonial past and a stark warning against authoritarian and nationalist tendencies in any political reality.

I have argued elsewhere that inherent in Kozhelianko's fiction is a deep-seated ambivalence about the importance of nationalist preferences in any nation and state building.[30] On the one hand, in a typically postcolonial gesture, the writer dismisses the old metropolis (Moscow) as a valid center and undermines that empire's historical significance; on the other, Europe also does not figure as a viable alternative. This is somewhat reminiscent of what Irvanets implies in his *Rivne/Rovno*, namely, while the persistence of the Soviet-style regime and its attendant cultural identity are loathed and disrespected, the presence of Western forces on Ukrainian territory is also implicitly criticized and in the end rejected. Bart Moore-Gilbert rightly concludes in his work on postcolonial theory: "Because colonialism has taken many forms and has many histories, and is accompanied by a plethora of at times internally and mutually contradictory discourses, decolonialization has been similarly multiform and complex—and its discourses may therefore at times be incommensurable with each other—as well as complementary."[31] Quite possibly the ambivalent and often contradictory realities found in Kozhelianko's texts are but his mechanisms of coping with the process of decolonization. By questioning the power of the supposed center (i.e., Russia), he also undermines the validity of a colonial inferiority complex. Juxtaposing these two perspectives and playing them off against each other are what makes Kozhelianko's work fresh and intriguing.

There is another aspect worth mentioning: Kozhelianko's parodic and equivocal approach to history places him squarely in the center of the postmodern camp. His method clearly adheres to Linda Hutcheon's take on postmodernism: "what I want to call postmodernism is fundamentally contradictory, resolutely historical, and inescapably political."[32] By ascribing imperialistic views to his protagonists, Kozhelianko risks appearing chauvinistic, if not for the fact that he wraps his narrative in a light, even humorous tone. There are plenty of typically postmodernist devices in his prose, including self-referential passages, as well as pastiche and parody. These techniques neutralize and deconstruct otherwise clearly exposed nationalistic sentiments. And this is precisely what is so intriguing about Kozhelianko: he always leaves an ambiguous trace with regard to his own views on nationalism. But there is nothing ambiguous as far as his narrative of place is concerned. The city of Chernivtsi lies at the center of most of the author's story lines. However, it is not contemporary Chernivtsi that fascinates the writer but Chernivtsi on the eve of and during the World War II period. Focusing on the significance of place in Kozhelianko's fiction, I will examine two of his novels, *A Parade in Moscow* and *Silver Spider* (*Sribnyi pavuk*, 2004).

The plot of *A Parade in Moscow* begins in November 1941 with a train approaching the Chernivtsi railway station. We are introduced to the main character, Dmytro Levytsky, an officer of the victorious Ukrainian Army, who is traveling back home to visit his aging father. Walking from the train station Levytsky contemplates the changes in his hometown: "It was tempting to observe Chernivtsi in its Ukrainian lineament. Signs on stores and cafes here and there were still in Romanian, but on the City Hall one can see the blue and yellow flag flapping ..."[33] This is but just one example of Kozhelianko's utilization of alternative history, whereby Ukraine is victorious and independent already in 1941. In his fiction the writer insists on making events that were in fact transient—like the proclamation of Ukraine's independence by Stepan Bandera on June 30, 1941—permanent fixtures of Ukrainian history.[34] He seems to be fixated on emphasizing glorious rather than defeatist occurrences in the Ukrainian past. Or, alternatively, he concocts the history in such a way as to create an impression of Ukraine's supremacy on the world's stage. In *A Parade in Moscow*, for example, Ukrainian agents capture Joseph Stalin in cooperation with Hitler's forces. Georgia overthrows the communists and aligns itself with Ukraine, which is considered a mighty partner. This mightiness continues well into the future. When Kozhelianko introduces a futuristic (science fiction) scenario in this novel, it points to the exceptional role of Ukrainians in defending planet Earth from alien unidentified flying objects.

It goes without saying that Chernivtsi plays a significant role in the novel *A Parade in Moscow*; after all, the main character comes from that place.

The city, however, even though presented in its multiethnic complexity, is depicted as fully Ukrainian and part of a greater Ukraine. In this sense the identity presented here has a national rather than a regional dimension. But the chapter devoted to the review of one issue of the Chernivtsi newspaper *Dzygarok* underscores specifically Bukovynian local events. Its heroes, writers and local history (like the Romanian occupation) are related and discussed.

In *Silver Spider*, Kozhelianko even more nostalgically describes the place and time first introduced in *A Parade in Moscow*, and the author's hometown of Chernivtsi plays an even more pronounced role than in his first novel. Similarly to what we encountered in Irvanets's *Rivne/Rovno*, Kozhelianko concludes his work with a section of photographic images of Chernivtsi, titled "Visions after Text." But unlike Irvanets, these are not contemporary pictures. "Visions after Text" is an interesting hodgepodge of newspaper clippings in the German language, photos of the city, and people from a number of different epochs: from the Habsburg period through the interwar period to the postwar period. But the time of action at the novel's outset is the eve of World War II. *Silver Spider*, however, does not dwell as much on the historical intricacies of the war as was the case in *A Parade in Moscow*. This novel is more of a detective story than a commentary on historical events. The writer, as before, consistently employs the familiar mix of science fiction and history. One almost feels that the devices he so skillfully introduced in his earlier works have exhausted themselves, and the author stands at the threshold of a new writing phase. But the detailed emphasis on the city landscapes is new and noteworthy. Through one of his protagonists Kozhelianko expresses his admiration for the city in which he spent considerable time but not without a humorous twist: "In a few decades a legend will be born that Chernivtsi is such an awe-inspiring city, so exotic and romantic, so artistic and refined that janitors sweep sidewalks with roses ..."[35] By borrowing and incorporating many elements of popular genres, such as science fiction, romance and suspense, the author's novels represent highly accessible and readable commentaries on nationalism, regionalism and identities.

Kozhelianko's Chernivtsi fascinates with its complexity and colorful past. The writer presents it as a multiethnic place where the traces of all previous rulers are visible and all non-Ukrainian inhabitants are acknowledged, from German (Austrian), Romanian, to Jewish, but his Chernivtsi also comes across as a place that nurtures Ukrainian nationalism. Hence no wonder his novels often read as offhand guides on how to overcome colonial inferiority complexes. Everything Ukrainian is inflated and, according to him, nothing could be more enticing than assuming Ukrainian identity.

Vynnychuk's Imagined Lviv and *Malva Landa*

Yuri Vynnychuk is a prolific and quintessentially Lviv author, who epito-
mizes this city as no other writer in contemporary Ukrainian fiction.[36] Active
in the 1970s and 1980s literary underground, he began to flourish as a man
of letters only in independent Ukraine, publishing a number of allegorical
short stories and novellas that often foreground totalitarian absurdity and
parody former Soviet rule. Vitaly Chernetsky focuses on two aspects of Vynnychuk's oeuvre, namely, on the writer's bent for magic realism ("of a more
macabre type,"[37] as he puts it) and daring sexuality, but Vynnychuk's narratives also present an excellent case study for those interested in the literature
of place. *Malva Landa*, a bulky novel published in 2003 (though written in
the early 1990s), offers a snapshot of Lviv in its local color not so much in
visual as in emotional terms. Vynnychuk's Lviv unfolds before our eyes as a
symbolic place, with deep roots in myth and history, yet preserves the basic
tenets of verisimilitude through language (employing a specifically Lviv
jargon),[38] people's attitudes and the local ambience. These aspects remain
constant throughout and survive a considerable dose of fantastic elements
interwoven into the narrative of the novel, which render actual city landscapes as secondary ones.

Discussing the properties and uses of place in literature, Leonard Lutwack
dismisses writing that celebrates places for their own sake and insists on the
importance of symbolic value:

> As with all literary materials, place has a literal and a symbolical value, a func-
> tion serving both geographical and metaphorical ends. But the literal and geo-
> graphic aspect of place is always under the strain that all literature feels to attain
> the condition of poetry, of symbol, and it is difficult to avoid the proposition that
> in the final analysis all places in literature are used for symbolical purposes even
> though in their descriptiveness they may be rooted in fact.[39]

This is particularly true for Vynnychuk and his treatment of place in *Malva
Landa*. He starts his novel in contemporary Lviv but soon transfers the action
to its periphery, first to the garbage dumps outside the city and then to the
provincial town S. He transforms those places into mythical enclaves where
space and time function according to a different set of laws. The peripheral
place becomes a refuge, in which the main protagonist discovers his heroic
potential and heals his ego from the wounds inflicted by the circumstances
in "real" Lviv. Moreover, a shift in place also triggers a shift in time (and
there are numerous time displacements in *Malva Landa*). It is as if "a geographically remote place awakens the memory of remote times."[40] Indeed,
the mountains of trash outside Lviv constitute a peculiar universe, which

remembers the past of the Habsburg Empire and in which historical memory continues to exist as symbolic formation and metaphor.

The hero of the novel, Bumbliakevych (we never learn his first name), a single, not particularly attractive, middle-aged man, pretends to his controlling mother that he is dating women (his mother desperately wants him to get married) and when pressed for details, he invents Malva Landa. But since his mother soon insists on meeting her, he is forced to make up a story of her illness and subsequent death. As it turns out later, Malva Landa happens to be not just a product of Bumbliakevych's imagination but also a pseudonym of a female poet, who published two collections of verse before World War II. Bumbliakevych, who has read both of them, admires her poetry and is on a mission to find out more about her as a person. In the meantime, his mother dies and he is free to devote his time to his favorite pastimes without anyone controlling his life. The hero manages to locate a friend of Malva Landa's, who maintains that she is still alive but advanced in age. The remainder of the novel is devoted to Bumbliakevych's quest to find Malva, and the leads he gathers direct him to the landfills outside Lviv.

Vynnychuk skillfully and with a considerable humor uses the universe of Lviv's trash heaps as a place where various transformations are not only possible but also desirable. One of the characters whom Bumbliakevych meets there at the beginning of the novel warns him about the place, saying that this is a labyrinth from which no one has ever been able to extricate herself/himself. But receiving some hope that he can find Malva there, Bumbliakevych continues his journey. In a way, it almost feels natural that the protagonist, while rummaging through the layers of garbage, finds himself in a different era, and moves backward in time a hundred years or so. This Bumbliakevych, unlike the one in Lviv, is extremely successful with women, and in the typical Vynnychukian manner the novel depicts numerous copulations: sexuality is out there, front and center. But in the end, Bumbliakevych's search for Malva becomes a path of creative self-discovery for the hero. She evolves into his muse, inspiring his creative urges, and the novel ends with Bumbliakevych becoming a writer and preacher to the inhabitants of Lviv's landfills. He finds love and a purpose in life outside the space and time offered by the real city of Lviv.

What is interesting to observe is that in Vynnychuk's fiction the mythological reality and symbolic value take precedence over the need to depict the urban life of contemporary Lviv. At a certain point in the novel, Bumbliakevych manages to escape the labyrinth of trash and returns to Lviv but soon discovers that six years have passed since he embarked on his journey, making him that much older, a fact he finds difficult to accept. No wonder, therefore, that time and space offered by the universe of trash is so much more appealing than the dreary reality. This spatio-temporal dimension moves slower (or is even timeless) and presents possibilities otherwise unachievable for such average mortals as Bumbliakevych.

Ultimately, *Malva Landa* is also a novel about writing and has all the attributes of a typical postmodern metafiction. Vynnychuk playfully juggles characters, epochs, sexual taboos and literary allusions, all in an effort to nostalgically capture the essence of the region of which he is so enamored, that is, Halychyna. The novel ends with Bumbliakevych scribbling on an empty page a poem and signing it "Malva Landa." He has merged his identity with that of his muse. Vynnychuk, on the other hand, having started the action of the novel in Lviv, ends it on the city's periphery, in a utopian trash space, where memory lives on, where everyone is welcome to dig layer upon layer in search of bygone days, but where, more importantly, all dreams come true—the writer's and his heroes alike.

Vynnychuk's Lviv retains local color through language but is synecdochically represented by the city's landfills. His Lviv, by focusing on its rummage, morphs into a symbolic, if not allegorical, place reminiscent of utopia. But Lviv in Vynnychuk's edition is also first and foremost the cultural center of Halychyna, the region in Western Ukraine, which continuously offers a vast reservoir of things Ukrainian, ready for consumption and emulation everywhere else in the country.

Neborak's Poetic Lviv

Viktor Neborak's poetic interactions with his hometown are intimate, occasionally contemplative, yet, at the same time, very concrete. The motif of a journeying hero is also present in his poetry. But we sooner find his lyrical hero taking a stroll through the city's streets rather than traveling long distances. When the latter happens though, Neborak often invokes Homer's Odysseus, seemingly his favorite character, and makes his lyrical hero assume the identity of the Greek protagonist to underscore the fact that whoever is lost will nonetheless eventually find his way home. In the poem "Maiatnyk" ("A Pendulum"), for example, the lyrical hero travels back and forth between Lviv and Kyiv, invariably drawing comparisons between these two cities, and his feelings about them:

In Lviv—I'm the dreamwalker Odysseus,
who got lost in line at a café,
plunging into mirage visions
that the city-coliseum collects.

In Kyiv I'm the most demure of guests.
From doors of rain I cross into doors

of strange snow, where a film relates
Salieri's confessions to me.[41]

Lviv emerges in this poem as more hospitable, cheerful and concrete; Kyiv,
on the other hand, appears distant and somewhat abstract, and fails to attract
because "the water grows dark and flows more ponderously, / and the cold in
a leaf, like nicotine."[42] In the end there is no doubt in the reader's mind where
the lyrical hero feels more at home, clearly in Lviv.

"A Pendulum" comes from Neborak's early collection *The Flying Head*
(*Litaiucha holova*, 1990). There are many allusions to urban landscapes in
this book, but the city of Lviv figures most prominently in a long poem, titled
"Karkolomni perevtilennia!" ("Stunning Reincarnations!"). It is Neborak's
homage to his hometown city, preceded by the following preamble:

VIKTOR NEBORAK
in an archmodern show of poems,
that from a bird's eye view
and to the depths of the once popular
café-bar
NECTAR
is dedicated to the nicest
of philistine cities
LVIV
and which is called
STUNNING REINACARNATIONS![43]

In "Stunning Reincarnations!" there are numerous references to Lviv's well-
known landmarks and places, among them the Opera House, the Adam Mickiewicz's monument,[44] the Poetry Bookstore, a few celebrated streets, but the
poem first and foremost conveys the general atmosphere of the city, which is
dynamic, chic, culturally diverse and bursting with youthful enthusiasm. No
doubt, the overall upbeat mood of the poem reflects the poet's own youthful
exuberance at the time. After all, the poem was written when Neborak was in
his twenties, a period in which he actively participated in the carnivalesque
shows of the Bu-Ba-Bu group. The poem also projects optimistic and antici-
patory feelings prevalent in the late 1980s when the expectation of a radical
change in the political situation was very high among artists and intellectuals.
Neborak gives a snapshot of contemporary Lviv and captures the moment in
which creativity awakens and the lyrical hero ends up writing his first poem.

In his 2009 poetic collection, *Poems from Vyhovsky Street* (*Virshi z vulytsi
Vyhovs'koho*), Neborak replaces his youthful enthusiasm with pensive reflections about his hometown, about continuous urban and social transformations,

and about an urge to rename places. By now, a family man and father of three daughters, he contemplates Lviv from a narrow prism of one of its streets, Vyhovsky Street, which also happens to be the street where he and his family live. Political overtones are clearly interwoven into the fabric of the poet's lyrical ruminations about Lviv, as are his concerns about the environment:

you can teach how to read, write, and count
and many other things as well
but can you really teach someone
how to correctly breathe poisonous air[45]

But the most characteristic feature of his mature poems about Lviv is the quotidian nature of his reflections. His story about Lviv is the story of its ordinary residents going about their daily errands, many a time missing transformations brought about by changing political realities unless they consciously take a stroll along the street to observe. It seems as if in *Poems from Vyhovsky Street* Neborak strives to slow down the urban tempo for people to notice, as he does, how history and power affect the development of the whole city, and of its component streets in particular. The poet's reflections about the renaming of his street from Empty (in the 1930s under Polish rule) to Tereshkova (in the 1960s under Soviet rule), and to Vyhovsky (since independence), spurs thoughts not only about particular turns of history but also about one's identity. After all, naming something entails ascribing to it certain distinctiveness, and renaming always happens for a reason. Understanding the fluidity of such junctures helps to open up new possibilities, and, according to Neborak, helps to be creative:

everything gets its name
to be renamed eventually
everything flows
from name to name
everything wants to be itself
and changes thus by renaming
a bright empty abyss
purifies itself of mixtures
dilutes borders
and frees itself
to create anew[46]

Neborak's Lviv—contemporary and concrete, also unfolds synecdochically, as in the case of *Malva Landa*, except that, unlike in Vynnychuk's novel, it is represented here by a street rather than by a landfill. Vyhovsky Street emerges in Neborak's poetry like a small parallel universe to be discovered and explored. More importantly, however, the poet strives to convince us that the knowledge we gain through such an exploration can provide us with an in-depth understanding of everything else the city of Lviv has to offer.

Makhno's New York

Vasyl Makhno, a Ukrainian poet who settled permanently in New York in 2000, immigrated to the US from the city of Ternopil in Western Ukraine. He does have a number of poems about his hometown,[47] as well as about other cities in Ukraine and abroad,[48] but the city that alone has left a notable imprint on his mature poetry is unquestionably New York, his adopted hometown. In 2004, he published a collection of poems almost entirely devoted to New York City, titled *38 virshiv pro N'iu-Iork i deshcho inshe* (*38 Poems about New York and a Few Other Things*). Three years later, in 2007, *Cornelia Street Café* came out, which in addition to his new poems also comprised selections from his previously published collections, including *38 Poems about New York*. The poet's most recent poetry book in English *Winter Letters* (2011)[49] is also in large part devoted to New York. The poetic propositions offered by these collections betray Makhno's utmost fascination with the cultural multiplicity of this most cosmopolitan metropolis of all American cities. The poet celebrates New York with all its ups and downs—at first he does so with a dose of considerable hesitation if not outright reluctance, but then with a growing attachment if not love. Makhno's New York comes across as a site of archaeological importance, a site in which he digs layer upon layer of textual deposits left by his predecessors and contemporaries, hoping to leave his own literary mark in the process.[50]

Makhno thrives on being a *flâneur* of sorts who observes the city and leaves behind a poetic record of New York's here and now like in the poem "Coffee in Starbucks":

in december—in downtown new york—
    drinking coffee in Starbucks—i watch
two mexicans laying marble wall slabs
    in the entrance to the building

an irksome Jingle Bells keeps playing in the café
new yorkers shimmer with their Christmas gifts and cars
street peddlers sell the tourists all kind of crap
the policemen snooze peacefully in their warm car[51]

This poem gives a poetic snapshot of a particular moment in New York. We are told at the outset that it is December and the café is in downtown New

York. We observe what is happening through the poet's eyes, yet he himself is almost invisible. Only in the middle of the poem does he re-emerge with his own reflections about the passage of time, the community of other poets and ars poetica but only for a brief moment, because the poem ends as it began: with the observation of two Mexicans working with stone on the entrance to the building. Makhno's New York could not be more concrete and alive.

Makhno's New York poems invoke literary traces left by other poets who either lived there permanently or were guests at some point of their lives. Federico Garcia Lorca, for example, becomes a central literary figure in Makhno's *Cornelia Street Café*. In Lorca's *Poet in New York* the creative elements are based on direct impressions, which in many cases could easily be localized. Makhno goes further: his direct impressions (often named and specified) also play a role but so do his textual appropriations. Lorca's images are not only implied but the Spanish poet himself becomes a protagonist in Makhno's poetic world. It is as if Lorca in Makhno's poetry assumes the same role as Virgil in Dante's *Inferno*.[52] The poet actively seeks all literary traces left on many surfaces of the city. He becomes an archaeologist who patiently digs and reveals all poetic layers imprinted on New York's walls. In that sense it is not only Lorca that he embraces but also the poets of the 1960s, including the New York Group of Ukrainian poets, as well as Americans Walt Whitman, John Ashbery and Frank O'Hara. In fact, Makhno's textual New York is simply a community of poets of all generations and of many different nationalities. They are present in Makhno's poetic texts either through his memory, which resurrects them to life in his New York, or through their own association with the city, which the poet conscientiously rediscovers and textualizes anew.

As I already mentioned, Makhno celebrates New York in all its literary, historical and ethnic peculiarities. From the Jewish Brooklyn to Manhattan's Chinatown, the specificity and local flavor dominate the tone and images in all his New York poems. In "Brooklyn Elegy" the poet's own persona becomes inconspicuous, it is only his detailed observation that we are offered:

each morning the jewish bakeries open up while it's still dark
the first thing that runs up to you—quick as a fox—
is the scent of cinnamon—beaten eggs with sugar—
to the brick synagogues—and this is the beginning of winter
because the dough smells of pine and jasmine picked yesterday
together with garlic and onions beckoning to you from the shelves[53]

However, on some occasions the ethnic coloring implies bias but, arguably, no malice, like in the poem "Chinatown: Seafood Store":

they cackle like Peking geese
here it is—Peking opera for free
when in the store they select
frozen or fresh fish
the Chinese buy fish everyday
vendors in rubber boots
like gray herons—
wipe their hands greasy with fish oil
on dirty white aprons[54]

Makhno embraces difference and locality with a typical postmodern acceptance. His New York, deeply rooted in the specific, reflects diversity, history
and allegiance. Makhno's community of others includes not just poets but
also ordinary men and women whom he observes while walking, or merely
drinking coffee in one of the city's cafes. The poet revels in idiosyncrasies
New York offers with all its local color, charm and incongruity. Moreover,
New York's multiethnic diversity reflects back on Makhno's own sense of
belonging. He is a Ukrainian poet who, nonetheless, feels at home in the
American city's cultural ambience. At the same time, however cosmopolitan
and worldly his views are, through language he is always thrust back to his
Ukrainian identity. Thus Makhno's American "now" is intrinsically linked to
his Ukrainian past. Whenever thoughts take him back to his place of origin,
they are inseparably interwoven into the context of his life in New York. In
many ways, the poet manifests a typical diasporic cultural hybridity in his
oeuvre, where the mindfulness of his East European roots is invariably etched
into his American life, revealing the artist who reflects on these parallel actu-
alities, enriching himself enormously in the process. This kind of hybridity
could potentially signal a condition tantamount to alienation or a state of
homelessness but this is not the case in Makhno's poems. His "outsider"
perspective imposed by diasporic circumstances engenders fresh approaches
to creativity and offers unique opportunities to evolve artistically and intellectually. And clearly, Makhno takes full advantage of such plural cultural
possibilities and makes himself a citizen of the world but with a Ukrainian
ethnic background.

THE REGION AS PROTAGONIST

In *Place in Literature*, Roberto Dainotto approaches the city and the region
as two opposing entities: "In search of a shared communal identity, region is
the rhetorical opposition to the modern city."[55] However, it is questionable
whether in the globalization era it is at all possible to ascribe pristine, ethnic

purity to any geographical enclave. And, as I indicated earlier, there are many examples in contemporary Ukrainian literature in which urban settings provide a set of beliefs, myths and historical accounts that go well beyond their city boundaries and exert influence on the adjacent territories. In such cases both the city and the region complement rather than oppose each other.

The regions that have attracted the most attention and are thus far best represented in literary texts come from both eastern and western parts of Ukraine. My focus here is on those few deemed most important: Slobozhanshchyna with Kharkiv as its center, the Carpathian Mountains, Zakarpattia and Halychyna, especially in Taras Prokhasko's and Yuri Andrukhovych's rendering. All four regions constitute geographical territories where the idea of a regional identity is nurtured and celebrated but the idea of a national identity is contemplated as well. In fact, Ukraine as an independent state becomes an indispensable background against which all other identities are played out.

East-West Dynamics

It is often acknowledged that there is a marked linguistic, ideological and intellectual divide between western and eastern regions of Ukraine. Halychyna (Galicia), for instance, in addition to an undeniable local coloring, prides itself also on being progressive and oriented toward the West, and takes Ukrainian identity for granted. The industrial southeast, on the other hand, perceives things Ukrainian with a dose of suspicion, viewing them as imports from Western Ukraine. No doubt, linguistic difference plays some role, but choice of language has never acquired a determinative value of self-identification. Two novels, by two different writers, both born in 1963, illustrate this east-west dynamic particularly well: one novel by Pavlo Volvach titled *The Class* (*Kliasa*, 2010)[56] deals with the industrial city of Zaporizhzhia, and another one, *Trees on the Roofs* (*Dereva na dakhakh*, 2010), by Oleksandr Vilchynsky depicts the city of Ternopil in Western Ukraine. However, even though these two novels predominantly focus on concrete cities, they both signify attitudes, beliefs and daily habits of their residents that are characteristic not only of these two urban centers but also of the respective regions of which they are an inseparable part.

Volvach's novel describes Zaporizhzhia on the eve of independence, in the late 1980s. The city itself, an industrial wasteland, polluted with smog and other environmentally hazardous substances, repulses rather than attracts. Ecological problems go hand in hand with social woes—drugs are widespread and youth by and large has limited prospects. The novel's main protagonist Pashek has aspirations to be a university student and secretly wishes to leave his work in the "Zaporizhstal," a widely known steel plant in

Zaporizhzhia, characterized as "hell" with "brown, yellow and pink smoke that merges into a poisonous smog, covering the sun and hanging over the city like a foggy tent."[57] But Volvach uses his hometown also as a metaphor for the whole industrial southeastern region, in which residents are forced not only to endure polluted air but are also kept misinformed, inadequately educated and ideologically indoctrinated.

On the eve of independence, however, the issues of identity necessarily take center stage. The region is overwhelmingly Russian speaking but Pashek's father, for instance, recalls the Soviet Ukrainianization efforts of the 1920s with its specific rules of orthography (later rejected)[58] and high-caliber cultural heritage. Clearly, Pashek's sense of belonging, nurtured by past memories preserved within his family circle, is well developed and he has no problem with self-identification issues. At some point in the novel, he even tells one of his friends, "we are Ukrainians."[59] His dreams of becoming a student eventually fulfilled, Pashek recalls visits and literary evenings by writers from Kyiv who read their works in Ukrainian. Such events in the late 1980s undoubtedly influenced the overall atmosphere of Zaporizhzhia and, perhaps, that is why the city's Russophone residents embraced independence with all its national symbols despite their initial suspicion toward activists coming from Western Ukraine.

Volvach's *The Class* presents the east-west dynamic in Ukraine as culturally entrenched but simultaneously fluid.[60] That is, the author implies that the Zaporozhian industrial region can be swayed toward nationally oriented democratic values if it perceives such a move to be in its own self-interest. In many ways, the novel concludes on an upbeat note—in the end the main hero contemplates his life as full of promise and potential. Of course, such expectations are more than justified when juxtaposed with the new beginnings of a new independent state. After all, it is natural at such junctures to assume changes for the better. Volvach does not dwell on potential conflicts but at the same time points out inherent differences in people's perceptions of what constitutes the pillars of nation-building activities. The author many a time alludes that the project of independent Ukraine will not prevail without engaging the proletariat of the industrial southeastern regions.

Vilchynsky's novel *Trees on the Roofs* takes independence for granted, which is understandable not only because its story line in contrast to Volvach's narrative unfolds close to two decades after Ukraine declared its exit from the Soviet Union but also because it takes place mostly in the city of Ternopil in Western Ukraine. Here the issue of indigenous language, history and culture does not have the same urgency as in the southeastern regions. Moreover, the novel's action comes about after the Orange Revolution and before the presidential elections of 2010, a five-year period known for its relatively democratic and liberal ways in politics and media. All these factors make the novel's political overtones markedly subdued and not as evident as in Volvach's case.

Vilchynsky's protagonists are by and large intellectuals and artists who cultivate a bohemian lifestyle, spend spare time in Ternopil's cafes, travel considerably not only within Ukraine but also abroad, yet are emotionally very much attached to their hometown. Ternopil and its environs indeed play an important role in the novel. In fact, Vilchynsky deliberately inserts passages about the city's history and urban development, names its streets, buildings, restaurants, hotels and places of recreation. But, all these topographic signposts seem to interrupt rather than complement the main story line. Evidently, the author aspires to underscore the significance of the locality but the way he treats the place in his fiction earns it an auxiliary rather than autonomous quality.

There is no doubt that the novel's chief protagonist, Yakiv Dovhan, is a local patriot who considers his Ukrainian identity a settled matter. What is worthy of underscoring, however, is the way Vilchynsky approaches identity issues because it alone separates him from other writers for whom regionalism and place in literature are relevant. In *Trees on the Roofs* the question of identity surfaces not so much because of a specific territorial affinity but because of race. The author introduces a woman of mixed race, Anzhelka, who grew up in an orphanage because her parents abandoned her while she was still an infant. Her Ukrainian mother got pregnant by a student from Africa and in the end refused to raise her own daughter. Anzhelka's orphanage located in the small town of Koropets in the Ternopil oblast conditioned the heroine to speak a very local dialect of Ukrainian. The combination of her dark skin and the idiosyncratic manner in which she communicates (the Galician dialect) makes her stand out in the provincial artistic milieu. Anzhelka becomes Yakiv's mistress and is readily accepted by his colleagues. The protagonist, it seems, is more concerned about introducing her to his mother than to his friends. When Yakiv visits his mother with Anzhelka for the first time he half-jokingly introduces her as an American journalist. But to his surprised friend Sashunia, the explanation about her is much simpler: "She is really Ukrainian, just dark-skinned."[61]

The love affair between Anzhelka and Yakiv allows Vilchynsky to inject a racial dimension into the novel. But more importantly, the author uses it to question the stereotyped perceptions about identity in post-independence Ukraine. By framing the issue of identity construction in terms of race, he is at the same time subtly underscoring tolerance and open-mindedness of western Ukrainians, at least among those who are educated. In the final analysis, as books by Vilchynsky and Volvach indicate, at the heart of the east-west dynamic lies, on the one hand, the tradition of a closed society, often guided by suspicion toward difference (the Soviet mentality), and on the other, the tradition of an open society, which appears to adjust to changing circumstances and has a sense of national belonging (the European mentality).

Serhiy Zhadan: Kharkiv and Beyond

Born in Starobilsk of the Luhansk oblast, Serhiy Zhadan (b. 1974) settled permanently in Kharkiv and is mainly known as a preeminent Kharkiv poet, writer and activist. However, his prose works are not thematically confined to Kharkiv alone but foreground the Slobozhanshchyna region, which encompasses territorially not only the provinces of Kharkiv, Sumy, and Luhansk but also parts of the Donbas region. And yet, it is undoubtedly justified to associate Zhadan first and foremost with Kharkiv because he himself cultivates this link in a rather pronounced way. One such example is his anthology of Kharkiv's new literature, titled *The Hotels of Kharkiv* (*Hoteli Kharkova*, 2008), which gathers together poets and writers expressing themselves in Ukrainian and Russian.[62] Despite the fact that almost all the texts included in the anthology do not thematize Kharkiv as an urban landscape, the literati presented there (in groups and individually) are all based in the city and it seems that Zhadan goes to great lengths to underscore the vitality of the literary circles in his adopted hometown. He considers himself very much part of the Kharkiv literary establishment and works tirelessly to promote his local colleagues.

Of course, Zhadan's oeuvre transcends a narrow regional character, yet I doubt if anyone would dispute that territorial considerations and/or referencing specific places do not play a major role in his narrative accounts, fiction and nonfiction alike. Interestingly though, unlike the other authors discussed in this chapter, it is impossible to pinpoint Zhadan to just one particular place. However attached to Kharkiv Zhadan is, what is most intriguing about his oeuvre is that he can easily shift his focus from Kharkiv of the 1990s (*Depesh Mod*,[63] 2004) to his birthplace Starobilsk of the 2000s (*Voroshylovhrad*, 2010),[64] and even invoke the 1920s and the Ukrainian War of Independence as he retraces activities of the anarcho-communist guerilla leader, Nestor Makhno (1888–1934) (*Anarchy in the UKR*, 2005). What emerges from these various narratives and memoirs is Zhadan's version of his own personal territory, as well as his vision of the Slobozhanshchyna region, which captivates with its contradictions and multiple identities.

Zhadan's manner of narrating often involves a journeyed hero. It is through his eyes that we see various places, including train and bus terminals, road diners, gas stations, hotels, both urban and countryside landscapes, yet these places never stand alone but are always viewed through the prism of people attached to them. For instance, in the *Anarchy in the UKR*, Zhadan's memoirs of sorts, the descriptions of places have a necessarily personalized angle—the protagonist inscribes his own experiences into familiar landscapes, because it is what his memory compels him to do. He first reminisces his childhood in Starobilsk, then adulthood in Kharkiv, and in the last chapter he even includes his trip to New York, all in an effort to capture not so much the essence of these places as geographical entities but to map out what can be labeled as "human landscapes," that is, places inextricably linked to particular people, if not a particular society. Growing up with a father whose work demanded being frequently on the road instills in young Zhadan a desire to go places, a curiosity to explore the unknown in order to make it his own. And this is precisely the attitude he assumes as an adult. He travels to reconnect with people he has lost touch, or to observe the way of life in any given place, and in the process he triggers self-identification impulses, or comments on the identity of others.

In *Depeche Mode*, Zhadan's first novel, three main protagonists are constantly on a move. They are united in search for their friend Karbiurator whose stepfather died and they need to notify him in time so he can attend his funeral. But this plot is a mere pretext to paint the generation coming of age in the early 1990s that appears to drift idly in the difficult economic times shortly after independence and whose only defense mechanism against external forces out of their control is their strong sense of collective solidarity. Their search for a friend is also their flight from the everyday realities encroaching upon them. We see them wandering the streets of Kharkiv, taking a train to a nearby town and back, yet as much as their journey in the city and its suburbs is front and center in the novel what really counts are not so much places visited as the encounters with people who motivate a trio of friends to continue with their pursuit. In the end, Karbiurator is found but the search for a missing friend can be taken as the protagonists' own quest for finding the right kind of destiny, their own dharma. Vitaly Chernetsky, for example, characterizes *Depeche Mode* as "a stunning stream-of-consciousness tour de force set among a gang of working-class youths in the early 1990s, an explosive hybrid of *Ulysses*, *Trainspotting*, and modern Ukrainian realia" and underscores the author's embrace of the writer-as-rebel image.[65] But there is also an underlining urge among that disadvantaged youth to search for meaning in life.

As Zhadan sees it, journeys can be open-ended or with a closure—in other words, with a sense of arrival. His novel *Voroshilovgrad* (2010) presents the latter scenario. As Pavlo Shopin aptly observes "the whole book is a journey in time and space during which the hero recollects his past and reconstructs his identity."[66] Herman, the novel's main protagonist, a thirty-three-year-old intellectual who works for some kind of organization in Kharkiv, receives a phone call from his brother's employee Kocha, informing him about the disappearance of his brother and ensuing difficulties his brother's business experiences because of this circumstance. Herman decides to make a short weekend trip to his hometown in order to find out more about this incident. It turns out that Herman's brother fled abroad fearing for his life when another local business clan decided to take over the gas station he owned.[67] Herman's one-day visit turns into a permanent stay. He makes a decision to resist a hostile takeover of local gas chain owners, then rebuilds contacts with his old childhood friends, and with their help successfully fights local corporate raiders. Here, like in *Depeche Mode*, places are meaningless unless they have a human dimension. Group solidarity, so pronounced in *Depeche Mode*, also plays an important role in this novel, except that here it is envisioned on a much larger scale.

The title *Voroshilovgrad* refers to an old name of Luhansk, the most eastwardly situated oblast city in Ukraine. And, at first, one might get an impression that the novel's story line unfolds indeed in Luhansk. But, as it turns out, *Voroshilovgrad* is really about the author's hometown Starobilsk, which is located in the Luhansk province.[68] Zhadan returns again to his hometown, this time in the work of fiction rather than memoirs,[69] seemingly in order to contrast two different social and economic realities in post-independence Ukraine. On one hand, there are people who are ready to play by the rules, however unstable or unenforceable they appear, on the other hand, there are those who form mafia-like structures, propped up by local authorities, whose main goal is control and enrichment.

Zhadan's preoccupation with "human landscapes" does not necessarily mean that he neglects painting the background and/or providing discerning descriptions of surroundings and actual localities. It is true that Starobilsk in *Voroshilovgrad* lacks clearly delineated city contours, although we do occasionally see fragments of urban space through the protagonist's eyes as he passes buildings that invoke specific memories from his past—a hospital where his brother stayed with an appendicitis, a monastery turned into army barracks where his father was stationed, and a school he attended as a child and youth. However binding these memories of the town of his childhood are, it is really Kharkiv that captures most of Zhadan's attention. He devotes an entire chapter to this city in *Anarchy in the UKR*. Being an activist who participated in the rallies supporting the Orange Revolution of 2004 and the Revolution of Dignity of 2013–2014, Zhadan always provides depictions of his home city with a commentary, many a time unflattering, ironic, if not outright sarcastic. He does not seem to endow Kharkiv with the same kind of admiration and love as Kurkov does the city of Kyiv in his novels. But Zhadan's emotional ties to Kharkiv are undeniable and often reflect his experiences in the city. He himself admits that much in his memoirs. The city is important to him because that particular urban space in many ways has designed his life, thereby creating in the process an unbreakable bond

between him and the place inhabited. Zhadan's sense of belonging is rooted
not so much in his attraction to concrete buildings, places and landmarks, as
is in his own remembrances of them:

> Only at first glance it appears that everything depends on memories, associa-
> tions, and reflections, but devil knows—these frightening numbers on the walls
> of buildings do not invoke any associations in me, no reflections whatsoever. It
> just happened that here, on these streets and squares, luck had it I spent fifteen
> years of my life, under these very arches of all that state industry I walked at
> five in the morning on one warm Sunday in June, when I alone in the whole
> city did not sleep, and because of these remembrances, I would be returning to
> this very place again and again, just like that, without any particular goal, or
> without any satisfaction. But, in the end—these are just associations.[70]

Zhadan's Kharkiv attracts and repulses at the same time. Writing about the
landmark hotel "Kharkiv" on the city's main square, for instance, he comments—not without a considerable dose of black humor—that it is so big,
with so many indistinguishable rooms, that it is a good place to hide dead
bodies, alluding subtly, perhaps, to the past Soviet and Nazi atrocities. The
author also alludes to the communist futurist aspirations of the 1920s, which
were reified in the constructivist architecture right in the Kharkiv downtown
area. Passing the Kharkiv university campus, the author reflects on students'
passivity, noting how much power ten thousand of them could master if not
for their habitual silence. Such commentaries are commonplace throughout
the chapter on Kharkiv, regardless of objects described—monuments, the
city's subway, public buildings and spaces. And this manner of narration
implicitly entails social concerns, which, ultimately, lead to the issue of
identity.

In Zhadan's imaginative world there are only two possible identity choices
for Ukraine's post-Soviet society, and, however unexpected for some it
might be, the main criterion of division does not necessarily involve a linguistic difference (Russian vs. Ukrainian). One identity embraces a new
independent reality and strives for a national consolidation, and another one
clings to old Soviet ways of being with everything it entails, in other words—
the Ukrainian identity vs. Soviet identity, still predominant especially in the
southeast. One could even argue that Luhansk (Voroshylovhrad), which is
really absent in the novel despite its title, signifies the latter, whereas Starobilsk—the author's hometown—stands for independence. The fight for a
gas station in *Voroshilovgrad* can also be construed as a struggle for and a
symbol of a basic human right to be independent and safe. Zhadan's quest
for personal freedom and territory no doubt equally applies to the nation he
represents.

The Carpathian Mountains Region: Poetic Visions of Herasymiuk, Midianka and Malkovych

No other contemporary Ukrainian poet is associated with the Carpathian Mountains as much as Vasyl Herasymiuk (b. 1956) is. He was born in Kazakhstan because his Hutsul[71] parents were deported there by the Stalinist regime in the early 1940s but they managed to return to their native village in the Kosiv district when the poet was still a child. Herasymiuk has authored ten books of poems, settled permanently in Kyiv, but from the very first published poetic line it has been clear that the Carpathians with its nature, people and specific Hutsul way of life have captured the poet's imagination for years to come. Herasymiuk transcends a mere description of the region's beauty—his connection with the mountains is deeply internalized, it is as if he hears the voices of his ancestors and feels responsible for staying faithful to their heritage. In his poetry, landscapes and people constitute an unbreakable ontological whole, and the mountains are often implied rather than straightforwardly depicted. We see them through metonymic associations—forests, streams, highland pastures, sheep and fog—in other words, the Carpathians are always there as poetic space, constantly present, as if they were air breathed by people and nature alike.

Herasymiuk displays a rare veneration for particular trees, fir and beech trees being most mentioned. A fir tree, for instance, becomes more than a symbol of the Carpathians, it becomes a kind of leitmotif, a symbol of life and vitality. In fact, his first collection of poetry bears the name of fir trees, *Smereky* (1982). His second collection is titled *Potoky* (1986), which means streams. The title of his third book, *Kosmach Pattern* (*Kosmats'kyi uzir*, 1989) also refers to the mountain region, this time employing in the title the name of a well-known Hutsul village Kosmach. In all these early collections the poet's attention is firmly rooted in the region he grew up in, providing poetic interpretations not only of the highland people's way of life but also creating his personal myths, his own idiosyncratic interactions with nature and the mountains.

Arguably, Herasymiuk's best mature poetry comes with the publication of his fourth book *The Children of Aspen Tree* (*Dity trepety*, 1991) and seventh, titled *Poet in Air* (*Poet u povitri*, 2002), for which he was awarded the Shevchenko Literary Prize, the highest honor for artistic achievement in Ukraine. *The Children of Aspen Tree* introduces a new dimension in Herasymiuk's poetry—his deeply felt religious sentiments, which reveal themselves through numerous biblical references as well as through a lyrical hero's longing for redemption. There are allusions to past sufferings: "I grew up with alphorns' despair. I cannot forget / that world",[72] but there are also allusions to a renewal and resurrection like in the poem "Young Forest"

(Molodyi lis): "It grew in place of primeval forest— / on a long postwar fell."[73] Herasymiuk nurtures memories of his own kin, however painful, writing poetry in his father's house in the village of Prokurava:

I write poems
  at night in Prokurava,
I write poems
  in my father's house,
as long as
  on the bench against the wall
my ancestors sit
  killed and cut.[74]

The award-winning book *Poet in Air* is thematically much more diverse than Herasymiuk's previous collections. It opens with a long poem of the same title, presenting a poetic biography of sorts, a long meditation on the birth of a poet. It is dedicated to the memory of the poet's father and once again brings to the forefront all the local beauty of the Carpathian region, as well as foregrounds the poet's attachment to his territory, including its painful past. Yet, the book also celebrates poetry and poets as such. There are many poems dedicated to Herasymiuk's friends and colleagues who share with him the same poetic craft. While *Poet in Air* continues thematizing the mountain region, underscoring its historical background even more deeply than previously and introducing many local words characteristic of Hutsul dialect, at the same time, it expands its thematic scope by including poems also about Kyiv, the poet's hometown since his student times. These two thematic currents, both referencing geographical entities, do not clash, however. On the contrary, they seem to coexist quite harmoniously, combining the poet's childhood and youth in the mountains with his adult life in the capital city Kyiv where he transformed himself from a Hutsul boy into a well-known poet.

    In the collection *Poet in Air*, Herasymiuk dedicates one poem, titled "1745— Petrivka," to Petro Midianka (b. 1959). Midianka is another poet whose connection to the Carpathian Mountains region is notably celebrated in his oeuvre. He was born in the Zakarpattia oblast and studied in Uzhhorod, the largest westernmost city in Ukraine but, unlike Herasymiuk, he returned to his native village Shyrokyi Luh to work as a teacher in a local school. By 2011 Midianka published ten books of poetry and, like Herasymiuk, he too was awarded the Shevchenko Literary Prize for the collection *The Ladder to Heaven* (*Luitra u nebo*, 2010). Despite this recognition, he is not a widely known poet and his poetry is often considered hermetic because of numerous dialecticisms. Yet, he is often perceived as a poet's poet since, judging by a number of awards, his work is indeed admired by his contemporary literary peers.

The Zakarpattia region is arguably the most ethnically diverse territory in Ukraine and has borders with four different countries: Hungary, Slovakia, Poland and Romania. Hence it has considerable Hungarian, Romanian, Russian, Roma, Slovak, and even German ethnic minorities. This ethnic diversity finds its ample reflection in Midianka's poems. The poet utilizes toponymy, specific Zakarpattian lexicon, and occasionally even Latin script, all in an effort to underscore the local multicultural reality. His poetry was translated into Slovak and Czech, and one of his collections, *Uzhhorod Cafes* (*Užhorodské kavárny*, 2004), a bilingual Czech-Ukrainian edition, was published in Prague.

Midianka loves the Carpathians—it is his refuge and his only true home. Hence his interaction with the mountains and nature is by and large solitary, if not intimate. At the same time, both the Carpathians and nature have a considerably more autonomous character than is the case in Herasymiuk's poetry. Midianka is not afraid to poetically paint contours of mountaintops with their forests, birds, plants, and name the places he feels attached to and which he likes to tread. One would almost think that this pronounced individualism would engender detachment to social issues but the poet is mindful of cultural and historical context, and, paradoxically, he populates his poems with plentiful examples of various intertexts—from Andy Warhol to Moulin Rouge, from many figures of local significance, be they of Hungarian, Czech, Slovak or Ukrainian descent, to numerous foreign words. The latter practice, for instance, is especially prevalent in the collection *Tax* (*Dyzhma*, 2003), published by Krytyka Publishing House in Kyiv. The language of the poems included there comprises words that are not part of standard Ukrainian vocabulary and that necessitate the inclusion of a short glossary of local and/or foreign terms. Arguably, no other Midianka's collection incorporates intertextuality to such an extent as *Tax* does. Here, the poet also adds a substantial name index of people and places of the Zakarpattia region that he readily employs, and which constitute the cultural and topographical content of the book.

From his debut collection *A Threshold* (*Porih*, 1987) to his 2011 *Poems from Below* (*Virshi z podu*), Midianka displays a peculiar talent to combine his solitary reflections about the beauty of the mountains and the haven they provide with the overwhelming knowledge of the multicultural context of his region. In fact, his poems are not only about the Carpathian Mountains but also about the cities of Zakarpattia—Uzhhorod, Mukachevo and Khust, to name just a few. The poet frequently alludes to the Rusyn population, which the Ukrainian government considers a subgroup of the Ukrainian ethnos but they themselves claim a separate national identity. The poems that thematize identity come mainly from the late 1980s—on the eve of independence these were indeed hot issues. But those poems also indicate that Midianka uses the designations Rusyn, Ruthenian or Ukrainian interchangeably, and thus does not think of the Rusyns as a separate ethnic minority. On the other hand, it is also true that the issue of Rusyn separate identity came to the forefront after Ukraine gained independence, and it is not clear from Midianka's later poetry where he stands on the issue since then. But there can be no doubt about his own identity. He is a local patriot of the Zakarpattia region but his sense of belonging to the Ukrainian nation is never questioned.

Midianka's poetic oeuvre is surprisingly contemporary and not in any way escapist despite his love of nature and the mountains. He does not dwell in the past to the same extent as Herasymiuk does, and in his oeuvre there is considerably less sentimentality than in his older colleague's poems. Whereas Herasymiuk is concerned with the metaphysics of time and space, Midianka is more concrete, or more postmodern, in the sense that he allows for and often juxtaposes elements otherwise incongruous and contradictory. Herasymiuk utilizes imagery, Midianka, on the other hand, employs self-reference, irony and subtle humor, especially when playfully referring to his own persona and to his own identity: "I will write myself down as a Serb or Greek ... / On my grave a fir tree will grow / With a beautiful sign—/ Petros Karpatoros."[75]

Both poets personalize the Carpathian region but each in his own unique way—Herasymiuk by looking back into the past, into the Hutsul traditions, attempting to reconcile his childhood memories with what a new independent reality has to offer; Midianka—by looking at the region through contemporary lenses, mixing past and present equally, juxtaposing various ethnicities indigenous to the region with the aim to embrace them all, and in so many ways to celebrate diversity and coexistence.

Unlike Herasymiuk and Midianka, Ivan Malkovych (b. 1961) does not dwell too much on the mountains in his poems, even though, he also claims the Carpathians as his native region and comes from a village near the well-known town of Kosiv. After settling down in Kyiv in the 1980s, he founded a private publishing house A-BA-BA-HA-LA-MA-HA in the early 1990s, specializing initially in children's books. Known primarily as a successful publisher, he nonetheless authored eight poetry collections and was recently awarded the Taras Shevchenko Literary Prize (2017) for his book titled *Plantain with New Poems* (*Podorozhnyk z novymy virshamy*, 2016).

Malkovych showcases his highland origin mostly in his early books, published in the 1980s, and only peripherally, often assuming a boy's gaze who keenly observes the daily lives of his Hutsul parents. But already in his second collection *The Key* (*Kliuch*, 1988), the poet alludes to the fact that his return to the mountains is impossible for "I lost my key: I named a pine needle / to be my key—and somehow I lost it."[76] His subsequent poetry books only occasionally invoke the Carpathians, and when they do, they evince a somewhat nostalgic reminiscence about the mountains and view the highland through the prism of people, including their rituals and traditions, rather than through the surrounding nature.

Taras Prokhasko's Halychyna

Taras Prokhasko (b. 1968) comes from Ivano Frankivsk and is part of the literary phenomenon known as the Stanyslaviv (Galician) School. He has published a number of books of prose, of which *For It's Like That* (*BotakIE*, 2010) represents a volume of his collected writings. His most accomplished work to date, however, is *UnSimple* (*NeprOsti*, 2002) with the story line taking place in the resort town of Yalivets in the Carpathian Mountains. But, Prokhasko, like Zhadan, does not align himself with just one geographical entity. The mountains, while important, do not capture his whole writerly imagination. Prokhasko's subtly experimental, often autobiographical, and at times lyrical narratives foreground Halychyna (galicia) in a very idiosyncratic way—the region acquires contours in his prose through the depictions of its cities and nearby mountains, through the interactions with its neighbors across the borders, and through the reflections and family memory about (among other things) resistance to Soviet rule. Yet Prokhasko's approach is too intimate, too magical or too singular to make his prose in any way politicized and/or didactic, even when he refers to specific political events. The precision and economy of his manner of expression (he loves short descriptive sentences and occasionally numbers his paragraphs, or even adopts a diaristic style of narration) underscore the writer's desire to tell his stories in the most efficient way, a trait of a scientist some would say. Prokhasko's prose also represents a clear change in the mode of narration. His story lines do not unfold sequentially but spatially, or "laterally," as author and art critic John Berger put it: "instead of being aware of a point as an infinitely small part of a straight line, we are aware of it as an infinitely small part of an infinite number of lines, as the centre of a star of lines."[77] Berger further states that such awareness is "the result of our constantly having to take into account the simultaneity and extension of events and possibilities."[78] And that, in turn, is the essence of what Edward Soja calls "postmodern geographies," a bold spatial turn or reassertion of space and geography in critical social theory.[79] The author of *UnSimple* fits this paradigm exceptionally well.

Prokhasko studied biology at the Ivan Franko National Lviv University but never really worked professionally as a biologist. He held a number of odd jobs before establishing himself as a journalist and writer in the early 1990s. In one of his interviews, Prokhasko made a connection between his writings and the subject he studied at the university by saying that he incorporates "biological methods of thinking" in his narratives.[80] It is quite possible that his love for plants and botany might be the reason for his contemplative, if not mystical, approach to narration. There is indeed a certain depth and timeless (spatial?) dimension in his prose. Whether he writes about people, nature, his beloved Carpathians, or any other place for that matter, a chronology, even if present, does not diminish an overall feeling that realities described in Prokhasko's oeuvre step out of the ordinary time-space and cross into the mythic realm. The latter is particularly true in *UnSimple*, a short novel in which protagonists are thrust into the mysteries of life unfolding in the Carpathian Mountains—a sacred territory that equally sustains shaman-like people (the UnSimple) and intelligentsia. The novel's main protagonists—Frantsysk, Sebastian, Anna (who appears in several incarnations) and Beda call the mountains their home and all live in harmony with the forces of nature. The story line spans close to four decades, from 1913 to 1951, but is presented out of sequence and set against the background that is historically accurate and magical at the same time.

UnSimple is a love story of sorts first between Frantsysk and Anna, then Sebastian and Anna-Stefaniia, and then again between Sebastian and Anna, and yet another Anna. She becomes a symbol of an eternal perfect woman/mother who after delivering a baby girl dies so there is only one Anna at any given time. The human life becomes as sacredly cyclical as the rest of nature. The incestuous character of Sebastian's relationships with his daughter and grand-daughter loses moral expediency in the world governed by a different set of rules. In the world of *UnSimple* the magic of life erases all taboos, transcends the linearity of time and populates the mountains with half-god creatures (sorcerers) that can be helpful or dangerous on a whim. In Prokhasko's imaginative writing time unfolds as a story and how it unfolds depends on the storyteller:

1. Sebastian told only of how things could be, and therefore things were as Sebastian told.
   All the years before starting to speak Sebastian actually did just one thing—he looked and thought about how to tell stories.
2. Sebastian told how he could tell people about their lives in such a way that they would want to live forever, without changing anything. And people really did want to live forever and changed nothing.[81]

But *UnSimple* is not only about the "round" time. It is really about the mysterious geography of the Carpathians, including an invented (fictional) place called Yalivets. Prokhasko opens the novel with a map of the mountains where Yalivets is situated right in the center and, in addition, provides a detailed toponymy of various places, real and imagined, that play an important role in his text. In many ways the Carpathian Mountains constitute an alternative world (reality) for the writer, a sacred place that sustains life not only on that particular territory but also in the neighboring environs.

In a collection of feuilletons, arranged in the form of a diary and titled *FM "Halychyna"* (2001), Prokhasko acknowledges that he cannot imagine his home city of Ivano-Frankivsk without the mountains. It is as if the Carpathians define the essence of the city:

> The mountains can become streets, courtyards, and squares of our urban outlooks. The mountains do not need us. They are all to themselves and perfect. We badly need them as our vision and point of reference. For the Carpathians are to our south and they are full of warmth and life. The Carpathians are for something that cannot be taken away. This is our knowledge about a hopeful haven, about the simplest relief, about the most perfect possibility of escape in case of necessity.[82]

In the same collection Prokhasko also alludes to the most beautiful, according to him, section of Ivan-Frankivsk in which there are parks, narrow streets and old villas from the times before the war, all of which nostalgically point to a different city life and to a different era. The author returns to his hometown again in his yet another collection of feuilletons titled *Port Frankivsk* (2006). Here Prokhasko re-envisions the mountains as a huge sea, which reaches with its shores a number of port cities, including his hometown Ivano-Frankivsk.

While Prokhasko focuses mainly on the Carpathians and his home city, one can get a sense of the whole region of Western Ukraine in his oeuvre. For example, he names seven oblasts-regions, Lviv, Frankivsk, Zakarpattia, Ternopil, Chernivtsi, Rivne and Volhynia, about which he encourages his readers to find out more information. He does assume a little bit of a preaching tone, like a father talking to a child, but it is all because he seems to know the geography of his "personal fatherland"—Halychyna, and would want to instill the same desire for knowledge about these places in his audience. In the final result, however, any search for one's roots is a function of self-identity and self-image. Prokhasko himself has no problem with that particular issue but is aware that the same self-confidence is not a domain of everyone.

YURI ANDRUKHOVYCH'S CULTURAL GEOGRAPHIES

Yuri Andrukhovych is one of Ukraine's most renowned contemporary authors whose books are always eagerly anticipated both at home and abroad. His oeuvre has been translated into many languages and awarded six prestigious international literary and non-literary prizes for his activities as a writer and public intellectual, five in Germany and one in Poland. Andrukhovych began as a poet and co-founder of the famed Bu-Ba-Bu poetic group, known for its carnival literary happenings and parodic performances, but in the early

1990s he turned to prose and it is the latter genre that gained him most of his recognition. By the end of 2011, he had authored five books of poems, five novels and a few volumes of nonfiction, including three books of essays and memoirs. He has also translated extensively from German, English, Polish and Russian.

Born in Ivano-Frankivsk in 1960, Andrukhovych's love for his home region, Halychyna (Galicia), is well documented in his texts, especially in his essays, but it is safe to say that cultural geography occupies a special position within the author's entire oeuvre. Arguably, he is quintessentially a writer of place whose reflections upon the connection between a geographical entity (urban or countryside) and flow of human events associated with it is always presented in the most intimate terms and always through a set of specific experiences. In his works he has described numerous cities and places but the bulk of his attention has invariably been directed to the region of his birth, including the Carpathians, his hometown Ivano-Frankivsk, and Lviv—the city where he studied. This is Andrukhovych's "last territory," as he coined it in one of his essays, a territory for which he invents private myths, inscribing them onto the map of his own personalized Europe.

From Chortopil to Venice: Debunking Colonial and Postcolonial Myths

The plot of Andrukhovych's first novel *Recreations* (*Rekreatsii*), published initially in the January 1992 issue of a preeminent émigré journal *Suchasnist'* that just moved its editorial office from New York to Kyiv, takes place in the small town of Chortopil in the Carpathian Mountains. It is not a coincidence that the author chooses the mountains as a background in which the stories of four aspiring Ukrainian poets unfold during the festival of the "Resurrecting Spirit." The Carpathians are venerated by Andrukhovych as much as by Prokhasko and, in many ways, symbolize a place of possibilities, the energizing source, out of which new national and personal beginnings can be launched. This is a territory that embraces the protagonists and prompts them to face their past, present and future—in other words, forces them to reflect upon their own personal myths and identity. In fact, one can almost conclude that the mountains in the novel, the way Andrukhovych sets it, constitute a theatre of sorts where a new national play is staged, a play whose ending is contingent and/or still to be written.

The action of *Recreations* occurs shortly before the collapse of the Soviet Union when the totalitarian system is still in place but already losing its grip on society, and the people are no longer afraid to speak freely. The festival of the "Resurrecting Spirit" in Chortopil ends in a faked coup, when for a brief moment the protagonists stare into the possibility of losing freedom again to the all-encompassing communist regime and are reminded what is at stake in the new movement for national awakening and liberation. Much had been made about the novel's prophetic aura to foresee the August 1991 events (a real coup) that resulted in independence proclamations for the majority of the Soviet republics but, more importantly, *Recreations* invokes a number of historical events that help us understand the writer's conceptualization of his own regional allegiance vis-à-vis his sense of national belonging. There is a nostalgic bias in Andrukhovych's flashbacks to the era of the Austro-Hungarian Empire, especially when contrasted with the ensuing Soviet atrocities during World War II in Halychyna, although both historical periods, as Andrukhovych has it, engender traps of which one should be aware.

Of the four main protagonists only two, Hryts Shtundera and Yurko Nemyrych, experience the shifts of time. What stands out in the case of Shtundera is his childhood memory relived during the festival when he visits a nearby village from which his family comes from. The protagonist retraces his father's story about massive deportations from Western Ukraine to Kazakhstan during the period of 1939–1941,[83] after Stalin and Hitler divided Poland between the Soviet Union and Germany. The change of rule from Polish to Soviet had enormous consequences for the Ukrainian population in Galicia and Andrukhovych, underscoring this event, delineates further the distinctiveness of the region. The second time shift occurs when Yurko Nemyrych visits a mysterious villa in Chortopil and is transported back to Halychyna of the Habsburg era, again alluding to the region's different points of political orientation or spheres of influence—Vienna and Europe rather than Moscow and Russia. But under the façade of etiquette and exalted courtesy are hidden deadly power manipulations and Nemyrych happily escapes back to the present time. All these historical digressions play a role of a regional marker, inscribing the specific regional experience onto the wider national context. Yet, even if at times nostalgic, Andrukhovych remains ironic and skeptical with regards to the impact of the Austro-Hungarian historical past.

Admittedly, *Recreations* is too complex a novel to be concerned with regionalism alone. It is also a novel in search of a new narrative voice on the eve of Ukraine's independence. Andrukhovych deconstructs the myth of a poet-prophet, which is in large part characteristic of all non-state (colonial) nations. His heroes—poets who all drink heavily, or spend a night with a whore, or sleep with a friend's wife—are not put on pedestals and do not conform to high moral standards normally expected from literary figures responsible for leading unaware masses.[84] Of course, Andrukhovych parodies the very premise of such a role for a poet. Moreover, *Recreations* begins a trilogy of sorts, with all three novels having a poet as the main protagonist and pointing to a spatial trajectory that originates in the Carpathians (Ukraine) and eventually leads to Europe (Venice to be exact), but not without first dealing with Moscow, an imperial center responsible for Ukraine's colonial woes.[85]

Andrukhovych's second novel *The Moscoviad* (*Moskoviada*, 1993) debunks the myth of Moscow as the only culturally valid and productive metropolitan center for its colonial subjects, including Ukrainians. We see the imperial city through the eyes of the novel's main protagonist, Otto von F., a Ukrainian poet studying literature at the Gorky Literary Institute in Moscow and living in a dorm with many other international students. One day in Otto's life in the capital city on the eve of his departure back to Ukraine exposes all the decay and malaise of the totalitarian and colonial system at its last gasp. Through grotesque, fantasy and black humor, Andrukhovych reveals the inner workings of Soviet rule, pointing out in the process its utter absurdity and cruelty. Otto von F. escapes this absurdity physically wounded but ideologically unscathed. In other words, Moscow was not able to morph him into a pliant colonized man. It is not a small detail that the protagonist's name is Otto. Clearly, the writer goes to great lengths to underline that such a compliance is a priori impossible simply because the hero's point of reference is rooted in Europe rather than in metropolitan Moscow.

However, Andrukhovych's third novel *Perverzion* (*Perverziia*, 1996), which thematizes westward orientation toward Europe, is also not as straightforward as it might at first appear. There is no doubt that the writer's worldview is tilted toward European democratic liberalism but he rejects the idea of outright emulation of European values by a former colony such as Ukraine.[86] By the end of the novel we get the impression that it is Europe who has the most to gain by embracing and accepting into the union its eastern neighbor—Ukraine. *Perverzion's* main protagonist Stanislav Perfetsky, a Ukrainian poet from Lviv, represents vitality, inventiveness and intelligence, which are put in contrast to cliché and somewhat predictable, if not snobbish, ways of Europeans. No wonder Perfetsky's company and approval are sought after by almost all conference participants.

The plot of the novel takes place mainly in Venice, at the conference "The Postcarnival Absurdity of the World: What Is on the Horizon?" and centers on the hero's interactions with the conference organizers, invited guests, as well as his guides and caretakers, Ada Zitrone and her husband Janus Maria Riesenbock. Perfetsky's ease and charm make Ada fall in love with him, and, as it turns out, her feelings are reciprocated. However, Perfetsky also falls in love with the city of Venice, which returns the favor by erasing all traces of his existence in the end and making the pursuit by unknown assassins vain and absurd.

All three of Andrukhovych's novels posit the special relationship between self and place. These places mark in turn a continuous process of shedding off colonial dependency, actively prompting the reexamination of identity issues.

The Carpathians, violated by the Soviets during World War II, still preserve enough "virginity" to be the source of a national renewal. But the patriotic rhetoric is not an answer, as Andrukhovych rightly concludes. Festivals, celebrations or festivities of any kind are expedient only if followed by inner transformations. Moscow—the empire that needs to be made irrelevant—will dominate as long as a colonized subject does not see a way out of its gripping spell. Europe also needs to be viewed through other than pink lenses and, even though its principles and values rooted in democracy are preferable, one should be judicial and intelligent in discerning flaws in its system as well. Places often demonstrate their own dynamics when it comes to decolonization and often contribute to undermining the stability of accepted norms—it is as if Andrukhovych, mindful of Frantz Fanon's wisdom that postulates: "Decolonization, which sets out to change the order of the world, is, obviously, a program of complete disorder,"[87] creates situations, in which protagonists embrace uncertainty and chaos because these are but the fertile ground of conceiving new territories, geographical and/or mental alike.

Andrukhovych's "Last Territory"

Andrukhovych returns to the Carpathian Mountains and his home region Halychyna in his fourth novel *Twelve Circles* (*Dvanadtsiat' obruchiv*, 2003) but with a twist. This time his home territory is looked at through the eyes of a foreigner, Austrian Karl-Joseph Tsumbrunnen, who likes Ukraine sufficiently enough to settle there permanently but only to face a tragic death. *Twelve Circles* constitutes a synthesis of sorts of all major thematic avenues expressed in the previous three novels, namely, representing a trajectory of dealing with decolonization and identity construction issues on the eve and shortly after independence, but especially underscoring the fact (so evident in *Perverzion*) how little Westerners know about Ukraine. As the writer has it—the only way to uncover this enigma is to actually take residence in the country and study its geography, and this is what happens to Tsumbrunnen in *Twelve Circles*. Andrukhovych's real return to the issue of his regional homeland unfolds, however, mostly on the pages of his essays, collected first in *Disorientation on Location* (*Dezoriientatsiia na mistsevosti*, 1999), then in *My Europe* (*Moia Ievropa*, 2000)—a book of essays co-authored with the Polish writer Andrzej Stasiuk, and, more recently, in *The Devil's Hiding in the Cheese* (*Dyiavol khovaietsia v syri*, 2006).

Disorientation on Location includes an essay titled "Time and Place, or My Last Territory" ("Chas i mistse, abo Moia ostannia terytoriia"), in which the author ironically defines Halychyna as "the most suspicious and scorned part of the world" whose very authenticity is dubious: "Halychyna—is non-Ukraine, a kind of geographical appendix, a Polish hallucination."[88] Of course, we soon learn that this is really the Others' perspective (that is, of those who are really hostile to the project of Ukrainian independence) rather than the author's but, nonetheless, through irony and wit, Andrukhovych accurately pinpoints all the historical incongruities that his home region encompasses and exudes. At the same time, he wholeheartedly identifies himself with this territory because it alone allows him to thrive as a Ukrainian writer. This is his "last territory," as he coins it, a cultural space of "normal" Ukraine, which he must defend because he has no other choice. In other words, his Halychyna becomes a synecdoche of Ukraine.

It is impossible to appreciate Andrukhovych's territorial self-identification with Halychyna without understanding his conceptualization of Europe. His Europe does not necessarily entail territory; his Europe is first and foremost a mental state, or Zeitgeist, culture, genealogy and people. And Halychyna, as Andrukhovych sees it, is entitled to partake in that cultural heritage of Europeans because of its history and the fact that at some point in time it was under Austro-Hungarian rule, when people could move freely, without any visa requirements, from his native Ivan-Frankivsk to Vienna, or even further to Venice. In the essay "Introduction to Geography" ("Vstup do heohrafii"), Andrukhovych boldly concludes that topography makes people: "Europeans were created by mountains and forests."[89] Hence, we can infer that his peculiar veneration of the Carpathian Mountains stems from such an understanding. But a close perusal of *Disorientation on Location* also foregrounds another fact—one can discern there more than one concept of Europe. By and large, the writer grapples with the concept of Central Europe, so in fashion in the early1980s and especially promoted by Milan Kundera. But this Central Europe, Andrukhovych admits, no longer exists after Poland, Slovakia, Hungary and the Czech Republic joined the European Union. In this context, cultivating the region of Halychyna as a small territorial remnant of the Habsburg Empire becomes a merely nostalgic habit that leads nowhere. Rather than to be stuck permanently in Eastern Europe, Andrukhovych prefers to be integrated with Western Europe. And, as he so eloquently expressed in *Perverzion*, Europe has much to gain by opening its gates to Ukrainians.

The connection between Halychyna and Europe is implied not only through topography and history but also through genealogy. Andrukhovych's Halychyna emerges in his essays as his own personal family history. The writer claims European roots through his German great-grandfather who arrived in Ivano-Frankivsk from the Sudetenland (a territory that is now divided between Poland and the Czech Republic) at the end of the nineteenth century to begin his new life in the provincial Galician town. That era knew different borders and different ethnic divisions. Interestingly, the writer's father returned to the land of his grandfather at the end of the Second World War as a young refugee boy but was repatriated back to the Soviet Union when his mother could not produce the necessary papers. Since the early 1990s Andrukhovych has had many opportunities to visit Germany, Austria, as well as many other European countries, and his writings evince a strong sense of attachment to Europe as a beacon of culture and democracy. But, at the same time, they also foreground his roots in Halychyna, his personally constructed homeland that invariably betrays the traces of old European ways of life for those who know where to look—architecture, multiculturalism, national identity and language are some of those traces, Andrukhovych alludes, that help to appreciate the past era.

According to the author of *Disorientation on Location*, Europe and Halychyna form but a weak opposition. They complement each other more than oppose. The relationship is not of the center and periphery. For it seems that the center of European gravity is fluid and unstable and that is why it is non-threatening and so enticing (unlike the constancy of Moscow as an imperial metropolis). Andrukhovych feels at home in both places—in Europe and Halychyna alike. Since being a European is a state of mind as much as a territorial marker, the writer feels European and Ukrainian simultaneously. Therefore the future integration of Ukraine with the European Union becomes for him an ultimate aspiration and priority, especially when he takes upon himself the role of a public intellectual. However, his tendency "to create his own, private myths of Stanyslaviv, Galicia, and Europe"[90] or his personally construed desires about the place of Halychyna (and Ukraine) on the map of Europe are not always rooted in geopolitical reality.

Geography of Intimate Places

Andrukhovych's book *Lexicon of Intimate Cities* (*Leksykon intymnykh mist*, 2011), conceived as memoirs of sorts about places visited, continues the author's fascination with cultural geography, with differences in ways of life and their relations to spaces and places. This time, however, the writer goes global, no longer confined to his beloved region of Halychyna. The book consists of short prose pieces, occasionally interspersed with poems, about 111 cities Andrukhovych had a chance to visit, arranged from A to Ya by geographical names in accordance with the Cyrillic alphabet. The spatial circle the writer delineates is vast—from Ukrainian to Russian, from East European to West European, and then all the way to North American urban landscapes, creating out of a mosaic of places a unique autobiographical atlas. Yet anyone expecting to receive extensive descriptions of those cities will be disappointed. Clearly, the author never intended to emulate a tourist guidebook. On the contrary, Andrukhovych's lexicon, as the title suggests, is for the most part about his own experiences and reflections upon various intimate interactions with a number of places and people during his frequent travels. These discontinuous, deliberately out of chronology and spanning almost half a century, reminiscences allow Andrukhovych to play with various stereotypes, popular local myths and even debunk his own views on the significance of history and "geopoetics."

In many ways *Lexicon of Intimate Cities* is a book of witty vignettes more about people rather than places, or, to put it differently, about how humans function spatially. Andrukhovych believes in the interdependence between landscapes and people's mentality. Each city represents for him a specific urban landscape. But the author rarely attempts to convey it holistically. Rather, he concentrates synecdochically on a chosen object and builds his story around it, whether it is a church, a train station, a street, a specific historical period or just a person, associated with that particular place. Sometimes Andrukhovych's stories are related as memoirs, at other times, he assumes a role of an indifferent but attentive observer diligently registering situations, adventures or mishaps of other people. In either case we receive a curious mixture of a contemporary panoply of events with a considerable dose of historical ruminations.

Of all the 111 places depicted in the book, two—Kyiv and Lviv—deserve closer scrutiny. Andrukhovych's attitude toward Kyiv is ambivalent and toward Lviv—full of unconditional adoration. The writer admits that he loves the capital city whenever it is in some way unrecognizable to him, or, whenever Kyiv attracts with its unpredictability and national upheaval such as the one during the Orange Revolution of 2004. But, otherwise, Kyiv for him is either a city of whores, or a city of close friends with whom he spends nights conversing at the kitchen table. What is also significant about the vignette on Kyiv is that it demonstrates that Andrukhovych does not view the city from the same historical perspective as he does Lviv. Despite Kyiv having over a thousand-year history, Andrukhovych alludes to only one historical episode, namely the times of the 1917–1921 independence war, underscoring the fact that Kyiv was changing its rulers twelve times during that period. It seems that he does so in order to emphasize his own fluctuating emotions about the capital—from utmost infatuation to heartfelt disdain. Andrukhovych concludes that Kyiv mirrors the national ambivalence (hybridity) about identity—it encompasses all the incongruities about language, awareness and the sense of belonging.

Lviv, by contrast, comes across as a city of depth, death and determination. The story about Lviv is related through its history (going back to the sixteenth century), as well as through its inhabitants, writers, location, commerce, executioners, dissidents, atrocities, cemeteries, patriotism and simulacra. These are by and large names of the subsections of the vignette on Lviv. This account, unlike many others in the book, is mainly about the city. The authorial experience becomes of secondary importance, although is not entirely absent. Lviv, according to Andrukhovych, lends itself especially well to be fictionalized. This is a city that begs to be turned into novels. And, he concludes, no matter how many of them he would write—there would still be plenty to cover. Lviv in that sense is an inexhaustible source of inspiration.

Andrukhovych's interest in cultural landscapes is inextricably connected to historical circumstances. The belonging to a particular territory entails constructing not only a regional identity but also developing an attachment to a larger cause such as building a nation. Andrukhovych is not interested in the politics of how to arrive at such a goal, at least not on the pages of his texts. Of course, that does not mean that he avoids activism and civic obligations, but he feels most comfortable in the space when all the expectant national accouterments simply (already) exist and allow him to evolve as a writer in his own native tongue.

NOTES

1. See, for example, Marko Pavlyshyn, "The Rhetoric of Geography in Ukrainian Literature, 1991–2005," in *Ukraine, the EU and Russia: History, Culture and International Relations*, ed. Stephen Velychenko (Houndsmills: Palgrave, 2007), 89–107.

2. Jim Wayne Miller, "Anytime the Ground is Uneven: The Outlook for Regional Studies and What to Look For," in *Geography and Literature: A Meeting of the Disciplines*, ed. William E. Mallory and Paul Simpson-Hously (Syracuse: Syracuse University Press, 1987), 12.

3. David Jordan, ed. *Regionalism Reconsidered: New Approaches to the Field* (New York: Garland, 1994), ix.

4. Ibid., xv.

5. Miller, "Anytime the Ground Is Uneven," 5.

6. Roberto M. Dainotto, *Place in Literature: Regions, Cultures, Communities* (Ithaca: Cornell University Press, 2000), 4.

7. Ibid.

8. Ibid., 5.

9. Miller, "Anytime the Ground Is Uneven," 17.

10. The Zhytomyr School, comprising of such writers as Yevhen Pashkovsky, Viacheslav Medvid, Volodymyr Danylenko, Mykola Zakusylo, Valerii Shevchuk and others, represents the "nativist" tendencies in Ukrainian literature, celebrating the richness of the language, including dialects, and views the Western orientation of the Galician School with skepticism and disdain. The Stanyslaviv School (Stanyslaviv is the old name of the city of Ivano-Frankivsk), refers to the group of writers gathered around the magazine *Chetver* and is considered as the main proponent of postmodernism in Ukrainian literature. The two best-known writers of this school, Izdryk and Yuri Andrukhovych, in their philosophy and outlook aligned themselves with the European cultural identity. For more on this, see Ola Hnatiuk, "Nativists vs.

Westernizers: Problems of Cultural Identity in Ukrainian Literature of the 1990s,"
Slavic and East European Journal 50 (2006): 434–51.

11. Dainotto, *Place in Literature*, 9.

12. Ibid., 14.

13. Referring to Michel Foucault, Edward W. Soja insightfully points out that the French philosopher "takes an integrative rather than deconstructive path, holding on to his history but adding to it the crucial nexus that would flow through all his work: the linkage between space, knowledge, and power." See his *Postmodern Geographies: The Reassertion of Space in Critical Social Theory* (London: Verso, 1989), 20. For Soja, Foucault's "ambivalent spatiality" is sufficient to label him "a postmodern geographer" (Ibid., 16) but Foucault himself lends credence to this by stating: "A whole history remains to be written of *spaces*—which would at the same time be the history of *powers* (both of these terms in the plural)—from the great strategies of geopolitics to the little tactics of the habitat, ..." See Foucault, *Power/Knowledge* (New York: Pantheon Books, 1980), 149.

14. Like, for example, Chervona fira in Kharkiv, Propala hramota in Kyiv, LuHoSad in Lviv or the most famous Bu-Ba-Bu, consisting of three members: Andrukhovych, Viktor Neborak and Oleksandr Irvanets, coming respectively from Ivano-Frankivsk, Lviv and Rivne. For more on this see Hnatiuk, "Nativists and Westernizers" and Michael M. Naydan, "Ukrainian Avant-Garde Poetry Today: Bu-Ba-Bu and Others," *Slavic and East European Journal* 50 (2006): 452–68.

15. Known in English as *Death and the Penguin* (2001).

16. Known in English as *A Matter of Death and Life* (2005).

17. A movie directed by Viacheslav Krishtofovich (1997) and based on Kurkov's novel.

18. Andrey Kurkov, "Narodzhennia novoho bez stresu ne buvaie," *Den'*, November 26, 2004, accessed September 11, 2008, http://www.day.kiev.ua/290619?idsource=128181&mainlang=ukr.

19. See Anthony Smith, *National Identity* (Reno, Las Vegas, London: University of Nevada Press, 1991).

20. See his 2006 J.B. Rudnyckyj Distinguished Lecture, presented at the University of Manitoba on February 23, 2006 entitled: "Independent Ukraine as a Function of Soviet Inertia," accessed September 11, 2008, http://umanitoba.ca/libraries/units/archives/grants/rudnyckyj_lecture/lecture_13.html.

21. Bohdan Tsiupyn, "Andrii Kurkov v hostiakh u Bi-Bi-Si," interview with Andrey Kurkov, November 5, 2005, accessed March 10, 2007, http://www.bbc.co.uk/ukrainian/forum/story/2005/11/051113_kurkov.shtml.

22. Ibid.

23. Andrey Kurkov, *Death and the Penguin*, trans. George Bird (London: Vintage, 2003), 228.

24. These dates refer to the first English editions. In the original they were published in 2002 and 2000, respectively.

25. Pavlyshyn, "The Rhetoric of Geography," 92.

26. Ibid.

27. However, choosing a penguin as the hero's pet makes the story somewhat unusual.

28. Including the allusions to the historically sizeable Jewish minority living in Rivne.

29. The concept of two Ukraines was especially advocated by Mykola Riabchuk back in the 1990s. The divide he proposed was not so much into eastern and western parts of Ukraine, or according to the language spoken, but more along the lines of what kind of value sets a given community identifies with: is it democratic, European (postcolonial) or the Soviet ("Creole"). Riabchuk uses the latter designation to underscore that community's hybrid identity or its ambivalent attitude in defining the national sense of belonging. See his interview "The Postcolonial Syndrome in Ukraine," *Euromaidan Press*, July 8, 2015, accessed December 18, 2016, http://euromaidan-press.com/2015/08/07/the-postcolonial-syndrome-in-ukraine/#arvlbdata. See also his *Dylemy ukrains'koho Fausta: hromadians'ke suspil'stvo i rozbudova derzhavy* (Kyiv: Krytyka, 2000) and *Postkolonial'nyi syndrom. Sposterezhennia* (Kyiv: K.I.S., 2011).

30. See Maria G. Rewakowicz, "Alternative History, Science Fiction and Nationalism in Vasyl Kozhelianko's Novels," *The Ukrainian Quarterly* 63 (2007): 70–78.

31. Bart Moore-Gilbert, *Postcolonial Theory: Contexts, Practices, Politics* (London: Verso, 1997), 203.

32. Linda Hutcheon, *A Poetics of Postmodernism: History, Theory, Fiction* (New York: Routledge, 1988), 4.

33. Vasyl Kozhelianko, *Defiliada v Moskvi* (Lviv: Kal'variia, 2001), 10.

34. Incidentally, Kozhelianko refers to this day as Ukraine's "real" independence day in more than one novel.

35. Kozhelianko, *Sribnyi pavuk* (Lviv: Kal'variia, 2004), 11.

36. See, for example, his *Lehendy L'vova* (Lviv: Piramida, 2000). Vynnychuk was born in Stanyslaviv (now Ivano-Frankivsk) but lives and works in Lviv.

37. *Mapping Postcommunist Cultures*, 202.

38. In fact, at the end of the novel he includes a short dictionary of words existing only in the Galician dialect. See his "Slovnychok halytsyzmiv," in *Ma'lva Landa* (Lviv: Piramida, 2003), 534–37.

39. Leonard Lutwack, *The Role of Place in Literature* (Syracuse: Syracuse University Press, 1984), 31.

40. Ibid., 55.

41. Viktor Neborak, *The Flying Head and Other Poems*, trans. Michael M. Naydan (Lviv: Sribne slovo, 2005), 231; 233. Reprinted with permission.

42. Ibid., 231.

43. Ibid., 63.

44. Adam Mickiewicz's monument in downtown Lviv was erected in 1900 and pays tribute to the Polish romantic poet (1798–1855).

45. Neborak, *Virshi z vulytsi Vyhovs'koho* (Lviv: Sribne Slovo, 2009), 31.

46. Ibid., 113.

47. In fact, in 2013, he published a poetry collection dedicated both to his hometown Ternopil and his adopted hometown New York. See his *Vybrani virshi pro Ternopil' i N'iu-Iork* (Selected Poems about Ternopil and New York).

48. Makhno has also published two books of essays, which oftentimes present cities and places the poet feels special connection with, both in Ukraine and beyond its

borders, but my main focus here is on his poetry. Cf. Makhno's essays collected in *Park kul'tury ta vidpochynku imeni Gertrudy Stain* (2006) and *Kotylasia torba* (2011).

49. Also published in Ukrainian as *Zymovi lysty* (2011). This is Makhno's second book in English translation. The first, titled *Thread and Selected New York Poems* (2009), included poetry mainly devoted to New York City. Orest Popovych rendered both collections into the English.

50. Leonid Rudnytzky, reviewing Makhno's two English collections, underscores his surprise that there is no reference in the poet's New York verses to the biggest tragedy the city experienced—the terrorist attack of 9/11. However, Makhno's New York, even though presented in all its everyday dynamics, is first and foremost a textual New York where traumatic events of the 9/11 effects are more likely deliberately blocked by the poet because they cannot be celebrated. Rudnytzky, "A Poetical Voice of the Ukrainian Diaspora: Random Notes on the Poetry of Vasyl Makhno," *The Ukrainian Quarterly* 67 (2011): 161.

51. Translated by Michael M. Naydan. Accessed May 13, 2012, taken from the site: http://ukraine.poetryinternationalweb.org. Reprinted with permission.

52. See Bohdan Rubchak, "Mandrivnyk, inodi ryba," in *Cornelia Street Café* by Vasyl Makhno (Kyiv: Fakt, 2007), 13.

53. Translated by Michael Naydan. Accessed May 13, 2012, taken from the site: http://ukraine.poetryinternationalweb.org. Reprinted with permission.

54. Vasyl Makhno, *Thread and Selected New York Poems*, trans. Orest Popovych (New York: Meeting Eyes Bindery, 2009), 53. Reprinted with permission.

55. Dainotto, *Place in Literature*, 22.

56. The novel was first serialized in the journal *Kur'ier Kryvbasu* (2003) and published by Dzhura Publishing House in Ternopil in 2004. I use the Folio edition of 2010.

57. Pavlo Vol'vach, *Kliasa* (Kharkiv: Folio, 2010), 22.

58. This is especially well illustrated by the novel's title: *Kliasa*. According to the current orthographic rules this word should be spelled: klas.

59. *Kliasa*, 400.

60. He expressed similar sentiments in his poetic collection about Ukraine's southeast *Pivdennyi skhid* (2002).

61. Oleksandr Vil'chyns'kyi, *Dereva na dakhakh* (Kharkiv: Folio, 2010), 289.

62. Those contributors whose language of expression is Russian are presented in the anthology in Ukrainian translation.

63. The title references an English electronic music band Depeche Mode that gained popularity in the 1980s. Zhadan on many occasions uses English original spelling for his book titles but in this particular case he decided to present the band's spelling in Cyrillic. However, referring to this novel from hereon I will switch to its original English version.

64. Published in English under the Russian spelled name *Voroshilovgrad* (2016), used hereafter as such.

65. Vitaly Chernetsky, "Ukrainian Literature" in "East-Central European Literatures Twenty Years After," *East European Politics and Societies* 23 (2009): 579.

66. Pavlo Shopin, "Voroshylovhrad Lost: Memory and Identity in a Novel by Serhiy Zhadan," *Slavic and East European Journal* 57 (2013): 385.

67. Or, as Shopin interprets: "One presumes that Herman's brother has died and gone to Heaven, not just Amsterdam" (Ibid., 383).

68. Since the Russian aggression of 2014 Starobilsk is in the Ukrainian government controlled territory, whereas Luhansk belongs to the separatists of the self-proclaimed Luhansk People's Republic.

69. Cf. *Anarchy in the UKR.*

70. Serhii Zhadan, *Kapital* (Kharkiv: Folio, 2009), 327. This excerpt comes from *Anarchy in the UKR*, included in Zhadan's volume of collected writings *Kapital* (*Capital*).

71. Hutsuls are an ethno-cultural group of Ukrainian highlanders who for centuries have inhabited the Carpathians.

72. Vasyl' Herasym'iuk, *Dity trepety: Poezii* (Kyiv: Molod', 1991), 20.

73. Ibid., 102.

74. Ibid., 100.

75. Petro Midianka, *Užhorodské kavárny* (Prague: Ukrajinská iniciativa v ČR, 2004), 11.

76. Ivan Malkovych, *Iz ianholom na plechi: virshi* (Kyiv: Poetychna ahentsiia "Kniazhiv," 1997), 62.

77. John Berger, *The Look of Things: Essays* (New York: Viking, 1974), 40.

78. Ibid.

79. Soja, *Postmodern Geographies*, 16.

80. See his interview with Iryna Slavinska "Taras Prokhas'ko: Ukrains'ka ideia pov'iazana z lahidnym sydinniam," *Ukrains'ka pravda*, January 10, 2011, accessed August 21, 2015, http://life.pravda.com.ua/person/2011/01/10/69933/.

81. Taras Prokhas'ko, *UnSimple,* trans. Uilleam Blacker, *Ukrainian Literature: A Journal of Translations*, accessed June 15, 2012, http://sites.utoronto.ca/elul/Ukr_Lit/Vol03/06-ProkhaskoUnsimple-Part-2.pdf.

82. Taras Prokhas'ko, *FM "Halychyna"* (Ivano-Frankivsk: Lileia-NV, 2001), 5.

83. This very much overlaps with the story of Vasyl Herasymiuk's family, discussed earlier.

84. Chernetsky, invoking Homi Bhabha's essay "DissemiNation: Time, Narrative and the Margins of the Modern Nation," underscores transgressive and hybrid qualities of all postcolonial writing. See his "Postcolonialism, Russia and Ukraine," *Ulbandus Review* 7 (2003): 59.

85. An insightful analysis of Andrukhovych's all three novels can be found in Mark Andryczyk's article "Three Posts in the Center of Europe: Postmodern Characteristics in Yuri Andrukhovych's Post-Colonial Prose," in *Ukraine at a Crossroads*, ed. Nicolas Hayoz and Andrej N. Lushnycky (Bern: Peter Lang, 2005), 233–52.

86. According to Michael M. Naydan, "Yuri Andrukhovych's 1996 novel *Perverzion*, perhaps, represents the most articulate embodiment of the younger generation's quest for a new Ukrainian identity within the newly reformulated Europe." See his "Ukrainian Literary Identity Today: The Legacy of the Bu-Ba-Bu Generation after the Orange Revolution," *World Literature Today* 79.3–4 (2005): 25.

87. Frantz Fanon, *The Wretched of the Earth*, trans. Constance Farrington (New York: Grove Press, 1963), 36.

88. Iurii Andrukhovych, *Dezoriientatsiia na mistsevosti* (Ivano-Frankivsk: Lileia-NV, 1999), 118.

89. Ibid., 36.

90. Lidia Stefanowska, "Back to the Golden Age: The Discourse of Nostalgia in Galicia in the 1990s (Some Preliminary Remarks)", *Harvard Ukrainian Studies* 27 (2004–2005): 187.

Chapter 3

Gender Matters

Women's Literary Discourse

Michael M. Naydan rightly notices that the Soviet period "witnessed a dearth" of influential female prose authors and ventures to speculate that one of the reasons for that could be that "prose fiction requires cultural and social stability, yet the repressive and congenitally patriarchal nature of the Soviet system may have stereotyped women from working in prose fiction."[1] The situation slightly improved in the second half of the 1980s under the leadership of Mikhail Gorbachev and his policies of glasnost and perestroika when a number of talented Ukrainian female authors, writers and poets alike, had their literary debuts, and changed even more dramatically after independence. In fact, authors such as Oksana Zabuzhko (b. 1960), Natalka Bilotserkivets (b. 1954), Liudmyla Taran (b. 1954), Yevheniia Kononenko (b. 1959) and Halyna Pahutiak (b. 1958) made a successful transition from the relatively stable but rigid Soviet system to the post-independence censorship-free and market-oriented but uncertain reality. In the 1990s and 2000s they have been joined by a cohort of younger and brilliant female talents whose sheer number makes them a force to be reckoned with within contemporary Ukrainian literary quarters. In truth, it is fair to state that female literary discourse since independence has acquired a considerable stature and, together with decentralization, regionalism and bilingualism, constitutes one of the determinative characteristics of the post-independence literary process. Thematically, contemporary Ukrainian women writers concern themselves with a wide range of issues, including representations of female subjectivity, feminism and the formation of national identity, postcoloniality and history, gender relations and the unequal distribution of social power between men and women.

In this chapter I want to offer a panorama of Ukrainian female voices of the post-independence period up until 2011, focusing equally on feminist, post-feminist and non-feminist approaches. I have intentionally excluded from my scrutiny those women writers who have excelled in popular genres and enter-tain a wide reading public—they will be examined in the chapter on popular literature. Here, I will begin my deliberation by first presenting the oeuvre of Oksana Zabuzhko, arguably the most important contemporary female author in independent Ukraine, and her recognition of gendered and postcolonial identities. Then I will move to discuss a variety of voices concerned with female subjectivity vis-à-vis the formation of national identity, including the European turn, a tendency toward a confessional mode of narration, as well as a preference for hybrid genres. Separately, I will relate the implicit post-feminist views of the three women authors of the younger generation, and, finally, I will introduce a few examples of belletristic works that go beyond the gendered pattern of writing.

OKSANA ZABUZHKO'S PARADIGM OF A POSTCOLONIAL WOMAN

Oksana Zabuzhko does not need much of an introduction in Ukraine even to people uneager to follow literary news. From the mid-1990s onward she has secured for herself a preeminent role of a public intellectual and spokesperson whose views on current affairs are keenly sought after by the national TV and print media, even if those views invariably turn controversial. Born in Lutsk, in the region of Volhynia in Western Ukraine, but raised in Kyiv, she graduated with a degree of philosophy from the Taras Shevchenko National University of Kyiv in 1982, defending her dissertation in aesthetics five years later. Soon thereafter she became a research associate at the Institute of Philosophy of the Academy of Sciences of Ukraine but eventually gave up her scholarly career to devote herself exclusively to writing. Zabuzhko's range of genres is indeed impressive—from poetry to fiction and nonfiction, from scholarly accounts to literary essays and journalistic columns in newspapers, all colored with the same unmistakable passionate intensity of her intellectual voice. However, that voice was not at first well-known. It was the publication of Zabuzhko's novel *Fieldwork in Ukrainian Sex* (1996), the first national bestseller that made her a celebrity of sorts almost overnight and firmly established her liter-ary career. Translated into a number of European languages and viewed at the time as a novel that forcefully advocated feminist agenda, *Fieldwork* acquired notoriety in some circles mainly because it "translated the issues of national and cultural identity and traumas into the language of a woman's body," as the author herself succinctly put it.[2] But Zabuzhko's feminism in *Fieldwork* reveals itself for the most part through the discussion of gender relations, in which Ukrainian intellectuals in general, male and female alike, are marginalized because of an inherited colonial syndrome, although women, no doubt, feel this marginalization more intensely than men, for they are often also subordinated to the latter. It is also clear that Zabuzhko's feminism has displayed dynamic qualities and evolved from a more radical version in her poetry to the so-called national feminism[3] in *Fieldwork* and *Notre Dame d'Ukraine* (2007), to, finally, what some feminists labeled cyberfeminism,[4] manifest especially in her short story "I, Milena" (1998), where we witness a breakdown of the boundaries between the natural and the technological. The heroine of the story, a TV talk show figure Milena, experiences a split in personality and seemingly turns into a cyborg of sorts—a hybrid of machine and human body.[5] That is evident when Milena's persona (image) on the TV screen (her "virtual self") begins to interact with her husband while the heroine's "physical self" witnesses the interaction.

Zabuzhko authored six books of poetry, two of which *May Frost* (*Travnevyi inii*, 1985) and *The Conductor of the Last Candle* (*Dyryhent ostann'oi svichky*, 1990) were published before independence. But it is her third collection *Hitchhiking* (*Avtostop*, 1994) that showcases her most mature and emblematic poems. Zabuzhko's next two collections *A New Law of Archimedes* (*Novyi zakon Arkhimeda*, 2000) and *The Second Attempt* (*Druha sproba*, 2005) consist mostly of selected poems spanning more than two decades of poetry writing.[6] By the late 1990s her creative energy was devoted almost exclusively to prose. Yet 1996 was doubly important for the author—not only her novel *Fieldwork in Ukrainian Sex* came out but she also had her poetry published in English translation in a volume titled *A Kingdom of Fallen Statues* that included some of her most representative feminist verses. The book's opening poem, "Clytemnestra," is Zabuzhko's no doubt most radical feminist statement. Drawing on the Greek mythology, the poet retells the story of Agamemnon's wife, Clytemnestra, who kills her husband as he comes back home after a long combat in the Trojan War. The lyrical heroine blames all the violence and oppression on male power and patriarchy, and is determined to reverse its dominance by establishing a new kingdom without men, a world without "Agamemnos." Such radicalism does not permeate the whole collection, after all *A Kingdom of Fallen Statues* also offers a number of lyrical love poems and its author does not reject heterosexuality outright, as some radical feminists do, but this English edition is indicative of Zabuzhko's early preoccupation with the issues of women's oppression (sexual and national) both in poetry and fiction, as well as with the relation between sex and violence, foregrounding her conviction that sexuality in general is a function of repression and power rather than mere pleasure. It is the latter point that lies at the heart of her novel *Fieldwork in Ukrainian Sex*. And in the process of deconstructing sex relations Zabuzhko imposes a gendered paradigm for dealing with colonial and national woes.

National Feminism and Gender Relations in *Fieldwork in Ukrainian Sex*

Uilleam Blacker in his essay on Oksana Zabuzhko comes to the conclusion that there are just two main preoccupations in her work: national identity and gender.[7] Tatiana Zhurzhenko, on the other hand, underscores Zabuzhko's role in the promotion and articulation of an indigenous feminism in Ukraine, a kind of feminism she labeled as "national."[8] From the perspective of an American critic, Andrew Wachtel, Zabuzhko's feminism "is attempting simultaneously to overturn a gender hierarchy in which women are subordinate to men and a literary hierarchy in which the Ukrainian language has been subordinated to Russian."[9] But the best clue how to read *Fieldwork* comes from the author herself. In her discerning essay "The Woman Author in Colonial Culture, or, Insights into Ukrainian Gender Mythology" ("Zhinka-avtor u kolonial'nii kul'turi, abo znadoby do ukrains'koi gendernoi mifolohii"), published in *The Fortinbras Chronicles* (*Khroniky vid Fortinbrasa*, 1999), her first collection of essays, Zabuzhko looks through a postcolonial lens at the case of a double marginalization of Ukrainian women writers. She argues that this marginalization takes place because women writers as colonial subjects experience the subaltern status, but as female subjects, living in a patriarchal society, they also experience gender inequality. While traumas of colonial and patriarchal subjugation affect Ukrainian women more acutely, and there can be no doubt that Zabuzhko's loyalty is largely with them, she deliberately broadens her discussion of gender relations to also analyze the historically unenviable situation of a colonized Ukrainian man whose "problem of national and sexual identity is even more entangled than that of a woman's, simply because his self-identification with his own country is not as straightforward as is for her but, rather, it is mediated by sexual difference: *for him* his country before all else comes forth as Mother."[10]

Zabuzhko surmises that imperial societal structures (be they tsarist or Soviet) do not leave much of a choice for Ukrainian men—they are forced to evolve to be either "sergeants" (an archetype which assumes a colonial psychology, thus becoming a pliant tool in imperial hands) or "bastards" (an archetype of a weak son, unable to stand for himself, who stays with his mother but loses his respect for her because in his mind she is a whore). In either case we witness the situation in which colonial (or totalitarian) domination and abuse not only degrades the dignity of colonized men but also transforms them into abusers themselves, especially when paired in relationships with women. And this is precisely the scenario reflected upon in *Fieldwork*, a novel about a tumultuous relationship between the main protagonist Oksana and her artist-lover Mykola K. Their romantic affair abruptly ends while they are both on a visit to the United States—she teaching at a university as a Fulbright scholar and he coming to stay with her as her guest. As Alexandra Hrycak and I already indicated in our 2009 essay, this relationship illustrates the plight of the male and female intellectual in post-independence Ukraine:

> Although M. is nationally conscious, he nonetheless suffers from inferiority complexes that leave him unable to satisfy her [Oksana]. Indeed, he is sexually abusive. The novel implies that his inability to fulfill her and his abusive behavior stem from the fact that a colonial subject is not a free subject. M. has interiorized imperial abuse and in turn becomes an abuser himself. Despite this tragedy, the heroine's voice exudes power and determination to transform her painful experience into something creatively meaningful.[11]

In many ways the novel's thematic scope is anything but new. It foregrounds the writer's attempt to turn her traumatic experience into literature (not unlike Kate Millett's story about her disintegrating lesbian relationship in *Sita* of 1977). What is new, however, is that Zabuzhko convincingly manages to conflate her heroine's personal drama with that of her nation. This dynamic interaction between the personal and the sociopolitical/national gives the novel considerable gravitas. To some extent it reminds us of previous attempts in this department undertaken by two prominent modernist Ukrainian feminists, Olha Kobylianska and Lesia Ukrainka, but it goes without saying that Zabuzhko's feminism is of a different kind. Hers is the case of all-out and unmediated self-exposure, writing her body and authorial self out in such a way that it becomes a cathartic and transformative experience. The stream-of-consciousness narrative is structured like a lecture to the imaginary, yet very present, audience. The author's frequent use of the salutation: "Ladies and gentlemen" underscores her willingness to tell all, including the most excruciatingly painful personal details. Despite the novel's title it is not the sexual scenes as such that raise eyebrows, but the protagonist's extreme forthrightness about female physiology, carnal pleasures (or, more precisely, displeasures), and her language, outpouring juicy curses, stripped of all niceties and/or purities. That they should come out of a woman writer's mouth stirred consternation among puritanically inclined Ukrainians for whom men/women of letters often serve as worthy examples and are put on pedestals as national heroes to whom readers can turn for moral guidance.

Gender relations, as presented by Zabuzhko in *Fieldwork*, go hand in hand with her concerns for the survival of her own nation, thus the author continues the long-standing Ukrainian tradition in which a writer feels responsible for the well-being of her/his country and expresses it in his/her works. But the way Zabuzhko conveys that concern might appear controversial to some because, as Maryna Romanets puts it, the novel "presents a pattern both of the sexually codified violence to which many women are exposed and of the victimization they seem to accept,"[12] and, again, I would add—because of the language used:

> What can I tell you, Donna-dearest. That we were raised by men fucked from all ends every which way? That later we ourselves screwed the same kind of guys, and that in both cases they were doing to us what others, *the others*, had done to them? And that we accepted them and loved them as they were, because not to accept them was to go over to the others, the other side? And that our only choice, therefore, was and still remains between victim and executioner: between nonexistence and an existence that kills you.[13]

One might be surprised how much information—historical, political and social—Zabuzhko manages to pack into a relatively short novel of 160 pages (in English translation). In the text there are allusions to the crackdown on the 1960s generation of Ukrainian intellectuals (including Zabuzhko's own father) by the oppressive Soviet regime; there is a mention about the Soviet man-made famine in the early 1930s, named *Holodomor* (death by starvation) by Ukrainians; there is a reference to the Battle of Kruty[14] and to the more recent tragedy of Chornobyl's nuclear accident, but topping all that there is just a simple desire on the part of the heroine and her lover "to reach [their] full potential."[15] Yet, she is well aware that reaching one's full potential is possible only in a country without colonial handicaps. Only then a Ukrainian writer would stop cursing his/her language of expression (that is, if s/he is determined to remain faithful to his/her mother tongue), aware how little of Ukrainian literature in Ukrainian has a chance to reach the world cultural scene:

> —because untasted, unused texts unsustained by the energy of reciprocal thought gradually cool down, and how!—if the stream of public attention doesn't pick them up in time and carry them to the surface, they sink like stones to the bottom and become covered by mineral waxes that can never be scrapped off, just like your unsold books which gather dust somewhere at home and in bookstores, this same thing has happened with most of Ukrainian literature, [...] but you, sweetness, you have no choice not because you're incapable of switching languages—you could do that splendidly with a little effort—but because a curse has been placed on you to be faithful to all those who have died, all those who could have switched languages just as easily as you—Russian, Polish, some even German, and could have lived entirely different lives, but instead hurled themselves like firelogs into the dying embers of the Ukrainian with nothing to fucking show for it but mangled destinies and unread books ... .[16]

And that desperate cry of the postcolonial author for the normal existence of Ukrainian imaginative works at home and abroad, combined with her concern for women's gender equality, constitutes the essence of Zabuzhko's national feminism.

Zabuzhko's Fiction and NonFiction Interpretations of National History

Zabuzhko's two other works that focus a great deal on the issue of national and gender identities, at the same time providing a window into the author's own reading of the national past, are *Notre Dame d'Ukraine* (2007), an intellectual biography of Lesia Ukrainka, and *The Museum of Abandoned Secrets* (*Muzei pokynutykh sekretiv*, 2009), a novel about resistance of the Ukrainian Insurgent Army during World War II, as viewed through a lens of a contemporary Kyivan couple, a journalist Daryna and her art dealer husband Rostyslav. In some ways *Notre Dame d'Ukraine* constitutes the final installment of a trilogy of sorts, Zabuzhko's project of reinterpreting populist and patriarchal readings of Ukraine's three most venerated literary figures: Taras Shevchenko, Ivan Franko and Lesia Ukrainka.[17] Both *Notre Dame d'Ukraine* and *The Museum of Abandoned Secrets*, although belong to two different genres—nonfiction and fiction, respectively, provide their author with ample opportunity not only to express her views on the complicated episodes of Ukrainian history and on the state of post-independence affairs, but also to create readable narratives that invest heavily in engendering a nationally marked collective memory with an appeal to the broader public.

Notre Dame d'Ukraine is considerably more than just a feminist retelling of Ukrainka's relatively short life (1871–1913) and her oeuvre. Zabuzhko turns her book into a vehicle for addressing contemporary Ukrainians' identity anxieties and provides them with an alternative reading of the national past, which, contrary to common beliefs, does have a deeply rooted aristocratic tradition, even if the latter survived only among a small number of Ukrainian families (and Lesia Ukrainka, according to the author, is its most representative member), thus deconstructing in the process the imposed conception of Ukraine as a solely "peasant nation." Zabuzhko's book is also "an indictment against the corrupt political and cultural elites of present-day Ukraine, and a call for Ukrainians to transform themselves into genuine citizens capable of self-determination."[18] It is through the juxtaposition of the aristocratic gendered voice of Ukrainka, a preeminent Ukrainian national heroine, on the one hand, and corrupt state officials of independent Ukraine (*khamokratiia*, as she coins it—brute democracy), on the other, that Zabuzhko maps out the path forward for her fellow citizens. As Ukrainka internalized and utilized in her works European literary themes, and practically considered herself belonging

to both the Ukrainian and European cultural traditions, so do Ukrainians
need to adopt, Zabuzhko reflects, a European course of development, for it
alone can offer them the way "out of captivity" and consolidate their sense
of national identity. By presenting a woman writer (Ukrainka) as an ultimate
"Europeanizing" model, the author of *Notre Dame d'Ukraine* (also a woman
writer) elevates the significance of female intellectuals and ascribes to them
(and thus to herself) an important role in the nation-building process and
gender education.

In *Notre Dame d'Ukraine*, like in *Fieldwork of Ukrainian Sex*, Zabuzhko
focuses again on the body of the woman as a site of traumatic, yet transformative experiences. She denies populist interpretations of Lesia Ukrainka
as a weak, sickly and asexual national heroine, and instead underscores her
passionate and carnal nature that preserves its vibrant core despite a chronic
illness and is capable of ignoring societal mores should they inhibit her love
interests.[19] Ukrainka's reevaluated body in *Notre Dame d'Ukraine* implicitly
entails the need for the similar reevaluation of the national body so to speak,
including the reevaluation of its history. Hence, that is why this particular text
by Zabuzhko so persistently foregrounds alternative interpretations of various
episodes in the national past, to the point that they themselves, as some critics
pointed out,[20] morph into new mythologies.

Zabuzhko's lengthy novel *The Museum of Abandoned Secrets* picks up
as its subject one of Ukraine's most controversial chapters of the Second
World War, mainly the guerilla-like combat of the Ukrainian Insurgent Army
(Ukrains'ka Povstans'ka Armiia—UPA) against the Soviets and the Nazis.
Being a military wing of the Organization of Ukrainian Nationalists (OUN),
UPA was accused of Nazi collaboration by the Soviet propaganda. The Insurgent Army's initial expectation that Nazi Germany would help Ukrainians to
establish an independent state was shattered rather quickly after Stepan Bandera's[21] premature proclamation of independence on June 30, 1941 in Lviv,
resulted in his arrest by the Gestapo and subsequent imprisonment. Despite
the fact that many Ukrainian nationalists, members of OUN and UPA, were
killed by the Nazis, the image of "banderites" as Nazi collaborators have
persisted, especially in southeastern regions of Ukraine up to this very day.
Zabuzhko's thematization of these controversial episodes in her novel indicates that she is more than ready not only to pick up a fight for gender equality
but also to rewrite pages of national history by portraying UPA soldiers as
national heroes.

However, *The Museum of Abandoned Secrets* is also a novel about the
reconstruction of the past thanks to a collective memory, which, as the author
suggests, needs to be nurtured and preserved by at least some groups in a
society, and made whole out of fragmented, incomplete and often scattered
personal stories, not unlike what Maurice Halbwachs outlined in his work

The Collective Memory. It is interesting to observe how Zabuzhko compares the ability to generate and retain memory by rural and urban populations—the city being so much more superior in that respect: "This was why the city was dangerous—it was a bottomless and unpredictable reservoir of *the past.* The woods—they were the opposite. The woods had a short memory; the woods—like the partisans, lived in the streaming moment; "[22] She fur-ther elaborates this point, insisting that the city constitutes a unique fortress capable of preserving memories of many successive generations:

> The city was a different beast—inside its walls, the city closely guarded the entire mass of time lived in it by its people, stashed it, generation after genera-tion like a tree growing new whorls. Here your past could pounce at you from behind a corner at any moment, like an ambush no reconnaissance could ever warn you about. It could explode in your face like a time-delayed bomb—with an old Gymnasium professor of yours, miraculously not exterminated by the Germans or the Soviets, or with a former friend from the German Fachkursen, later recruited by the NKVD, or simply with someone who had once been a witness to an old fragment of your life, which was, at the moment, of absolutely no use to you and thus subject to being expunged from your memory—but not from the city's. Because this was the city's job—to *remember:* without purpose, meaning, or need, but wholly, with its every stone—just as to flow is the job of rivers, and to grow is the job of grass. And if you take the city's memory away—if you deport the people who'd lived in it for generations and populate it, instead, with relocated squatters, the city withers and shrivels, but as long as its ancient walls—its *stone memory*—stand, it will not die.[23]

While both *Notre Dame d'Ukraine* and *The Museum of Abandoned Secrets* engage in reconstructing and reevaluating the national past, the former does so from a clearly feminist and postcolonial perspective. Zabuzhko's bulky novel, on the other hand, is arguably her least feminist work to date. Femi-nism, it seems, no longer occupies here as central position as was the case in the beginning of the author's literary career. On the contrary, the main protagonist, Daryna, is involved in a loving relationship with a man, who not only loves her very much but also understands her needs to fully real-ize herself as a female intellectual. Moreover, unlike Oksana in *Fieldwork in Ukrainian Sex*, Daryna becomes pregnant thus her dream of experiencing motherhood is fulfilled. But that in itself again brings the focus back to the female body. Hence, the interpretation of the female body as a repository of memory is equally intimated in both novels. All in all, as Uilleam Blacker aptly observes, "through her engagement with the space of the body not only as inextricably linked with language, memory and identity, but as a metaphor for the national-cultural space and simultaneously a space for the inscription of colonial and anti-colonial narratives, [Zabuzhko] gives a distinctive, if paradoxical, expression of the post-colonial female subject's traumatic, complex experience of body, sex, and gender."[24]

FEMINISM AND NATIONAL IDENTITY IN BELLES-LETTRES OF WOMEN AUTHORS

The link between feminism and national identity in works of literature by contemporary Ukrainian female writers is subtle but, at the same time, pervasive. By and large, women authors do not champion nationalist concerns, but a preoccupation with identities—national, gender and class—is certainly there. As I already pointed out, the most celebrated female writer in post-independence Ukraine, Oksana Zabuzhko, in her novel *Fieldwork in Ukrainian Sex* skillfully stresses the parallels between the national and the personal, focusing with equal passion on both feminine and masculine points of view. The failed masculinity of Zabuzhko's male protagonist moves in tandem with Ukraine's impotence as a nation. In this sense *Fieldwork* goes beyond purely feminist concerns. Zabuzhko's feminism projects itself more as a vehicle to engender a discursive space in which both national and feminist issues are taken up rather than any attempt on her part to produce a typical feminist novel.[25]

Often perceived as Zabuzhko's disciple, Svitlana Pyrkalo (b. 1976) intimates her own vision of society's inner workings with regard to the position of women in contemporary Ukraine. Her short novel *Green Margarita* (*Zelena Marharyta*, 2001), in comparison to Zabuzhko's *Fieldwork*, approaches feminist and national identity issues with humor and casualness. Pyrkalo's offhand and fragmentary manner of narration, quite in line with postmodernist premises, helps her to debunk entrenched gender stereotypes, as well as allows her to parody the trivialities found in a number of women's magazines. Consider for a moment the following ad titles: "A Debate: How to Become a Star, A Textbook for a Businesswoman"; "The Best Makeup Foundation for Brains: Now in a New Container"; "Man as a Particularly Useful Creature"; "The Mobile Telephone as a Measure of Sexual Dignity," to mention just a few. They all point to Pyrkalo's penchant for playfulness and to her mastery of handling controversial issues in a very unimposing way. At the same time, Pyrkalo's protagonist Maryna, a self-proclaimed feminist, when faced with a choice either to go abroad to study or stay in Ukraine, chooses the latter, tacitly acknowledging the importance of the sense of national belonging in a postcolonial setting.

Pyrkalo's second novel *Don't Think about Red* (*Ne dumai pro chervone*, 2004) presents a different scenario, however. Here the main protagonist, Pavlina, actually leaves Ukraine for England in order to take up a position as a BBC journalist. Putting aside the motivation for that decision, what is worth mentioning is that despite a number of acquaintances and colleagues, and despite having a satisfying job, Pavlina feels lonely in England without her Ukrainian friends. In the end she convinces one of her close male friends from Kyiv to join her in London so that she can have a companion, someone of the same background to converse with.

Another woman author, Natalka Sniadanko (b. 1973), also presents a female protagonist with a connection to the West, to Europe, to be precise. Sniadanko's novel *Collection of Passions* (*Kolektsiia prystrastei*, 2001) in a humorous and ironic way portrays Olesia's love relationships with men of different ethnic backgrounds, thus inextricably linking the personal with the national. The main protagonist, who ends up in Germany first as an au pair and then as a student, dates men of other than Ukrainian background. Yet having experienced relationships with Russian, Italian and German men, she returns to her native Lviv and settles for a Ukrainian. The issue of national identity is intentionally woven into sexual relationships, as if the author wanted to underscore the fact that there is a direct correlation between ethnicity and the way carnal pleasures are experienced.

Oksana Lutsyshyna (b. 1974) goes beyond Europe and even beyond heterosexual relationships, and places one of her lesbian protagonists in the novel *The Sun Sets So Rarely* (*Sontse tak ridko zakhodyt'*, 2007) in the United States, in the Florida Everglades. The author explores in her oeuvre both homosexual and heterosexual relations, focusing on cases in which sex and violence go hand in hand. Her explicit depictions of the body and sexual organs are always put in the context of feminist debates about gender equality and power struggle. Lutsyshyna's choice of geographical location might be explained in part by the fact that she herself immigrated to America in the early 2000s and began her Ph.D. studies in comparative literature at the University of Georgia. No doubt, the author's take on feminism is informed both by her literary interests and her own personal experience as someone who grew up in the provincial town of Uzhhorod in Zakarpattia, where female assertiveness was viewed with considerable skepticism, if not suspicion, as one of the heroines in *The Sun Sets So Rarely*, an aspiring writer, found out for herself. The novel relates the story of three different women, two living in Ukraine and one in Florida. All three aim at radically changing their unbearable situations: a lesbian Yunona in Florida is determined to reunite with her lesbian girlfriend Victoria despite contrary demands of her mafioso father; Tania, an aspiring writer, manages to leave her town for the West to study, and Yulia, after the homelessness and hardship on the streets, finds a man she is happy with.

Lutsyshyna's texts published since she has settled in the United States[26] display more affinity with the feminist and national concerns advocated by Oksana Zabuzhko than with the lightheartedness and irony embraced by

Pyrkalo and Sniadanko. The novel *The Sun Sets So Rarely*, tells not only the story of three women but also foregrounds social and national issues, including language choice and usage. For example, Lutsyshyna subtly underscores the fact that in criminal circles in Uzhhorod prevails either *surzhyk* or Russian. And thus the issue of belonging and self-identification come to the forefront.

In the realm of poetry, Ukrainian female authors, especially those of the younger generation, shy away from a direct thematization of questions pertaining to nationalism or national identity. But implicit, interiorized responses both to feminist and national concerns are certainly there. For example, the early poetry of Marianna Kiianovska (b. 1973) foregrounds female self-sufficiency and autonomy and avoids a thematic representation of woman as mother. In her collection *Mythologizing* (*Mifotvorennia*, 2000), any inference of a woman's auxiliary role in society is not only kept out of her poetic vocabulary but also is viewed as incompatible with Being: "There is I, there is you, and there is the permanence of God."[27] Kiianovska's lyrical heroine does not reject love or relationships, but makes them subordinate to her own subjectivity. However, in her subsequent collection *Ordinary Discourse* (*Zvychaina mova*, 2005) she underscores the importance of both carnality of intimate relations and her own experience as mother:

mother's body an edge of bed a wall

what are words
when one needs to scream?

not one woman
in labor
even one that is incapable of
that knows all knowing nothing
even I
remembering this poem[28]

Mariana Savka (b. 1973), on the other hand, ironically deconstructs the patriarchal myths of women yearning to give themselves to "real" men. She also reminds her readers of the ways in which women are not understood because they remain "unread" so to say:

Woman has always been
Opened on the first page
And left unread[29]

But in her 2006 collection *Cumin Flowers* (*Kvity tsmynu*), Savka turns to reminiscences and brings forth her recollections about female family members and close friends. Her poetic portraits of various women, real and fictitious, from her grandmother, mother and sister to literary characters of Donna

Anna (from Lesia Ukrainka's play *Stone Master—Kaminnyi hospodar*) point to the poet's attempt to create something of a universal sisterhood, a collective female voice in her oeuvre. A successful publisher and businesswoman, Savka toned down her feminist rhetoric in her later poetry.

Gender relations lie at the heart of Halyna Kruk's poetry,[30] another woman poet based in Lviv (like Kiianovska and Savka). By 2011, Kruk (b. 1974) had published three collections of poems but her most mature poetic works come from her volume titled *The Face beyond the Photograph* (*Oblychchia poza svitlynoiu*, 2005). Even though in one of her poems she provocatively declares: "poets don't have gender," every line in her oeuvre is marked by her ostentatious femininity:

genius doesn't have gender
  just a throat raw from shouting
    between the legs[31]

Kruk is also one of the very few female poets concerned with social ills, especially if they affect women: "… listen, Halka, / millions have already died of AIDS / more than in the last war / but, you and me, we're alive / this has to mean something."[32] At times, there is a sheer brutality in Kruk's poetry bordering on the grotesque, as in her description of a woman's suicide and overall contemplation about women worrying about their looks in a society that demands beauty and youth, turning females into mere sexual objects:

the woman cuts into her veins
with a kitchen knife simply
as she would open a can of sardines
  because she doesn't want to grow old
a feeble angel
a corpulent doctor and a four-eyed assistant
are a dubious group for this dirty work
their idealism makes the head spin
and the stingy sun set behind the kiosk across from the road
how can she escape
  how can she flow through the knife's narrow cut
and which pathway should she surrender to when
  everyone, without exception, is against it
a whirlwind carries her through the spiral of the aorta
  with such ease …
the doctor brings a mirror to her mouth
  he thinks—the woman often reconsiders
but, get out of here, never, because when her mind is made up
  then her mind is made up

the woman, you know, is a stubborn soul—
God forgive her[33]

Yet among the poems so completely dominated by issues of gender equality, women's position, power and bodies, one can also encounter a verse with an ironic title "Love for One's Fatherland" ("Liubov k otchyzni") and a line expressing the author's seeming concern for her nation's political aspirations: "I have to tell you, Ukraine: / be careful, you little girl, / in your relations with Europe / there's a bit too much pink."[34] By comparing Ukraine to a little girl, Kruk possibly signalizes her country's inexperience and naivety when it comes to dealing with Europe but does not seem to question the westward direction.

Liudmyla Taran (b. 1954), a poet, journalist and prose writer representing an older generation of female writers, who is especially active in shaping feminist discourse in post-Soviet Ukraine, also betrays an obsession with gender relations. For example, in her book *A Collection of Lovers* (*Kolektsiia kokhanok*, 2002), she experiments with gender reversals, assumes the male gaze and contemplates female sexuality from a mostly desirous male perspective. She uncovers and simultaneously debunks male tendencies to treat the female body as an object, yet does not reject the possibility of a real dialogue between the sexes:

Women are the Other. Protect
Your pensive and luscious eyes:
In your gaze, they
Desire to see themselves.

But you, men—are the same!—
You added, laughing and calling me.[35]

These are but just a few examples of female poetic voices and their need to address some of the concerns relating to women's role and place in a transitional society such as post-Soviet Ukraine. What is most striking and deserves emphasis is the sheer number of those voices. Never before in Ukrainian literary history has there been such a number of talented female writers, poets and intellectuals producing so many interesting and diverse works. Despite the prevalent misogynist rhetoric coming from contemporary male authors, women of letters in present-day Ukraine have managed to carve an influential space for themselves. What they have to say is not always approved but is heard nonetheless. This is no small achievement. The voice of women in contemporary literature constitutes an island of progressive attitudes and ideas in an otherwise vast ocean of artificially engineered myths and stereotypes confining women to narrowly formulated prospects. But there is a notable shift, and at least in belles-lettres this island is growing bigger and the ocean is shrinking.

Autobiographical Turn and Hybrid Genres

Much of the criticism about texts produced by Ukrainian female authors in the first two decades of independence underscores its autobiographical bias.[36] Autobiography as a literary genre was quite widespread among American and British feminist writers in the 1970s and 1980s. Some examples of women's confessional writings include: Erica Jong's *Fear of Flying* (1973), Kate Millett's *Flying* (1974) and *Sita* (1977), Alice Koller's *An Unknown Woman* (1982), and Ann Oakley's *Taking It like a Woman* (1984), to name just a few. These pioneering feminist confessions were full of elements that deliberately problematized the distinction between autobiography and fiction. They were all very much influenced by the women's liberation movement and reflective of women's changing perception of self. Rita Felski, for example, thinking of reasons for this blurring of genres in feminist literature, comes to the conclusion: "Feminist confession exemplifies the intersection between the autobiographical imperative to communicate the truth of unique individuality, and the feminist concern with the representative and intersubjective elements of women's experience."[37]

In Ukrainian contemporary literature, the trend toward an autobiographical approach in fiction and a penchant for hybrid genres is best represented by writings of Oksana Zabuzhko and Nila Zborovska. Zborovska's *Feminist Reflections*, published in 1999, three years after the appearance of *Fieldwork in Ukrainian Sex*, constitutes an elaborately constructed reaction to the stormy aftermath fomented by Zabuzhko's bestseller. Not only does she provide her own critical evaluation of *Fieldwork*, she also deciphers, at times wickedly, the prototypes of Zabuzhko's protagonists via a series of so-called literary rumors whose function is (among other things) to present a deliberately excursive, behind-the-scenes background for the novel's emergence. But even more unexpected is Zborovska's open mystification, which allows her to playfully emulate Zabuzhko's exhibitionism. This idiosyncratic metanarrativization of the female intellectual's contemporary experience would not have been possible had Zborovska adhered to a strictly scholarly exposition.

Zabuzhko's *Fieldwork* came to prominence as a work of fiction. The writer deliberately strove to minimize the novel's autobiographical elements.[38] Yet, no matter how emphatically the author would want us to forget her text's autobiographical underpinnings, they surface nonetheless. In fact, Zabuzhko herself injects a considerable dose of ambiguity. For example, her ironic introductory note ("From the Author") playfully considers the possibility of potential lawsuits from people who read a photocopied version and happened to be implicated in the novel. This strategy only reinforces the perception that perhaps not all the characters and events are truly fictional. Otherwise, why would anyone want to challenge her in court? On the other hand, she diligently reminds the reader that a novel is a work of fiction and a seeming factual resemblance is a mere coincidence from which she a priori exempts herself. In spite of that, Zabuzhko makes her central protagonist bear the name Oksana, thus signaling the autobiographical bias through the identity of names. Moreover, her heroine (not unlike the author herself) is also a poet, an intellectual, a Fulbright scholar in the United States, and visiting professor at the University of Pittsburgh. Her male character, introduced in the novel as Mykola K., turns out to be the artist Mykola Kumanovsky, as Zborovska eagerly explicates in her *Feminist Reflections*. Clearly, Zabuzhko delights in this intricate play of identities and mystifications in which it is implied that the author might be both creator and subject matter of the literary text.

The confessional character of *Fieldwork* cannot be denied.[39] It is precisely this authorial openness that has stirred reactions and made the novel such a compelling subject for interpretation. Zabuzhko's confession foregrounds the private to the point of sounding clinical: a forceful penetration, painful intercourse and getting a period—all is revealed and reflected upon and there is a certain yearning for transcendence (if not self-therapy) that can be only achieved through confession, which is nothing else but a subgenre of autobiography.

While Zabuzhko undoubtedly problematizes the distinction between autobiography and fiction in *Fieldwork*, as well as presents her own unique account of a woman's experience, "the shift toward a conception of communal identity" (using Felski's words) is conspicuously absent. One does not easily discern solidarity with women's lot in general. Zabuzhko's character is too much of a special person: an exceptional woman seeking an exceptional man, dreaming of an exceptional child (a hint of eugenics is simply unmistakable here). This elitist bias permeates the novel and makes the heroine's rather commonplace experience, a crisis caused by the lover's departure, anything but common. All the more, Zabuzhko herself expressed surprise that so many women identified with her story. In her interview with the translator, Halyna Hryn, she states:

> My greatest, I would say, "cultural shock" came from my hundreds of female readers, ranging in age from early twenties to early sixties, who responded with the same exclamations—in letters, at meetings—"This is my story!", "It reads as though you were sitting in my kitchen, and I was pouring my heart out to you!", "I feel as though I wrote it!" etc. I didn't expect that, honestly. It stunned me.[40]

One can only speculate, but it appears that Zabuzhko's female readers predominantly identified themselves with the sexual abuse the heroine experienced. Domestic violence is still, unfortunately, a very common problem in Ukraine. But what is different here is that despite her personal drama, the protagonist's voice exudes power, strength and determination—attributes traditionally associated with male discourse and not the attitude commonly found among battered Ukrainian women.

There can be no doubt as to who is the active agent in the novel and who wants to be in control (the heroine's lover is silenced and reduced to a passive object). On the other hand, this projected masculinized manner of the protagonist's demeanor clashes with her at times masochistic moments of submission to the sexual abuse. However weak her artist-lover is, he still manages to inflict serious scars on the protagonist, both physical and psychological. Maryna Romanets provides an interesting psychoanalytical reading of this male character: "[his] identity is defined by the phallic and heterosexual economy of lack both on the psychological and physical, perfomative level, since he experiences a metaphorical form of castration. Simultaneously, he suffers the castration trauma that is characteristic of the dispersed and dislocated subjectivities of the colonized."[41] There is a leitmotif of sorts throughout Zabuzhko's novel stating "slaves should not bear children."[42] All the more, one is surprised that the heroine longs to form a union with a man who has clearly interiorized imperial abuse but whom she perceives (at least initially) worthy of her attention and worthy of fathering her child. One could almost surmise that her old-fashioned yearning (as radical feminists would put it) to have family entails dependence rather than freedom and equality but the heroine's desire "to have beautiful children, an elite breed"[43] seemingly mars her good judgments.

What is fresh in Zabuzhko's texts is her willingness to touch controversial, taboo subjects and her flair to subvert the form. Unlike the feminists of the 1970s, she weds fiction and autobiography not in order to express her solidarity with the women's liberation movement, but in order to come up with a convenient channel to convey contradictory premises. *Fieldwork* manifests both failure and victory. Its heroine fails to form a meaningful relationship, but its author is catapulted to fame following the novel's publication. The notorious controversy surrounding *Fieldwork* (which is a blessing for any publicity campaign) came about in large part because of Zabuzhko's well-thought-out and pretended unwillingness to discuss the autobiographical provenance of the novel. One could argue that this work thrives mainly because of its unacknowledged hybridity. It is precisely this hybridity of genre that allows Zabuzhko to skillfully debunk both the male- and female-dominated discourses.

Zborovska's *Feminist Reflections* champions hybridity as well, but its effects function differently than those in Zabuzhko's work. Her account lacks Zabuzhko's spontaneity; it is at times too constructed and explicatory, although structurally quite inventive and considerably more polyphonic than Zabuzhko's tale. The second part of *Feminist Reflections*, written

by Zborovska's alter ego, Mariia Ilnytska, includes among others, a story
"Dzvinka," which looks at parenthood and the tragedy of losing a child both
from a female and male perspective. In this short story one can discern a
subtle polemic that Zborovska carries out with Zabuzhko's way of representing female sexuality. Gone are the painful intercourses of *Fieldwork* and the
allusions to the oppressive nature of sexual experience. What we have in
"Dzvinka" is a sample that admits the possibility, if not celebration, of carnal delights between man and woman. However, this story is also important
because it provides a link to Zborovska's work of fiction entitled *The Ukrainian Reconquista* (*Ukrains'ka Rekonkista*, 2003). This anti-novel, as Zborovska insists, is not without a hint of the author's own personal struggles,
including the depiction of her exceptionally close relationship with her grandmother, but it is not as transparently autobiographical as was the case with
Zabuzhko. *The Ukrainian Reconquista* by and large unfolds as a story about
a woman in search of her identity as a wife, daughter, mother and intellectual,
but the idea of national rebirth also figures quite prominently. The heroine
faces a variety of choices that directly point to the issues of self-identification.
When faced with the dilemma to stay or to leave Ukraine, she chooses to stay.
Unlike her ex-husband who emigrates to the United States, Dzvinka, the main
protagonist, is determined to build her life in her own country, because only
there she feels she can realize her intellectual potential.

I have focused intensely on autobiographical turn and hybridity in Zabuzhko and Zborovska mainly because of their pioneering efforts in these areas.
However, there are other female writers who also succumb to autobiography's seductive possibilities. For example, Pyrkalo's second novel, *Don't
Think about Red*, openly draws on the author's own experience as a BBC
journalist in England. The protagonist, as indeed Pyrkalo herself, lives and
works in London. It is left to the reader's imagination to sort out what is fiction and what is real.[44]

Still another approach we find in Yevheniia Kononenko's work *Without
a Man* (*Bez muzhyka*, 2005). The author of two successful novels *Imitation*
(*Imitatsiia*, 2001) and *Betrayal* (*Zrada*, 2002), as well as numerous short
stories and essays decided to come up with a seemingly straightforward autobiography. That is, by design it is not an autobiography parading as fiction.
However, in an interview with Liudmyla Taran, the author of *Without a Man*
demonstrates that her autobiography is not so straightforward after all and
she openly declares that the genre of autobiography gives her an opportunity
to play with the audience, to actually tell lies.[45] She further asserts her right
not to be truthful even though the mode of narrative is confessional. In other
words, she clearly debunks the premise of the confessional approach, fashionable in feminist writings, especially when female sexuality is concerned.

European Turn, or, In Search of New Identity

In 1989 when Natalka Bilotserkivets published an untitled poem with the now well-known line, "we will not die in Paris I now know it for sure,"[46] which openly echoed and paraphrased Cesar Vallejo's famous line, "I will die in Paris," she in a way expressed her generation's despair over the long-kept divide and provincialism imposed on them by the Soviet authorities with regard to the Western cultural heritage and the deep, implicit longing to be culturally part of Europe. The overall pessimistic tone of the poem would indicate that the poet did not harbor any hope for a different turn of events. And yet, some ten years later, the younger generation of Ukrainian poets and writers made Europe if not their home (though in a few case that too), then certainly a point of destination and/or reference. The generation that reached adolescence after independence seemingly does not suffer from the complexes of those who grew up under the Soviet communist ideology. Travel to different cities of Western Europe is common, as is the sense of personal freedom to create wherever possible, without any obligation toward the homeland. Paradoxically, however, these younger literati do not dispense with the feeling of belonging. To the contrary, their identities as Ukrainians congeal more notably when juxtaposed against the European paradigm. Consider, for example, a poem by Halyna Petrosaniak (b. 1969) in which she underscores her heroine's Ukrainianness set against the Vienna suburban landscape:

To remain at the Dominican school near Vienna forever,
To pray just in Ukrainian to the surprise of the nuns.
To write letters sometimes to family after vespers,
Asking how their health is, and how their gardens are doing.
To go to the market every day along Schlossbergstrasse,
To get used to having enough, to buy a car,
To live in harmony with yourself, thanking the Savior
For the fact that all has turned out so well. And suddenly
After about twenty years, when no one
Any longer recognizes the foreigner in you, to wake up at dawn,
To pray in Ukrainian again, surprising people,
And not removing the garb of a Dominican nun,
Knowing well what and for what you're changing,
To set off on the road intending not to return,
Surprising those who didn't think the work "homeland" has
Such an inconceivable dimension
And surprised yourself.[47]

In the novel *Don't Think about Red* Svitlana Pyrkalo's protagonist Pavlina shares to some extent the author's own experience as a London-based journalist covering stories about Ukraine for the BBC. As mentioned earlier, there are obvious autobiographical parallels between the heroine and Pyrkalo, but what is particularly striking about the story as it unfolds is the easiness with which Pavlina, the main protagonist, adapts to the host country, England. Of course, it helps that she is fluent in English, intelligent and articulate. One could expect that the cultural differences between Ukraine (with the Soviet legacy still being quite pervasive) and a Western country such as England could undermine the adjustment, but it never happens. Pavlina seems to fit in without any problem and in some situations she even outsmarts her local male as well as female friends. Yes, she might miss her Kyiv friends, but she feels as much at home in London as in Kyiv. The contrast between Bilotserkivets's poetic contemplation about a Europe that seems to be unreachable and Pyrkalo's outright experience as a successful journalist in London could not be more pronounced.[48]

Natalka Sniadanko in her novel *Collections of Passions* also insists on a European connection for her heroine Olesia from Lviv. Unlike Pyrkalo's Pavlina, Olesia, a student at Lviv University, leaves for Germany to work as an au pair with a young German family. After a year, having learned the language well, instead of going back to her hometown she decides to stay in Western Europe and study at a university. Of course, being a student without much money for support is not as easy as being a journalist. Yet Olesia makes the most of her Western experience, mainly because she manages to immerse herself exclusively in a foreign milieu, in which, again, she does not necessarily feel inferior. The mere fact that she is from Eastern Europe does not prevent her from having meaningful interactions with her foreign peers. But Germany is for her only a temporary abode. After a series of romantic affairs the protagonist returns home and marries a local man. Interestingly, when Sniadanko sets her heroine on a trip to Western Europe she cannot but intertextually refer (ironically it seems) to Bilotserkivets's nostalgic line "We will not die in Paris": "Who among us, overly confident, young and utterly naïve, did not dream of dying under the Mirabeau bridge in Paris, London's Tower, or at least under the ruins of the Berlin Wall?"[49] Again, what seemed impossible in the 1980s became a reality in the post-independence period.

Still younger than Pyrkalo and Sniadanko, Irena Karpa (b. 1980) builds her literary image as a young female rebel, ignoring rules and etiquette. Her prose is deliberately outrageous, full of expletives but also full of language experiments, and therefore not as straightforward as is the case with Pyrkalo and Sniadanko. It seems that Karpa, too, cannot resist having a European connection in her works. She generously intersperses her narratives with English words and phrases, and emphasizes her protagonists' ease and cosmopolitanism. In her novella *Hunting in Helsinki* (*Poliuvannia v Helsinki*, 2004),[50] Karpa makes her female protagonist play with the notion of what it means to be a European. On the one hand, at one point the heroine ironically states: "now we can start writing a new book: HOW WE LOST EUROPE,"[51] on the other, she clearly indicates that she feels quite at home there, or to be more precise in Helsinki: "We were walking down Helsinki's streets to the hostel at night. It felt like I had been walking here my whole life."[52] Karpa appropriates Europe not just in a geographical sense, but, more importantly, in a psychological one. Europe is no longer something unreachable out there, but as interiorized personal experience in the here and now.

Even though Yevheniia Kononenko is closer in age to Bilotserkivets than to the three female authors of the younger generation discussed above, her European orientation and experience puts her firmly in their company. All three of her novels (*Imitation*, *Betrayal* and *Nostalgia*) depict relationships between Ukrainian women and foreign men. It must be rooted, at least to some extent, in her personal experience, because in *Without a Man* Kononenko openly reveals her three-year relationship with a non-Ukrainian man and her consequent frequent trips abroad. She had an opportunity to stay in the West, but knew that that would mean the end of her writing career and she did not want to sacrifice her creativity for everyday comforts. But, as she herself admits, this experience allowed her to see Europe and life there from within rather than without. After all, she lived there for some time and was not a mere tourist.

If one looks at women's literary discourse in post-Soviet Ukraine in its totality, that is, criticism and belles-lettres alike, one is struck by its overall Western orientation. This orientation is not just thematic, but entails many sources of inspiration—from theoretical to literary, and it implies a general awareness of one's own place and belonging within a society. The female critics I discussed in chapter 1 in many ways revolutionized literary scholarship by making it subjective on the one hand (Zborovska) and theoretically challenging, on the other (especially Hundorova). Employing feminist, psychoanalytic and phenomenological approaches and being at home within the parameters of what is perceived as poststructuralism, these female scholars introduced novel modes of reading and literary analysis, and reinterpreted quite a few classic works and authors of Ukrainian literature.

The issue of national identity in Ukrainian literature figures rather strongly in the post-independence period, in large part because of discursive formations around two literary schools, one called the Zhytomyr School and the other one the Stanyslaviv (or Galician) School, the former perceived as being anti-Western or "nativist" and the latter as Western or postmodern.[53] However, regardless of whether one agrees or disagrees with this classification, it must be emphasized that the key authors representing the respective schools are all men and therefore they overwhelmingly project a male perspective. A similar divide, that is, between those striving for modernization (read: the

West) and those looking for native sources of inspiration, simply does not exist in texts produced by female writers in post-Soviet Ukraine. Women's oeuvre, as indicated above, is uniformly pro-Western and progressively minded in terms of advancing a just society, a society in which the welfare of women as well as of all citizens steadily and surely improves.

POSTFEMINISM OF WOMEN AUTHORS OF THE YOUNGER GENERATION

While the paradigm of an oppressed or victimized woman, championed by authors of Zabuzhko's generation, dominated the literary discourse in the 1990s, in the 2000s, there is a tendency among younger female writers to reject such a pattern. Here I want to focus on prose works of three Ukrainian women authors, all born in the early 1980s, whose literary propositions fit the conceptual framework of what is commonly labeled as postfeminism, even though the term itself is not always consistently used. And since it indeed evokes various understandings and reactions,[54] let me announce at the outset that I am not inclined to define postfeminism as "anti-feminism," or to agree with the belief that "feminism is dead" because it succeeded in tempering the extent and effects of sexism. Rather, I subscribe to the concept of postfeminism as the cultural space in which women (especially young women) take gender equality for granted and shun the activism of the women's rights movement, especially as represented by the second-wave feminism. Postfeminists take feminism into account (as Angela McRobbie suggests in her works) but then promptly push it away. McRobbie's take on postfeminism as a subversive or undermining force is somewhat too negative in my opinion, but she rightly observes that "one strategy in the disempowering of feminism includes it being historicised and generationlised and thus easily rendered out of date."[55]

The views and works of three Ukrainian writers, namely Irena Karpa (b. 1980), Sofiia Andrukhovych (b. 1982) and Tania Maliarchuk (b. 1983), fit the above description particularly well. All three, each in her own unique way, position themselves as postfeminists in the sense that they as authors do not foreground issues of women's rights in contrast to their older female colleagues. They also dispense with the discourse of victimization and draw on progressive ideas of empowerment and choice as substitutes for political activism. Their female characters, by and large liberated and independent, enjoy their sexuality and freedom, and yet, at the same time, dream to find a right man. Another characteristic that these women authors share is their reluctance to identify with feminists and, if the word "feministka" (the feminist) is invoked in their works at all, it is used in a pejorative way. For example, Karpa's main protagonist in the novel *Freud Would Cry* (*Froid by plakav*, 2004), Marla Friksen, when called a feminist by one of her male friends, responds to him offended saying he would pay for this. Clearly, as Karpa sees it, naming someone a feminist is not only undesirable but offensive as well.

There could be several explanations for a postfeminist turn among Ukraine's female authors of the younger generation. One such explanation could be that they just follow a general trend against feminism that commenced in the early 1990s in the West, when promoting and building a consensus that women are free to choose their values (be they conservative or liberal), relations, career and/or family life gained currency. Of course, it is an entirely different story how such supposedly free choices have worked in real life. But one thing is certain, these three women writers are self-confident, believe in taking charge of their own success (which is especially true of Irena Karpa) and do not want to be perceived as victims of patriarchal whims. They act as if gender equality has already been achieved and there is no need for collective action to defend it. If anything, they rely first and foremost on their own competitive individualism. Thus, this attitude could indeed point to a generational divide because those Ukrainian female authors who were actively writing in the decade of the 1990s, by contrast, demonstrated a strong penchant for feminism not only in belles-lettres but also in literary criticism. Oksana Zabuzhko's bestselling novel *Fieldwork in Ukrainian Sex* and her nonfiction work on Lesia Ukrainka, *Notre Dame d'Ukraine*, foreground gender inequality through a postcolonial lens and engage, as I have already indicated, in what has been often labeled as "national feminism." Karpa, Andrukhovych and Maliarchuk do not see themselves as Zabuzhko's "daughters" because they do not champion oppositional constructs, that is, an "us vs. them" mentality. And it is not that these young women eschew national concerns.[56] On the contrary, they do, but choose not to thematize them in their works.

Another explanation of postfeminist inclinations among younger female authors could be that the stigma of the word "feminism" is quite real in Ukrainian society. It could indeed well be that avoiding it altogether is these writers' way of not jeopardizing their own positions. However, I am inclined to think that it probably has more to do with their beliefs; namely, that feminism has a tendency to divide sexes rather than unite them, and that is why they prefer to talk about women and men alike, often narrating from a male point of view.[57] Hence women are de-centered, or, to put it differently, "women are people," and not a special case.

Irena Karpa: A Woman as Rebel

Irena Karpa, chronologically the oldest among the three and in many ways a transitional figure, has been exceptionally prolific as a writer, all the more that she has also been active as a singer. By 2011 she authored eight books of fiction, four of which have been translated and published in Polish, Czech, Bulgarian and Russian. Karpa made her name not just as a writer and a singer, but also as an actress, filmmaker, TV personality and journalist. She has traveled extensively and her journeys in Europe, India and Southeast Asia became subjects of her mostly autobiographical works. With her older feminist colleagues she shares a reliance on autobiography for generating plots. She differs though in the way she portrays her protagonists. They are never portrayed as victims. They are always in charge, deliberately outrageous, anti-glamorous, sexually liberated (often bisexual), involved in several romantic affairs at the same time. Feminism appears redundant simply because Karpa's characters are already empowered, smart and seemingly lacking nothing. They sexually enjoy men and women alike, and do not demand commitment. Or, to be more precise, they fear commitment though secretly yearn it.

Karpa's novels *Freud Would Cry* (2004) and *Pearl Porno (A Supermarket of Loneliness)* (*Perlamutrove porno [Supermarket samotnosti]*, 2005) constitute fictionalized travelogues, which allow the writer to construct an image of a new liberated woman who is not afraid to trespass morality (as in carrying on a romantic affair with a married man) and has the same sexual appetite as her male counterparts. Hence having a monogamous relationship is not sufficient for her. Karpa debunks gender stereotypes and seems to reject common binary oppositions such as man vs. woman, or feminist vs. non-feminist. Instead, she prefers to populate her fictional world with either strong or weak individuals regardless of what gender they belong to. Being informed or being ignorant also plays an important part in Karpa's literary domain, as does her insistence on dispensing with glamour so much imposed on women by the media.

Karpa's fifth novel *Bitches Get Everything*[58] (2007) intends to shock and scandalize. Its main protagonist, Trisha Tornberg, is a young film director, whom we meet in the process of making a provocative movie, forbidden in advance for general distribution. Shown in underground screenings, it manages to win a prize at the Venetian film festival but Trisha is shot there by one of her former lovers. The plot itself is rather simple and does not reflect the real fabric of the narrative, which is dynamic, interspersed with expletives and language experiments. Trisha, not unlike Karpa herself, is very social, has lots of friends, straight and homosexual, and cultivates her image as a female rebel, ignoring rules and etiquette.

Karpa is one of the very few authors in Ukraine whose private life provides plenty of material for Ukrainian tabloids. Her marriage to journalist Anton Friedland and a subsequent divorce, followed immediately by her second marriage to American businessman Norman Paul Hansen made news, as did her giving birth to two daughters in 2009 and 2011, respectively.[59] Karpa's willingness to accept an invitation to pose nude in such magazines as *Playboy* and *Penthouse* also gained considerable attention. Nudity was not a problem for her, more likely she used it as a publicity stunt. Karpa has thus managed to become a celebrity of sorts whose personal moves have been scrutinized and debated, a quality rather uncommon for literary figures in Ukraine. It is worthwhile to point out that unlike her protagonists, who often proclaim that they do not need a husband (which does not entail that they would go without men), Karpa herself is a twice-married woman and mother of two daughters. Quite in line with the postfeminist spirit that a woman can and deserve to have all, both career and family life, Karpa demonstrates that it is indeed achievable and, perhaps unintentionally, sets herself as a model for emulation.

Sofiia Andrukhovych and Female Individualization

Sofiia Andrukhovych, the daughter of a well-known Ukrainian writer, Yuri Andrukhovych, and the wife of a well-known Ukrainian poet, Andrii Bondar, could not have more of a literary milieu to grow up in than the one granted her by family circumstances. What is refreshing about her work is that it does not appear to be as openly autobiographical as was the case with Karpa. During the period under consideration here Andrukhovych produced four volumes of prose, of which *Salmon* (*S'omha*, 2007) is best known. Called a novel by the author, it resembles more a book of loosely tied short stories rather than a narrative account with one coherent plot. In fact, one should note that Andrukhovych's talent, as manifested to date, reveals itself better in short fiction than in novelistic work. She also weaves into her prose the elements of fairy tale, the fantastic and the macabre.

Two early novellas *Milena's Summer* (*Lito Mileny*, 2002) and *Old People* (*Stari liudy*, 2005)[60] present the world that is deliberately placed outside of a recognizable time period. This is true especially for *Milena's Summer*, which has all the attributes of a fairy tale or utopia, with an ending that "they all live happily ever after." Both works emphasize the importance of family relations but also reverse the accepted notions of what it is that constitutes family. In *Old People*, for example, the main protagonist Luka has a romantic relationship with his grandmother's stepsister Marta who supposedly has only 102 days to live when they meet again, and she imposes her will on him but in such a way that in the end he accepts it as his own and cannot imagine it to be any other way. A more common in real life "sugar daddy" relationship is turned on its head here to become a "sugar mammy" tale. Andrukhovych empowers her female characters but, ideally, in this fictional world man and woman, equal and understanding, tend to live harmoniously, loving each other till death does part them.

Her book *Salmon* decisively departs from this paradigm. First, it makes
female sexuality its focal point[61] and second, it de-idealizes relationships
between men and women. Six chapters of this novel, or rather six separate
short stories, all narrated from the female point of view and all except one
having a first-person narrator, present the world of skewed expectations,
mistrust and detached sex. Through the narrator Andrukhovych reminisces
her childhood, adolescence and womanhood, and manages to build some
suspense in the process. Introducing a mysterious voyeur in the first story
gives impulse to a transformation of sorts. In the following chapters the main
heroine assumes that role herself, observing her own body and sexuality,
yet incapable of discovering the essence of her femaleness in the end. The
last story of the book, "I want to comprehend your inner world" ("Ia khochu
piznaty tvii vnutrishnii svit") in which we see the heroine gruesomely killed
by a man (perhaps the same voyeur introduced in the first chapter?), becomes
the metaphor of such impossibility. The ritualistic murder that concludes
Salmon bears some likeness to hara-kiri (except that in Andrukhovych's work
it is not a suicide unless we accept an interpretation that this unknown man
"who wants to warm his hands in the entrails of his victim" is her imaginary
double) and, in many ways, underscores the fractured identity of the individual in postmodern society regardless of his/her gender and/or sex.

How does Andrukhovych's oeuvre fit the postfeminist rhetoric? Explicitly
and discursively feminism is nowhere to be found in her works, nor is even
invoked as a teaser and/or pretext to get offended as was the case in Karpa's
novel, unless her visible preoccupation with the female body is perceived
as such. The way the main protagonist is presented in the novel clearly has
not much to do with feminist concerns. It appears that Andrukhovych relies
on what McRobbie refers to as "female individualization," that is, the belief
that "individuals must now choose the kind of life they want to live,"[62] again,
invoking postfeminist ideas of taking charge of one's own success. McRobbie further articulates that because old social structures with fixed gender
roles no longer hold, young women need to have a "lifeplan" and "become
more reflexive in regard to every aspect of their life."[63] This kind of reflexivity, I would add, a confessional reflexivity, is abundantly present in Andrukhovych's *Salmon*.

Tania Maliarchuk's Gendered Allegories

Tania Maliarchuk, the youngest and stylistically the most diverse writer
among the three analyzed here, has authored seven books of prose and
received considerable critical acclaim for someone still relatively young.[64] In
comparison to the other two she is a very private person and does not like to
share things of personal nature too much in the few interviews she has given

so far. After completing her university studies in Ivano-Frankivsk she moved to Kyiv where she worked as a TV journalist for a few years. She was married to a fellow journalist and writer Oleh Kryshtopa but they divorced and since 2011 she has been living in Austria.

Her fiction represents a gamut of various styles, from the stream-of-consciousness to satire and allegory. Her third book *How I Became a Saint* (*Iak ia stala sviatoiu*, 2006), for example, experiments with the surreal and the fantastic, whereas *To Speak* (*Hovoryty*, 2007) returns nostalgically to the author's childhood and experienced hardship of growing up in Ivano-Frankivsk in the period immediately following the collapse of the Soviet Union. But such a reliance on autobiographical moments is rare in Maliarchuk's oeuvre, which successfully manages to transcend confessional trappings and instead weaves personal experience in a subtle and hardly perceptible way.[65] Interestingly, each of the books published by Maliarchuk thus far is stylistically different and focuses on a different set of issues. Her book of short stories *Bestiary* (*Zviroslov*, 2009) illustrates the author's affinity with postfeminism most directly and convincingly.

Bestiary consists of ten tales, each having as its title the name of an animal. Of course, this is not a book about animals but about people. Maliarchuk uses the medieval tradition of bestiary (but restraints a moral comment) to point out the foibles of contemporary Kyivites—by and large marginal and lonely people, men and women alike. She simply shows them in various situations, some quite comical, others grotesque or even tragic, and paints a rather bleak picture about the urban landscape of the capital city. In other words, *Bestiary* is a book about different kinds of loneliness and the ways to cope with it. Sometimes just dreaming alone helps, sometimes pure luck brings two people together and their isolation is alleviated, or, more often than not, there is no remedy available and Maliarchuk's protagonists are left to their own devices. What is interesting about this work is that it debunks common perceptions about gender. The author shows that not only women dream of their princes and endure loneliness, men too experience that. Maliarchuk deconstructs such stereotypes and concludes that this "disease" (loneliness) is suffered equally by both genders.

Let me quote Maliarchuk's own words as far as her stand vis-à-vis feminism is concerned. In one of her interviews when asked what is her attitude toward feminism and women's emancipation in general, and whether or not the classification of literary works into "male" and "female" is justified, she replied:

All this feminist talk, in my opinion, is passé. It makes no difference who authors a book—whether a man or a woman, and what this book is all about,—what is important that this book is interesting and new. I am not a feminist. I do not divide people into men and women, nor do I divide literature into female or male with some kind of warring literary aim in sight. However these literatures are indeed different. They are about a different way of seeing things but this is good. And women's emancipation? Oh, Lord! One needs to go through this in adolescence and then live in peace.[66]

All three women authors discussed here clearly make an effort to distance themselves from the feminist rhetoric but, at the same time, there is no outright repudiation of it either. The reluctance to be associated with the movement appears to have its roots more in the perception that feminism is somehow no longer fashionable rather than in the desire to reject all its achievements. And this is precisely what is at the core of postfeminism: taking for granted things that not so long ago required fighting on women's part. Karpa, Andrukhovych and Maliarchuk cannot be blamed for not wanting to be associated with feminism if they themselves feel that their rights as women are in no way threatened or denied. After all, they indeed seem to have accomplished all, a literary career and, at least in two cases, a fulfilling family life. Certainly, all three assume a privileged position and therefore their lives cannot be reflective of the society at large but their attitudes do signal important shifts in the perceptions about women's role in contemporary Ukraine. Whether or not there will be other female voices in the Ukrainian literary milieu wanting to champion specifically women's concerns such as equal pay, domestic violence and/or workplace harassment, remains to be seen. Increasingly, postfeminist and genderless approaches in belles-lettres compete with the previously dominant feminist discourse.

BEYOND FEMINISM AND POSTFEMINISM

While feminist and postfeminist concerns dominated female literary discourse in the first two decades of post-independence Ukraine, some women authors have succeeded to go beyond the standard thematization of gender relations, by moving into less readily exploited territories of fantasy, metaphysics and urban social fringes. Among them four writers merit closer scrutiny, especially since they constitute the most representative and interesting examples of genderless voices in imaginative writings. Halyna Pahutiak's combination of magic realism's hermetic style with popular genres and vampire themes makes her contributions stand out, winning her the 2010 Shevchenko Prize in Literature for the novel *The Servant of Dobromyl* (*Sluha z Dobromylia*, 2006). Two sisters, Dzvinka and Bohdana Matiiash, although employ different literary genres (prose versus poetry, respectively), both explore the philosophically inexhaustible themes of life and death, love and God, mourning and forgiveness, focusing especially on the connection between the human and the spiritual. Finally, Svitlana Povaliaieva in her dense and stream-of-consciousness narratives exhumes the city's youth margins, revealing in the process the remarkably egalitarian and equitable world of drug addicts, a world in which gender relations appear irrelevant.

These four female authors could not possibly offer more distinct or differing styles, yet what connects them all is their irresistible desire to establish in their works boundaries of well-defined spatial constructs, or alternative worlds of sorts, that can act as safe havens. Invariably, in each case we are dealing with some kind of an escape or a movement toward a space (be it a particular place, God or drug-induced deliriums) that alleviates protagonists' anxiety and brings them solace. In all four writers the passage from one state of being into another is always accompanied by a certain casualness, as if they want to convince the reader that nothing is more natural than to turn into a vampire, or to converse with God, or to actually die. Pahutiak's insistence on the ever-entrenched Manichean struggle between evil and good comes in sharp contrast to all embracing love of Christian agape kind put forth by the Matiiash sisters on one hand, and Povaliaieva's Buddhist questioning of the ego, on the other.

Halyna Pahutiak's Magic Realism

Born in the Drohobych region of Western Ukraine, Halyna Pahutiak is the prolific author of short stories, novels, young adult fiction and essays, best known for incorporating in her fiction mythic, dreamlike and fantastical elements, and popularizing the world of vampires, based on the local mythology. In one of her interviews she states: "I want everyone to know that in this gray everydayness there are many doors leading to different worlds."[67] And her works indeed show the path to alternative realities, at the same time embracing and relying on historical facts.

Pahutiak graduated from the Taras Shevchenko National University of Kyiv with a degree in Ukrainian philology but returned back to her hometown and eventually settled in Lviv. Her parents moved from the village of her birth, Zalokot in Lviv oblast, to Urizh when she was still a little child, a place that she later often thematized in her prose.[68] Urizh happens to be situated near the village of Nahuievychi, Ivan Franko's birthplace, and there is no question that Pahutiak feels certain affinity with the oeuvre of the most important author of Western Ukraine, who was active in the fin de siècle era and in the first decade of the twentieth century, and whose ethnographic study on the actual incident of burning vampires in his native Nahuievychi in 1831 became the source of inspiration for her novel *The Urizh Gothic* (2009).[69] In that particular work Pahutiak's vampires are reluctant to use their special powers, and they too, not unlike humans, can be of good or evil dispositions.

But it is her award-winning novel *The Servant of Dobromyl* (2006) that brought Pahutiak widespread recognition. The novel juggles multiple planes of reality and, thanks to the introduction of the immortal realm of vampires, presents its protagonists against the background of almost eight centuries of Ukrainian history. Interweaving real historical figures and events (and their mere selection already implicates the author in the process of national identity formation) with fantastic attributes (vampires) allows Pahutiak to add her voice to the overall national mythmaking. Indeed, *The Servant of Dobromyl* constitutes a new phase in the author's writing in the sense that she devotes equal attention to time and space. Pahutiak's earlier tendency to divorce her spatial constructs—be they concrete places or imaginary havens (or, as Hundorova puts it, "virgin lands"[70])—from any reference to time frame made her oeuvre fairly abstract and deliberately philosophical in nature. That is especially true in such works as *Notes of a White Little Bird* (*Zapysky biloho ptashka*, 1999) and *Scribe of the Eastern Gates Refuge* (*Pysar Skhidnykh Vorit Prytulku*, 2003), where the story lines unfold in imaginary places and mythic reality, thus making time a somewhat redundant category. *The Servant of Dobromyl* lacks such abstractness—all events happen not only within a recognizable historical period but also have concrete dates assigned to them. In terms of place, as the novel's title itself suggests, the plot evolves in and around the real town of Dobromyl in the Lviv vicinity and expands further to cover the whole of Halychyna region.

The story line of *The Servant of Dobromyl* begins in the fall of 1939 in the Lavriv monastery, shortly after the onset of World War II. Ukrainian monks anxiously await the arrival of the Soviet Army, which invaded and annexed the Galician territories of eastern Poland on September 17 as a result of the Molotov-Ribbentrop Pact signed between Nazi Germany and the Soviet Union on August 23, 1939. An elderly monk convinces the young novice Ilko to flee to Lublin in Poland, and the remaining monks, knowing that they all will be killed, in haste manage to hide many valuable old books that are in the monastery's possession. The story then moves forward in time, to 1949, and we see that another monastery, the one in Dobromyl, has been converted to a psychiatric ward by the Soviet authorities and placed under the management of a young psychiatrist Oleksii Ivanovych. Among his patients is a man who calls himself the Servant of Dobromyl and claims to be born in 1287 out of wedlock of a witch and her dead husband. Children who come out of such unions are endowed with special powers and can use them to perform either good or evil deeds. The Servant of Dobromyl becomes a good vampire. His mission in 1949 is to help a young Ukrainian resistance fighter Ilko, wounded in battle with the Soviets. This Ilko is the same novice that escaped from the Lavriv monastery in 1939 but rather than to become a monk in Lublin he fell in love with a local girl and became involved, like her, in the Ukrainian underground resistance movement (UPA), fighting the Soviets well after the war ended. Thanks to the Servant's magic ability to put everyone to sleep in his proximity by playing his flute, he takes Oleksii Ivanovych to a hideout to treat Ilko of his injury. The psychiatrist reluctantly agrees and while Ilko is recuperating and all are asleep, the Servant of Dobromyl tells the doctor the story of his life.

By placing the action of her novel in a psychiatric ward, Pahutiak adds another layer of ambiguity, yet at the same time creates circumstances, which can rationally explain the presence of fantastic elements—after all, mentally ill patients can come up with all kinds of stories. But such an explanation does not do justice to the novel's import. What is significant here is that incorporating magic plot lines provides the writer's with the right tools to connect different planes of reality simultaneously, revealing in the process the deeper substance of the narrative. For *The Servant of Dobromyl* is a novel about finding one's destiny, both on an individual and collective level. And finding the right path, according to Pahutiak, is only possible when one comes to grips with one's own identity. Ilko, for example, becomes an UPA fighter rather than a monk, quite consciously sacrificing his life for Ukraine's liberation. The Servant of Dobromyl, on the other hand, supposedly serves the Merchant of Dobromyl (also a vampire) but, in fact, throughout many generations his main concern has been the well-being of Ukraine (synecdochically represented in the text by the town of Dobromyl) and protecting its destiny from the evil vampire (empire), embodied toward the end of the novel by an NKVD captain, who is no other than simultaneously the Russian Tsar's and eventually the Soviet Union's loyal servant. Liberated Ukraine is nowhere on the horizon in 1949 but by framing the struggle in such Manichean terms, the author implicitly suggests that the good will prevail in the end.

This plot no doubt betrays ideological underpinnings but, by being so thoroughly immersed in the technique of magic realism, it nonetheless exudes the sense of the marvelous and the mystical, even though it is so utterly rooted in history. First, the author dispenses with linear time structure and avoids a clear-cut ending, thus preserving the overall mystery, and second, although her underlying ideological sympathies are not that difficult to decipher, she also strives to reveal the connectedness of all things, however uncanny they might be, exposing again and again her ingrained philosophical bias. But, as Konstiantyn Rodyk aptly observes, in *The Servant of Dobromyl*, Pahutiak moves away from a reflective mode of narration of her earlier works to a more readily suspenseful and action-packed emplotment, thereby making her prose considerably more popular and accessible to the average reader.[71] Finally, the writer seemingly dabbles in metafiction when at the end of the novel she implies that the whole story related by the Servant (employing first-person narration) might be actually written down by no other than the psychiatrist

Oleksii Ivanovych himself. And that strategy, I would argue, elevates the importance of ideas at the expense of the novel's characters who in the end clearly morph into the servants of history, or, more accurately, become carriers of national mythology, as envisioned by Pahutiak.

Metaphysics of Two Sisters

Dzvinka Matiiash (b. 1978) excels in engendering meditative, stream-of-consciousness narratives that mysteriously combine seemingly incompatible realities. On the one hand, we see her protagonists deeply rooted in everyday existence, on the other—they all long to transcend the physical world and move closer to God. Her two books of prose *A Requiem for November* (*Rekviiem dlia lystopadu*, 2005) and *A Novel about Fatherland* (*Roman pro bat'kivshchynu*, 2006) offer the writer's reflections on death, love, family and everyday existence.

In *A Requiem for November*, dedicated to the memory of the author's mother, she reflects: "One should not fear death. Perhaps death is just a dream in God's palms, so Daryna no longer worries for those who passed away, including her mother."[72] *Requiem*'s main protagonist Daryna loves walking on the streets of her city, observing people's lives and meditating on the flow of time. Matiiash preserves the reality of things (there is by design no magic or fantasy in her texts, although dreamlike states abound) but avoids ascribing to them the concreteness of a specific locality or situation. There are also clear signs of autobiographical elements in this work but they unfold with a considerable dose of detachment and free of a confessional bias. One can surmise that for Daryna, like for the author herself, things observed become secondary to the act of mourning after her mother. Or, to put it differently, a detached observation becomes a way to cope with death. And while the writer does not reveal any details about how her (or Daryna's) mother's passing came about, one can get some clue from the rather pronounced focus on women's breasts, including her reflections on mastectomy:

> Women with breasts cut off worry a lot if their husbands would still love them as before. Wouldn't they become lesser women? Would their husbands still want to kiss their scars? Wouldn't they now feel disgusted? And what will now happen in bed? Perhaps nothing at all, for when you want to feel hands on your breasts, and breasts are no longer there? Women feel pain in their breasts that are no more.[73]

Despite this focus on the female body and its image from the angle of the male gaze, Dzvinka Matiiash does not really dwell too much on gender relations. Hers is a world of deep-seated existential concerns that go way beyond standard feminist issues of discrimination, equality or oppression. Her prose is more about the understanding of what lies behind the everydayness of things, why in our existence "the door opens and closes,"[74] as she puts it, but life still goes on. It is also about the process of writing and its reception and, finally, about a compelling desire to be heard (or read) by God, because He alone, as Dzvinka theorizes, is the most attentive reader.

Communicating with God becomes even more pronounced in Dzvinka's second book *A Novel about Fatherland*. Here, amid the narrator's reminiscences about her father and grandmother (kin relations are always implicated in Matiiash's texts), we have many direct invocations to God, at times emulating regular prayers, at others—reading like poems. The title of the book, indicating that it is a novel about a fatherland, might be somewhat misleading because this slight volume is anything but the author's rumination on her country. True, early on in the text Dzvinka provides a poetic, roundabout explanation of what fatherland means to her. For example, she says that among other things fatherland, *"is when the door to your home is not locked; I come in and need not look for a key, I step over the threshold and close my eyes because it smells as it always has, smells never change, they do not get old like people."*[75] But, *A Novel about Fatherland* is for the most part a novel about the heroine's metaphysical longing while she copes with everyday existence, still wanting ordinary things from life, still wanting to love and to be loved, wanting to communicate with her deceased mother, writing letters to her and reflecting on old age. To Dzvinka—life is the most mysterious in its ordinariness.

Dzvinka's younger sister Bohdana Matiiash (b. 1982) expresses poetically similar concerns and even has a collection titled *Conversations with God* (*Rozmovy z Bohom*, 2007). However, she is more abstract, if not more philosophical in her poems, and makes considerably fewer references to her family than her older sister (though Bohdana's first collection *Unrevealed Pictures* (*Neproiavleni znimky*, 2005) is dedicated to the memory of her mother as was the case with Dzvinka's first book). Clearly, both sisters were profoundly affected by their mother's untimely death and, possibly, their dwelling on metaphysics has its provenance in that traumatic event. But Bohdana is no doubt more circumspect than her sister about expressing her feelings about it overtly.

Thematically and formally, her first collection shows a versatile poet who offers a number of beautifully crafted poems about women, ars poetica, and life in the city, but it is her second volume, *Conversations with God*, that presents a remarkably mature poetic voice at a relatively young age. These predominantly long elegiac poems about establishing communication channels with God, though monothematic, reveal a lyrical heroine whose inquisitive personality and monologic acumen truly hypnotizes. Bohdana's conversations with God constitute an unstoppable flow of words, without any pause, as if in one breath. She asks complicated questions, yet knows that such inquiries cannot be answered. But she begs for enlightenment nonetheless:

21 (64)
every pain if you wished it my Lord could turn to joy
when the world falls asleep and when I cannot distinguish your features
I think how joy feels to the touch what color it is and how it smells
I think how the human smile is born and how it dissolves just tell me
why it dissolves my God why can't it disperse across a sky like a
seven-colored rainbow or spill forth in the chirping of birds it would be
so nice my God so endlessly happy so transparent you know sometimes
I think you created this world with amazing joy and then I get so
sad that among your mountains and rivers birds and animals fish and bugs
trees and grass there is so much pain that day and night and morning
and evening are filled with it and it shows up even in the sweetest embrace
I think of those who are grieving and those who are rejoicing and those
who are dying and those who are being born those who are giving
and those who are accepting you know their slightest move each thought
each breath from first to last and also you know how overwhelmingly
and sharply I now feel every joy and how I live every loss and how I
suffocate among false things and how few real ones I have how I am
afraid to do harm and afraid to hug because to hug is sometimes the same
as to harm teach me my God to turn all these pains to joys if you teach me
I will almost not want anything I will almost not ask for anything
I will almost not need anything if only you will wish this my Lord[76]

However, what is particularly striking about Bohdana's version of God is how thoroughly traditionally envisioned he is. He assumes the role of all-knowing and loving father figure whose presence is coveted by a lyrical heroine because that provides her with a sense of security and belonging, and with a feeling of being anchored, thereby endowing her with a well-defined identity. Bohdana's God "says good day my child he says / that he will always call me his child even when I am over eighty."[77]

For both sisters finding a way to simply be, to exist, brings them solace and catharsis of sorts. Their metaphysical bias is not just a mode of expressing their creative energies, but constitutes a determinative factor of their sense of identity. Turning to a higher Being allows them to cope with pain and suffering but also shows them the way out, recognizing that this is the nature of all forms to emerge and disappear, so succinctly put by Dzvinka by her metaphor of opening and closing doors. It is rather remarkable that two sisters would produce works that complement each other both in themes and moods to such an extent. Their oeuvre is unmistakably feminine in tone but concerns they are raising and their attitude toward them go beyond feminist and postfeminist rhetoric.

Svitlana Povaliaieva's Poetics of Liminality

While Halyna Pahutiak finds her niche in fantasy and myth, and sisters Matiiash in metaphysics, Svitlana Povaliaieva (b. 1974) seeks more down-to-earth ways of situating her protagonists. She prefers settings that are placed in temporally and geographically well-defined frames. Her novels deal largely with young adults, often students, coming of age in urban milieus, mainly in Kyiv, in the economically difficult decade of the 1990s, and who encounter unprecedented personal freedom after the collapse of the Soviet Union but use it to indulge themselves in substance abuse and sex, happily embracing hippie existence, many a time emulating behaviors of their Western idols in rock and pop music. In that sense her work, especially her first two novels *The Exhumation of the City* (*Ekshumatsiia mista*, 2003) and *Instead of Blood* (*Zamist' krovi*, 2003), resonates greatly with Serhiy Zhadan's novel about the Kharkiv youth in *Depeche Mode*, however, unlike Zhadan, Povaliaieva more consistently embraces social fringes as a recurrent theme in her prose.

Born and raised in Kyiv, Povaliaieva works as a TV journalist and has some half a dozen books of fiction to her credit. Her prose is dense, poetic, polyglot and rough both in terms of language—curses and obscenities abound, and issues employed. Her novels thematize heterosexual relationships among drug addicts that are completely devoid of any gendered power struggle. In fact, she even occasionally introduces a male first-person narrator like in her novel *Instead of Blood*, as if wanting to transcend common parallels drawn between authors and narrators. Povaliaieva's protagonists, young women and men, not only share needles, sex, dwelling and food, but also each other. There is a surprising degree of empathy developed among them regardless of what gender they belong to. And if there is any male abuse at all, it is often a female protagonist who provokes it, and then we invariably must see a female in the role of an abuser, as if the author makes a special effort to underscore the fact that abuse is really gender neutral and can go either way. Perhaps that is why it does not really matter if Povaliaieva's narrator assumes male or female identities. In her third novel *Origami-Blues* (*Origami-bliuz*, 2005), for instance, the main protagonist Mriia invites her boyfriend Flesh to hit her because she wants to see how he would manage to strike a woman. He does as commanded but afterward immediately feels guilty and begs her for forgiveness. Then in another scene it is Mriia who kicks Flesh without any mercy after he falls drunk on the sidewalk. Thus, contrary to common perceptions, Povaliaieva apparently insists that abuse is not a function of innate gendered predisposition but rather a function of character or induced by substance intoxication.

What we find in Povaliaieva that is missing in Pahutiak's or sisters Matiiash's texts are numerous references to Ukraine's current affairs. As I already mentioned, the author situates her plots predominantly in contemporary Kyiv, and events of such magnitude as the presidential elections of 2004 and the Orange Revolution are referenced in her 2006 novel *Simurg*, as are her views on such diverse subjects as Ukraine's potential membership in NATO, or the Orthodox Church of Moscow Patriarchate's influence on Ukrainian society, mentioned in her 2009 novel *Bardo Online*. Moreover, Povaliaieva also invokes in her works well-known newspapers (e.g., *Dzerkalo tyzhnia*) or names of national and private companies (e.g., Naftohaz and RosUkrEnergo), thereby lending her prose decisively activist overtones and endowing her protagonists with an unmistakably nationalist bias.

What unites Povaliaieva with the other three authors discussed here is her conspicuous focus on death. However, unlike Pahutiak's or sisters Matiiash's treatments, Povaliaieva's thematization of death comes mostly as a result of her characters' substance abuse. Her protagonists often die young because of drug overdose, or, possibly, because of their uncontrollable desire for self-destruction. To be annihilated, to be no more, becomes perversely attractive.[78] Yet, there is also a more mystical side to death, as Povaliaieva further contends in the very same novel. For death, as her heroine Mriia finds out, facilitates the "desire to merge with the harmony of all surroundings."[79] The altered, liminal, states of consciousness (regardless whether mystical or drug-induced) create an opening of sorts to help transcend intractable hurdles of everyday existence.

One can speculate that the coming-of-age in the 1990s generation, as Povaliaieva so consistently depicts it, being constantly on edge and often bordering on self-destruction, entails and simultaneously symbolizes the very transitionality experienced by a young state—Ukraine. The liminality of growing up applies equally to youth as it does to countries. In that sense, the persistent metaphor of the door in various configurations—opening or closing, difficult to find[80] or leading to alternative worlds—present in all four authors can readily signify choice(s) faced not only by their fictional characters but also by the political elites of all-too-real independent Ukraine.

NOTES

1. See his "Emerging Ukrainian Women Prose Writers: Twenty Years After Independence," *WLT* (November–December 2011), accessed October 27, 2011, http://www.ou.edu/worldlit/11_2011/essay-naydan.html.

2. From Oksana Zabuzhko's interview, conducted by Alexandra Hrycak and Maria G. Rewakowicz in June 2008, excerpts of which were subsequently utilized in their article "Feminism, intellectuals and the formation of micro-publics in postcommunist Ukraine," *Studies in East European Thought* 61 (2009): 327.

3. See Tatiana Zhurzhenko, "Feminist (De)Constructions of Nationalism in the Post-Soviet Space," in *Mapping Difference: The Many Faces of Women in Contemporary Ukraine*, ed. Marian J. Rubchak (New York: Berghahn Books, 2011), 175; 180–81.

4. Cf. the section on Technologies in *Feminisms*, ed. Sandra Kemp and Judith Squires (Oxford: Oxford University Press, 1997).

5. See Donna Haraway's "A Manifesto for Cyborgs: Science, Technology, and Socialist Feminisms in the 1980s," in *Feminisms*, 427.

6. The same is true of her last book *Selected Poems, 1980–2013* (*Vybrani virshi 1980–2013*) published in 2013.

7. Uilleam Blacker, "Nation, Body, Home: Gender and National Identity in the Work of Oksana Zabuzhko," *Modern Language Review* 105.2 (2010): 487.

8. Zhurzhenko, "Feminist (De)Constructions of Nationalism," 174–78.

9. Andrew Wachtel, *Remaining Relevant After Communism: The Role of the Writer in Eastern Europe* (Chicago: Chicago University Press, 2006), 113.

10. Zabuzhko, *Khroniky vid Fortinbrasa: vybrana eseistyka 90-x* (Kyiv: Fakt, 2001), 164.

11. Hrycak and Rewakowicz, "Feminists, intellectuals," 326.

12. Maryna Romanets, *Anamorphosic Texts and Reconfigured Visions: Improvised Traditions in Contemporary Ukrainian and Irish Literature* (Stuttgart: ibidem-Verlag, 2007), 106.

13. Oksana Zabuzhko, *Fieldwork in Ukrainian Sex*, trans. Halyna Hryn (Las Vegas: Amazon Crossing, 2011), 158.

14. The Battle of Kruty took place on January 29, 1918, near Kruty railway station (Chernihiv oblast), about 130 kilometers northeast of Kyiv, which took the lives of several hundred Ukrainian military cadets and students who fought to stop the Bolshevist army of Russian Lieutenant General Nikolai Muravyov from advancing on Kyiv.

15. Zabuzhko, *Fieldwork*, 74.

16. Ibid., 36–37.

17. See her *Filosofiia ukrains'koi idei ta ievropeis'kyi kontekst: Frankivs'kyi period* (The Philosophy of the Ukrainian Idea and the European Context: The Franko Period, 1992) and *Shevchenkiv mif Ukrainy: Sproba filosofs'koho analizu* (Shevchenko's Myth of Ukraine: An Attempt at a Philosophical Analysis, 1997).

18. Hrycak and Rewakowicz, "Feminists, intellectuals," 330.

19. For example, she stayed with and cared for a man she loved, Serhii Merzhynsky, despite the fact that they were not married and that he was in love with another woman at the time.

20. See Yevheniia Kononenko's "Heroine or Bad Girl?" in her *Heroini ta heroi* (Kyiv: Hrani-T, 2010), 96–103.

21. Stepan Bandera (1909–1959), a Ukrainian politician and leader of the nationalist movement in Western Ukraine, assassinated by the KGB agent in Munich after the war, remains a controversial figure in Ukrainian politics to this day. In

January 2010, the outgoing president of Ukraine Viktor Yushchenko, awarded him posthumously the title of Hero of Ukraine, which was revoked by President Viktor Yanukovych a year later. Bandera's activity has been variedly assessed, from praise to condemnation. The publication of Zabuzhko's novel coincided with this political controversy.

22. Zabuzhko, *The Museum of Abandoned Secrets*, trans. Nina Shevchuk-Murray (Las Vegas: Amazon Crossing, 2012), 429.

23. Ibid., 430.

24. Blacker, "Nation, Body, Home," 501.

25. That was also noticed by Blacker: "… while Zabuzhko is generally regarded as a pioneer of feminism in Ukraine, in actual fact her work displays an ambiguous attitude toward feminist ideas, precisely because of its cultural agenda. The attitude of the narrator of *Pol'ovi doslidzhennia* to feminism is distanced, mistrustful and even scornful, and she sees both men and the role of wife and mother as necessarily desirable to women" (Ibid., 492).

26. In addition to the mentioned novel, she also published a collection of short stories *Without Blushing* (*Ne chervoniiuchy*, 2007), a poetry collection *I Listen to the Song of America* (*Ia slukhaiu pisniu ameryky*, 2010), and more recently another novel *Love Life* (*Liubovne zhyttia*, 2015).

27. Marianna Kiianovs'ka, *Mifotvorennia: Poezii* (Kyiv: Smoloskyp, 2000), 29.

28. Kiianovs'ka, *Zvychaina mova* (Kyiv: Fakt, 2005), 60.

29. Mar'iana Savka, *Hirka Mandrahora* (Lviv: Vydavnytstvo Staroho Leva, 2002), 71.

30. On the site of Poetry International Rotterdam where Kruk's poems in English translation are posted her last name is spelled Krouk.

31. This and other excerpts by Kruk, quoted here, unless indicated otherwise, are in Olena Jennings's rendition, reprinted by permission. The translation posted online on the site of Poetry International Rotterdam: http://www.poetryinternationalweb.net/pi/site/poem/item/5556/auto/POETS-DONT-HAVE-GENDER, accessed September 30, 2013.

32. Halyna Kruk, *Oblychchia poza svitlynoiu* (Kyiv: Fakt, 2005), 118.

33. See http://www.poetryinternationalweb.net/pi/site/poem/item/5564/auto/0/THE-WOMAN-CUTS-INTO-HER-VEINS, accessed September 30, 2013.

34. Kruk, *Oblychchia poza svitlynoiu*, 126. My own translation.

35. Liudmyla Taran, *Kolektsiia kokhanok* (Lviv: Kal'variia, 2002), 36.

36. This bias is especially evident in critical writings by Liudmyla Taran. See her "Obzhyty vnutrishnii prostir: Do problemy avtobiohrafizmu v suchasnii ukrains'kii prozi zhinok-avtoriv," *Kur'ier Kryvbasu* 6 (2005): 222–28 and "Buty samii sobi tsilliu: Do pytannia pro avtobiohrafizm suchasnoi zhinochoi prozy," *Suchasnist'* 3 (2006): 139–55. See also Nila Zborovska, "Feministychnyi tryptykh Ievhenii Kononenko v konteksti zahal'noukrains'koi tematyky," *Slovo i chas* 6 (2005): 57–73.

37. Felski, *Beyond Feminist Aesthetics*, 93.

38. This is made especially clear in her polemical exchange with George G. Grabowicz in *Krytyka* 2.12 (1998): 26–30.

39. Zborovska herself underscores this aspect of the novel: "We have here a striking example, unknown until now, of a surprisingly open female confession" (*Feministychni rozdumy*, 116).

40. See Halyna Hryn, "A Conversation with Oksana Zabuzhko," *Agni* 53 (2001), accessed September 28, 2013, http://www.bu.edu/agni/interviews/print/2001/zabu-zhko-hryn.html.

41. Romanets, *Anamorphosic Texts*, 108.

42. Zabuzhko, *Fieldwork*, 76.

43. Ibid., 85.

44. Pyrkalo has been more forthcoming about her personal life in London with her American husband Darrell in her book of short essays on love of cooking titled *Egoist's Kitchen* (*Kukhnia ehoista*, 2007). Interestingly, in her trademark offhand fashion the writer not only provides recipes and shares with the reader her learning about various cuisines but also comments on a variety of topics, from the traumatic historical episodes such as the *Holodomor* to current affairs in Ukraine and Europe.

45. See her "Mizh namy, zhinkamy ... Rozmova Liudmyly Taran z Ievheniieiu Kononenko," *Kur'ier Kryvbasu* 2 (2006): 150.

46. *Hotel' Tsentral'* 59. This poem was originally included in Bilotserkivets's collection *Lystopad*, published in 1989.

47. Translated by Michael M. Naydan. Available online: http://www.poetryinternationalweb.net/pi/site/poem/item/8086/auto/0/To-remain-at-the-Dominican-school-near-Vienna-forever, accessed May 29, 2014. Included with permission.

48. One of the subjects that is not readily thematized in women's belles-lettres but surfaces in essays and travelogues is the issue of Ukrainian migrant female workers in the European Union. Pyrkalo, for example, depicts her encounters with such women in Italy in her book *Kukhnia ehoista* (53–55), and Liudmyla Taran in her *Liubovni mandrivky* (Love Journeys, 2007) relates about a similar meeting with Ukrainian migrant workers while visiting Portugal (223–28).

49. Natalka Sniadanko, *Kolektsiia prystrastei, abo pryhody molodoi ukrainky* (Kharkiv: Folio, 2004), 117–18.

50. Published in her *50 khvylyn travy (koly pomre tvoia krasa)*.

51. Irena Karpa, *50 khvylyn travy: koly pomre tvoia krasa* (Kharkiv: Folio, 2004), 224. The capitalization is Karpa's own.

52. Ibid., 231.

53. See Ola Hnatiuk, "Nativists vs. Westernizers: Problems of Cultural Identity in Ukrainian Literature of the 1990s," *Slavic and East European Journal* 50 (2006): 434–51.

54. One such reaction is the conceptualization of postfeminism as an ongoing engineering process promoted most vigorously by the political right and aided by the corporate media. Postfeminism is crucial to the latter because they so heavily rely on advertising.

55. Angela McRobbie, "Post-Feminism and Popular Culture," *Feminist Media Studies* 4.3 (2004): 258.

56. Karpa, for example, turned activist under the Yanukovych presidency by regularly writing columns in the Internet newspaper *Ukrains'ka pravda*, participating in various political actions, like in a rally in defense of the Ukrainian language before the building of Verkhovna Rada in 2010, or by paroding the political regime with a lollipop bearing an image of Ukrainian President Viktor Yanukovych on TV's "Shuster Live" political talk show in 2011.

57. For example, the first-person male narrators are found both in Andrukhovych and Maliarchuk.

58. This title is in English in the original.

59. She split with Hansen in 2014.

60. Both were republished under one cover in 2008 by Lileia-NV in Ivano-Frankivsk. The reprinted book assumed the title of the second novella *Stari liudy*.

61. Incidentally, the book's cover depicts the cut salmon that resembles female genitalia.

62. McRobbie, "Post-Feminism," 261.

63. Ibid.

64. Her most recent novel *Oblivion* (*Zabuttia*, 2016) won the 2016 BBC Prize for Ukrainian literature.

65. In her 2011 interview Maliarchuk declared little interest in autobiographical narratives, although does not deny that an author's individual experience shapes his/her way of artistic expression. See her "Piznaiu vpovni prynady immihrantstva" at: http://litakcent.com/2011/11/25/tanja-maljarchuk-piznaju-vpovni-prynady-immi-hrantstva/, accessed October 6, 2013.

66. Oleh Kotsarev, "Tania Maliarchuk: Literaturoiu maibutn'oho stanut' maliunky iedynorohiv na skeliakh" Available online: http://ukrlit.blog.net.ua/2007/05/22/tanya-malyarchuk-literaturoyu-majbutnoho-stanut-malyunky-jedynorohiv-na-skelyah/, accessed October 6, 2013.

67. Halyna Pahutiak, "Nasha literatura skhozha na khvoroho, shcho rozuchyvsia rukhatysia," *Sumno*, March 23, 2008, accessed October 10, 2013. http://sumno.com/article/galyna-pagutyak-nasha-literatura-shozha-na-hvorogo/.

68. See especially her collection of short stories and novellas titled *Zakhid sontsia v Urozhi* (Sunset in Urizh, 2003; 2nd ed. 2007) and novel *Uriz'ka hotyka* (The Urizh Gothic, 2009).

69. This information is taken from the Forward written by the editor Oleksandra Chaus. She cites Franko's essay "Spalennia opyriv u seli Nahuievychakh u 1831 rotsi" published in the book *Ukraintsi: narodni viruvannia, povir'ia, demonolohiia* (Kyiv: Lybid', 1991) (*Uriz'ka hotyka* 5).

70. Hundorova, *Pisliachornobyl's'ka biblioteka*, 135.

71. Kostiantyn Rodyk, "Halyna Pahutiak: perevantazhennia," *Ukraina moloda*, May 11, 2011, accessed October 6, 2013, http://www.umoloda.kiev.ua/print/84/45/66727.

72. Dzvinka Matiiash, *Rekviiem dlia lystopadu*, 2nd rev. ed. (Kyiv: Fakt, 2007), 7.

73. Ibid., 60.

74. Ibid., 140.

75. Dzvinka Matiiash, *Roman pro bat'kivshchynu* (Kyiv: Fakt, 2006), 17. Italics are in the original.

76. Bohdana Matiiash, "21 (64)," trans. Oksana Lutsyshyna, *Ukrainian Literature: A Journal of Translations* 3 (2011), accessed October 13, 2013, http://sites.utoronto.ca/elul/Ukr_Lit/Vol03/04-Matiash-Lutsyshyna.pdf. Reprinted by permission.

77. Matiiash, *Rozmovy z Bohom* (Lviv: Vydavnytstvo Staroho Leva, 2007), 12.

78. See her *Origami-bliuz* (Kharkiv: Folio, 2007), 60.

79. Ibid., 99.

80. Povaliaieva, for example, ruminates: "I move along the walls and cannot find the door. I can't remember how to get out of here." See her *Bardo Online* (Kharkiv: Folio, 2009), 223.

Chapter 4

Language Choice and
Language as Protagonist

The political and social strategies employed by the successive post-Soviet governments in Ukraine appear to privilege the plurality and hybridity of national and cultural identities. In the post-independence period, especially during the first two decades, the language issue continued to stir passions and seemed to be a divisive tool in the hands of politicians manipulating the electorate in hopes of winning extra votes in parliamentary and/or presidential elections. Thus far Ukrainian remains the only official state language (a constitutional guarantee since 1996)[1] and yet, as many have argued, the status of the Ukrainian language has not been visibly improved since independence.[2] Many visitors to Ukraine have to concede that the Russian language represents the preferred means of communication, with the sole exception of Western Ukraine (Halychyna) where Ukrainian dominates. However, the correlation between ethnic and linguistic identities is not always straightforward.[3] By and large, it coincides in the case of ethnic Russians. However, in the case of some ethnic Ukrainians, Ukrainian does not necessarily constitute their native language. In other words, the Russian ethnic minority, that is minority according to official statistics, does not appear to be a true minority if gauged only by linguistic practice. Volodymyr Kulyk sums up this as follows: "In Ukraine, ... language identity is embodied in the concept of native language that was imposed by the Soviet institutionalisation of ethnicity and came to mean ethnic belonging as much as linguistic practice."[4] In other words, he contends that the linguistic diversity of Ukrainian society should be measured both in terms of language identity and language use for they do not always overlap.

It goes without saying that the language situation in Ukraine, which, to be fair, is not unlike that of any other former colonies whereby there is a visible discrepancy between language practices and ethno-cultural identities, has direct implications for the development of the post-independence literature. For those writers who want to express themselves in Ukrainian this situation is problematical because it invariably affects their pool of potential readers. On the other hand, there is also a large group of writers expressing themselves exclusively in Russian who nonetheless, by citizenship, are Ukrainian, and who too feel often marginalized, without critical resonance and, perhaps, in their minds not nurtured enough by the former metropolis. The dilemma, which up to now has not become a "hot issue" but which might in the future, depending which way linguistic self-identification of the majority of the population goes, is how one arrives at some kind of agreement as to what is or will be the body of texts that can be considered a national literature: will it be literature written only in Ukrainian or literature written by Ukrainian citizens regardless of what language is being used.[5]

This chapter will focus on two opposing ends of the language spectrum as practiced in contemporary belles-lettres: on the one hand, I will discuss a handful of Ukrainian Russophone writers, on the other—authors for whom the Ukrainian language constitutes the essence of their artistic identity and itself becomes a hero of sorts. In between these two extremes lies a vast majority that uses variants of language(s) for stylistic purposes, employing as many linguistic devices as creatively justified—from *surzhyk* to various dialects, from standard Ukrainian to other foreign languages—with Russian and English being the two most prevalent ones.

UKRAINIAN RUSSOPHONE WRITERS

In his informative article "Children of a Soviet Widow" ("Dity radianskoi vdovy"), Ihor Kruchyk analyzes the situation of Russophone authors in Ukraine shortly before and after independence (focusing mostly on poets) and makes an interesting claim—independent Ukraine has allowed them to thrive artistically more so than the previous Soviet regime.[6] His assertion is backed up by some publishing statistics that shows a considerable increase in a number of Russian language publishing houses, literary magazines and various anthologies being issued on the territory of Ukraine since 1991. Kruchyk also reminds the reader that the literary elite of the Soviet Union, almost exclusively centered in Moscow, was never really interested in supporting its Russophone colleagues in the provinces.[7] Hence, whoever had an ambition to proverbially "make it" as an all-union writer, was forced to seek his/her position among the literary circles in Moscow.[8] With the collapse of the Soviet Union and the disappearance of censorship such cultural and political orientation toward the metropolis has been in steady decline, though many authors still look up to Moscow as an ultimate gauge of value and success.[9] More importantly, however, evaluating the situation of Russophone writers since independence, Kruchyk comes to the conclusion that their biggest concern is how to tackle the issue of self-identification because sooner or later their living in Ukraine, regardless of language chosen for artistic expression, compels them to make a decision whether to be part of the Ukrainian or Russian spheres of culture.[10] In a few cases, authors indeed try to assert themselves in both realms simultaneously but such a situation is not easily maintained in the long run, as the example of a spousal team of Russophone Ukrainian co-authors of fantasy literature, Maryna and Serhiy Diachenko, has revealed.[11] As Marco Puleri rightly observes in his insightful article on Russophone authors in Ukraine: "We are dealing with a genuinely hybrid phenomenon that grows out of the passage from Soviet domination to national independence and produces a narrative of displacement."[12]

The authors analyzed in this section—Andrey Kurkov, the Diachenkos and Lada Luzina—all function (or functioned) within the Ukrainian cultural space, although some more decisively than others (for instance Kurkov), and all have attained a high degree of popularity in their respective genres both at home and abroad. One significant factor that affects their overall sense of belonging, I contend, is their choice of a publisher. Both Kurkov and Luzina are firmly rooted in Ukraine in this respect,[13] whereas the Diachenkos early on began to rely on Russian publishing houses instead.[14] True, most of their books have been translated into Ukrainian and published (often simultaneously) in Ukraine by a number of well-respected houses but, apparently, the Diachenkos' main bet on the readership has been placed in the Russian Federation—prompting them in the end to move there for good.

The crucial question faced by authors expressing themselves in the language of the former metropolis is whether they want to consider themselves Russian or Russophone writers—if the latter, then, it seems, they can embrace their hybrid identity more readily and easily than those who aspire to see themselves as part of the Russian cultural space. The question faced by Ukrainian literary institutions, on the other hand, is whether or not such Russophone writers deserve their place in the national canon. During the first two decades of independence this dilemma had not yet found its resolution and the struggle with self-identification issues continues to stir Russophone literary circles.

Andrey Kurkov as Ukrainian Writer

The figure of Andrey Kurkov, I argue, is central to the debate about what constitutes a national literature in independent Ukraine and how to reach a consensus about criteria to be adopted in such considerations. This is so not only because of his commercial success in the West (mainly in Western

Europe) but also because of his clearly defined position as to who he is as a writer and what national identity he assumes. He conveys his identity directly or through his protagonists; the main hero of the novel *Penguin Lost*, when asked who he is, says: "Ukrainian of Russian parents."[15] As a public figure Kurkov is forcing the issue. He has engendered an important discursive space around his oeuvre vis-à-vis identity politics, a space that simply cannot be ignored in contemporary literary quarters in Ukraine. And even though the question of national literature with regard to new Ukrainian literature at this juncture is still somewhat academic,[16] it becomes more and more visible and current because of Kurkov's stand and vocal statements. In the West he identifies himself as a Ukrainian writer who writes in Russian, because Russian happens to be his mother (native) tongue. However, as I already indicated in Chapter 2, he is also fluent in Ukrainian and consistently uses the official state language in public, whether communicating with his Ukrainian literati peers or in interviews with Ukrainian journalists. And it is not without significance that he likes to emphasize that his mentality is Ukrainian (see his interview with Bohdan Tsiupyn).

Such statements, given at various times and on various occasions, leave very little doubt that Kurkov has a keen interest in fashioning the image of his literary persona in a certain way. He does not belong to those writers who guard their private life and do not like to share personal details. To the contrary, Kurkov readily and willingly discloses his past and present. Perhaps one reason is that his biography is anything but ordinary. Having graduated from the Kyiv Foreign Languages Institute majoring in Japanese language, he was supposed to be deployed to Kamchatka and the Kuril Islands assisting KGB (the notorious Soviet security agency) to do radio espionage, but thanks to the intercession of his mother (a doctor in the police hospital), he did his military service as a prison guard in Odessa. A polyglot (he boasts of speaking seven languages), he married an English woman who agreed to move and live with him in Ukraine. They have three children and, as Kurkov often says, his household is trilingual, with all three languages: English, Russian and Ukrainian each having its niche. A prolific author of fiction, known in the West primarily for his surreal depictions of criminal and political mafia-like realities in Ukraine immediately following the collapse of the Soviet Union, Kurkov underscores (sometimes overzealously) the fact that his prose, despite being written in Russian, is part of contemporary Ukrainian literature.

This view has not been universally shared among Ukrainian writers, although it is fair to state that these debates, acute especially in the early 2000s, dissipated over time. For example, Vasyl Shkliar, in an interview given to the magazine *Knyzhnyk-Review* in 2003, explicitly states that language should be a decisive criterion. That is, only works written in Ukrainian should be considered part of Ukrainian literature. Expressing his opinion on contemporary Russian-language writers living as citizens in Ukraine, he says: "I respect the refined, remarkably elegant prose of Maryna and Serhiy Diachenko, I like Kurkov, ... but I will never say that Andrey Kurkov is a Ukrainian writer."[17] Volodymyr Yavorivsky, on the other hand, representing the literary establishment of the Writers' Union and belonging to the *shistde-siatnyky* generation, happens to take a different position on the matter. In an interview given to the newspaper *Dzerkalo tyzhnia*, he states: "We've had a tradition in Ukraine for centuries whereby Russian-language writers live and work here. Their prose and poetry are based on Ukrainian material, characters, and realities. There are Russian-language writers of whom our literature should be proud. For example, Andrey Kurkov—a renowned literary figure whose works are published in many countries. We have to define our stand clearly—this is our intellectual property."[18]

The above opposing statements might appear brand-new in the post-independence period but there is a precedent in the history of Ukrainian literature, when several languages were used interchangeably. This is true, especially for the Renaissance and Baroque periods. The literature of that era was multilingual and not based on the vernacular: not only Latin and Polish were employed regularly but also a Ukrainian version of Old Church Slavonic. From a more contemporary perspective—a vast array of literatures known as "postcolonial" typically use the languages of former metropolises. These examples do not intend to dismiss the position of those Ukrainian writers who oppose such an idea and insist on Ukrainian as a sole literary language. Such writers often feel, and one could argue justifiably so, like "endangered species" in their own country. Even Kurkov admits that the book market in independent Ukraine favors Russian-language publications.[19] Ukrainian publishing houses are at a disadvantage vis-à-vis their Russian counterparts because they do not enjoy comparable government subsidies. Hence some Ukrainian writers do feel resentful toward Russian-language literary production on Ukrainian territory.

However, the situation in the publishing industry should not shape the debate on language choice when it comes to factors defining a national literature. For Kurkov, as I have already indicated, the language itself is not a sufficient criterion. He advances the view in which a territorial approach seems to take precedence. This is the view he has expressed many a time in a number of interviews thus far, and also indirectly through his novels, because, despite writing in Russian, his fiction, at least thematically, is deeply rooted in Ukrainian reality. In fact, his novels published in the late 1990s and the 2000s are arguably even more "Ukrainian" than his early works.

Two novels, written eight years apart, *Good Angel of Death* (*Dobryi angel smerti*, 1997) and *The President's Last Love* (*Posledniaia liubov prezidenta*, 2005),[20] stand out in this regard in particular. *Good Angel of Death* describes a hero, Nikolai Sotnikov, who by chance inherits a copy of *Kobzar*, a book of poems by the renowned Ukrainian national bard Taras Shevchenko, with handwritten comments placed in the margins. He decides to learn the identity of the author of the scribbled notes and in the process discovers more papers, which eventually send him to Kazakhstan in search of a hidden treasure. He is determined to visit the places where Shevchenko served as a soldier in the tsarist army, a punishment he received for writing anti-tsarist poems. As it turns out, he is not the only one looking for this treasure. A couple of young Ukrainians also embark on the same mission. In the end, Nikolai Sotnikov and the two Ukrainians become allies and together find Shevchenko's original love letters written to a married woman, no doubt an interesting discovery, but, more importantly, the main protagonist also finds a personal treasure, his future wife. She is a Kazakh girl, whose family saved him from an imminent death in a desert storm. All in all, *Good Angel of Death* is an adventurous novel with many twists and turns, but there are two things that stand out in particular. First, Kurkov uses the iconic figure of Shevchenko to debunk nationalist tendencies to put him on a pedestal and make him a saint. In Kurkov's novel Shevchenko is depicted as a man who, like everyone else, has his weaknesses and flaws. Second, it is the only novel in which Kurkov makes some protagonists actually speak Ukrainian (but he uses Russian letters to convey the Ukrainian pronunciation). In one of the interviews, the writer admitted that in the mid-1990s he felt pressure to switch languages and express himself in Ukrainian, and that is why he partially introduced the official state language in *Good Angel of Death.*

Kurkov's novel *The President's Last Love* also dwells on Ukrainian experiences. It is a Bildungsroman of sorts because we see the maturation process of the main protagonist, from his youth in the mid-1970s to his middle age in 2016. The novel's narrative does not unfold in a linear, chronological manner. Instead, we deal with a time-shifting plot comprising three separate stories, each being devoted to a different time frame in the hero's life. The novel is about a president of Ukraine, poisoned by his political enemies, in which his personal life is described against the background of intricate corrupt dealings of the Ukrainian elites. The novel was written shortly before the Orange Revolution, and Kurkov's president—rather passive and ineffectual, suffering from a heart disease, bears some resemblance to the third president of Ukraine, Viktor Yushchenko. It is no doubt a mere coincidence, but Kurkov skillfully shows the workings of the whole image-building apparatus. His president, although a good man, is depicted more like a puppet in the hands of clever officials (oligarchs) than a strong leader.

Following the publication of *The President's Last Love* Kurkov continues his preoccupation with Ukrainian politics in the novel *The Milkman in the Night* (*Nochnoi molochnik*, 2008),[21] focusing this time on members of the

Parliament (Verkhovna Rada). As usual in Kurkov, we have here an intriguing mix—a murder mystery, love story and many other strange plot twists, including the case of a young single mother from the countryside outside Kyiv selling her breast milk to a special clinic in the city. Her milk, as we eventually learn, is bought by a parliamentary deputy who uses it for baths believing that breast milk is a new elixir of youth that keeps off aging. Of course, these bizarre happenings are but a pretext to show a society riddled by stupidity and insatiable appetite for luxury, and its political elite immersed in utter corruption. Kurkov's novel is written in the best tradition of political satires, except that he intertwines his story line with comic interludes and keeps the overall mood lighthearted.

By engaging Ukraine's current affairs in his fiction Kurkov wants to underscore the fact that he is very much part of the contemporary Ukrainian literary scene. Moreover, he not only closely follows the developments in new Ukrainian literature but also understands the literary process behind them. He is outspoken about his views on national culture, including national literature, and talks a great deal about a variety of factors that might contribute to its further betterment. No other Ukrainian contemporary writer has managed to be as commercially successful in the West as Kurkov. It remains to be seen if literary critics of today and tomorrow will be equally generous toward his oeuvre and find a niche for him in the national canon.

Fantasy Genre: The Diachenkos and Lada Luzina

The Russophone writers—the husband/wife team Serhiy (b. 1945) and Maryna (b. 1968) Diachenko,[22] and Lada Luzina[23] (b. 1975)—adopt fantasy literature as their favorite genre with all its magic and supernatural phenomena but approach it differently and draw their inspiration from different sources. Luzina's characters are at the outset placed in a real world setting and then only accidentally stumble into a fantasy realm, the Diachenkos' protagonists, on the other hand, from the very beginning exist in an alternative fantastical universe. Hence, it is instructive to compare some of their works because they yield two different models of cultural appropriation and hybridization. In this respect two novels stand out in particular. Both invoke witchcraft and both reference various East Slavic mythologies but their settings and plots unfold in two different imaginary worlds. The Diachenkos' novel *Age of Witches* (Ved'min vek, 1997),[24] inspired by the Ukrainian mythology of the Carpathians, depicts a dystopian society, ruled by the Great Inquisition that is responsible for controlling (destroying) the witch population, accused of destructive and subversive activities. Situated somewhat abstractly in the contemporary setting of a place called Vizhna (there is public transport available there—buses, metro, as well as telephones and other contemporary gadgets), *Age of*

Witches nevertheless incorporates the institutions of the deep past (the Inquisition) and unexpectedly combines them with various supernatural creatures, all found in Ukrainian folklore such as *chuhaister* (a forest faun) and *mavka/niavka* (a wood nymph). The plot of Luzina's novel, titled *Kyivan Witches. Sword and Cross (Kievskie ved'my. Mech i krest*, 2005),[25] on the other hand, is firmly set in recognizably contemporary Kyiv, although numerous time shifts also reveal other epochs in the development of Ukraine's capital, going back all the way to the medieval times of Kyivan Rus'. Luzina maps out the city's streets and architectural monuments through a historical lens, with accuracy and love similar to that found in Kurkov's oeuvre. But, for the most part, her Kyiv intertextually belongs to the Russian cultural space. Luzina's witches, three young Kyivan women, relish Mikhail Bulgakov's famous work *Master and Margarita* and appreciate artistic contributions to the city of Kyiv made by Russian painters Viktor Vasnetsov and Mikhail Vrubel.

Age of Witches, arguably the Diachenkos' most acclaimed work, tells the story of Ivha,[26] a young woman who is a witch and in love with her boyfriend Nazar but hides this fact from him. Klavdii, a friend of Nazar's father, discerns her true identity and that prompts her to run away from Nazar, hiding for a while on the streets of the hostile city. Ivha lives in constant fear of being recognized for what she really is in a society that ruthlessly and systematically prosecutes witches because of their power to allegedly destroy the established order of things. Her dreams of a normal family life with a man she loves are shattered and, apparently, she is left with only two choices: either to become an initiated witch by joining the secret sisterhood, or to become a "registered" witch and cooperate with the authorities. Neither choice appeals to her, because in reality, she has no desire to accept her witch identity. However, thanks to the intervention of Klavdii, a Great Inquisitor, who promised to help her shortly before her flight from Nazar, another possibility opens up to her. Ivha goes to Klavdii's house and accepts his protection. That way she learns of his methods to fight the sisterhood of witches and also intuitively (being a witch with special powers) learns more about him.

Both protagonists are exceptionally ambivalent. Klavdii has personal secrets too. Back when he was young he was in love with Diunka who, after dying tragically, turned into a *niavka*, a wood nymph. Such nymphs are routinely hunted by *chuhaisters* whose only responsibility is to destroy them after frantically dancing with them. Thus Klavdii, the Great Inquisitor, whose main duty is to untangle the conspiracy of witches by all means necessary, including torture and death, tries to protect his *niavka* from being hunted by her prosecutors. In the end, however, he is not only unable to save Diunka but also loses Ivha who, after staying with him for a while, realizes that she is not really in love with Nazar but rather attracted to Klavdii despite the difference in age. His mission to uncover a grand conspiracy of witchcraft also misfires, as it turns out that it is Ivha who has special powers and becomes the witches' leader.

But the above plot does not do justice to the depth and range of moral questions posed by the Diachenkos in this work. The most interesting passages in the novel include the discussions between Klavdii and Ivha about methods ethically justifiable to secure the desirable outcome when it comes to securing someone's safety. Do the ends justify the means, or, more specifically, is it acceptable to torture witches if they possess knowledge that can prevent future major disasters? Such questions are not new in ethics but in light of the terrorist attacks of 9/11 and many other around the globe they have acquired special currency in the era of globalization and war on terror. One can only admire the authors' prophetic acumen to foresee such dilemmas back in the mid-1990s, at the time when the novel was first written and published. For despite a seeming semblance of rule and law in *Age of Witches* (for example, we learn that the existing law forbids torturing witches under eighteen—not much of a justice by any measure), this gloomy dystopia comes as a warning of sorts and one is under the impression that the authors' intention is to underscore the consequences of what happens when difference as such, regardless of its provenance, is criminalized.

However, the most unexpected feature of the novel is its wide utilization of Ukrainian folk material. As I have already alluded, the story line unfolds in a locality that bears hardly any geographically recognizable characteristics, and yet because the authors incorporate the supernatural creatures—*chuhaistyr* and *niavka*—popularly known to Ukrainians through such literary classics as Mykhailo Kotsiubynsky's *The Shadows of Forgotten Ancestors* (*Tini zabutykh predkiv*, 1911) and Lesia Ukrainka's *A Forest Song* (*Lisova pisnia*, 1911), *Age of Witches* undoubtedly betrays Ukrainian roots. In fact, the Diachenkos, both born in Kyiv, skillfully appropriate Ukrainian folk mythology and in the process create a fictional work that is intertextually immersed in the Ukrainian cultural space. They again asserted their "Ukrainianness" when they published the fantasy novel/fairy tale *Wild Energy. Lana* (*Dikaia energiia. Lana*, 2006), inspired by and dedicated to the Ukrainian pop singer Ruslana who won the Eurovision Song Contest in 2004. Winners of multiple literary awards in the genre of fantasy and science fiction, the Diachenkos settled as writers only after being first involved in theatre and film.[27] Like Kurkov, Maryna and Serhiy identify themselves as Ukrainian Russophone writers, speak fluent Ukrainian, and believe in the civil model of national identity.[28] But, it is not inconceivable that their move to Moscow in 2009 might gradually influence their sense of belonging and eventually affect their popularity in Ukraine.[29]

Lada Luzina's popular fiction embraces contemporary Kyiv with utmost love and attention. In this respect, her Kyiv, like Kurkov's, mirrors post-independence reality with all its everyday struggles and widespread corruption. She provides extensive descriptions of individual streets, buildings, churches and monasteries, while simultaneously and conscientiously studies the city's past, uncovering multicultural layers in art, architecture and literature. True, her focus is overwhelmingly on the Russian contributions to the capital's cultural heritage but, at the same time, she does not avoid the context of independent Ukraine and its national heroes. Hence, alongside Mikhail Bulgakov there is Lesia Ukrainka (though her presence figures less prominently); moreover, side by side with Russian artists Viktor Vasnetsov and Mikhail Vrubel who worked in Kyiv under imperial rule in the late nineteenth century, there are important notables of the Ukrainian past—a medieval warrior-turned-monk of Pecherska Lavra (Kyivan Cave Monastery), Illia Muromets, and two figures of the seventeenth century, Hetman Ivan Mazepa and Metropolitan Petro Mohyla, the latter known primarily as the founder of the Kyiv Academy, Ukraine's first university, later renamed Kyivan Mohyla Academy. Written in the popular genre of fantasy, mixed with adventure and murder mystery, *Kyivan Witches. Sword and Cross* manages to subsume a surprisingly large corpus of relevant historical detail about the capital. Luzina skillfully relates and amalgamates multiple cultural layers of her beloved city, and presents it against the background of a suspenseful, page-turning plot in which three young women—Masha Kovalova, Dasha Chub and Katia Dobrazhanska[30] inherit magical powers from the witch Kylyna whose murder in an apartment on Andriivskii Uzviz they witness, and from that moment onward all three women embark on an adventure that reveals to them many past and present secrets of their city.

The novel begins with a detailed description and history of one of the most famous streets in Kyiv, Andriivskii Uzviz, related to a group of foreign tourists by Masha's history professor. Then we are introduced to three main protagonists—a history student (Masha), a recently fired club singer (Dasha) and a successful businesswoman (Katia). They all converge in Kylyna's apartment, but before they have a chance to enter her office, each separately meets with a good-looking fellow waiting in the hall who mysteriously disappears after each woman receives from him a golden necklace in the shape of a snake. The heroines then witness Kylyna's strange death and, unaware of what powers they just acquired, all flee from the crime scene. This incident on Andriivskii Uzviz triggers all subsequent happenings in the novel that include puzzling murders in the Church of St. Cyril (which itself is part of the St. Cyril Monastic complex that also houses a psychiatric hospital); talking cats; magic potions; satanic rituals; broomstick flying; and time traveling, to name just a few. Luzina's talent for seamlessly blending fantastical elements with extensive historical digressions, simultaneously endowing various episodes with a rich intertextual subtext that draws both from Russian and Ukrainian sources, makes her fiction exceptionally hybrid. And even though the author nostalgically goes back to Kyiv of the late nineteenth century, depicting the late imperial period when two famous Russian painters Vrubel and Vasnetsov work on the murals in St. Cyril's and St. Volodymyr's Churches, respectively, she also strives to preserve the verisimilitude of contemporary life in the capital, which unquestionably unfolds in modern-day Ukraine.[31]

Luzina's three main protagonists are considerably more than just newly initiated witches. They become "Kyievytsi," protectresses of Kyiv, whose provenance goes back at least to the times of Kyivan Rus', and whose main life mission is to defend the city from all potential calamities. Thus, they not only solve a series of murders committed on the territory of St. Cyril's Monastery but also find a way to prevent the imminent destruction of the capital city. *Kyivan Witches* enjoys enormous popularity and Luzina has so far created a whole series based on the same protagonists. By 2011 three more sequels occurred: *A Shot in the Opera* (*Vystrel v opere*, 2007), *Princess Greza* (*Printsessa Greza*, 2011) and *Nikola Mokry* (2011). As in the first novel of the series, in the sequels Kyiv emerges as a protagonist in its own right, as if the author embarks on a mission to underscore the cultural significance of her native city.

What especially strikes in the popular novels of Luzina and the Diachenkos is their ability to hybridize cultural content. The Diachenkos reach out to the sources of native folklore but situate their fiction by and large in an abstract, site-unspecified locality. Still, judging by content alone they seem to be more "Ukrainian" than Luzina, although, unlike her, they publish their oeuvre predominantly, if not exclusively as of late, in Russia. Luzina's fantasy works, all published in Ukraine, espouse cultural hybridity eagerly and enthusiastically. Her overt love for Kyiv manifests itself in her digging out various legends, myths, and historical facts and curiosities about the capital that comprise different national realities but, in the end, she seems to be embracing and mixing them all. However, one cannot deny the fact that she clearly privileges the Russian perspective over the Ukrainian one. Could it be that it is because she resents cultural exclusion and attempts to preserve traces of the Russian input in the otherwise overwhelmingly Ukrainian capital city? Luzina—a Russophone author[32] presents herself as a local patriot who is somewhat detached from current political realities but who nonetheless cultivates the topography of her native city. There are obvious similarities between her and Kurkov in their literary treatment of Kyiv—both authors love their hometown and both strive to put it on the cultural map. But, unlike Luzina, Kurkov actively engages Ukrainian current affairs themes both on the pages of his books and well beyond them, in the real world so to say, explicitly commenting on the issues of identity, whether it concerns him personally or his fictional heroes. Luzina, on the other hand, prefers to immerse herself

in fantasy and history, and rarely touches upon the issue of national belonging in her oeuvre. Yet, expressing her views on the occasion of the twentieth
anniversary of independence, she leaves little doubt that she is concerned
about Ukraine's geopolitical direction and sees her literary output firmly
within the Ukrainian cultural milieu.[33]

TEXTUAL *SURZHYK,* POLYGLOTS AND BILINGUALS

Opinions vary as to the saliency of future Russophone literature in independent Ukraine. No one doubts that Russian language belletristic works will
continue to be published there but, as Kruchyk and other critics surmise, a
vast majority of them might not have enough of a critical resonance to evolve
further in any meaningful way. Sooner or later such authors are compelled to
seek publishing opportunities in Russia—a move that potentially undercuts
their visibility and competitiveness at home. While a handful of Ukrainian
Russophone writers enjoy widespread popularity (Kurkov, Luzina) and are
undeniably part of the domestic literary mainstream, others (the Diachenkos,
G.L. Oldi, Volodymyr Puzii-Arenev, and Anastasiia Afanas'eva, to mention
a few) rely mostly on the Russian publishing industry and exist on the margins of Ukrainian literary establishment. Equally an unenviable situation is
that of bilingual writers who can rarely achieve the same degree of attention
and acceptance in two different linguistic spheres, and eventually choose
one over the other (e.g., Yana Dubynianska, Dmytro Lazutkin and Andrii
Kokotiukha). However, for a vast majority of Ukrainian-speaking authors
the question is not so much of a language choice but, rather, how effectively
to express themselves in the official state language that de facto functions in
the bilingual and hybrid cultural space. They desire their literary production
to be convincingly authentic and shy away puristic artificiality; therefore,
they make themselves open to a variety of linguistic devices, including the
utilization of frequently despised *surzhyk* and/or many foreign words and
expressions. These measures can at times betray a dose of snobbism, on other
occassions—a mere playfulness or satire, but many a time they also fulfill a
clearly delineated aesthetic purpose.

Textual *Surzhyk*

Surzhyk entails a hybrid form of Ukrainian and Russian languages that devi-
ates from the accepted standard norms in vocabulary, phonetics or grammar.
Historically, this mixed language has its roots in the migration of Ukrainians
from the countryside to the cities and their subsequent contact with Russian,
used overwhelmingly in urban centers both before and after the Bolshevik

revolution. Under Soviet rule the policy of Russification, introduced first by Stalin in the 1930s and continued almost until independence, also had a profound impact on the way people communicated. In the post-independence period, *surzhyk* still thrives in everyday communication despite the official status of Ukrainian, mainly because in a de facto bilingual country there are plenty of opportunities to facilitate interference of one language over another, and this time it is also Ukrainian that is impacting Russophones who are attempting to express themselves in the state language and in the process make a variety of errors.[34] What is perhaps somewhat surprising is not that *surzhyk* still remains a means of communication for some strata of the society but that after independence it has become a popular stylistic device for a number of writers and entertainers who use it for various aesthetic and/ or ideological ends, from comical effects to social critique. For this kind of intentional linguistic hybridity (as Bakhtin put it) I will apply the term "textual *surzhyk*."[35] While *surzhyk* commonly refers only to Ukrainian-Russian mutual language interference, I am inclined to include here also a habitual language mixing between Ukrainian and English, found especially in texts of writers of the younger generation.

There seems to be a generational difference in literary attitudes toward *surzhyk* as a stylistic device. Bohdan Zholdak (b. 1948) and Les Poderviansky (b. 1952), for example, known for a wide utilization of this mixed language in their texts, employ it both to underscore a lower-class (marginalized) status of its speakers and to implicitly critique reality that engenders rise of such a speech variant. By and large, their ironic texts refer to the late Soviet period and make use of what Bilaniuk calls "Sovietized Ukrainian surzhyk"[36] but there are also substantial differences between the two of them. Poderviansky, a painter and author of a series of short, absurd plays, written mostly in the late 1980s, mixes *surzhyk* with obscenities and vulgar swearing in order to make his protagonists easily recognizable within the Soviet context and, simultaneously, to subversively laugh at the grotesqueness of the Soviet system and its iconic figures (Pavlik Morozov, Maksim Gorky and Nikolai Ostrovsky, to name a few). Zholdak's textual approach to *surzhyk* is more varied and complex. First, he does away with obscenities, and second, his *surzhyk* bears all the attributes of a literary construct that in many ways is only peripherally relatable to present-day Ukraine's linguistic realities. For example, alongside short stories, which are written almost entirely in standard Ukrainian with only occasional interferences of *surzhyk* whenever it is plausible that a given character would use it (like a lower-class mother-in-law or a taxi-driver), there are also stories conceived entirely in *surzhyk*, that is, both the third-person narration and characters' direct speech are in a non-standard form.[37] Zholdak, incidentally, has a whole cycle of short stories titled *Farewell, Surzhyk!* written in the mixed language with a "homo sovieticus" as its narrator, as Hundorova put it.[38] In his collection *Anti-Climax*, Zholdak has a few political stories about Stalin and Hitler and, because they are related entirely in *surzhyk*, we encounter a paradoxical situation in which both Stalin and Hitler converse in this mixed Ukrainian-Russian language. By literally putting *surzhyk* into the mouths of such odious villains the author implicitly expresses his contempt for hybridized language practices.[39] Hence Zholdak's *surzhyk* stories come across more as a warning of sorts rather than an encouragement or legitimization of dispensation with any norms. Podervian-sky—outrageously shocking, by contrast, appears more playful and open to transgressions.

Pavlo Volvach in his novel *Class* (*Kliasa*, 2010) adheres to a more tradi-tional textual practice with regard to *surzhyk* by making his working-class youth protagonists speak it in industrial Soviet Zaporizhzhia, because this is precisely how they would communicate in real life. To preserve the verisi-militude of youth's attitudes and behavior in the heavily Russified city of the late Soviet period, Volvach not only introduces *surzhyk* but also generously intersperses it with common profanities and inserts whole Russian phrases. However, by spelling the latter in Ukrainian he automatically textually hybridizes them, otherwise, when pronounced, they would reflect the stan-dard form. For example, the phrase: "Та ета малалєткі" (in Russian: "Та это малолетки" which means "But these are underage girls") is spelled in Ukrai-nian but phonetically constitutes the correct Russian pronunciation. On the other hand, the following italicized words in: "Так а *шо* він, не *чуствував*, коли його *роздівали?*" (And what, he did not feel when they were undress-ing him?) are typical linguistic hybrids, where "sho" (what) is a combination of Russian "chto" and Ukrainian "shcho"; "chustvuvav" (he felt) is really a Russian word, except that the grammatical ending is Ukrainian (in Russian it would be: "chustvuval"); and finally "rozdivali" (they were undressing) mixes Russian "razdevali" and Ukrainian "rozdiahaly." Unlike in Zholdak's and Poderviansky's, in Volvach's *surzhyk* there is a pronounced naturalness in direct speech. It sounds real and justified within a given context rather than constructed and artificial as in the practice of his older colleagues.

Yet another approach to *surzhyk*'s textualization we can observe in Svit-lana Povaliaieva's and Svitlana Pyrkalo's texts. Both of them use *surzhyk* as one of many possible ways to experiment with language. And both also represent the category of "polyglots," as I have coined it to denote the incor-poration of more than one foreign language in belletristic works. Pyrkalo occasionally hybridizes Russian textually by using Ukrainian spelling, similarly to what happens in Volvach's text. For the most part, however, she simply prefers to switch to standard Russian spelling. Her interspersing of *surzhyk* has a definite parodying effect. As a postmodernist, Pyrkalo even ironically and playfully laughs back at herself, especially when she claims her regional identity and says that the Poltava oblast (where she comes from) should separate from the rest of Ukraine and proclaim *surzhyk* as a new state language.[40] Pyrkalo's offhand manner of narration allows her to incorporate *surzhyk* both as a decorative "spice" of sorts and as a necessary signifier of linguistic reality in post-independence Kyiv.

Povaliaieva too hybridizes Russian by spelling it in Ukrainian (in addition to using straightforward *surzhyk*), but, moreover, she also hybridizes English words by similarly expressing them via Ukrainian spelling.[41] Hence she offers textual *surzhyk* that is understandable to almost everyone in Ukraine if it is Russian spelled in Ukrainian, but only those with the knowledge of English can grasp the full meaning of her text if it is an English word or phrase spelled in Cyrillic letters. That way Povaliaieva a priori defines her reading audience—clearly, her texts are mainly addressed to students who in the post-independence period massively began to study foreign languages, especially English. Thus, for example, she would use "трабл" (trabl) instead of "trouble" or in Ukrainian "клопіт" (klopit) and "драйвер" (draiver) instead of "driver" or in Ukrainian "водій" (vodii). These are direct borrowings spelled in Cyrillic but occasionally Povaliaieva not only borrows a word from English but also declines it in Ukrainian, thereby constructing a genuine hybrid: "побачив на його фейсі"[42] (pobachyv na ioho feisi), which means: "he saw on his face." The latter word underwent a double hybridization: first, the English word "face" (instead of Ukrainian "обличчя" (oblychchia)) was spelled in Ukrainian, and second, it acquired an ending "–i" for a locative case. Examples of this kind of intentional hybridization between English and Ukrainian abound in Povaliaieva's prose. In many ways, she introduces a new paradigm of language hybridization in the Ukrainian context—an interesting reversal in social status with regard to linguistic language mixing. Whereas original Ukrainian-Russian *surzhyk* is by and large associated with an uneducated speaker, Povaliaieva's English-Ukrainian *surzhyk* (or mixed language) signals someone "initiated," someone knowledgeable linguistically and culturally to comprehend the author's subtle nuances in code-switching.

Polyglots

By far the two most popular foreign languages utilized by contemporary Ukrainian authors in belles-lettres are English and Russian. In many ways, these languages mirror two different cultural paradigms (or Others)—the West (Europe) versus Russia (the former colonizer), which compete for primacy on many different levels within the Ukrainian post-independence context. Of course, incorporating one or the other does not necessarily denote the writer's political orientation. Rather, Russian and English passages within otherwise Ukrainian texts often become authors' way to mark ideological struggles ingrained in Ukrainian society. Not to mention that interweaving English phrases is supposed to signal to the reader certain worldliness, sophistication and openness. Russian or *surzhyk* inserts, on the other hand, evince a quotidian quality rooted in everyday postcolonial reality, totally devoid of the unfamiliar or the exotic.

One of the first to incorporate English phrases into her narratives was Oksana Zabuzhko. Her main protagonist O. in the novel *Fieldwork in Ukrainian Sex* is depicted spending some time in the United States as a Fulbright scholar, hence throwing English phrases here and there (and corresponding footnotes with Ukrainian translations) seems to be justified by context. Yet, Zabuzhko's English interpolations are not only utilized for reasons of verisimilitude, but more importantly, they betray the worldly and knowledgeable author-narrator, signaling that she herself is fluent in the language of the host country and understands its cultural underpinnings. Addressing her imaginary audience as "Ladies and Gentlemen," the heroine creates an aura of downright sophistication and western civility, which is in such a short supply in her own country, and which also comes as a stark contrast to her being physically and psychologically abused by a Ukrainian partner with deep-seated colonial complexes. According to Svitlana Kobets:

> The extensive use in the text of English, and to a lesser extent Russian expressions is both functional and symbolic. For example, one of the functions of English is to challenge the peripheral thinking and mode of existence of the narrator's countrymen and countrywomen. The use of Russian by Ukrainians becomes a target of the narrator's sarcasm. She mocks Ukraine's dependence on the Russian idiom, exemplified by her lovers' sexual discourse.[43]

All in all, Zabuzhko's embrace of English (or Russian for that matter) is not parodic or playful. She treats it with a scholarly seriousness and, moreover, her English inserts come about as her own personal defense mechanisms against backwardness and incivility, and, predictably, appear in the text at moments of conspicuous tension.

Svitlana Pyrkalo's use of English, Russian and *surzhyk*, by contrast, is all about play and parody. In *Green Margarita* she creatively and seamlessly incorporates various advertisements (by and large written in standard Russian), journalistic commentaries, interviews and questionnaires. Pyrkalo's protagonist Maryna, journalist by profession, muses on consumerism, feminism, gender equality and many other hot topics of the day, utilizing all linguistic devices accessible to her. Her English inserts are readily explained in footnotes (although some, especially curses, are left untranslated) but, overall, one must admit that her text inevitably implies the sophisticated reader who can appreciate both her nuanced play of identities through language(s) and her restraint of judgment on language practices. Published in 2001, *Green Margarita* can even be perceived as Pyrkalo's unconventional response to all the debates on language purity, raging so pervasively in Ukraine of the 1990s.[44]

No one is weaving English words and phrases in contemporary Ukrainian literature as consistently as Svitlana Povaliaieva. They appear in her novels rather profusely either as straightforward English passages or as textual hybrids, that is, transliterated in Cyrillic letters. The author does not even make an effort to translate or explain her English interpolations, as if she takes for granted that her prose will be comprehensible to the reader. Povaliaieva's first three novels describe mostly Kyiv student groups, hooked on drugs and enamored by Western pop music and rock bands (e.g., Nirvana and Metallica). By all accounts, her protagonists have interiorized English to such an extent that it constitutes for them a kind of lingua franca, which, interwoven together with a specifically youth jargon that equally incorporates Russian and *surzhyk*, arguably represents a nod for postmodern inclusiveness and an acknowledgement of issues with global implications (youth substance abuse being one of them). In addition to hybridizing English and Russian by spelling them in Ukrainian, she also occasionally transliterates Ukrainian into Latin script, and then mixes it further with words in Cyrillic and English:

Tanya-sexy bujnyj parostok akseleratciji z такими сідницями, що ... . O! o! o! o!-baby-baby-baby-beiba'—the-all-people-in-the-tramves'-tramvaj-vtratyv-gluzd!-tcherez oblipleni- розумієте! ОБЛІПЛЕНІ ЩІЛЬНО ВЕЛОСИПЕДНИМИ ШОРТАМИ-пружні-рухливі-динтьки-сідниць- Tanya-a-a hirko platche—zagybybyla [sic] mjatchyk—tyhshe, Tanetchka, ne platch, ne potone mjatch—М'ЯЧ ВОБШЕ НЕ ТОНЕ!!!... .[45]

Yet the above concoction of multilingual words by Povaliaieva does not convincingly evince parodic qualities. Rather, it signals that her prose is directed to those few "initiated," or to those who feel at home in the world swallowed up by global media, clichés and an ever-increasing sexualization of culture.

Irena Karpa follows in the footsteps of her older polyglot colleagues and also incorporates extensive passages in English and Russian, occasionally augmenting her fiction with German and French phrases. She differs from Pyrkalo and Povaliaieva, however, in her reluctance to employ *surzhyk*. While Karpa hybridizes her prose by multilingual interpolations in her narrative, she offers her inserts in foreign languages mostly in their standard literary forms, rarely transliterating them into Ukrainian.[46] The author is not consistent with providing parallel translations in footnotes—sometimes they are present, and sometimes they are not. Again, similarly to Povaliaieva, Karpa too expects her readers to be linguistically prepared, if not culturally sophisticated. One could well argue that her autobiographical novel-travel-ogues provide ample justification for introducing foreign words and phrases; after all, traveling around the world and putting her protagonists (who know and use other languages) in global contexts, especially in Europe and Asia, is only natural since it enables communicating with the people of the countries visited. It would be a mistake, however, to think that Karpa's polyglot narra-tives are ideologically neutral and only contextually motivated. By far Eng-lish prevails, although Russian passages figure prominently as well. While the latter phrases do not need translations for the general Ukrainian public, those in English do. All the more, it is surprising that in one case, Karpa pro-vides a footnote explaining a Russian phrase she used.[47] The writer goes to great lengths to underline linguistic difference between these two East Slavic languages. It is her way to demarcate identities, especially abroad where she notices how easily Ukrainians and Russians are perceived as the same people. It almost seems that Karpa's extensive traveling only reinforces her sense of national belonging and that, in turn, affects her main protagonists who, by any measure, do not appear to be confused as to their national identity. They all speak good literary Ukrainian (including plenty of the native cursing), at the same time are also fluent in other languages. It is as if Karpa provides a perfect linguistic formula for her compatriots to follow.

Another widespread tendency among contemporary Ukrainian authors is to come up with English titles (be they for books or individual works), by either using exact wording or by transliterating it. For example, Serhiy Zhadan's third collection of poetry is titled *Pepsi* (1998), spelled in Cyrillic; his first book of short stories—*Big Mac* (*Big Mak*, 2003); his first novel—*Depeche Mode* (*Depesh Mod*, 2004), both also spelled in Cyrillic; and his memoirs—*Anarchy in the UKR* (2005), using original English. There are some paral-lels in his use of language in the novel *Depeche Mode* with that of Svitlana Povaliaieva. Both are attracted to Western bands and music, and both attempt to capture the essence of youth jargon in Kharkiv and Kyiv, respectively, clearly informed by Western cultural influences of the mid-1990s.

Makhno is another poet who readily adopts English for the titles of his books (e.g., *Cornelia Street Café*, 2007) or individual poems (e.g., "McSorley's Old House"). Unlike Zhadan, Makhno left Ukraine in 2000 to settle permanently in New York. Hence, at least contextually, his English interpolations are geo-graphically justified. By and large, the poet borrows directly from English whenever he refers to local places or institutions (for instance, Staten Island, Coney Island, Astor Place, Jewish Center, La Mama Theater, and New York University, to name a few), or widely known brand names such as Toyota, CNN and Starbucks. Not surprisingly, living in New York Makhno also comes into contact with Spanish. Quotes from this language are rare but in the poem "Coney Island" he inserts a few random words: "mañana mujera i rojo" (tomorrow, woman, red) when he introduces homeless character Pedro. Overall, Makhno does not overindulge with interspersing foreign words and phrases in his poetry; his embrace of "foreignness" is motivated by context alone and bears no signs of hidden subtexts.

An interesting case in the polyglot category represents the poetry of Andrii Bondar (b. 1974). Based in Kyiv, he too occasionally weaves in English phrases and titles (e.g., his poem "Jogging"). In his collection *Primitive Forms of Ownership* (*Prymityvni formy vlasnosti*, 2004), we find both original English words put in quotes and left unexplained ("soft," "brother and sister," "mature," "pregnant," etc.) and those transliterated into Ukrainian: "ай джаст вона філ ріел лав," meaning: "I just wanna feel real love." Their inclusion is largely motivated by themes taken up in individual poems, referring in some cases to movies watched or songs heard. He also experiments with introducing Latin script in Ukrainian poetry and, in fact, has a poem titled "The Roman Alphabet" ("Latynka"), written entirely using Latin letters. It is a highly ironic and politically engaged verse, critiquing rampant corruption and lawlessness of post-Soviet society, and, in the end, implicitly defending the existing Cyrillic script for Ukrainian letters:

I've long had
the urge
to write at least one poem
using the roman alphabet
one of my friends thinks
that if we switch to the roman alphabet
our people will steal less
and immediately
our messy byzantinisms
our obnoxious sovietisms our endless ugro-finnisms
(sorry ugrics, sorry finns)
will disappear and something will snap in our heads
—and "voila!" we are part of europe
[...]
if every living ukrainian poet
writes one poem in the roman alphabet
it will be possible to make an anthology
of contemporary ukrainian poetry written in the roman alphabet
what a pity that Ivan Malkovych won't be able to write a poem
about the crescent moon of the letter є
and the slender candle of the letter ї [48]

Bondar's poetic language—very colloquial and accessible—is surprisingly free of *surzhyk* and Russian, even when the thematics of the verse would warrant it. True, his poem "To Russia with Love" ("Rosii z liubov'iu") provides a handful of Russian words in Ukrainian spelling but they are included only as examples of the game the lyrical hero used to play with his brother in their childhood. The poem itself is again highly ironic and political, and this time it muses on the fact why in the football match between Wales and Russia the lyrical hero roots for distant Wales rather than neighborly Russia.

All the cases discussed above point to three categories of polyglots: (1) those who incorporate foreign words and phrases to underscore the verisimilitude of the circumstances described (Zabuzhko, Makhno, Karpa); (2) those who use it for parodic or ironic ends (Pyrkalo, Bondar); and (3) those who embrace it as a differentiating marker for countercultural inclinations of post-Soviet youth, affected by similar movements in the West (Povaliaieva, Zhadan). Looking at these belletristic trials from an aesthetic angle, all polyglots included here share a penchant for postmodern inclusiveness and a sensibility rooted in globalism. Their writings and experiences also reflect the enormous progress made in freedom of movement around the world since independence. The journeys described in their works, real and imaginary, naturally entice them to cross not only geographical boundaries but linguistic as well.

Bilinguals

While all contemporary Ukrainian authors are practically bilingual, very few of them express themselves artistically in Ukrainian and in Russian simultaneously. Usually, for their artistic expression they choose one language or the other, although in their everyday communication they can easily switch between the two. And even those few writers who at some stage publish in both languages, sooner or later end up with one language taking over and being the predominant one. The poet Dmytro Lazutkin (b. 1978) and science fiction/fantasy writer Yana Dubynianska (b. 1975) are the case in point. Lazutkin, born in Kyiv, first established himself as a Ukrainian poet, and then also started to publish poetry in Russian. However, his published output in Ukrainian is considerably more voluminous than that in Russian. Dubynianska, born in Crimea, began as a Russophone author,[49] then switched to Ukrainian only to return later to publish in Russian with Moscow publishing houses. Both authors reflect the typical postcolonial ambiguity and hesitance in linguistic practice precipitated by the unequal status of two languages under colonial rule at the crucial for them time of adolescence but, invariably, because they are both based in Ukraine (and residing in the capital city for that matter), it should not surprise us that they see themselves as primarily belonging to the Ukrainian cultural sphere.

Dmytro Lazutkin first published three books of poetry in Ukrainian: *Roofs* (*Dakhy*, 2003), *Sweets for Reptiles* (*Solodoshchi dlia plazuniv*, 2005) and

Grass Stuffed Sacred Cows (*Nabyti travoiu sviashchenni korovy*, 2006) before his Russian collection *Sweet Pepper of Dreams* (*Paprika grez*, 2006) came out in Moscow. Thus far this is his only book of poetry in Russian but he regularly appears in print in quite a few prestigious literary magazines in Russia. His Ukrainian poetry for the most part shuns away from political commentary, so prevalent in Andrii Bondar's oeuvre, but is nonetheless remarkably contemporary by being playful, urban and with a lyrical hero representing "the society of consumption," as Bohdana Matiiash succinctly put it.[50] Yet at times he can be surprisingly lyrical and intimate, although his overall ironic tone often undermines the trustworthiness of his declarations of love (no wonder his lyrical hero calls "conscience—a last dinosaur"). In many ways, his Russian poetry seems to be less brutal, less playful, and more subtle and lyrical. It deals mostly with love relationships going nowhere and, in this respect, reverberates with his Ukrainian poems. Arguably, the inability of Lazutkin's lyrical hero to commit to a more serious relationship mirrors the poet's own linguistic bifurcation and lack of unconditional devotion to one literature. He is seemingly capable of keeping his literary involvement in two cultural spheres neatly apart, avoids any language hybridization, and, I assume, for the Russian reader, if not for a biographical note identifying him as a poet from Ukraine, it would be hard to find any reference to his Ukrainian roots. However, even though Lazutkin does not hybridize in either of the two linguistic niches in which he expresses himself artistically, his overall bilingual output is a pure example of post-Soviet cultural hybridity.

Yana Dubynianska's Ukrainian literary debut in 1999 with a collection of short stories *Three Days in Syrenopol* (*Try dni u Syrenopoli*), followed subsequently by four novels in Russian, from the outset established her as a bilingual author. However, in contrast to Lazutkin, her Russian literary output clearly outgrows her Ukrainian one. And even though her most popular Russian novels have been translated into Ukrainian and published in Ukraine, a majority of her more recent oeuvre in the genre of fantasy has been coming out in Russia. In the end, she chose commercial success abroad over a less profitable domestic book market.

Among Dubynianska's early Russian novels, *A Staircase Platform* (*Lestnichnaia ploshchadka*, 2003), translated into Ukrainian as *Skhodovyi maidanchyk* (2005),[51] is arguably her best. Published simultaneously in Moscow and Donetsk, this science fiction novel about the possibility to switch realities with the help of a special machine, invented by an elderly professor Richard Stranton, primarily dwells on relationships and love, despite some initial emphasis on fantastic setting. The author chooses English sounding names for her protagonists (Greg, Liza, Ed, Inga and Steven)—as if longs for some kind of distance or estrangement—but does not situate them within an easily recognizable foreign context. Time and place are deliberately vague for in the world of interchangeable realities, exact coordinates are clearly redundant. Dubynianska manages to keep suspense going to the very end while at the same time probes the psychology of desire fulfillment. It seems that no matter how enticing and transformative inventions can be, if there is no cooperation and love among people, then switching realities is not much of an accomplishment.

There is one fundamental difference between polyglots and bilinguals. The latter do not accept hybridizing languages. Rather, they prefer to express themselves separately in two linguistic mediums, making sure that in each there is a convincing artistic message to be conveyed.

LANGUAGE AS PROTAGONIST

It is understandable that for postcolonial states the existence of a separate language helps to construct a necessary differentiation from the former metropolis. And even though arriving at political independence can be accomplished without linguistic demarcation (the United States is the best example of such a model), having a national language makes striving for cultural difference for newly independent states seemingly that much easier. Hence one can argue that protecting the status of Ukrainian as the only official state language after independence facilitates the process of national identity construction, mainly because it engenders the feeling of sameness among the formerly colonized people and points to the otherness of the former colonizer. Yet, the situation in Ukraine, as I have already indicated on many occasions, is considerably more complicated than that. The widespread non-reciprocal bilingualism and/or the existence of many types of *surzhyk* complicate achieving homogeneity in terms of ethnolinguistic identity. Of course, it is unlikely that in a country as large as Ukraine such homogeneity can ever be accomplished, or if it should be even desirable, but no one questions that the government ought to do all it can to promote parity and harmonious coexistence among its ethnically diverse population. Nevertheless, the linguistically challenged situation of the post-independence period poses real dilemmas for a Ukrainian writer.[52] First, s/he is faced with a language choice and, second, if Ukrainian is chosen, then how pure it should be. Many contemporary authors love to experiment with all kinds of linguistic possibilities—*surzhyk*, dialects and even foreign languages (the latter practice is especially widespread among postmodernists). However, there is also a small group of writers for whom language constitutes more than just a communicative tool, for them language becomes a hero of sorts, the very essence of the identity they claim for themselves.

While the "language as protagonist" categorization can be applied broadly, I am inclined to reserve it only for the chief representatives of the so-called

Zhytomyr School—Viacheslav Medvid and Yevhen Pashkovsky, simply because it is the phrase Medvid himself coined in one of his interviews. Speaking of his novel *Blood on Straw* (*Krov po solomi*, 2002) in an interview given to *Knyzhnyk-Review,* he said: "Language is also one of the main protagonists of my novel."[53] I am mindful that other authors, or critics for that matter, could claim the "language as protagonist" category as applicable in other cases as well. And the critic Yevhen Baran, for example, analyzing Yuri Andrukhovych's *Perverzion*, comes to this very conclusion: "And if we were to talk about the protagonist of the novel *Perverzion* ... it is the language, and not just as a means of communication but as a work of art."[54] However, in my analysis, I draw a distinction based on what language aspect (communicative or intrinsic) prevails in the author's attitude toward his or her material.

Contrary to what Baran says about the language of *Perverzion*, Andrukhovych, undoubtedly privileges the communicative and performative aspects of language, incorporating a variety of intertexts, genres, word games and insisting on a dialogue with the reader. Such approach entails interaction and invariably opens up to the audience. Medvid, on the other hand, insists on the intrinsic value of the Ukrainian language, presenting it as a somewhat insular repository of people's collective memory and their experience in history, and can hardly count on a wide readership. Both Pashkovsky and Medvid, unlike Andrukhovych, do not explicitly thematize identity concerns but they do celebrate the richness of their native tongue. The Ukrainian language becomes for them not just a medium of expression but an aim and center of its own, a protagonist. Though, admittedly, this attitude is more characteristic of Medvid than of Pashkovsky.

In his essay "With the Name of Other Loneliness" ("Z imenniam inshoi samotnosti"), Medvid writes: "It is the language, which emerges as a separate being, that is a justifiable agent of any changes in its dwelling, and it is the language, the most patient and divine initiation and essence, that awaits the coming of someone ready to awake it for a new conception and a new life."[55] I have no doubts that Medvid sees himself as that someone special who has the power to awaken the language and to give it a new life. The clear messianic tone of the above excerpt betrays the author's somewhat romantic, if not old-fashioned, belief in the unique mission of intellectuals to be the national vanguard on behalf of their compatriots. Language is also in the epicenter of such a vanguard. And, in line with such views, the language of his novels indeed becomes central and an end in its own right. Medvid underscores the language's ability to be the carrier of the native (or local) culture and dismisses the importance of establishing a rapport with the reader.

There is an apparent incongruity between Medvid's style, the main attribute of which is a stream-of-consciousness narrative, and the thematics of his works, often characterized as neo-populism.[56] It begs the question: who is the main recipient of his texts? Clearly, it is not someone from the milieu depicted in his prose, that is, his beloved hometown called Kodnia in the Zhytomyr region.[57] Rather, Medvid constructs his own implicit (or ideal) reader for whom language is a sacred entity and the only determinative factor in self-identification process. One cannot but notice yet another interesting thing: both geography and language in Medvid's texts are first and foremost imaginary constructs that only peripherally relate to the reality on the ground. In the already mentioned interview, Medvid admits that in his novel *Blood on Straw* he treats language somewhat haphazardly: "I tried ... to put words into mouths of certain people that they would never articulate in real life."[58] The constructed character of his narratives, which are by and large plotless, undermines the strength of his populist rhetoric. Moreover, Medvid's language is static, opaque and borders on some kind of exhaustion.[59] To put it differently, I have doubts if it is possible to evolve this kind of style any further, or in some other, diametrically opposed, direction. The impression one gets is that from here there is nowhere to go. Consider, for example, the following excerpt from Medvid's *Pro domo sua*, as he reveals his "ars poetica": "I have always composed my books in such a way that having read them through, a person with great pleasure returns to individual chapters, pages, perceiving them as a separate whole and that way rewards himself for the previous labor; I myself do not read [my books] through because it is difficult for they do not have a classic plot but how one can arrive at a plot if it does not exist in life ... ."[60] Clearly, the author feels compelled to justify his writerly approach.

Pashkovsky's prose displays similar qualities though, to be fair, his first novel *Holiday* (*Sviato*, 1989; 2nd ed. 2005) presents a rather straightforward story line of a young man Andrii, born in a village but moving to and seeking his dharma in the city. Disappointed with his romantic relationships, first with his girlfriend Nadia, then with his lover Anna—in the end, he embarks on yet another journey. This hero's odyssey, however, resembles more of a flight than an ordinary outing—a desperate escape both from himself and from the realities of everyday existence. In fact, Pashkovsky's protagonists seem to be on the constant run, never content and always restless. Consider, for example, Serhii's ruminations in the novel *The Wolf's Star* (*Vovcha zoria*, 1991):

Thinking of his tormenting wanderings, Serhii always tried but never managed to imagine all the ferocious magnitude of an ichorous river that floods and will flood, that sweeps and will sweep people from their houses protected by dams, apparently, these exiles are still lost in the desert darkness and call their unblessed kin to be rescued from the temple of sorrow, brother after brother, accompanied by loud prophecies of terminals, will fall down like golden bedbugs from the hot and sour fur of the wolf, running it rescues itself by a mere habit of flights, chattering with fangs it hews out flesh from its own enraged blood, and on the paved road, under the thorny shadow, on the stone, in the good land, we will remember you, oh implacable arch-father of ours.[61]

Pashkovsky's prose style, like Medvid's, is dense and opaque, and the writer's relationship with the reader not particularly engaging.[62] But, unlike Medvid's, Pashkovsky's novels are more contemporaneous and rarely attempt historical digressions, which are profuse, for instance, in *Blood on Straw*. In many ways, one can also discern signs of style's exhaustion in Pashkovsky but it is spatial rather than temporal. Time for Medvid is nonlinear and unfolds through language, and this is what characterizes his overall output. His language suffers from overindulgence and has nowhere to go and, arguably, it is because the author of *Blood on Straw* has an obsessive tendency to historicize the present and to mythologize the past. In other words, his desire to embrace the totality of Ukrainian experience, although through the prism of the local, pushes his language to the edge of abyss: "I am like a dystrophic that cannot remember the right word; after all, the history of a society is really the history of its language; a few elementary language structures, learned back in school and preserved in the people's discourse, turn alright, but then one stands as if on the edge of abyss in the universe."[63] Or, to use a different metaphor, his language behaves like a river that overflows its banks and devours everything in its path. In the end, all you see is water. By the same token, all one sees in Medvid's prose is the language with voracious qualities.

The aforementioned exhaustion is present in Pashkovsky's oeuvre but it is of a different kind. Rather than temporal, it is more spatial. He is more concerned with place and its dangers (be it a village or a city) than with time. Neither of these two types of human dwelling—rural or urban—constitutes a haven in Pashkovsky's imaginary world. Contrary to what some critics have been advocating,[64] his texts do not really privilege the village over the city. In fact, both places represent a dead end. A protagonist with rural roots, bound to make it in the city, has in reality no choice of going back to the place of his origin because that in itself signifies a failure: "... and not revering the village, he was more and more thinking of returning, but imagined scorns of villagers kept him at bay—'oh, he's back, it didn't take him long' ... ."[65] Pashkovsky's village is not an alluring place. It is not Arcadia. In his novel *Holiday*, the author sees all the foibles among the country dwellers and does not have any kind words to say about them:

... pushing through the dike, he's been thinking that any village is just a village—rumors, superstition, maybe that's not a chaffing but a good warning, for here everyone knows about everyone, it's hard to keep secrets for long and a collective invisible conscience looms up, that is why people slope off to new places where no one knows them or their kin, where no one bad-mouths anyone; and that is why his father did not get better, spat angrily and left for non-trouble, foretelling his children that they too would scatter like sparks from a honing stone.[66]

Medvid, for that matter, also does not idealize the countryside because for him it lacks the spirit it used to have in the past: "It is frightful to think what kind of people once lived in the village that now one can only glimpse them on photographs; you would think there's the same language, the same work as before in Ukraine but the spirit's clearly different, something got swept away."[67] There is a clear note of nostalgia in Medvid's ruminations that would indicate the author believes that things were considerably different in the past, if not better. Yet there is no evidence that he is advocating some kind of restoration of the long bygone values and times. Rather, there is an overwhelming allusion to the consistent persecution of peasants under the Soviet regime. Therefore, I am not so convinced that the ascribed neo-populism is an apt designation in his case. Medvid insists on the importance of collective memory, preserved by means of language and oral history, especially in the countryside, mainly because it is through such channels a new future can be created. But he has no illusions as to the real state of affairs in contemporary Ukrainian villages. Hence, his writings do betray some quixotic qualities.

Pashkovsky is less nostalgic in his works, quite possibly because there is nothing positive in the past or in the present that he can nostalgically refer to. According to him, there is no center, no reference point, and all that life has to offer is a trap. His heroes oscillate on the village—city continuum and seemingly cannot find a niche for themselves anywhere. At first, they feel lost, and then quite angry. But the angry rhetoric of *Daily Baton* (*Shchodennyi zhezl*, 1999), for instance, sounds rather artificial. This anger only reveals the author's utter impotence to affect changes, or to make life any different for ordinary people and intellectuals alike. And, despite Pashkovsky's desire for power, as ascribed to him by the critic Roksana Kharchuk, his rhetoric in *Daily Baton* is simply tragic and empty at the same time. The writer's compulsion to blame someone or something for his own (and in his imagination) his native land's woes is in line with the experience found in other postcolonial societies. Edward Said puts it beautifully:

> The tragedy of this experience, and indeed of so many post-colonial experiences, derives from the limitations of the attempts to deal with relationships that are polarized, radically uneven, remembered differently. The spheres, the sites of intensity, the agendas, and the constituencies in the metropolitan and ex-colonized worlds appear to overlap only partially. The small area that is perceived as common does not, at this point, provide for more than what might be called a *rhetoric of blame*.[68]

Thus, Pashkovsky's "post-imperial public discourse" (using Said's terms) is a typical postcolonial reaction to the unbearable hybridity, impurity and contradictions left by the legacy of imperialism.

Medvid's rhetoric of blame in this respect is more refined and turned inward rather than outward (he certainly does not denounce the West in the same way as Pashkovsky does), but he is also compelled to seek scapegoats for the overall apparent national and cultural decline of Ukraine, and in the process reveals his deeply conservative and openly misogynistic views. For, according to Medvid, one such scapegoat is a Ukrainian woman. In his essay "State and Woman" ("Derzhava i zhinka") he contemplates:

> Hence that is why the state in its destruction of the aboriginal tradition has such a reliable partner in the body of an "emancipated" woman.
>   The history of human species is first and foremost the history of its language, and right now it is the language that suffers the most. To begin, the ancestors of hybrid ethnos reify the hybridity of its psyche in the traditional structure of discourse (consider the Ukrainian-Russian *surzhyk*) and destroy it from within. [...] A woman—mother readily cultivates this hybrid in her child because of its convenience in social interactions.[69]

However, to be fair, Medvid does not spare intellectuals, writers and artists either: "We create out of hatred for each other and you cannot hide that from others. [...] I will not be surprised when an artist will be cornered in such a way that all he will be left with will be his delusions and renditions of his own words."[70] The gloomy outlook, as well as the rhetoric of blame, well documented in both authors' texts, undoubtedly stem from the tangled colonial experience. Both Pashkovsky and Medvid, eager to shed the imperial trappings, consciously or unconsciously, uphold the imperial experience by assuming typically imperial postures: intolerance and self-righteousness.

Finally, I would like to address the well-established practice of classifying Medvid and Pashkovsky as neo-modernists.[71] Admittedly, at least on the surface, this designation appears more fitting than another common label reserved for them, namely "neo-populists." Reading both writers closely I became more and more convinced that both neo-modernism and neo-populism do not adequately convey what is happening in these two authors' texts. While they are fond of a stream-of-consciousness technique, a mode of narration indeed characteristic of literary modernism, they lack a modernist spirit, which, by definition, is anti-traditionalist, and with sight directed into the future rather than into the past. Medvid and Pashkovsky do not champion the new, the progressive or the futuristic, on the contrary, they certainly dwell mostly in the days gone by. And this turn toward the past puts them closer to postmodernists than modernists. To Linda Hutcheon, for example, "the presence of the past"[72] is one of the defining principles of postmodernism. This past, according to her, needs to be problematized, otherwise it becomes a mere nostalgia. Medvid's essays are quite telling in this respect because they often criticize the very approach he then applies in his own fictional works, namely utilizing various historical sources, borrowed texts and facts (this is especially evident in the novel *Blood on Straw*). In his essay "Erotic Zones of Ukrainian Elitism" ("Erohenni zony ukrains'koho elitaryzmu") Medvid contemplates: "the relentless penetration into the past and inert inferring from it lessons for today—a characteristic of a sick organism is an attempt to seek in the past something that heals and to which there is no return."[73] Clearly, the past can also be harmful, if approached uncritically, Medvid asserts. Yet, at the same time, the past is the place where the author himself looks for inspiration.

As for Pashkovsky, there are critics who are ready to classify his works as postmodern.[74] Indeed, his profound metaphysical doubt (despite a considerable Christian flavoring and Biblical allusions), displayed in the impossibility to find home (or the center, if you will), arguably expels him from the modernist project. In many ways, Pashkovsky and Medvid, while shying away from parody and pastiche (typical postmodernist devices whose subversive qualities are mainly on the surface), are both engaged in constant undermining of "the center" from within. In other words, the values and beliefs they are promoting do not resonate precisely because they are questioned and doubted at the same time. How can one seriously accept their proclivity for *narodnytstvo* (populism) as the guiding philosophy, if the way they convey their ideas is the most elitist and abstruse among contemporary Ukrainian authors? They can claim discursively populist positions as much as they want but stylistically their texts tell a different story. The language of their narratives does not strive to communicate easily and thus can never count on massive reception and influence. Therefore, the "language as protagonist" choice becomes for them, paradoxically, a curse rather than reward, if viewed from the perspective of effective national identity construction.

NOTES

1. Amid the widespread opposition, fistfights in the Parliament, and countless rallies across Ukraine, President Viktor Yanukovych signed new language legislation on August 8, 2012, passed by the Parliament controlled by the Party of Regions, and reluctantly signed by the Speaker Volodymyr Lytvyn. The new law, called "On the principles of state language policy," aims at giving Russian, or any other minority language, the status of a "regional" language, thus allowing it to be adopted by courts, schools, and government institutions in areas of Ukraine where ethnic minorities

constitute at least 10 percent of the total population of a defined administrative district. Although the new legislation did not reverse the existing law on the official state language as guaranteed by Article 10 of the Constitution, it provided a considerable break for Russian-speaking southeastern provinces. Critics of the law claim that the Russian language is already widely used and giving it a privileged status in some areas would only further depress the usage of Ukrainian and become a contributing factor in furthering a split between eastern and western parts of Ukraine. Following the Revolution of Dignity in 2014 and Yanukovych's flight to Russia, the temporary Ukrainian government rescinded that law only to reinstate again to prevent a backlash in the southeastern provinces. Unfortunately, violence in the Donbas commenced nonetheless.

2. For example, Maksym V. Strikha provides a very interesting statistics for the first decade of independence: "... according to 2001 census only 39.1 percent of Ukrainian citizens speak Ukrainian at home (in 1992 thirty-seven percent did). ... But the proportion of citizens speaking only Russian at home has increased from twenty-nine percent in 1992 to thirty-six percent in 2000." See his "Language and Language Policy in Ukraine," *Journal of Ukrainian Studies* 26 (2001): 244–45. However, a decade later, in 2011, according to the statistics provided by the Razumkov Center in Kyiv, 53.3 percent of Ukrainian citizens speak Ukrainian at home, whereas 44.5 percent speak Russian. See "Bil'she polovyny hromadian Ukrainy hovoriat' ukrains'koiu u pobuti" http://www.pravda.com.ua/news/2011/08/23/6524063/, accessed August 23, 2011. But, amid this improved statistics, there are also numerous examples of discrimination against citizens asserting their constitutional right to speak Ukrainian in the public sphere. See Oleksandr Shelukhin, "Shche odyn oksiumoron. Chomu v Ukraini nebezpechno rozmovliaty ukrains'koiu?," *Ukrains'ka pravda*, March 12, 2012, accessed March 13, 2012, http://www.pravda.com.ua/columns/2012/03/12/6960434/.

3. See Viktor Stepanenko, "Identities and Language Politics in Ukraine: The Challenges of Nation-State Building," in *Nation-Building, Ethnicity and Language Politics in Transition Countries*, ed. Farimah Daftary and François Grin (Budapest: Open Society Institute, 2003), 114 and Volodymyr Kulyk, "Language identity, linguistic diversity and political cleavages: evidence from Ukraine," *Nations and Nationalism* 17 (2011): 628–29.

4. Kulyk, "Language identity," 628.

5. Tamara Hundorova touched on that point briefly in one of her articles: "The reverse canon of the 1990s embraced not only Ukrainian-language but also Russian-language mass literature. The preceding canon was monocultural and excluded works by Ukrainian authors written in Russian. ... Some Russian-language authors, such as Andrei Kurkov and Marina and Sergei Diachenko, live and work in Ukraine and call themselves Ukrainian writers." See her "New Ukrainian Literature of the 1990s," *Journal of Ukrainian Studies* 26 (2001): 269.

6. Ihor Kruchyk, "Dity radians'koi vdovy," *Krytyka* 16.5 (2012): 25.

7. But, worth noting, the government of the Russian Federation assumed a diametrically opposed stand, and considerably increased its support for the Russian-language production in the so-called near abroad in the 2000s, not only with words

but also with money. Kruchyk provides a stunning statistics—during the period of 2009–2011 Russia spent over 1 billion rubles in grant money for those who cultivate Russian culture in the former republics of the Soviet Union . See Kruchyk, "Dity," 26.

8. The same dynamic seems to be in place also in the post-independence period. See Marco Puleri's article "Ukrains'kyi, rosiis'komovnyi, rosiis'kyi (Ukrainian, Russian-speaking, Russian): Self-identification in post-Soviet Ukrainian literature in Russian," *Ab imperio* 2 (2014): 379–80. Puleri comes to the conclusion that "the most popular Ukrainian Russian-speaking writers were those who publish their works abroad, mainly in Russia" (Ibid., 380).

9. For example, Igor Klekh, born in 1952 in Kherson, Ukraine, moved to Moscow in 1994 and published four books there. While his early writings deal with Galicia and the city of Lviv (where he studied and worked for a while), he considers himself a Russian writer. Cf. his *A Country the Size of Binoculars* published by Northwestern University Press in 2004. Another Ukrainian Russophone writer of the younger generation, Volodymyr Puzii (b. 1978), publishes his fantasy fiction in Russia because of better financial rewards, he even agreed to assume a more Russian sounding pen name "Vladimir Arenev" on the suggestion of his Russian publisher.

10. Or, as Puleri indicates in his article, for quite a few of the most popular Russophone authors living in Ukraine, it is difficult to find the unequivocal sense of national belonging, and they sit on the fence, so to speak. Aleksandr Kabanov (b. 1968), for example, states that he is a Russian poet and a Ukrainian citizen (Ibid., 379), Aleksei Nikitin (b. 1967) wants to identify with both cultures (Ibid., 387), whereas Donetsk-born Volodymyr Rafeyenko (b. 1969) sees himself first and foremost as a human being and seems to dismiss the importance of national self-identification outright (Ibid., 390). Rafeyenko lives now in Kyiv and his poems are included in the anthology *Letters from Ukraine* (2016), published in Ternopil. It appears that in the end he chose to be part of the Ukrainian cultural space.

11. They moved to Moscow in 2009; since 2013 reside in the United States. See https://ru.wikipedia.org/wiki/Дяченко,_Марина_и_Сергей

12. Puleri, "Ukrains'kyi," 368.

13. It is not without significance that Luzina's first book *Moia Lolita* (*My Lolita*, 2002) was published by the Ukrainian Cultural Fund. Since then, all her novels are published by Folio in Kharkiv. Kurkov's beginnings in the early 1990s, on the other hand, were marked by his own entrepreneurial self-publishing efforts until he managed to find a Swiss publisher for his *Death and the Penguin* in 1997. Since his commercial success in the West, he regularly publishes with Folio in Kharkiv.

14. Their first two books were still published in Ukraine (*Privratnik*, 1994, and *Ritual*, 1996). But after that the only other work (besides a couple of books for children) that was published in Ukraine (both in the original and translation) was the novel inspired by the songs of Ruslana, the Ukrainian pop singer who won the Eurovision Song Contest in 2004, titled *Dyka enerhiia. Lana* (*Wild Energy. Lana*, 2006). This book was published by Teza Publishing House in Vinnytsia.

15. Kurkov, *Penguin Lost*, trans. George Bird (London: Vintage, 2005), 253.

16. Published in 1998 *Istoriia ukrains'koi literatury 20 stolittia*, a collective work under the general editorship of Vitalii Donchyk, focuses mainly on the Soviet writers

rather than those debuting in the glasnost and post-independence periods. This seems to be a systemic problem, put plainly—literary scholars of the older generation or conservative proclivity simply do not take up a new literature.

17. Vasyl' Shkliar, "Ia ... 'poslav' legionera v Chechniu," *Knyzhnyk-Review* 9.66 (2003): 4. However, Shliar's views in this regard must have changed dramatically by 2010, as I witnessed his participation in a literary event at Knyharnia Ye in Kyiv together with Kurkov and Larysa Denysenko. Shkliar admitted at that time that he embraced Kurkov's oeuvre as Ukrainian.

18. Volodymyr Iavorivs'kyi, "Kompleks tiazhiie nad ukrains'kym suspil'stvom," *Dzerkalo tyzhnia*, January 4, 2002, accessed October 21, 2013, http://gazeta.dt.ua/SCIENCE/kompleks_tyazhie_nad_ukrayinskim_suspilstvom.html.

19. See his lecture "Independent Ukraine as a Function of Soviet Inertia," first mentioned in Chapter 2.

20. Published in Ukrainian as: *Ostannia liubov prezydenta* (Ternopil: Bohdan, 2005). This is the edition I used for this study. Also published in English as *The President's Last Love* (2007).

21. Published in Ukrainian translation in 2008 by Nora-Druk in Kyiv and in English translation in 2011 by Harvill Secker in the United Kingdom. For this study I used the Ukrainian edition in Ostap Slyvynsky's rendition.

22. Another team of authors that also excels in fantasy genre is G.L. Oldi, the pseudonym of two Russophone Kharkiv writers—Dmitrii E. Gromov (b. 1963) and Oleg S. Ladyzhenski (b. 1963).

23. This is her pen name. Her real name is Vladislava Kucherova.

24. Published in Ukrainian as *Vid'oms'ka doba* by Kal'variia in 2000. It has been translated into English and e-published by Amazon in 2014.

25. Published in Ukrainian as *Kyivs'ki vid'my. Mech i khrest* by Folio in 2012. This is the edition I use for this study.

26. I am using the Ukrainian edition of this novel and that is why all proper names have the Ukrainian spelling.

27. Maryna Diachenko worked previously as an actress and occasionally lectured at the Kyiv National Institute of Theatre Art. Serhiy Diachenko, a psychiatrist turned screenwriter (after graduating from the Moscow Film Institute), continues to be involved in film. In fact, the couple's move to Moscow in 2009 was prompted in part by an invitation for Serhiy to work on a TV screenplay *Belaia gvardiia* (White Guard).

28. See their interview with Paweł Laudański, "Wywiad z Mariną i Siergiejem Diaczenko," *Esensja*, February 9, 2005, accessed November 10, 2013, http://esensja.stopklatka.pl/ksiazka/wzw/tekst.html?id=2008&strona=1#strony.

29. Since the mid-2000 all the Diachenkos' new works have been published simultaneously in Ukrainian translation. Their latest novel *Stokrat* (Hundredfold, 2012) has been so far issued only in Russian. Whether or not this is the beginning of a new phase, in which Ukrainian publishers are no longer eager to render the Diachenkos' works in Ukrainian translation, remains to be seen.

30. The translator Viktor Boiko makes these names sound Ukrainian in his Ukrainian rendition of the text. Hence instead of Masha and Dasha we have Marika and Daryna.

31. For example, there is a bizarre scene in the novel, in which Dasha, all naked, rides through the streets of Kyiv on her red motorcycle with the blue and yellow national flag of Ukraine in her hand.

32. She also works professionally as a journalist.

33. See Iryna Slavinska, "20 rokiv nezalezhnoi ukrains'koi literatury." It is not without significance that she agreed to participate in Slavinska's survey alongside other well-known Ukrainian authors, thereby signaling her cultural orientation. On the other hand, she was the only one among them expressing her views in Russian.

34. Laada Bilaniuk calls it "a post-independence surzhyk" and differentiates it from those types that involve language shift from Ukrainian to Russian. See her detailed typology of *surzhyk* before and after independence. *Contested Tongues*, 103–41.

35. Taras Koznarsky also uses this term in his extensive analysis of *surzhyk* in Bohdan Zholdak's collection of short stories *Ialovychyna* (Beef, 1991), although calls it a cultural oxymoron since, as he explains, any written text a priori entails a certain normativity. See his "Notatky na berehakh makabresok," *Krytyka* 2.5 (1998), 28.

36. Bilaniuk, *Contested Tongues*, 130.

37. This seems to be Zholdak's strategy in most of his short story collections. See especially *Ialovychyna* (*Beef*, 1991), *Boh buvaie* (*God Is*, 1999) and *Antyklimaks* (*Anti-Climax*, 2001).

38. Hundorova, *Pisliachornobyl's'ka biblioteka*, 122.

39. In fact, Hundorova quotes Zholdak himself who admits that he addresses his *surzhyk* stories to intelligentsia, hoping that it will act as some kind of therapy for them, that is, helping them to overcome this "stupid" (as he puts it) language practice (Ibid., 121–22).

40. See her *Kukhnia ehoista* (Kyiv: Fakt, 2007), 58.

41. That practice we also find in Pyrkalo but not as consistently and visibly, as it is encountered in Povaliaieva.

42. All three examples are from her novel *Instead of Blood* (*Zamist' krovi*).

43. Svitlana Kobets, "Review of *Pol'ovi doslidzhennia z ukrains'koho seksu*, by Oksana Zabuzhko," *Slavic and East European Journal* 41 (1997): 184.

44. And discussed by Bilaniuk in *Contested Tongues*, 117–21.

45. Povaliaieva, *Zamist' krovi* (Lviv: Kal'variia, 2003), 53. The quotation is provided in the original to illustrate Povaliaieva's approach to hybridizing language. The italic script and caps are in the original text. The quoted excerpt clearly betrays performative qualities and more likely imitates a song. It can be paraphrased roughly as follows: "Sexy Tanya, you are a lush sprout of acceleration, with such buttocks that … . Oh! Oh! Oh! Baby, baby, baby, all the people on the streetcar, the streetcar went crazy because of covered—understand! TIGHTLY COVERED WITH BIKE SHORTS buttocks, like resilient and quick melons, Tanya cries, she lost a ball, be quiet, little Tanya, do not cry, your ball won't drown, A BALL IN GENERAL NEVER DROWNS."

46. In *Freud Would Cry* she has a footnote, informing the reader that the author reserves the right not to transliterate Russian and other foreign languages into Ukrainian. See *Froid by plakav* (Kharkiv: Folio, 2004), 73.

47. Ibid., 218.

48. Translated by Virlana Tkacz and Wanda Phipps, reprinted by permission. Available at: http://www.poetryinternationalweb.net/pi/site/poem/item/5552/auto/0/0/Andriy-Bondar/THE-ROMAN-ALPHABET, accessed November 17, 2013. Incidentally, Bondar alludes here to the poem by his contemporary Ivan Malkovych about those Ukrainian Cyrillic letters that are unique to the Ukrainian alphabet.

49. Actually, she debuted with a Ukrainian collection of short stories published in Ukrainian by the Smoloskyp Publishing House in 1999. However, she established herself as an author with subsequent four novels written in Russian.

50. See her article "Lazutkin as Lazutkin as Lazutkin—Traces Remain" translated from the Ukrainian by Chrystyna Kuzmych for the website "Poetry International Rotterdam." http://www.poetryinternationalweb.net/pi/site/cou_article/item/8846/Lazutkin-as-Lazutkin-as-Lazutkin-traces-remain, accessed November 18, 2013.

51. This is the edition I used for this study.

52. An excellent summary of the challenges faced by Ukrainian writers is provided by Mark Andryczyk in his Ukrainian article "Proza movnoi identychnosty" in *Krytyka* 9.3 (2005): 23–24.

53. Viacheslav Medvid', "Ukrains'ka liudyna dlia ukrains'koi literatury ie vse shche nerozhadanoiu materiieiu," *Knyzhnyk-Review* 6.63 (2003): 3.

54. Ievhen Baran, *Zoilovi treny* (Lviv: Lohos, 1998), 57.

55. Medvid', *Pro domo sua: shchodennyky, ese* (Kyiv: Ukrains'kyi pys'mennyk, 1999), 148.

56. See especially Ola Hnatiuk's arguments in her *Pożegnanie z imperium* (Lublin: Wyd. Uniwersytetu Marii Curie-Skłodowskiej, 2003).

57. The following passage from his *Pro domo sua* describes this the best: "The more I think about it, regardless of who I am or where I come from, I do feel the need to be a patriot of a certain locality" (Ibid., 76).

58. Medvid', "Ukrains'ka liudyna," 3.

59. I am mindful of the allusion to John Barth's article "The Literature of Exhaustion," published in 1967. In many ways this early postmodern manifesto corresponds to Medvid's interest in the processes of the narrative itself. Medvid, like Barth, comes to the conclusion that the conventional modes of literary representation had been exhausted (hence his focus on the language rather than plot or characters), at the same time, he readily employs modernist techniques while exploring their extreme possibilities.

60. Medvid', *Pro domo sua*, 24.

61. Ievhen Pashkovs'kyi, *Vovcha zoria* (Kyiv: Molod', 1991), 70–71.

62. Marko Pavlyshyn pointed this out in his article "Dva khudozhni tila suchasnoi prozy," *Svito-vyd* 3 (1997): 103–10.

63. Medvid', *Pro domo sua*, 61.

64. See, for example, Nila Zborovska, "Pro romany Ievhena Pashkovs'koho," in *Feministychni rozdumy*, 144–45; or, R.B. Kharchuk, *Suchasna ukrains'ka proza: Postmodernyi period* (Kyiv: Akademiia, 2008), 82.

65. Pashkovs'kyi, *Vovcha zoria*, 156.

66. Pashkovs'kyi, *Bezodnia: romany* (Lviv: Piramida, 2005), 73.

67. Medvid', *Pro domo sua*, 23.

68. Edward Said, *Culture and Imperialism* (New York: Vintage Books, 1994), 18.

69. Medvid', *Pro domo sua*, 182.

70. Ibid., 209.

71. See Hundorova, *Pisliachornobyl's'ka biblioteka*, 254–55, and Kharchuk, *Suchasna ukrains'ka proza: Postmodernyi period*, 74–106.

72. Hutcheon, *Poetics of Postmodernism*, 4.

73. Medvid', *Pro domo sua*, 217.

74. See an entry under Pashkovsky in *Pleroma* 3 (1998): 87.

Chapter 5

Ways of Social Marginalization
in Post-Independence Fiction

Ideology, Disease and Crime

The collapse of the Soviet Union and the emergence of independent Ukraine in 1991 brought about a profound social and political transformation that affected not only the society's attitudes toward the printed word but also impacted the social role of the writer and what subject matters he or she wanted to explore in his/her narratives. The explosion of artistic freedom, a tiny bit of which was already tasted under Gorbachev's policies of glasnost and perestroika, blossomed enormously in the 1990s. But while that period saw the end of censorship, making subjects previously taboo—be it for political or moral reasons (e.g., erotica, homosexuality, obscenity and nationalism, to name a few)—profusely utilized in literary texts, the psychological and thematic grip of the "Sovietness," aka *Sovok*, was still very much in play in a number of narratives produced shortly after independence.

In this chapter I want to examine various manifestations of social marginalization as represented in fiction of those authors who grapple with issues of identity construction but in such a way that they are set against the background of a new social and political reality. What interests me in particular are narratives that focus on societal margins—misfits, outcasts, madmen, rebellious youth, religious zealots and criminals. And even though the marginalization in each analyzed text unfolds according to different suppositions, what unites them all is their protagonists' yearning for redemption of sorts—they all seek an exit from otherwise unbearable situations, though rarely being successful in finding one. Faced with a profound social change these characters are forced to find for themselves new outlets for coping with anxiety and stress, and depending on their early conditioning and subsequent circumstances such outlets can be at times socially constructive, but more often than not—maladaptive, if not outright dangerous. Social marginalization routinely comes about because of protagonists' faulty application of coping strategies, which, rather than to alleviate problems, only further exacerbate them and morph into various forms of deviations—mental and/or criminal. On the other hand, as some texts below assert, madness or violent crime can be quite liberating, mainly by engendering a chasm with the existing order, causing a radical break from power relations imposed by the current of life. As Deleuze and Guattari poignantly point out, "Madness need not be all breakdown. It may also be breakthrough ... ."[1]

However, not all mental deviations are created equal and manifest themselves in the same way. Some are directed inwardly and can be quite innocent (mainly of neurotic types), often intellectualizing the creative process itself, while others—psychopathic types—are outwardly by their very nature and therefore invariably pose some danger to society, as they often result in criminal acts. To what extent the collapse of a known political and social order (as the collapse of the Soviet Union very much embodied) triggers an outpour of deviations, marginalizations, and criminality among youths and adults alike becomes the subject of many fictional accounts, produced by a number of Ukrainian post-independence authors of different generations, from Volodymyr Dibrova (b. 1951) to Liubko Deresh (b. 1984).[2] The thematization of social misfits, youth transgressions and various traumas many a time goes hand in hand with questions concerning a sense of national belonging and, at the same time, underlines the shakiness of the process of decolonization and constructing a new Ukrainian identity. A diseased society in which corruption and oppression reign supreme allows for the buildup of resentment that eventually finds an outlet in rage and rebellion. For socially minded authors probing the extent to which oppression, hopelessness, destitution, failure and humiliation figure into the aggregate of causes that result in mental breakdowns and/or violent crimes has become the new creative dictum following the emergence of independent Ukraine. But the examination of social woes without implicit or explicit references to the Soviet colonial past has been unavoidable and they figure quite prominently in many post-independence literary texts.

SHEDDING THE SOVIETNESS (*SOVOK*): TRAUMAS OF SOCIAL CHANGE

Dealing with the Soviet past inevitably amounts to dealing with the trauma of social change. For some, the psychological adjustment that a new order demands morphs into an insurmountable barrier, blocking paths forward, often pushing into delinquency or even suicide. Three novels by three different authors—Volodymyr Dibrova, Oles Ulianenko and Yuri Izdryk, respectively, examine such adjustments (or, more accurately, failures in adjustments), quite vividly, forcing their protagonists to undergo various degrees of traumatic experience.

Dibrova's *Burdyk*, written in the mid-1990s, is a novel about the lost generation of the 1970s intellectuals (to which the author, born in 1951, himself belongs—"Suffocated Generation,"[3] as he put it) who, when confronted with sweeping ideological shifts on the eve of independence, are unable to adapt to new social and political circumstances. Burdyk, a Ukrainian intellectual hero who manages to cleverly navigate the absurdities of the Soviet system, in the absence of an ideological adversary becomes a social misfit, a "Superfluous Man"[4] as the novel's narrator and Burdyk's friend states right at the outset. The narrator too, as he relates his friend's life to the imaginary reader, betrays similar qualities—his previously meaningful underground existence morphs into a literary redundancy in post-Soviet Ukraine. In fact, he can be easily taken as Burdyk's double, desperately trying to reconcile two different realities that are naturally unbridgeable and constantly rupture.

Dibrova's protagonists yearn for change and fear it at the same time. Burdyk dies in a tragic accident while waiting for a friend, killed by a bus on one of Kyiv's streets, shortly before independence. At the end of the novel the narrator reunites with Burdyk in his dream and thus, arguably, also fades into oblivion or dreamlike existence. Burdyk's death becomes the symbolic exit of the whole intellectual generation from a literary scene that in its thinking, as Dibrova contends, has been equally incompatible with ideological premises offered by the Soviet regime as with those, proposed by the newly installed post-independence authorities. In his monograph *The Intellectual as Hero in 1990s Ukrainian Fiction*, Mark Andryczyk correctly observes that: "In post-Soviet Ukraine, the Eighties Writers did indeed fade from the public eye. This, however, transpired not because they became subservient to the government, but because their views on Ukrainian identity were incompatible with the views of those who had rapidly accumulated political power."[5]

While the marginalization in *Burdyk* is socially and politically situated, in Izdryk's *Wozzeck*, written at the approximately same time as Dibrova's novel, it comes across more abstractly (if not existentially), signifying, I argue, the main character's inner imperative, his compelling desire to be left alone, to be on society's margins by choice. But Izdryk's postmodern intellectual hero, not without allusions to his namesake predecessors—real and imaginary (from the historical figure of Johann Christian Woyzeck, the former soldier, who in a jealous rage murdered his lover in Leipzig in 1821, to Georg Büchner's unfinished drama, *Woyzeck*, based on that incident and written in the 1830s but published in 1879 but, to, finally, Alban Berg's atonal opera *Wozzeck* premiered in 1925 and exploring the same theme)—is not a superfluous or allegorical man. He is a man thrust into existence,[6] in pain most of the time, his suffering closely reflecting the imperfect physical

world. Clearly distrustful of others and not at ease with his own disintegrating (schizophrenic?) self, Wozzeck nonetheless refuses to give up looking for
coping strategies, even though it is safe to conclude that he fails in the end to
find the right answer for himself or, using religious terms, to find redemption.
But it is not without significance that both chapters, called Night and Day,
end with the Lord's Prayer. One can at first speculate that the disintegrating
self seemingly finds solace in Christian faith but both concluding prayers,
themselves disintegrating into syllables and separate sounds, more likely
signify the impossibility of finding the center, the truth or the coveted union
of one self to another.

There is not much of a plot in Izdryk's postmodern novel. His Wozzeck is
in love with A. but unlike his historical prototype, he does not murder her.
Instead, he locks her and her son up in the basement in order to protect them,
as he confesses, from an unkind world. It is a Manichean world of Darkness
and Light (hence the two chapters appropriately named Night and Day), or
Good and Evil, with which Wozzeck constantly struggles, diseased by it both
physically and mentally. His act of imprisoning his family, criminal by any
social measure, emerges in his mind as an act of kindness:

> To be sure, Wozzeck believed that only by imprisoning his family in the base-
> ment—an illegal act in the opinion of the authorities—could he protect his son
> and his wife from the menace of a decadent, evil, lascivious world; and although
> psychiatrists are still unsure how convinced he was of his claim, one can concur
> that he loved them—his son and his wife. He loved his son. He loved his wife.[7]

Indeed, the character elicits plenty of sympathy. Perhaps, it is partly
because he is depicted as mentally ill and in care of psychiatrists. Or, perhaps,
it is because that throughout the novel he comes across as a knowledgeable
subject, doubting the very essence of his own existence and being in constant
dialogue with his contemporary and past heroes. There are not that many
explicit references to Soviet or post-Soviet realities, nor there are any covert/
overt complaints about the state of national culture in Ukraine, including the
language situation, as was the case in Dibrova's *Burdyk*, but there are ample
allusions (intertexts) to the European intellectual tradition and to the local
artistic milieu in which the main protagonist functions. Wozzeck's crime is
forgiven and his "dis-ease" with the world is rather benign, as his mental illness is directed more toward his own annihilation rather than toward that of
others. Moreover, the whole text can be read as a witty game of wordplay,
or a deconstruction of various philosophical premises, or, possibly, even a
parodic indulgence in intertextuality, without any far-reaching moral consequences and/or certainty about what is real and what is imagined, quite in line
with a postmodern sensitivity.

The same cannot be said about the events depicted in Ulianenko's novel *Satan's Dauphin* (*Dofin Satany*, 2003). Written in the realist tradition, this novel depicts gruesome murders committed by the serial killer, Ivan Bilozub, over the period of ten years, and an obsessive hunt to stop him by a detective, captain Raksha. The story line of *Satan's Dauphin* begins in 1989 with a horrific quadruple murder in one of Kyiv's apartments by Bilozub, who annoyed by a noisy neighbor, goes to his place and beheads everyone inside. This exceptionally horrendous act, depicted by Ulianenko with an utmost grisly naturalistic detail, acquires religious overtones when the reader learns that Bilozub commits murder through the encouragement of an Angel that descends upon him in his apartment in the body of a beautiful young man with female facial features, dressed all in radiant white, and declares to him that he is the chosen one:

I came to help you. Why are you afraid? You humans are all so strange: you want to be free but stand here like a post and don't know what to do. Go and free yourself, liberate your own self. If that neighbor of yours does not yield to you, then you must get rid of him. How otherwise? And you must do the same to everyone else present there. How you ask? By all means necessary, even if you must kill them all. Do you think that we visit just anyone? Go and free yourself. You are the chosen one.[8]

Izdryk and Ulianenko, both born in 1962, not only reflect upon a causal connection between mental illness and crime, but also do so within the framework of religious symbols emanating from Christian faith. However, Ulianenko, unlike Izdryk, places his deliberations within a clearly defined social context. Bilozub's murders come about right on the eve of independence, at the time of radical social and political change, and continue well into the post-independence period. In his mentally twisted mind Bilozub believes that his violent acts constitute God's vengeance for all the injustices inflicted upon him by various individuals under Soviet rule and through murder he is able to break the shackles that hold him in bondage. He also maintains that he is authorized by higher powers to punish selected groups of people for all the runaway debauchery and filth rampant everywhere since independence. Bilozub's extreme acts of violence, not only murders but also occasional cannibalism, occurring at times randomly, at other times—transpiring as part of a well-thought-out plan, are all prompted by the angelic voice he hears in his head and which he takes as a command to carry out God's will. The fact that he is not caught and that someone else (a homeless man Kometa) is tried and executed for those first beheadings only reinforces in him the belief in his own special power and status.

In the best tradition of naturalistic writing, Ulianenko attempts to determine the underlying forces of Bilozub's mental/criminal deviations by focusing on the social environment and heredity as factors influencing his actions. Hence we are provided with his childhood biography, including the abuse in the hands of his equally cruel parents and school friends, spiced up with cases of underage rape, homosexuality, incest, theft, all insinuating the reasons for Ivan's transformation from the abused into being the abuser himself. More adversities follow in his youth and adulthood that include, among other things, many unhappy relationships with the opposite sex. While not an intellectual or aspiring writer as was the case with Dibrova's or Izdryk's protagonists, psychotic Bilozub is nonetheless well-educated, highly intelligent, quite charming and seemingly well-adjusted to his however tenuous circumstances, the qualities that make him so much more elusive to the authorities. He is also bisexual and eventually becomes involved with a gay man Richchi with whom he colludes to seduce and kill as many homosexuals as they can physically handle.

Ulianenko, in the Manichean fashion, counterbalances the forces of Evil with those of Good. Thus the novel has two other important characters that represent the latter, namely the captain Raksha and his lover Lilit. They are not by any stretch of the imagination faultless agents of Good (after all, perfection is conceivable only in the realm of the spiritual world) but together they manage to outsmart Bilozub and finally bring him to justice. In the end, it turns out that Bilozub, a notorious serial killer and psychopath, is but a coward who is afraid to die. Despite his decade-long horrid acts of violence committed seemingly without fear of retribution, following his capture he employs delaying tactics as his legal defense, expecting at any moment an imposition of a much talked-about moratorium on capital punishment. And indeed, Ukraine officially abolished capital punishment on December 29, 1999. However, Bilozub is asphyxiated two days prior to that act by a fellow prisoner, Abkhazian Muslim Romodan, who on his way to be executed demands to see Bilozub as his last wish. Romodan's final act of vigilante is so swift and unexpected that prison guards are unable or unwilling to intervene. The last paragraph of *Satan's Dauphin* informs the reader that Raksha married Lilit, left the law enforcement agency and became a private detective. Yet despite a happy family life that included two children, "life lost meaning for him. He knew one thing: whatever it was waiting for him on that other end he must live his life regardless of how horrible it seemed."[9]

Dibrova's and Ulianenko's narratives quite overtly link their protagonists' maladaptive coping with the corruptive influence of the "Sovietness," which endures, both authors contend, under different guises in the post-Soviet space even though the communist regime as such no longer exists. However, they do so rather differently. Dibrova's Burdyk, unable to adjust to new circumstances, falls victim to substance abuse becoming an alcoholic, but does not pose any physical threat to others. His cleverness and raison d'état under Soviet rule lose expediency when faced with change. Ulianenko's Bilozub, with tons of unresolved sexual issues and mania of righteousness, turns to killing innocent people, becoming a dangerous psychopath. Social marginalization in both cases has roots in the totalitarian system but, ideologically, is framed differently. Dibrova's text is a thoroughly secular account, its characters do not view religion as a remedy or universal cure, and, if they look for an exit (escape) at all from the unbearable "here and now," they find it sooner in emigration rather than in faith. Ulianenko, on the other hand, places his story line within the context of evil and good, amply referring to Christian symbols. He depicts Bilozub's Angel (who is obviously a Satan) as a gay man. There is some psychological justification for such a representation because the reader eventually learns that Bilozub is in fact bisexual, so his delusion could easily materialize in the embodiment of the effeminate male. Dibrova's and Ulianenko's main protagonists end dead as if to suggest that there is no escape other than death for those afflicted with misconstrued ideological fixations. However, other characters in these two respective novels also do not fare much better—though not dead, they are far from feeling content. We see the narrator in *Burdyk* at a crossroads after he comes back to Ukraine from working abroad and resigns from his job, or the captain Raksha in *Satan's Dauphin*, despite his "mission accomplished" performance, perceives life as futility if not a heavy burden. Even Raksha's wife Lilit, a beautiful and glamorous woman who equally shares his obsession to capture Bilozub and manages to allure him to her lover's apartment, cannot resist the killer's charm in the end and has sex with him shortly before he is arrested. Her odd transgression aside, it seems that all these characters are marked by the impossibility of breaking the bondage of their psychological past, deeply rooted in the Soviet reality.

Izdryk's *Wozzeck* differs in this respect substantially because its points of reference or overall contextualization are so decidedly, at least on a surface, non-Soviet. It is also not without significance that the novel's central character, Wozzeck, ends up being locked up in a mental institution rather than being dead. One can almost surmise that in his case madness and intellectual prowess go hand in hand, perhaps invoking Michel Foucault's work *Madness and Civilization* (1964) in which the French philosopher claims that in the Renaissance "madness fascinates because it is knowledge."[10] Wozzeck's madness fascinates too because it betrays an intimate knowledge of the European intellectual tradition, from Descartes to Heidegger, but, on a less positive note, it also implicitly suggests that that kind of orientation can easily become the source of social marginalization in the milieu unaccustomed to view affairs through philosophical lenses. And that leads straight to the issue of self-identity. Marko Pavlyshyn observed Izdryk's European affinity back in 2001 in his article "Choosing a Europe: Andrukhovych, Izdryk, and the New Ukrainian Literature." Comparing Andrukhovych's and Izdryk's European entanglement he concludes:

Both Andrukhovych and Izdryk choose a Europe, and the choice for each of them is no easy matter. Both engage with Europe, each in his own way savoring its blandishments and suffering its impositions. [...] Both recognize that they are not of the East, Andrukhovych through explicit declaration, and Izdryk through silence concerning it. Andrukhovych struggles to preserve the joy of seduction by Europe, to retain it as a familiar and beloved Other. In his efforts to remain detached—a tourist, a Europhile—he admires, enthuses, describes, classifies, and interprets. Yet, in the end, he acknowledges that he cannot but be involved. Europe is his, warts and all—not only its rococo palaces, but also its genocides. Izdryk, less ambivalent, has no comparable detachment. Europe's great problems are his problems. He is not a Europhile, but a European.[11]

All three novels under scrutiny here display various manifestations of social marginalization as their major themes: mental illness versus criminal activity; substance abuse, including drugs; alcoholism; death; religion and crime; social fringe groups—prostitutes, homosexuals, criminals, all intertwined in the chaotic and unstable reality of the post-independence reality. These novels are dark, gloomy and macabre, especially in Ulianenko's rendition. Yet, strangely, what connects them all besides the above social ailments is their protagonists' unquenchable desire for redemption. And all the main characters, Burdyk, Wozzeck and Bilozub, seek that redemption through love. True, Wozzeck's love for A. partially leads to his demise, but she is also the best thing that ever happened to him. Bilozub, falling for Lilit, makes love to her and in his sick mind fantasizes of a new happy life, a life without killing, with a woman he truly loves. Finally, the narrator of *Burdyk*, dreaming of the reunion with his friend learns from him that all that really matters in life is love: "... whom did you see there?" I asked Burdyk as if reciting a poem—"She's not there!" "There is!" He answered me in the same manner. "Love—that's what always is!"[12] These desperate cries for "the lightness of being" (as Kundera put it), signified by love, remain in the realm of the unattainable for all three protagonists, but the recognition that this is the only way out of the unbearable darkness is definitely there.

NEUROTICS, PSYCHOPATHS AND MENTALLY DISTURBED

The plethora of Ukrainian novels depicting characters with various personality disorders, and/or mentally disturbed that came out in the 1990s and 2000s, quite possibly reflects the overall social disorientation and revaluation of moral beliefs following the collapse of the Soviet Union, compounded, moreover, by ensuing extremely difficult economic conditions, especially in the first five years of independence. While psychologists generally agree that genetic predisposition plays a role in many mental illnesses, it is often an adverse environment that triggers antisocial behavior. An inability to adapt to one's environment might result in neurosis, whereas being physically neglected as a child, having poor supervision or coming from a low-income family, might give rise to psychopathy.

The most compelling psychopathic characters are found in Oles Ulianenko's fiction, which most deeply explores the connection between mental disorders and criminality, delving into the post-Soviet social decay with a breathtaking attention to detail and gruesome naturalism. But other writers, such as Izdryk, Anatolii Dnistrovy (b. 1974), and to a lesser extent Kostiantyn Moskalets (b. 1963), also display in their prose characters with mental disorders, though the degree of severity of their psychological issues varies. Izdryk, Dnistrovy and Moskalets focus more on neurotic types, for the most part intellectuals, whose behavioral patterns cause them suffering and/or lead to their inability to function in life. These protagonists are in search and need of finding coping mechanisms, capable of alleviating the overwhelming feeling of emptiness, meaninglessness and anxiety. Whereas neurotics look inward and dream of self-realization, psychopaths, on the other hand, seek sensation and control, demand immediate gratification, lack empathy and betray aggressive tendencies. Each behavioral pattern generates different responses and comes with a different set of consequences. What comes as a surprise (or, perhaps, it should not) is that regardless of the severity of mental disorders, the afflicted individuals—characters in fictional works—reflect the larger context, that is, the milieu in which corrupted behavior does not appear out of order but, on the contrary, seems to blend naturally in the overall social fabric.

Anatolii Dnistrovy's novel *A Fruit Fly over Kant's Volume* (*Drozofila nad tomom Kanta*, 2010) does not delve into societal margins but instead concentrates on the most educated strata, choosing an intellectual, an assistant professor of philosophy, as his main protagonist. And yet, we do not necessarily partake of highbrow philosophical debates. Rather, through the hero's inner neurotic musings we glimpse into the academic system of Ukrainian higher education that is degraded, corrupt and of quality that leaves much to be desired.[13] However, it does not seem that the novel's main goal is to come up with a social critique of the Ukrainian academic milieu. *A Fruit Fly* is too intimate for that, although, by default, it does reveal the corrupt system of higher education in post-independence Ukraine. What we witness in the novel are by and large inner dialogues of the much-conflicted neurotic protagonist Pavlo who presumably chooses isolation and passivity. He yearns for love, daydreams about an intimate relationship with a woman he is in love with but, in the end, apparently sabotages his own happiness by not showing up at his own wedding. His personal freedom and single way of life are seemingly more important to him than marriage and commitment. Pavlo's inability to change his life patterns no doubt points to his neurotic condition but it is less clear why he seems to be so stuck in the first place.

Pavlo clearly does not condone the corrupt Ukrainian educational system but being passive as he is we do not see him trying to change it in any meaningful way. On the contrary, he is very much part of the corrupt system— sleeps with female students and/or accepts in kind donations like produce in exchange for a favorable exam outcome—a very widespread practice among underpaid faculty members in the 1990s. He often dreams of dead flies and repeats the phrase "again the same thing," as if to underline the social decay around him. While not suicidal, Pavlo oftentimes repeats in his head that he does not know how to live: "I ended up in a desert, all by myself among motionless sands of my despair and loneliness."[14] He is aware that one way out of this depression is to work, yet he has a problem with that too. A proposition to write a popular study on Kant is enticing and he accepts it, yet we will not know by the end of the novel whether or not he manages to complete it. By all measures a womanizer, Pavlo often blames women for his intellectual impasse and ennui, simultaneously nurturing his daydreams about love and that perfect relationship with someone special because "a man without love amounts to a slow and relentless atrophy."[15]

It is difficult to know for sure whether the protagonist's conflicting desires about love relationships stem from some deep psychological issues he struggles with, or are simply triggered by unenviable external circumstances in which university teachers are inadequately compensated and thus not particularly eager to have a family. One thing is certain—Pavlo sees his profession, that of a scholar and philosophy professor, as being exceptionally marginalized, if not a totally useless occupation. In fact, in one of his inner musings he puts it on the same level as being homeless or a drug addict: "I think sometimes that Ukrainian scholars in this current social environment of very poor and very rich turned themselves into corpses on leave. It is the same risk group as homeless or drug addicts."[16] No wonder then that Dnistrovy's hero has escapist inclinations and drowns in neurosis. On the one hand, he idealizes love and thoughts of his beloved act like a safe haven for him; on the other hand, he is frightened by intimacy and real bond that necessarily come with commitment. He soon realizes that having casual sex is one thing but marriage, quite another. Life seems to lose its meaning and the constantly reflecting hero almost becomes envious of a little drosophila that has a short lifespan and yet such an enormous capacity to adapt to various conditions and environments. Pavlo questions his knowledge, his utility as an intellectual, and compares himself to a fruit fly that can only hover over the Kant's volume but produce hardly anything of value.

The theme of intellectuals' uselessness to society is also pursued by Kostiantyn Moskalets in his novel *Evening Mead* (*Vechirnii med*, 2009). It is perhaps best captured by the scene in which one of the protagonists, Kostyk, makes a decision to incinerate the entire printing of his poetry collection, turning it into a spectacle of sorts, or some kind of performance, all recorded on camera by a professional director. Shortly before setting his oeuvre on fire, Kostyk browses through his book, thinking, "it must be burned together with its depressing aura of marginality."[17] The act of destruction of intellectual property in *Evening Mead* mirrors self-destructing tendencies of its author and/or protagonist, whose alcohol addiction can turn deadly for him at any moment. Alcohol consumption masks *Evening Mead* protagonists pervasive neurosis and inability and/or unwillingness to adapt to changing circumstances. Mark Andryczyk, discussing the novel's main characters, puts it this way:

> Both Lord Krishna and Trotskyi are delusional men who respond to their marginalization by destructing themselves; this adds the sense of a vicious circle that Moskalets continually induces in this novel. The more these intellectuals fade from society's respect, the more they act in a deviant and anti-social manner and, thus, end up themselves fleeing from society. Moskalets presents the reader with an entire group of self-destructive and damaged intellectuals. They are unable to function normally in society—they are *ab*normal.[18]

And yet, as in the case of Dnistrovy's protagonist in *A Fruit Fly*, Moskalets's intellectual hero in *Evening Mead* also seeks salvation in love. His existential musings are interwoven with inspiring letters and paeans to his love interest, Andrusia, all in hope that she alone can pull him out of his debilitating neurosis. However, unlike Pavlo in *A Fruit Fly* Moskalets's hero does not walk out on her; it is Andrusia who apparently leaves him and, at the end of the novel, we learn that she moved to the United States, to the state of Arizona to be exact. Despite such a turn of events Kostyk still thinks highly of her and clearly suffers because of her already two-year absence. The novel ends in an imagined conversation between Kostyk and Andrusia, facilitated by an angel who sits on the hero's arm while he rides a train. We can easily surmise that this whole scene is either alcohol-inspired (hence hallucinatory) or of oneiric provenance. It certainly underscores the fact that the main character is unable to transcend his overwhelming feeling of neurotic impotence. What Pavlo and Kostyk share as intellectuals is that they both appear totally harmless to others. In other words, they do not pose any danger to society and their neurosis, while sickening for them, has no consequences outside their immediate bohemian milieu.

Neurotic types also populate Izdryk's novels. In his first novel *Wozzeck* he invoked Georg Büchner's *Woyzeck*, the nineteenth-century unfinished drama, and utilized it as a base for his new story line with a mentally disturbed hero.

In his other two works, *The Island of Krk* (*Ostriv Krk*, 1998) and *Double Leon: The History of an Illness* (*Podviinyi Leon: istoriia khvoroby*, 2000), considered, together with *Wozzeck*, a trilogy of sorts, he relied more on a contemporary backdrop and reiterated his interest in heroes that are conflicted, hopelessly in love, and on a verge of self-annihilation, either through alcohol addiction or madness.

The theme of illness constitutes a strong undercurrent in all these works but in *Double Leon*, as the subtitle poignantly indicates, it becomes its raison d'être. By focusing on the disease and its impact, especially on creative individuals, Izdryk explores the issue of personal responsibility and studies the boundaries of the self in relation to others. What is particularly fascinating about his approach is that he implicitly draws parallels between the protagonist's sickness and the deficient and/or fraudulent system that attempts to cure it. Izdryk's hero pretends to desire to get better and his caregivers pretend to offer him an effective treatment. It seems that there is a double game of deceit constantly being played by both sides. Leon's explanations in psychotherapy as to why he drinks—because he has fallen in love, yet is unable to leave his wife and family, hence an inner conflict he is not able to cope with—are immediately debunked by him in his head, denying that this is really the case:

> A girlish psychiatrist listens to me attentively and with understanding, and I think to myself that I lie to them all and they are not any better than me in this respect, actually I have really mastered self-deception. What has my falling in love to do with drinking? It is just a consequence of lack of will, indecisiveness, and unconscious desire to see myself a victim of a sad drama. Yet this drama looks more and more like a farce—tragic but the farce nonetheless.[19]

One can speculate that underlying his alcoholism is the pressure from the artistic milieu with which he identifies himself and which glorifies alcohol as one way to cope with the harsh reality. Discussing "the sick souls" in his monograph, Andryczyk sums this up as follows: "Izdryk, in essence, implies that alcoholism is inevitable for the artist, as is the need to escape both real and fictional worlds."[20]

Thematizing disease in *Double Leon* Izdryk focuses on a few of its possible variants: addiction, neurosis and schizophrenia. While neurosis and alcoholism provide escapist opportunities, they only slightly undermine a rational perception and do not necessarily offer a release from legal responsibility. Mental disorders such as psychosis and schizophrenia, with their hallucinatory and delusional alternative worlds, on the other hand, allow the afflicted to dwell in the interstices of what is forbidden and taboo, mindless of legal consequences. As Leonid Kosovych comments in his "Postscript" to *Double Leon*, Izdryk's protagonist apparently yearns for that kind of freedom: "chronically neurotic Leon constantly attempts to break through into inaccessible for him spheres of classic psychosis."[21] But despite a fragmented self that occasionally crosses into schizophrenic territory, what we predominantly witness in this novel is a typical neurotic artist who often observes and comments, with a considerable dose of detachment and clarity, on his many bouts of depression, anxieties, lack of energy and love sickness. And yet, regardless of his skepticism, Izdryk's hero allows himself to undergo a variety of treatments without actually believing in their effectiveness. There are in fact quite a few healing procedures depicted in the novel, from acupuncture, injections, psychotherapy to substance abuse interventions, all trying to alleviate dependence and burdensome addiction symptoms. In the end, however, it is not clear if the protagonist himself is that eager to leave his state of "abnormality," using Andryczyk's characterization. For sickness itself becomes part of his identity and it is very difficult to fathom Leon healed—then, needless to say, he would no longer be the same Leon.

Ulianenko's protagonists also struggle with self-identification issues. In his most acclaimed novel *Stalinka* (2000),[22] the writer reverses the common understanding of what it means to be mentally disturbed. The novel begins with the escape of two mentally ill patients—Lord and Lopata—from a mental institution. Lopata soon dies of exhaustion and Lord, after his companion's unexpected death, assumes a new identity and a new name, becoming Yona. Contrary to all expectations, Yona is depicted as the most gentle and humane person in the otherwise cruel and decaying world. His freedom turns illusory, however, because on the other side of the walls life is as much, if not more, disturbed than in the madhouse itself. In fact, another parallel story line that Ulianenko offers in the novel, the one of the Piskariov family that unfolds in the Kyiv's Stalinka district, only underscores the maddening reality in which the boundaries between a locked population of mental patients and a decaying society, living in depressed neighborhoods, are exceptionally fluid and murky.

While supposedly mentally disturbed Yona represents positive forces in the novel, Horik Piskariov, another important character of *Stalinka*, is the embodiment of marginalized and delinquent youth that has no qualms whatsoever to steal from someone or kill another human being, deal drugs and/or hang with a gang of likewise criminals. Prostitution is rampant in this dark world, especially among teenage girls, and the whole moral barometer of society's values in the Stalinka neighborhood is at a record low. Ulianenko paints a bleak picture of the capital city, attempting to show that the so-called ordinary life in one of Kyiv's districts is more mad, evil, or mentally disturbed than at any psychiatric institution. In this context Yona comes across as someone who is misunderstood and underappreciated; he has a capacity to love and to forgive—both traits denoting the highest human values. In fact, having met a woman who provided him with shelter, he is ready to transcend all evils and forgive any wrongdoing done to him. It is telling how each of the two main characters of *Stalinka* fare at the end of the novel: Horik is mauled to death by a pack of homeless dogs and Yona, free of fear, meditates on nature and seasons, and believes he still has time to transform and grow spiritually. The religious allusions are unmistaken here, suggesting that having a strong faith is the key factor in any transformation. Although the novel ends ambiguously, the image of an old woman praying in the window might point toward that direction.

Ulianenko's novel *Serafyma* (2007) approaches mental disorders in a more nuanced way but it also underscores their awful consequences if uncontained. *Serafyma* is more representative of a new style the writer assumes in the post-*Stalinka* period. Stylistically, it is considerably more accessible than *Stalinka*; thematically—more concentrated on presenting social decay at its most raw. In his later novels, such as *Serafyma*, Ulianenko often connects criminal behavior to either personality disorder or mental illness. Madness here is no longer of an innocent kind. In *Satan's Dauphin*, Bilozub, a psychopath killer, murders innocent people believing he fulfills the angel's command; in *Serafyma*—it is a female serial killer who lures and poisons men who either betray her or are standing in the way toward her personal enrichment.

In many ways, *Serafyma* is a coming-of-age novel that portrays the evolution of a female psychopath from her early teenage involvement in prostitution, drugs and murder to being finally locked up in a mental institution where she dies. In between these two points in her life we witness a heroine who meticulously plans and kills her victims and, thanks to her utmost precision and care, is capable of continuing her murderous spree for quite some time. Ulianenko, again, like in *Satan's Dauphin*, introduces in *Serafyma* a detective Reus who, after initially falling for Serafyma, eventually solves the puzzle of her murderous inclinations. The psychiatrist who treats Serafyma calls her an "ingenious psychopath," mainly because she has managed to avoid detection for so long.

All four writers present novels with characters that are clearly mentally disturbed. In some of them we witness neurotics—by and large harmless individuals who redirect all their conflicts and frustrations into their own inner psyche, rarely posing any danger to society. Still in others, we see highly intelligent and attractive psychopaths getting away with murders for a considerable period of time. Either way, both camps of writers paint a rather bleak picture of what transpires in the social fabric of Ukraine after independence.

YOUTH TRANSGRESSIONS: DRUGS, SEX AND VIOLENCE

The theme of social decay among youth in Ukrainian literature of the post-independence period was vigorously pursued by authors of the younger generation whose target audience was often their peers—college students, many still in their teens. It reflected on the difficulty with which teenagers and young adults had to readjust to the social change they witnessed in the 1990s and to their own growing up under such trying conditions. The generational divide in capturing creatively these processes is quite evident, as Maxim Tarnawsky in his essay on Serhiy Zhadan and Anatolii Dnistrovy aptly points out:

> Perhaps the most striking feature of the second wave of post-independence Ukrainian literature is its distinct appeal to a youthful, socially conscious but culturally "hip" audience of specifically Ukrainian readers. For Serhii Zhadan, Anatolii Dnistrovy, Iryna [sic] Karpa, Liubko Deresh, and a sizeable circle of their friends and colleagues, the intended audience for their works is clearly somewhat different from what it was for some of their older counterparts in the 1990s, such as Andrukhovych and Zabuzhko.[23]

Tarnawsky, moreover, correctly observes that the younger generation of writers shuns the individualism of their older peers and focuses instead on collective identities, frequently combining them with descriptions of socially deviant behavior, as is often the case among various street gangs of adolescents. The theme of youth transgressions is indeed perhaps best captured by Zhadan and Dnistrovy, as Tarnawsky attests, but Liubko Deresh's and Svitlana Povaliaieva's fiction also merits attention, as they both forcefully thematize violence and delinquency among young adults.

Before *A Fruit Fly over Kant's Volume* was published in 2010, Dnistrovy was better known for his poignant fiction depicting the underworld of youth culture. His novels *The City of Deferred Action* (*Misto upovil'nenoi dii*, 2003) and *Pathetic Blunder* (*Patetychnyi blud*, 2005)[24] introduce the themes of adolescent criminality, on the one hand, and harsh realities of student life, on the other. Both represent pioneering efforts on the part of the author to illuminate issues that young adults grappled with following the collapse of the Soviet Union, especially in the absence of a new system of social values.

The main protagonist of *The City of Deferred Action*, Oleh Zuiev, nicknamed "the professor" because of his aspirations to enroll at a university, vacilitates between two diametrically opposed social milieus—that of the youth gang comprised mainly of school dropouts—dangerous, primitive but stimulating, and that of the upper-middle-class family of college academics—cultured, refined but boring. Clearly, his desire to study and thus become someone in life underscores the contingent character of his association with the gang; on the other hand, time and again Oleh displays a considerable loyalty to his gang buddies. Despite his private reservations and not always condoning the gang's behavior, he acknowledges the authority of its leader,

Tiulia, and never openly questions any deviant actions undertaken by him or the gang. Oleh constantly seems to be torn between his intellectual ambition and the sense of belonging that his gang friends provide him with. This inner conflict that the hero struggles with is resolved only after he leaves the town to pursue his studies.

The novel opens with the murder of a man who offends the gang and thus receives a fatal blow from one of its members, forcing the entire group to secretly dispose the body in the river in a secluded section of the park. While some gang buddies seem to be quite shaken by the killing, Tiulia, the gang's leader, retains composure and instructs them to carefully cover the traces, including disposing their shoes, if necessary, to avoid being caught. And, indeed, the gang gets away with murder, even though this semi-accidental slaying affects each individual gang member differently. Yet the trivialization of death in Dnistrovy's novel only further underscores a total collapse of the value system among city youths shortly after independence. Being promiscuous (incidentally, Dnistrovy truly excels in his depictions of copulations), or using drugs, and/or drinking is one thing but killing another human being quite another. While at first shaken by this criminal act, each gang member goes on with his/her life soon afterwards, as if nothing has happened.

The gang loyalty means not only covering for each other in their socially deviant and/or criminal acts but also in honoring the existing relationships within the group. For example, Oleh is attracted to Tiulia's girlfriend, Roma, but hesitates to reveal his feelings to her precisely because he knows that Tiulia, being violent as he is, would not tolerate sharing her with anyone else. Encouraged by Roma, however, he does have sex with her eventually, thus breaking with the code of gang loyalty. Monogamous relationships at this age, as Dnistrovy sees it, simply would not ring true. As it turns out, Roma is not Oleh's sole sexual interest, as Oleh is to Roma but a diversion.

Wavering between the primitive, if not frightening, world of the gang existence and the civilized world of intellectuals that the family of his girlfriend, Inha, represents, Oleh seems to be utterly conflicted about his desires and loyalties. Inha is well-behaved, cultured and devoted but does not stir in Oleh the same degree of arousal than Roma does. Besides, even though on some level Oleh aspires to be part of that "highbrow" milieu, he simultaneously despises it. That feeling of contempt is best reified in Oleh's act of forced sex (if not rape) with Inha. By almost raping her, Oleh attempts to show her his contempt for rules and correctness, thereby undermining his own image of being morally "better" than his other gang buddies.

Dnistrovy's next novel *Pathetic Blunder* continues to study the youth underculture, but this time concentrating on university students, living in a high-rise dormitory. The main character of the novel—Vitalii, a young man, struggling financially, appears as conflicted about his feelings and relationships as Oleh has been. Vitalii begins a love affair with an attractive female college professor Lidia, which enables him to escape a dreary dorm life, even though he breaks the heart of his student girlfriend Nastia in the process. In the end, he is incapable of bonding and seems to alienate his friends. While not as violent as *The City of Deferred Action*, *Pathetic Blunder* also creates situations that confront its young protagonists with moral choices. They all seem to be craving for strong role models but are finding pale substitutes instead. According to Tarnawsky,

> The core dilemma in the lives of Dnistrovy's young characters is the choice between conformism and self-fulfillment. But the actual parameters of this dilemma appear to be malleable. Dnistrovy's heroes have difficulty identifying the value system that defines their present and future choices. Thus personal loyalties become a handy substitute for thoughtful choices in making complex personal and ethical decisions.[25]

In Dnistrovy's fiction, personal attachments and loyalties, however fleeting and/or contingent, act as a moral compass. In its attitudes and behaviors, the youth simply reflects the social malaise at large. After all, in the early 1990s, not only youngsters struggled with their own sense of identity and direction— their parents grappled with the same dilemmas as well.

Svitlana Povaliaieva's novels dwell on urban youth, by and large students, who coming of age in the difficult 1990s experience an unprecedented degree of freedom but, unable to utilize it in any meaningful way, misdirect it toward socially unacceptable behavior: drugs, alcohol and violence. The author many a time underscores the fact that her heroes have prototypes but the majority of them are no longer alive. The main culprit is substance abuse that frequently leads to drug overdose, thus cutting many young lives short. In fact, Povaliaieva's thematization of death emerges as one of the most conspicuous characteristics of her oeuvre. Her protagonists seem unable to stop their uncontrollable desire for self-destruction. Induced by drugs, the altered states of consciousness are not only "hip" but also help transcend the difficulties of everyday existence.

Perhaps the best examples of such tendencies are described in her early novels *The Exhumation of the City* (2003) and *Instead of Blood* (2003). The latter novel in particular yields scenes of drug orgies and addiction with an excruciatingly gruesome detail. It is telling that the very first chapter of her second novel *Instead of Blood* is titled "The History of the Disease in Slides and Toponymic Beginning." But it is in the third chapter "This Music Will be Forever if I Change the Batteries" that we witness the main protagonist's daily ritual of injecting into his veins an addictive cocktail of heroin and the immediate "high" his body experiences:

I felt my pupils as if they were basketball balls. Contrasts and lighting reached their maximum. I breathed so deeply that with each of my gasps the kitchen was pulsating and bursting—a muscle schizophrenia. For an hour and a half, which felt like a minute and half, I loved the universe without bounds, admired the back of my chair merely for its existence and also because it prevented my fall onto the floor, possibly hitting my head in the process. I loved Mike as my brother, and Tsypa as my sister. I preferred to listen to the music, write, paint, run to the store, race to the highway bound to Crimea as if I was a champagne cork straight, or just sit and have orgasms by simply contemplating contours of the dilapidated kitchen wall. I felt as if I were an Icy God of Reified Intensity. I wanted all and could do ANYTHING! And for that very reason I did nothing.[26]

Yet this "high" does not mask its devastating awakening. The first-person narrator warns in fact that he is not actually trying to promote narcotics but admits that once a certain line is crossed it is very difficult to stop being a junkie. The "high" is a kind of disease, a state in which one can experience boundless creativity but which can also lead to heinous acts such as murder.[27] Death, as Povaliaieva has it, can come from many different quarters, murder being an ultimate demise, but it can also occur either by getting infected with AIDS with rampant needle sharing among addicts, or by accidental overdosing.

Povaliaieva's novels are remarkably egalitarian and gender neutral. Her characters, regardless of sex, display a considerable degree of loyalty among them and seem compelled to share with each other not only needles, dwelling and food but also each other. One is struck by a high degree of their allegiance, as well as the ability to feel empathy toward each other. They seem to be drunk with the freedom surrounding them and totally in love with their city—Kyiv. Arguably, the capital city becomes an indispensable co-conspirator and witness to all socially deviant acts among the counterculture youth. One of the characters in *Instead of Blood* even states that they are not homeless really because they have Kyiv as their home. In many ways, Povaliaieva embraces Kyiv's youth underworld without any judgment; moreover, she even seems to be somewhat nostalgic about that very first post-independence lost generation.

As much as Povaliaieva's heroes are enchanted by Kyiv, Serhiy Zhadan's characters in *Depeche Mode* are likewise attached to the city of Kharkiv, with both authors sharing the same fascination with Western rock music and instilling it in their respective protagonists. Even though there is a high dose of violence in Zhadan's fictional youth world,[28] still, one is under the impression that there is more hope there than in Povaliaieva's oeuvre. His protagonists—mostly idle and lost—appear confused about what to do with the newly obtained unbounded freedom but are guided by the strong sense of camaraderie and collectivity. While in Povaliaieva's fiction freedom by and large leads to substance abuse and self-destruction, in Zhadan's world—it engenders drifting and petty crimes.

Depeche Mode presents many acts of cruelty not necessarily committed by criminals. Yes, there is a drug dealer who shoots at a trio of friends when they question the quality of his marijuana, as well as the mafia, guarding its turf at the Kharkiv train station and threatening anyone encroaching on its territory, but there are also policemen abusing their power and a train conductor displaying sexual aggression toward the youth. These examples of lawlessness and aggression coming from those who are supposed to uphold law and order demonstrate a total collapse of values and mechanisms of law enforcement. Yet, despite such a gloomy portrayal of the post-Soviet reality, there seems to be light at the end of the tunnel. When the Kharkiv teens look for a missing friend Sasha, they learn a lot about themselves, and when in the end one of the trio friends locates Sasha, he realizes that Sasha no longer cares about the past and wants to start anew. At this point it becomes irrelevant that the whole search was undertaken to communicate to him about the death of his stepfather. Since the past no longer exists for Sasha, that piece of information is simply redundant.

Zhadan shows that it is possible to embark on a different path in spite of many social roadblocks. His approach is well summed up by Tarnawsky:

> In Zhadan's world, assorted acts of human kindness and charity, from gift giving to saving invalids from the police, are part of a pattern of innate human goodness that society either cannot accept or cannot capitalize into a state of redemption. The faults Zhadan observes and depicts are not only the product of decades of Soviet misrule and the misguided materialism of the West: they are an inherited blemish on the moral fabric of Ukraine's society. Zhadan does not explore the possibility of redemption in his works, but clearly it involves a reestablishment of moral underpinnings in society.[29]

Restoring a sense of social justice, if not moral underpinnings, is something that preoccupies Liubko Deresh (b. 1984), an author whose literary debut with a novel *Cult* (*Kul't*, 2001) at the age of seventeen caused quite a stir in literary quarters, not to mention the fact that it instantly brought him recognition and resonance among a younger audience. In his early novels, he focuses on a variety of youth transgressions, or as Izdryk succinctly put it in his Foreword to Deresh's fifth novel *Intent* (*Namir*, 2009)—on "sex, drugs & rock'n'roll."[30] What strikes in Deresh's writing in particular is that his characters are not typical hard-core juvenile delinquents. They all appear to have a solid middle-class background, that is, to be from so-called good families, and yet they are often involved in unspeakable violence and murder, as if these were but commonplace occurrences. The casualness of criminal acts, on the one hand, and their unexpectedness, on the other, is what sets Deresh apart from his older literary peers who also foreground similar issues in their works.

His first novel *Cult* is a case in point. Its main protagonist, Yurko Banzai, who is about to graduate from the Ivan Franko National University of Lviv with a degree in biology, takes a teaching position at a college in a provincial town Midni Buky. Soon after his arrival he gets romantically involved with one of his female students—Dartsia Borkhes. While he is aware that this is against the rules and feels at first bouts of guilt because of his involvement with a teenage girl, they are not strong enough to prevent him from not only having sex with Dartsia but also experimenting with drugs in her presence, all in search of altered states of consciousness. The college's permanent faculty is not particularly exemplary either. Its school psychologist smokes marijuana in his office and ends up hospitalized because of an antidepressants overdose. Then there is the mysterious Roman Korii, a former sailor and an alcoholic whose association with the college is not entirely explained but who plays an important role in Banzai's dreamlike states. But the worst crime that occurs on the grounds of the college—a triple murder in fact, involves the school's director, Andrii Yaroslavovych Vaisgott. Unable to control his passion for a young school nurse Aliska, he attempts to rape her but she fights him back cutting his face and one of his eyes with a razor. The gruesomeness of the depiction how the director's slashed eyeball bursts out of the socket and yet he still has enough strength to pierce Aliska with calipers before she manages to lock herself in the neighboring room, clearly has a shocking effect. In the end, eager to get out of the trap, she leaves the room with a piece of glass from a broken vase, and thinking that a kneeling man in the corner is her rapist cuts his neck. By then she has lost enough blood to die herself shortly thereafter but not before realizing that the man she attacked was not the direc-tor but one of the teachers, Myrko. Deresh describes the murder scene with a ghastly detail, yet by also incorporating elements of fantasy and dreamlike states he attempts to turn his first novel into a tale about the forces of light and darkness, seemingly only partially interested in realistic representations of social ills as they relate to the secondary educational system.

While the described murder in *Cult* can be characterized as a crime of passion involving two adults that happened because of an attempted rape, in Deresh's second novel *The Adoration of Lizard* (*Pokloninnia iashchyrtsi*, 2004) we witness a murder that is premeditated and executed by teenag-ers. The novel's three main protagonists—Dzvinka, Mykhailo and Hladkyi Khippi are determined to kill Fiedia, a local "gopnik"[31] who at some point almost raped Dzvinka and is known for his violence and brutality. After tell-ing Mykhailo about this incident, Dzvinka tells him that she wants Fiedia dead. What follows is a careful planning of a murder by three teens who are otherwise seemingly good students coming from a solid middle-class background of nationally conscious Ukrainians.[32] However, as it turns out, the killing of Fiedia is not as simple as the trio of friends initially hoped, and Mykhailo, left alone with him, morphs from a perpetrator to a victim himself. In the end, the whole premeditation process becomes meaningless, as Mykhailo fights for his life. Fiedia eventually drowns in a swamp, carried there unconscious by Dzvinka's friends but not before he tortures Mykhailo and almost hangs him. What was supposed to be a premeditated murder turns to a murder in self-defense. Again, Deresh seemingly delights in presenting excruciating details of horrific acts, as if insisting that revealing them has a therapeutic effect.

His subsequent two novels *Arkhe* (2005) and *A Little Bit of Darkness* (*Trokhy pit'my*, 2008) focus more on substance and sexual abuse among youths than on outright criminality. Deresh displays an interest in various degrees of the "high" state experienced by his protagonists through the experimentation with a variety of drugs. In many ways, *Arkhe* also comes across as the novel that depicts the Lviv underworld, similarly to what Povaliaieva and Zhadan did for Kyiv and Kharkiv in their novels, respectively. Deresh's characters in *Arkhe* often appear to be bored, apparently nothing can surprise them anymore after trying everything that the existing counterculture could offer them. No wonder then that instead of murders, we witness suicides, more than likely resulting from a chronic substance abuse:

> The whole toxic summer Kursant was wearing a cap with earflaps: he said it was because he was afraid that his head might be swept away. And no one seemed surprised as everyone knew Liolik was injecting himself nonstop for a month, and in the process *saw* something BIG, which completely threw him off. He went bonkers. There is a version that Kursant found out why Jesus had O blood type but Terezka thought that it must have been something more serious. Then they said that Liolik stopped taking "arche" and went to Shypit in the Carpathians. And it was there, on the night of the Kupalo festival, he undressed himself next to the bonfire and just in trunks began to dance on embers. Then all of the sudden he thrust a knife into his stomach and walked away wet with blood toward the river. Never came back. They said that his cap with earflaps punks took.[33]

In the novel *A Little Bit of Darkness* Deresh devotes even more attention to suicidal impulses and analyzes relationships as they evolve from abuse toward a more communal way of life. The novel depicts a camp of punks from various regions of Ukraine who come to the festival in Shypit in the Carpathian Mountains. One of the protagonists, Vika, meets there Herman who claims to be a gynecologist. Vika opens up to him, revealing her suicide attempt following the abuse she experienced in the hands of her former boyfriend, Vitas. Despite Vitas' cruelty toward animals, she felt compelled to stick with him until she realized that his actions are the result of mental illness. He was convinced that he could feed on his own purulence but was in fact on the path to self-destruction, forcing Vika to join him in that endeavor.

The festival in the Carpathians facilitates all kinds of confessions, true and false, as long as there are others willing to listen. The event of this nature also encourages promiscuity and having sex with many partners. Sharing narcotics comes as an extra bonus. Deresh's heroes seem to tread on the thin line between life and death, as they all display suicidal tendencies and carefree attitudes. What keeps them in check, however, is the comforting sense of collectivity regardless of how volatile and transitory that sense might be.

All four authors present the Ukrainian youth counterculture as a deeply urban phenomenon that arose on the ruins of the communist collapse. For that very reason in all four authors the stories told are invariably connected to their respective cities: in the case of Dnistrovy—provincial cities of Ternopil and Nizhyn; in the case of Povaliaieva and Zhadan—Kyiv and Kharkiv, respectively; and in the case of Deresh—the metropolitan Lviv with its suburbia. They all seem to cherish their hometowns, as their narratives provide generous space for descriptions of respective urban landscapes, often linking them to the regional flavor and character that each city exudes.

POST-SOVIET CRIMINALITY AND SOCIAL MISFITS

As the analyzed texts indicate, the provenance of post-Soviet criminality can be manifold. It might arise as a consequence of social change and the inability of some segments of society to readjust to new circumstances; it can also be engendered by mental illness and various personality disorders; as well as by challenges of growing-up manifesting themselves in youth violence and substance abuse. But the most prevalent crime in the first decade after independence comes as a result of infighting among mafia-like clans that in their quest for power and personal enrichment entangle themselves in corruption and chain assassinations. As Andrey Kurkov skillfully demonstrated in his fiction of the 1990s and early 2000s, the control of state resources in post-independence Ukraine rests not so much in the hands of democratically elected officials as in the hands of those who are not afraid to use guns to achieve a desirable outcome.

Kurkov's novels from that period provide an interesting commentary on the evolving political and economic situation in post-Soviet Ukraine. The author of *Death and the Penguin, A Matter of Death and Life* and *Penguin Lost*, among others, often points to the widespread criminality indirectly, one could almost say reluctantly, and in the majority of cases—only because his protagonists knowingly or unknowingly get entangled in shady affairs. Many a time Kurkov's hero is a man in the early thirties who is well-educated but totally unable to make a living and adjust to the new post-Soviet situation. And when at last he does, as, for example, in the case of Viktor from the novel *Death and the Penguin*, it turns out that his substantial income does not come from legitimate sources. Notable and ordinary people die left and right under mysterious circumstances but it is happening as if somewhere on the periphery, and for a long time Viktor pretends it has nothing to do with him until he himself is faced with the possibility of being next in line for assassination.

Even more startling is the tale of Tolya (Anatolii) from Kurkov's novel *A Matter of Death and Life*. Incapable of coping with his wife's adultery and his own uselessness as an unemployed translator, Tolya (another thirty-something male character) plans his own assassination, except that in the process he changes his mind and is now forced to kill his own assassin. Finding someone willing to do it for him is not difficult at all as long as cash (preferably in dollars) is on hand. Kurkov's darkly tale alludes how cheap and unpredictable life in Ukraine has become after the fall of Communism, especially when friendships are being replaced by business transactions. People are ready to do anything for money, often assuming multiple identities to help compartmentalize incompatible aspects of their personalities. One can be a contract killer, a caring husband and a devoted father all at the same time. Although, arguably, the ending of the novel leaves some hope as it signals that the same circumstances that push one toward crime can also morph into feelings of responsibility and perhaps even love.

While *Death and the Penguin* and *A Matter of Death and Life* confine themselves solely to the realities of post-Soviet Ukraine, Kurkov's other two novels *The Case of the General's Thumb* and *Penguin Lost* expand their geographical reach to also incorporate Russian criminal circles. In the first of these two novels the writer makes sure that there is no confusion as to the identity of Russian and Ukrainian secret services, but he does simultaneously underscore the cultural affinity of their relationship that the common Soviet past imposes upon all of them. In *Penguin Lost*, on the other hand, Kurkov raises the issue of cruelty in the Russian-Chechen conflict, questioning the motives of both sides and concluding that any war engenders profiteering and criminal behavior: "Some Fed regulars raped and beat up a Chechen girl, and shoved her in my furnace. Alive. Chechen guerillas caught up with them, got the truth out of them, chopped their heads off, and then burnt your friend Seva alive. So we shot the guerillas. You burnt the bodies. And I've enforced my neutrality."[34] Whether on the individual or state level, criminality in Kurkov's edition has an absurdist or even surreal tinge, yet in its blackish, grotesque and exaggerated modality it carries a powerful message about the consequences of weak institutions in general, and those of law enforcement in particular.

Kurkov's fiction is remarkably readable despite its dark subject matter. His peculiar sense of black humor and suspense sets him apart from other writers who also pursue topics dealing with mafia, corruption and contract killings. Whereas Kurkov paints the post-Soviet criminality with a broad brush, Oles Ulianenko, on the other hand, puts everything under the microscope. In his novel *Son* (*Syn*, 2006), for example, he describes the evolution of violence and corruption from the level of small business all the way to the highest echelons of government officials with an excruciatingly repulsive detail. As Ulianenko sees it, the extent of societal decay is such that there is no possibility for correction. His fiction leaves no hope and its incessant brutality desensitizes in the long run. Leonidas Donkins in his conversation with Zygmunt Bauman put it aptly: "Violence shown every day ceases to provoke amazement, or disgust."[35] Yet, Ulianenko's take on the ugliness of corrupt ways of doing business in post-Soviet Ukraine also brings to light eternal questions of evil in everyday life. Arguably, no other author deals with moral sensibilities (or the lack thereof) with such a passionate and harrowing fervor.

In Ulianenko's novel *Son* there are only villains. He devotes each chapter to a different character, each being part of a vast criminal network, though the most attention is paid to Yukhym Blokh, his girlfriend Lizka and his partner Klovsky. Blokh's rise from a small drug dealer to a mafia-like boss of a large criminal enterprise within a short period of time indicates the underlying weakness of the country in transition, in which corruption is rampant and the main attraction of a market economy is self-enrichment. Ulianenko's catalog of crimes committed by his protagonists is staggering: drug and sex trafficking, brutal killings, fake passports, prostitution, control of city beggars, illegal alcohol and human organs trade, and enslaving illegal migrants, to name just a few of them. The author describes scenes of unspeakable brutality, especially involving women. Blokh's first girlfriend Liuska is left to her own devices when she goes into labor with his child, and it is clear that she will die at childbirth because no one cares to help her. His second girlfriend Lizka, shot in the crotch by Klovsky, becomes an invalid for the rest of her life. While being successful for a considerable period of time, thanks in large measure to the right connections at the highest government levels, Blokh ends up in jail, with no one rushing to his rescue despite his enormous bribes paid in the past to various officials and their wives. Of the three main protagonists, only Klovsky escapes unscathed, knowing when to disappear before being caught. Perhaps the fact that he is a highly educated killer (with two advanced degrees to his credit) helps him navigate the system the best.

Ulianenko paints a picture of post-Soviet Ukraine that is repulsive, brutal and drowning in criminality. He captures some of the essence of fraud and collusion between criminal circles and government officials, so widespread shortly after independence. However, one also feels that his dark image of newly independent Ukraine is somewhat hyperbolic and exaggerated, focusing exclusively on social ills. While Kurkov only hints at criminal activity and simultaneously depicts many acts of kindness and generosity among his protagonists, Ulianenko, on the other hand, oftentimes with gruesome details, reveals the insides of the beast, so to speak. His characters and their acts do not evoke sympathy in the reader, or any other feeling for that matter. One is left wondering, if the plethora of violence and killing, described in his novels, is perhaps there merely to desensitize us from overbearing brutality.

Serhiy Zhadan's second novel *Voroshilovgrad* depicts the nature of criminality in the Donbas region before it got itself entangled in the separatist insurgency and Russian aggression. Like elsewhere in the country at the time, criminal clans acted there without any fear of ill consequences, often bribing local officials and using them as pliable instruments to blackmail and/or destroy legitimate businesses. However, unlike Ulianenko's oeuvre, Zhadan's prose presents a glimmer of hope. The novel's main protagonist Herman not only manages to outsmart the local mafia but also retains his own sense of dignity and worthiness. He is not alone in his fight against local thugs because he knows how to attract good and like-minded people with whom it is possible to resist racketeering and blackmail. There is still another difference between Zhadan and Ulianenko, and it has to do with how each approaches religious matters in their works. While there are many religious allusions in Ulianenko's fiction, they are by and large presented in terms of the Manichean dualism between good and evil, except that the latter so thoroughly takes over. In Zhadan's *Voroshilovgrad* things are not as straightforward and it is clear from the outset that the author avoids painting the world in black and white. For example, Herman befriends a protestant pastor who overcomes drug addiction and for whom forgiveness, gratitude and responsibility are even more important than faith alone:

> What I'm trying to say is that certain things are more important than faith. Things like gratitude and responsibility. Actually, it was an accident that I joined the church. I just didn't have any other place to go. I couldn't turn to my sister any longer, because she'd just send me right back to the loony bin. I had no real other choice. But the church and I didn't really get off on the right foot. I mean, the church can do wonders, sure, but nobody besides you can fix your problems. Basically, I didn't think I was in it for the long haul. I thought that the holy brothers would give me the boot sooner or later, as soon as they caught on to my act. They knew my history, but they never made a big deal about it. And then they sent me up here.[36]

In Zhadan's fictional world there are no perfect human beings. After all, the same is true in real life. But what is even more impressive about Zhadan's vision is that his attitude toward other human beings, be they enemies or not, is so decisively all-embracing and magnanimous. His protagonists do fight injustice when they see it but do so in such a way as to avoid violence as much as possible. Moreover, the writer creates enough space for his fictional social misfits to transform and become useful again in society.[37] And that optimistic take on life, ability to forgive, evident throughout this novel, is uniquely Zhadan's. No other contemporary Ukrainian writer strives to bridge the ideological chasm in the Donbas as much as he does and with such forcefulness. In many ways, Zhadan's fiction prophetically foresaw tragic events of 2014 by underscoring what Bauman called "the absence of state as an effective instrument of action and change."[38] When governing institutions display structural weakness, then it becomes more of people's responsibility to maintain social order. Yet, in situations of social uncertainty and confusion such a task might be too difficult, or even impossible to carry out. Ideologies can easily be "privatized," as Bauman and Donskis assert, cut out to fit whatever niche is required at the time, and thus very alluring to certain segments of society. One counts on the reasonableness of those in power, but, as Donskis puts it, there is no guarantee:

> It turns out that a "healthy and normal person" can for a time turn into as much of a moral idiot as a sadistic sociopath slowly killing another human being, or one showing no sympathy for a tortured human being's suffering. One doesn't even need clinical terms—moral insanity can befall even the healthy. The routinization of violence and killing during war leads to a condition in which people stop responding to war's horrors.[39]

Andrey Kurkov's depictions of cruelty during the Chechen war in *Penguin Lost* immediately comes to mind after reading the above statement but even in Ulianenko's and Zhadan's fiction, where there is no direct reference to any kind of war, we can also witness acts of unspeakable violence not only from mentally disturbed but also from individuals deemed otherwise "normal." What is not disputed by any of the three authors discussed here is the need for a radical transformation in order to combat Ukraine's social decay and its ability to marginalize whole segments of society.

NOTES

1. Gilles Deleuze and Felix Guattari, *Anti-Oedipus: Capitalism and Schizophrenia* (Minneapolis: University of Minnesota Press, 1983), 131.
2. Michael M. Naydan noticed such a tendency back in 1995: "... one can observe that the paradigm of dysfunctional individuals and families is prevalent in contemporary Ukrainian prose and reflects the unfortunate reality of current society."

See his "Ukrainian Prose of the 1990s as It Reflects Contemporary Social Structures," *The Ukrainian Quarterly* 51.1 (1995): 61.

3. Volodymyr Dibrova, *Vybhane* (Kyiv: Krytyka, 2002), 294.

4. Ibid., 287.

5. Mark Andryczyk, *The Intellectual as Hero in 1990s Ukrainian Fiction* (Toronto: University of Toronto Press, 2012), 86.

6. See Lidiia Stefanivs'ka, "Pisliamova," in *Votstsek & Votstsekurhiia*, by Izdryk (Lviv: Kal'variia, 2002), 194.

7. Izdryk, *Wozzeck*, trans. Marko Pavlyshyn (Edmonton: Canadian Institute of Ukrainian Studies, 2006), 74.

8. Oles' Ul'ianenko, *Stalinka. Dofin Satany: romany* (Kharkiv: Folio, 2003), 120.

9. Ibid., 381.

10. Michel Foucault, *Madness and Civilization: A History of Insanity in the Age of Reason*, trans. Richard Howard (New York: Vintage Books, 1988), 21. Interestingly, Andryczyk also makes reference to Foucault's work when he discusses Izdryk's oeuvre: "Madness here is one that Michel Foucault would see as representing a minority status" (*The Intellectual as Hero*, 80).

11. Pavlyshyn, "Choosing a Europe: Andrukhovych, Izdryk, and the New Ukrainian Literature," in *Contemporary Ukraine on the Cultural Map of Europe*, 261.

12. Dibrova, *Vybhane*, 449.

13. See Neborak, "Chytachi nad tomom Dnistrovoho," *Molodyi bukovynets'*, April 8, 2001, accessed July 3, 2016, http://molbuk.ua/vnomer/kultura/36630-chitachi-nad-tomom-dnistrovogo.html.

14. Anatoliii Dnistrovyi, *Drozofila nad tomom Kanta: roman* (Lviv: Piramida, 2010), 76.

15. Ibid., 93.

16. Ibid., 96.

17. Kostiantyn Moskalets', *Dosvid koronatsii: Vybrani tvory* (Lviv: Piramida, 2009), 117.

18. Andryczyk, *The Intellectual as Hero*, 76.

19. Izdryk, *Podviinyi Leon: istoriia khvoroby* (Ivano-Frankivsk: Lileia-NV, 2000), 95.

20. Andryczyk, *The Intellectual as Hero,* 80.

21. Leonid Kosovych, "Postskrypt," in *Podviinyi Leon*, 177.

22. The novel was written in 1994 but first published in 2000. The title refers to the name of the neighborhood in the capital city of Kyiv in which the action of the novel takes place and that was in use from the 1920s to the 1960s, clearly adopted from the name of the Soviet leader, Joseph Stalin. Today, this neighborhood is called Demiivka.

23. Maxim Tarnawsky, "Images of Bonding and Social Decay in Contemporary Ukrainian Prose: Reading Serhii Zhadan and Anatolii Dnistrovy," in *Contemporary Ukraine on the Cultural Map of Europe*, 265.

24. The second edition of this novel was published under a different title: *Tybet na vos'momu poversi* (Tibet on the Eighth Floor, 2013).

25. Tarnawsky, "Images of Bonding," 270.

26. Svitlana Povaliaieva, *Zamist' krovi* (Lviv: Kal'variia, 2003), 47.

27. Povaliaieva indeed describes how one of her characters—Dzhanis—kills her boyfriend Diubel under the influence simply because he wanted to have sex with her. Cf. *Zamist' krovi*, 123.

28. Tarnawsky, for example, states: "Malice, aggression, injury, and violence accompany boys wherever they go" (Ibid., 268).

29. Ibid., 274.

30. Izdryk, Foreword to *Namir!*, by Liubko Deresh (Kharkiv: Klub simeinoho dozvillia, 2009), 8.

31. A pejorative term used in Russian and other post-Soviet countries to denote aggressive young lower-class suburban male dwellers, often coming from families of poor education and income.

32. Deresh is quite playful and ironic writing about Dzvinka's background: "Dzvinka comes from an ideal Ukrainian family, so ideal in fact that it could have only been invented by Yurko Vynnychuk" (*Pokloninnia iashchirtsi*, 9). It is quite telling that Deresh invokes here the best-known Lviv author—Vynnychuk, as if the latter alone can vouch what it means to be a Ukrainian patriot.

33. Liubko Deresh, *Arkhe: monoloh, iakyi use shche tryvaie* (Kharkiv: Folio, 2009), 117–18.

34. Kurkov, *Penguin Lost*, 156.

35. Zygmunt Bauman and Leonidas Donskis, *Moral Blindness: The Loss of Sensitivity in Liquid Modernity* (Cambridge: Polity, 2013), 39.

36. Zhadan, *Voroshilovgrad*, trans. Isaac Stackhouse Wheeler and Reilly Costigan-Humes, 422–23.

37. It is worth noting that one of protagonists in *Voroshilovgrad*, Kocha, working for Herman at the gas station, is a former petty criminal.

38. Bauman and Donskis, *Moral Blindness*, 87.

39. Ibid., 37.

Chapter 6

Popular Literature and National Identity Construction

Much has been made about the distinction between high and popular culture. In fact, modernist literature or art thrived on the principle of cultural exclusivity and geared up its artistic production for the elites rather than the masses. José Ortega y Gasset, for example, worried back in the 1930s that mass culture represented a threat to difference, excellence and individuality, as well as undermined social and cultural authority, although he disregarded the importance of social class, claiming that his "mass man" could equally come from "upper" or "lower" classes.[1] Pierre Bourdieu, on the other hand, makes clear that there is a visible link between cultural taste and social class:

> In fact, through the economic and social conditions which they presuppose, the different ways of relating to realities and fictions, of believing in fictions and the realities they stimulate, with more or less distance and detachment, are very closely linked to the different possible positions in social space and, consequently, bound up with the systems of dispositions (habitus) characteristic of the different classes and class fractions. Taste classifies, and it classifies the classifier.[2]

And then he adds: "That is why art and cultural consumption are predisposed, consciously and deliberately or not, to fulfill a social function of legitimating social differences."[3] But, as John Storey aptly observes, cultural consumption is not a static thing by any measure and very often what used to be popular (like opera or Shakespeare) was "*made* unpopular" by being "actively appropriated from their popular audience by elite social groups determined to situate them as the crowning glory of their culture (so-called high culture). In short, opera and Shakespeare were transformed from entertainment enjoyed by the many into Culture to be appreciated by the few."[4] However, referring to the work of the American sociologist Richard Peterson,[5] Storey also points out that more recently we are witnessing a democratization of taste, meaning that the dominant social class is not necessarily limited solely to the consumption of high culture but is open to a wide range of cultural practices:

> The elite-to-mass model assumes a hierarchy in which the dominant social class has a well-defined pattern of consumption in terms of what, how, and where to consume, together with an attitude of contempt for mass culture and those for whom mass culture is culture. What is changing is this: rather than consume only high culture, members of the dominant class now also consume much of what they had previously dismissed as mass culture.[6]

In other words, in the postmodern environment the distinction between "high" and "low" (mass) culture loses its prominence and cultural elitism becomes out of fashion.

The rehabilitation of popular culture as valid culture bears important ramifications for the formation of identities. After all, what is widely consumed (as Storey puts it, "consumption is also a form of production"[7]) affects the overall sense of cultural, if not national identification. Reaching out to as wide an audience as possible and in an accessible way allows a writer and/or an artist to influence in part the process of individual self-formation. Popular literature that deliberately probes the resources of national history, language and culture necessarily assumes a role of an educator of sorts in addition to being merely entertaining. By the same token, a writer engaging popular genres cannot be easily dismissed, especially in the postcolonial context, for his or her works might bring to light past events of significant value to the overall understanding of collective self.

In the case of Ukrainian post-independence popular literature I discern three main tendencies: first and foremost, a willful attempt to popularize national traumas by producing highly accessible fictional accounts of historical events that are not that well-known; second, an emergence of a new type of female protagonist—a successful professional and/or businesswoman, thematized primarily by women authors; and, finally third, an appropriation of popular genres, such as, for instance, a detective story, as a vehicle to channel various identity construction issues.[8] Each of these three main categories addresses specific questions, from collective memory and role-playing to individual empowerment and national political power. Regardless of what topic is engaged and what theme explored, what connects all these texts is their universal popularity and high accessibility. Moreover, some of them display a certain constructed quality, that is, one senses that there is an implied mission of sorts underlying the plot and overall composition—perhaps ascribing to pulp fiction an additional function, one that enables the construction of a new sense of national belonging. It is also important to keep in mind that popular literature, at least the way I refer to it in this chapter, is popular either because of its wide readership or because it utilizes specific genres, those that are traditionally considered popular—romances, detective stories, fantasy, science fiction, to name a few. Sometimes these two aspects coincide, sometimes do not, but either way, they will be both indicative of the vast literary realm that popular literature assumes.

POPULARIZING NATIONAL TRAUMAS

Three novels deserve attention in particular for they have managed to popularize historical events that have often been forgotten and/or deliberately misconstrued but proven seminal in the understanding of what are the "roots and routes" (using Stuart Hall's popular phrase) as far as Ukrainian identity is concerned. They are: *Black Raven* (*Chornyi Voron*, 2009)[9] by Vasyl Shkliar (b.1951), *Sweet Darusia* (*Solodka Darusia*, 2004) by Mariia Matios (b.1959), and *Notes of a Ukrainian Madman* (*Zapysky ukrains'koho samashedshoho*, 2010[10]) by Lina Kostenko (b. 1930).[11] All three rely heavily on collective and/or individual memory to convey traumatic experiences from the 1920s, World War II, and the increasingly authoritarian Leonid Kuchma presidency leading to the Orange Revolution of 2004, respectively.

Shkliar's *Black Raven* is arguably the most revealing, especially for its strong national bias. Based on real events, it relates little known facts about the continued armed struggle of Ukrainian partisan regiments with the Soviets, mainly in the central provinces of Ukraine, following the collapse of the Ukrainian National Republic[12] and its Army in 1920. Pressed militarily by the Bolshevik Army on the eastern front, the leaders of the Ukrainian Republic, such as Symon Petliura, allied with newly independent Poland to fight the Soviets in April 1920, seeing it as its last chance to preserve independence. Known as the Treaty of Warsaw, it stipulated the establishment of a new border between Ukraine and Poland along the Zbruch River and the joint offensive against Soviet Russia. The ensuing Polish-Soviet War, culminating in Poland's victory in the Battle of Warsaw (August 1920), led to the Peace of Riga, signed on March 18, 1921, which de facto annulled the earlier Polish-Ukrainian alliance. The Ukrainian government and its army ended up in internment camps in Poland, feeling utterly betrayed. That setback did not discourage Ukrainian fighters back home who against all odds continued resisting the Soviet government throughout the 1920s, considering it an occupying force. Shkliar's novel foregrounds that struggle by focusing on one such commander in particular—known as Chornyi Voron (Black Raven) who does have its prototype in a real-life fighter, Ivan Yakovych Chornousov.

Such "village otamans," having their paramilitary troops recruited mostly from local peasants, were especially widespread in the early 1920s in the Cherkasy and Kyiv regions and represented bastions of resistance against the newly established communist regime.

The issue of national identity is front and center in the novel not only because the writer frames that fight more in national than ideological terms but also because he draws distinct ethnic fault lines between Russians and Ukrainians.[13] There is no doubt who the enemy is, or who the Other in *Black Raven* is—it is not merely a communist regime but, more importantly, a Russian communist regime. Accordingly, the assessment of these paramilitary units in the 1920s Civil War that raged following the collapse of the Ukrainian People's Republic differs substantially depending on whose point of view the assessor represents. The Soviet historiography viewed these paramilitary formations as bandits and murderers but in Shkliar's novel they emerge as national heroes who fought for national liberation.[14]

What is rather unusual in the novel is that its author interweaves his main narrative in Ukrainian with real and relevant archival documents, released from the KGB stacks after the collapse of the Soviet Union, the vast majority of which are in Russian, thus turning the novel into a bilingual account. These archival inserts describe separate incidents of real fights in various villages around the woodland known as Kholodny Yar in the Cherkasy region. For example, the main protagonist of Shkliar's novel, Chornyi Voron, escapes from the Soviets into the underground labyrinth of caves under the Motronynsky Monastery that, as the legend has it, links the monastery with the far-off defensive walls on the edge of the Kholodny Yar forest. There is no definitive record of Chernousov's death; according to some—he died in the fall of 1922, according to others—in June 1925, and that discrepancy allowed Shkliar to imply at the end of the novel that Voron did not die but managed to escape through the cave labyrinth, eventually making it to Poland by crossing the border along the Zbruch River. He is depicted as an intelligent and loyal leader, a Ukrainian patriot and national hero. By showing the 1920s insurgency from the perspective of the Ukrainian liberation movement, Shkliar seemingly single-handedly rehabilitated the forgotten pages of the Ukrainian past, although, as he admitted, he had some personal motivation. The writer himself comes from the Cherkasy region and was eager to find out why in his family's collective memory there were stories circulating of his grandfather being a "bandit." It turned out that his grandfather was a teacher and served in the Army of the Ukrainian National Republic, and that fact alone was sufficient for the Soviets to distort his past. Afraid of being persecuted and coined as traitors by the Soviet regime, Shkliar's relatives easily internalized the Soviet narrative of having a "bandit" in the family.[15]

However, exposing mere facts about the struggle for independence back in the 1920s would not be sufficient in and of itself to turn *Black Raven* into a bestseller that sold a quarter of a million copies—something unheard of for Ukrainian language belles-lettres. It had to be a very readable account, a page-turner, if you will, to achieve such a feat. And it has been indeed, with renewed interest in it, especially after the Russian aggression in 2014. Shkliar has produced a historical novel with an interesting plot that includes not only depictions of battles but also underscores the importance of humanity, kindness and love in the midst of brutality, killing and torture. There are stories of betrayal and love, stories of self-sacrifice and rejection, fictional stories and fact-based stories, all interconnected to create a highly engaging reading. For example, a love story between Tina and Voron alone injects a very romantic subplot, with many erotically charged scenes. But there is also a love story between another otaman, Veremii, and his wife Hannusia whose infant son Yarko is later adopted by Tina and smuggled to safety in Poland, thanks to Voron's plan in which he helps Tina and the child cross the Zbruch River. Hannusia's tragic death at the hands of Soviet perpetrators touches the heart of every insurgent fighter and they all are eager to save her son. Veremii never returns back home, having been most likely killed, but his and his wife's devotion to the cause, makes the insurgent slogan "Freedom to Ukraine or death" sound doubly true. That immense loyalty to his fighters and national liberation makes Voron return back to Ukraine after he helps Tina and Yarko cross into Poland. No doubt all these stories and subplots vastly contributed to the novel's enormous popularity. *Black Raven* has managed to reach and appeal to a wide audience by exploring little known pages of the national past at a time when a sense of national identity was heightened and sought after.

Mariia Matios' *Sweet Darusia* comes across as considerably more intimate and less panoramic than *Black Raven* but, similarly to the latter work, it also foregrounds issues of traumatic memory, this time by invoking the turbulent times of World War II in the Carpathian Mountains of the Bukovyna region. Published in 2004, this relatively short and popular novel thematizes the trauma experienced by a ten-year-old girl as she inadvertently betrays her parents before a Soviet NKVD officer, revealing to him their participation in the resistance against Soviet rule put up by the Ukrainian Insurgent Army (Ukrains'ka Povstans'ka Armiia—UPA). Matios' reference to UPA before it became commonplace under the presidency of Viktor Yushchenko (2005–2010) points to the author's courage to take on controversial, if not taboo subjects at the time. For UPA insurgents, fighting against the Soviets long after war ended, not unlike Voron's fighters in Shkliar's novel some thirty years earlier, were labeled by the communist regime as nationalists, fascists and bandits, and such designations had lingered in the collective memory of

Ukrainians even after independence was proclaimed. The enormity of the human suffering unfolding quietly in the novel in one of the Bukovynian villages—Cheremoshne, the region that the author herself comes from, encompasses events during and after World War II. But it is only at the end of the novel that the extent of the main heroine's tragedy is fully comprehended. Witnessing her mother's horrendous death, Darusia never recovers from that trauma, losing ability to speak and forfeiting her chance to lead a normal productive life.

Matios structured *Sweet Darusia* as a novel in three parts, with the first two unfolding after war, and the last one—the longest—mostly during World War II. This inverse order, rejecting chronology, allows for the slow buildup of drama, eventually culminating in the revealing of the cause of Darusia's predicament—her inability to speak and her periodical migraines triggered by candies and other sweets. We see the heroine first as an adult woman living alone in the house she inherited from her parents, mute and different, hence considered by many as mentally retarded. Her neighbor Mariia appears to be the only one who treats her with understanding and is by and large sympathetically predisposed toward her. Everyone in the village knows that Darusia does not speak but it is Mariia who accidentally overhears that, while visiting the grave of her father, Darusia is actually able to say one word: "daddy."

The first part is devoted exclusively to Darusia. In the second part, we see her with Ivan Tsvychok, a vagrant man of unknown origin who plays an instrument called a *drymba* in Ukrainian (jaw harp) and seems totally oblivious to what others think of him. To villagers he looks dumb and useless but to Darusia he is kind and helpful. She is taken by his music and allows him to stay with her. Ivan too finds Darusia's difference attractive and wants to help and take care of her. Together the two of them form a couple, however strange and unlikely, that could have probably lasted, if not for the unfortunate incident in which Ivan unintentionally sets off Darusia's memory of her painful past and that alone is enough for her to let him go. As we learn, it is not just candies that trigger her headaches but also an officer's uniform. Having offended local law enforcement figures, Ivan is sent to prison for two weeks and upon his release the prison sergeant, taking pity on Ivan's tattered clothes, gives him his own uniform. Not knowing Darusia's past, coming back to her in such an attire, Ivan opens the wound that cannot be healed. Interestingly, the story of adult Darusia ends with Ivan's departure—we do not see her life past that incident, for the third and last part of the novel takes us back in time to 1939 and relates the story of Darusia's parents, exposing in the end the reason for the heroine's long-lasting trauma.

The novel draws its historical significance from depicting the horror of war, as it touched the lives of innocent people in remote mountain villages of Bukovyna. Matios addresses frequent changes of government in the region at the time, from Romanian to Soviet rule, then German and Romanian again, and back to Soviet, and what impact these changes had on the local population. She also describes the support given by the locals to the Ukrainian Insurgent Army and what were the consequences for families whose members joined its ranks—they were evicted from their homes and transported to Siberia. But her most effective narrative emerges when she focuses on individual lives and relates the tragic story of one family, Darusia's parents, as they attempt to muddle through those trying times. The first setback comes when Matronka gives birth to Darusia but three months later is abducted by the Soviets, mistakenly accused of helping Ukrainian nationalists. She is raped by one of the officers and let go under the condition that she will not tell anyone about the incident. She keeps her word, even when her husband Mykhailo beats her to find out the truth, prompted by allusions from Lupul, a local Romanian official. He eventually learns the truth from Matronka but by then it is too late for both of them. When the Ukrainian Insurgency Army fighters come to their house to get some food, Mykhailo and Matronka do not refuse helping them, intending to convince the authorities that it was a forced robbery. But those who come to investigate do not believe the story, especially the same officer who raped Matronka back in 1940. He cleverly approaches Darusia, tempting her with a candy and uncovers the deception from her because her father always taught her to tell the truth. Matronka hangs herself afterward and Mykhailo is arrested.

Sweet Darusia earned Matios in 2005 the highest state-sponsored literary prize in Ukraine—the prestigious Taras Shevchenko National Award. The novel has gone through several editions and retained its popularity both in print and on stage. Its theatrical adaptation, premiered back in 2008, continues to attract wide audiences in many different Ukrainian cities, but especially in Chernivtsi, the capital of Bukovyna.

In contrast to Shkliar and Matios, Lina Kostenko's novel *Notes of a Ukrainian Madman* (2010) concentrates on post-independence Ukraine, narrowing its focus to four years preceding the 2004 presidential elections between Viktor Yanukovych and Viktor Yushchenko, fraudulent results of which led to the Orange Revolution. In fact, the time framework of Kostenko's first and only novel to date is precisely delineated, beginning in September 2000 with the discovery of the gruesome murder of the Georgian-born Ukrainian journalist Georgiy Gongadze and ending with the repeat presidential elections thanks to the Orange Revolution with Yushchenko prevailing.

Notes is a novel written in a diary-entry format, with the expected first-person narration, a novel in which Ukraine's affairs and its place in the world are viewed through the eyes of a computer programmer—a family man in his mid-thirties who has a difficult time to adapt to new circumstances despite his education and professional skills. We learn that he and his wife—a literary

scholar specializing in Nikolai Gogol (Mykola Hohol)[16]—met as students
when they were both involved in a hunger strike, a protest action by young
pro-independence Ukrainians in 1990, demanding, among other things,
the resignation of Prime Minister Vitalii Masol. This student action was
successful, as the Ukrainian authorities, still under Soviet rule, caved into
students' demands. These details indicate that the couple is well aware of
their own sense of national identity. The main protagonist even mentions that
some of his co-workers call him a nationalist for his insistence on speaking
only Ukrainian. But he also has a tendency to view things through a catastrophic lens, as he scrupulously enumerates murders, assassinations, freak
or suspicious accidents, terrorist attacks and various catastrophes, not only in
Ukraine but also around the world. One such catastrophe that emerges as a
main traumatic event in the lives of Kostenko's characters is the Chornobyl
nuclear power plant accident of 1986. They are touched by it personally, as
the main protagonist's father-in-law is buried in the exclusion zone and visiting his grave becomes a challenge, whereas his mother-in-law experiences
nightmares about the accident, dreaming of radiation. No wonder then that
the Chornobyl catastrophe figures prominently in the hero's diary as a particularly painful memory and trauma, and we see him counting impatiently
days to the plant's decommissioning. President Leonid Kuchma officially
shut down the plant on December 15, 2000.

Another issue that seems to be central to the main protagonist, though
perhaps not as traumatic as the Chornobyl accident, is the language issue. It
is quite clear that Kostenko channels her own views on the subject through
her hero. First, we witness his harsh criticism about the widespread usage
of *surzhyk* not only among less educated classes (something to be expected)
but also among high-ranking politicians, including Ukraine's president—the
guarantor of its Constitution, where according to Article 10, Ukrainian is the
only official state language. Second, he complains about the continued perception of the Ukrainian language as being less prestigious than Russian in
urban centers, despite its official state status:

> In all countries language is simply a communication tool but here it is also a
> factor of alienation. A dumb enmity surrounds our language even now, in our
> own state. We are like an ethnic minority—every jerk seemingly has the right to
> offend you. Wherever I go I attract attention, true—sometimes in a positive way
> but that does not make it any easier. Because in the very nature of this attention
> there is something unnatural and humiliating. A man expresses himself in his
> own native tongue and people turn their heads.[17]

Finally, toward the end of the novel, with the events of the Orange Revolution taking center stage, there seems to be a slight improvement, a correction

in social attitudes toward Ukrainian in the capital city, where, as Kostenko's "madman" observes, even his neighbors, a nouveau riche widow called Glamur and her son Borka (Boris), have begun speaking the language. The aftermath of Chornobyl and the language situation are not the only issues consuming the main protagonist—he is also concerned about the epidemic of AIDS and the poor economic climate in Ukraine that forces many highly trained professionals to leave the country (the so-called brain drain). In fact, he corresponds with his friend, also a computer engineer, who left for California, having obtained a well-paying job there, and oftentimes entices the hero to do the same. This is especially tempting after he loses his job in Kyiv and for months cannot find employment. But he resists emigration for various reasons, family obligations being one, as well as having this at times irrational sense of responsibility for the well-being of his nation, though often dreams of going to the Canaries. That incessant mantra of invoking the Spanish islands becomes a metaphor for him of wanting something that is highly desirous and yet totally unachievable, not unlike the unattainable dream that Gogol's character Poprishchin has in "Diary of a Madman," having the audacity to fall in love with his boss's daughter. However, the dream of Kostenko's "madman" goes beyond of being just personal—it encompasses the national dream, so to speak, which in the end is reified in the Orange Revolution.

Shortly after its publication, Kostenko's *Notes* was harshly criticized by Lviv literati for inaccurately presenting the protagonist's profession and for using him as a mask to channel her own subjective views on different issues, many a time of a conservative tinge, among other things.[18] That harsh criticism, incidentally, interrupted her book tour in the early months of 2011, resulting in the author's refusal to continue promoting the book in person. But other critics, such as Dmytro Drozdovsky, praised her new work for experimenting with the genre, especially its hybridization, and for exposing the absurdities generated by the media and new virtual space. He even claimed that the real protagonist of her novel is not an unnamed computer programmer but a twenty-first-century information overload that invariably contributes to neurosis, if not real madness.[19] Kostenko's hero, of course, is not a madman but a highly sensitive individual who interiorizes past and present traumas, and because of it feels emotionally overwhelmed. At some point, he muses about Ukraine going through a genocide, linguicide and, following the Chornobyl disaster, also ethnocide, as a large segment of population from the Polissia region had to be evacuated because of radioactive pollution. Not being able to cope, whether in personal or professional life, leads to his suicide attempt. In the end, he finds catharsis in love and in Kyiv's Maidan during the Orange Revolution.

What connects all three novels analyzed here, besides being bestsellers, is their overwhelming national bias and focus on events, both historical and contemporary, bringing out the heroic and the civic in otherwise passive communities. Wars necessarily dehumanize and traumatize, as do rampant corruption and authoritarian rule. Despite that, Shkliar, Matios and Kostenko make an effort to show the importance of basic humanity and dignity in the midst of brutality and violence. Their protagonists also become in large part carriers of the national idea, or "Ukrainianness" if you will, and thanks to the novels' wide reach, that in and of itself exerts enormous power and influence on the formation of national identity.

THE RISE OF PROFESSIONAL WOMAN
AS A NEW TYPE OF HEROINE

As I have previously indicated, one of the leading characteristics of post-independence literary trends is a powerful contingent of women authors. This is also true in the realm of popular fiction. In fact, this niche is over-whelmingly dominated by female voices. Such writers as Iren Rozdobudko (b. 1962) and Liuko Dashvar (b. 1957) have developed their own following and enjoy multiple printings of their works. Still others, who also dabble in popular genres such as Larysa Denysenko (b. 1973), and to a lesser extent Yevheniia Kononenko (already discussed in Chapter 3), while not as popular, nevertheless produce examples of very readable and accessible prose. Each of these authors approaches social and national issues somewhat differently but, not surprisingly, all of them tend to generate strong female characters. One type of heroine that appears particularly prevalent across their oeuvre is that of a well-off professional woman, oftentimes a businesswoman. The latter type of female character could only have developed in the new economic environment of independent Ukraine, when the centrally planned economy was replaced by market rules. As depicted in fictional works, these women tend to be professionally very successful either through their own talent and hard work, or thanks to the connections provided to them by their husbands. Either way, despite their fortune these professional women often display considerable vulnerabilities capable of undoing their hard-earned success in no time. Whether they play a role of heroine or villain, they always exude power; have substantial resources at their fingertips; and are more than ready to use all means necessary to obtain a desired outcome.

Born in Donetsk, Iren Rozdobudko moved to Kyiv in 1988 and worked first as a journalist. In her late thirties she began to write fiction and her first two detective novels *Dead Bodies* (*Mertsi*)[20] and *Escort into Death* (*Eskort u smert'*), published in 2001 and 2002, respectively, brought her consider-able resonance. Incorporating the best elements of mystery fiction, these two novels not only present highly suspenseful narratives involving a series of mysterious deaths, but also foreground a new type of heroine—that of a successful businesswoman. What is also characteristic of these two novels is that they both provide links between the Soviet and post-independence realities, that is, to solve the mysteries in both of them, the author offers clues hidden deep in the Soviet past.

The main protagonist of *Dead Bodies*—Vira, a successful journalist and TV personality earned her success by her own perseverance and hard work. Vira struggles with her past, as her own mother was accused of murdering an old wealthy widow of a Soviet diplomat, Aloiza Abelivna, who was giving Vira French lessons as a thank you gesture for her mother's housekeeping chores. It was little Vira who discovered Aloiza's body and that incident left her severely traumatized and in need of psychiatric care. Vira's mother subsequently committed suicide by hanging herself in a prison cell and her daughter was forced to grow up in an orphanage. Despite these setbacks she managed to receive a good education resulting in a prestigious job that allowed her to thrive professionally. At that point of her career, Liliana Povolotska approaches her with a proposition to join her as her assistant director in the Department of Cultural Relations at a Press Agency that she is heading. The conditions were such that Vira could not refuse. Liliana Povolotska represents yet another powerful female character that has connections and substantial resources at her disposal. However, shortly after Vira joins Povolotska's department, her co-workers begin mysteriously dying. As it turns out at the end, there is no coincidence as to who works for Liliana—she puts a lot of effort to assemble her team out of her childhood friends from the early 1980s, all of whom lived in the same neighborhood in Kyiv in which Vira also resided at the time, in order to find out who has a box with diamonds they stole from old Aloiza after killing her. The novel concludes when all the perpetrators of the old crime are dead and Vira is ready to begin a new life with a newly found love.

Rozdobudko's second detective novel *Escort into Death* is almost entirely populated by strong businesswomen.[21] Some of them are on the receiving end of service provided by an escort firm, still others—are owners and managers of that very business. Owned by Dana Viacheslavivna and managed by Maryna with the help of invalid Lana, the dispatcher who works from home, the Escort-Service Firm is engaged in finding and employing good-looking and educated men willing to work as escorts to powerful and rich women.[22] Since the compensation for such a service (that excludes sex) is so much more lucrative than otherwise, Maryna does not have any problems recruiting such men. However, when they begin to be murdered one by one, the firm understandably goes on edge and the mystery begins. This novel, unlike *Dead Bodies*, provides a considerably more visible role for a detective, named Roman Marchenko, who takes over the investigation and solves the crime.

To catch the serial killer he involves his good-looking colleague Orest as a lure but, in the end, discovers the truth himself. As Marchenko gets strangely attached to facially disfigured Lana, he eventually realizes that the invalid woman is behind all the murders. She prompts other people to carry out killings on her behalf, by using her power of persuasion in the case of Maryna and that of blackmail in the case of Dana's husband. Lana orchestrated all that crime to bring back to her life a man with whom she was very much in love as a teenager back in the 1980s and who happens to be the detective Roman Marchenko.

The dynamic plots of both novels offer highly readable accounts but, more importantly, allow Rozdobudko to channel her own views on many social issues, including feminism, ostentatious greed of the nouveau riche class, and low earning power of highly educated individuals. Despite employing popular genres, such as a detective story, she clearly aspires to be taken seriously as a writer. Her female characters are all educated and well read; Vira in *Dead Bodies*, for example, reads a book by the Argentinian author Julio Cortázar, Maryna in *Escort into Death*, on the other hand, salutes works by Milorad Pavić, Erich Maria Remarque, Mario Vargas Llosa and also quotes Akhmatova. Moreover, Rozdobudko interweaves her narratives with poetic lines of a few contemporary Ukrainian poets, such as Volodymyr Tsybulko and Vasyl Herasymiuk. All that makes her prose appear intellectually attractive and intentionally very Ukrainian, though, one could argue, somewhat lacking in authenticity precisely because of that. After all, Kyiv urbanites, especially business elites, overwhelmingly interact in Russian in real life, whereas in Rozdobudko's fiction they all speak perfect literary Ukrainian. There is hardly any hint in her texts that people in that particular social milieu might interact in a language other than Ukrainian. Rozdobudko's faithfulness to the language is all the more telling, if we take into account that she comes from Donetsk, a very Russian-speaking city. Finally, the author seemingly wants to acknowledge Agatha Christie's inspiration by invoking the latter's famous fictional character of Miss Marple, an elderly spinster who acts as an amateur detective. In *Escort into Death*, however, Rozdobudko assigns this name, perhaps half-jokingly, to the professional detective Roman Marchenko, calling him Mister Marple.

Yevheniia Kononenko, on the other hand, without direct allusions to Christie's protagonist, creates a Marple-like amateur detective in the character of Larysa Lavrynenko. Unlike Miss Marple, Larysa is a professional woman in her thirties, an art historian who works for a Western foundation "Gifted Child International," based in Kyiv. The character of Larysa appears in Kononenko's three detective novels *Imitation* (*Imitatsiia*, 2001), *Betrayal* (*Zrada*, 2002) and *Nostalgia* (*Nostal'hiia*, 2005),[23] not always necessarily playing the role of chief protagonist. Whereas Rozdobudko's "whodunits" portray successful female characters from Kyivan business circles, Kononen-ko's novels explore such women characters from within the context of Kyiv's intellectual milieu. Some critics view her novels as pseudo-detective stories[24] because their "whodunit" element does not appear to be the most important driving force for plot development, but setting genre demands aside, Kononenko does produce mystery fiction in which the process of find-ing crime perpetrators is as material as probing the depths of psychological handicaps of each character involved.

In the novel *Imitation* Kononenko presents a highly accomplished Ukrai-nian female intellectual, Mariana Khrypovych, who, thanks to her education, contacts and numerous travels abroad, thrives professionally in the capital city of Kyiv and helps her other female friends to find their feet as well. A liter-ary scholar and poet, Mariana is engaged to an American Jerry Bist, her boss (and Larysa's) at the "Gifted Child" foundation. The importance of Western funds in having a relatively comfortable life in Kyiv of the 1990s cannot be overstated. In fact, it seems that Mariana gets romantically involved with Jerry precisely for financial security reasons, simultaneously having an affair with Anatolii Sumtsov, a music teacher from Donetsk. The work at the Kyiv foundation entails finding and supporting artistically gifted children from various social strata anywhere in Ukraine with the goal of helping secure future generations of Ukrainian artists. This kind of work requires frequent travels to provincial towns and villages, and during one such trip Mariana is found dead on rail tracks in what appears to be a suicide, according to the local authorities. But her friends at the foundation doubt that conclusion and the private investigation ensues, resulting in finding out who really is behind Mariana's death. But pursuing justice or punishing perpetrators seems less interesting to Kononenko—instead, she is keen on motivation and psychol-ogy, paying considerable attention to gender issues, Western materialism and rampant elitism (if not snobbism) among Kyivan intellectuals.

Kononenko's second novel *Betrayal* continues some of the themes first introduced in *Imitation* but widens the social circle of her protagonists to include professionals beyond the narrow niche of highbrow Ukrainian intel-lectuals. The chief protagonist of this novel, Veronika Raievska, aspires to be a theater director. She leaves her controlling husband, Dmytro Stebelko, taking with her their teenage daughter Viktoriia, after he hits her in the face for allegedly betraying him. Dmytro loses contact with them for more than a year and when thanks to an anonymous phone call tip he finally finds Veronika in the hospital sick with the flu, she unexpectedly dies the following day. Viktoriia, now a student at a university, blames her father's visit for her mother's untimely death but her aunt Larysa Lavrynenko, Dmytro's sister-in-law, manages to convince her otherwise, deducing that someone else must have been behind Veronika's demise. They all join forces to solve the crime but, as in *Imitation*, in the end, it seems less important how and if the actual perpetrator is punished.

Dmytro, who helped Veronika leave her crime-ridden neighborhood when she was barely sixteen, could not imagine that she would thrive professionally without his financial support. He sacrificed his career as a scientist turning to construction in order to provide for his family and secure an apartment for all of them. And yet, Kononenko makes an effort to underscore in her novel that talented women do find a way to realize their potential. Veronika returns to her old neighborhood to find her father, realizing that her childhood home is now in Kyiv's highly desirable district and a developer is willing not only to provide them with a replacement apartment in a prestigious downtown quarter but also to pay her extra cash. Having solved a housing dilemma, Veronika pursues her professional dream, becoming a director of an amateur theater, which is invited to perform in the United States. She surrounds herself with like-minded people and collaborates with a playwright Zhenyk (or Yevhen Murchenko) who falls in love with her. Zhenyk, trying to free himself from the embrace of his domineering mother, Tetiana Viktorivna, a well-known Kyiv physician, eagerly investigates the mysterious death of his beloved, joining forces with Viktoriia and Larysa. In the end, the senseless crime turns to be the result of an unhealthy passion of a controlling mother for her son.

Once a crime is solved Kononenko is not interested in its legal aftermath. We never see law enforcement officials investigating or arresting anyone for that matter. Incidentally, there are many other strange deaths in *Betrayal*, but mostly on Dmytro's family side. These subplots play a rather minor role in the overall fabric of the narrative, although Dmytro's mother Mariia provides yet another example of a strong female character for whom professional life (being director of a local agroforestry) takes precedence over her family life and who is supposed to curse her husband and wish him dead after he abandoned her. And indeed he is killed in an accident. However, a most interesting twist in the novel comes when Viktoriia, an aspiring businesswoman, admits to her father that she is guilty in her grandfather's demise because she deliberately left a door open to an unfinished balcony in their new apartment, knowing well that in his confusion he would fall down to his death. There are no perfect or ideal protagonists in Kononenko's fictional world. Their deeds or misdeeds are as significant as the motivation behind them.

Both *Imitation* and *Betrayal* foreground the importance of having one's own space (understood literally and figuratively), especially for a woman of talent to realize her dreams. Kononenko thematizes perseverance, personal drive and dedication that each of her professional women characters put on display. These women stay faithful to their calling, even if that means failure in their personal lives. They all crave for meaningful relationships with men but only with those willing to understand and support their creative passions. Of all female characters in Kononenko's detective novels Larysa Lavrynenko seems the luckiest. First, she stays alive; second—in the novel *Nostalgia* she not only helps solving a twenty-year-old murder-suicide mystery but also falls in love with and wins the heart of a man who is directly affected by the case.

Unlike in her previous two detective stories, in *Nostalgia* Kononenko presents a murder-suicide crime involving an elderly Kyivan couple whose son Alex Hayer, a gifted pianist, left the Soviet Union for the West and never returned home. When he eventually comes back to Kyiv from Germany, Ukraine is independent and, seemingly, at least in his mind, no longer as backward as it used to be under Soviet rule. Alex is eager to find out what prompted his father first to kill his mother and then himself. And it is Larysa Lavrynenko, now in her forties and still working for the same "Gifted Child" foundation that helps him solve the mystery. In *Nostalgia* she is the novel's chief protagonist, a driving force behind the crime investigation and a recipient of another man's courtship. Kononenko, keeping suspense running, simultaneously uses her protagonists' situation to explore the beauty of Kyiv's urban landscapes and the transformations—both positive and negative—that the city experiences after independence. Being born and raised in Kyiv herself, Kononenko offers cityscapes that bear marks of an insider. The author also depicts everyday life in Kyiv with a realistic and accurate detail, free of any needless sentimentality and shows what it takes for a woman of Larysa's talent to succeed.

Whereas Kononenko and Rozdobudko frequently utilize a detective story to portray images of strong professional women, Liuko Dashvar employs straightforward narratives, relying more on the development of character within or without its social milieu than on the set conventions of the crime tale. Her first two novels *A Village Is Not People* (*Selo ne liudy*, 2007) and *Milk with Blood* (*Moloko z krov'iu*, 2008) depict village life in southern Ukraine, often foregrounding its backwardness and superstition, but her subsequent novels *Paradise. Downtown* (*Rai. Tsentr*, 2009), *To Have Everything* (*Maty vse*, 2010) and the trilogy *Beaten Are: Makar, Maks, Hotsyk* (*Byti ie: Makar, Maks, Hotsyk*, 2011–2012) depict an urban way of life in the capital city Kyiv. Born in Kherson, Liuko Dashvar (a pen name of Iryna Chernova) grew up in a Russian-speaking family and worked as a journalist in her hometown before moving to Kyiv in the early 2000s. She entered the Ukrainian literary scene relatively late, published her novel at fifty but ever since then her novels have drawn considerable attention of critics and readers alike, winning her a number of awards and generating huge print runs, measured by Ukrainian standards.[25] While strong female characters can also be found in her early novels about village life, it is predominantly in *To Have Everything* that we can observe lives of powerful professional women and witness their character evolution.

Dashvar no doubt deliberately plays with the novel's title, as "maty vse" can be read as both "to have everything" or, alternatively, "mother is everything." One could even argue that the latter rendition explains what is happening in the story line of the novel more convincingly, but the beauty of such playfulness is that either one conveys to some extent the significance of the family bond.

We are introduced to the Verbytsky family of Kyiv renowned physicians, Petro Hryhorovych, his wife Ivetta and their two children Lida and Platon. When the novel commences Petro Hryhorovych is already deceased and the whole family is under firm command of Ivetta, a well-off and highly esteemed doctor in her own right who is taking care of her mentally disturbed eighteen-year-old son Platon. Her daughter Lida is a medical doctor as well, already living separately as she is married to Stas who works as a disinfection control officer. We soon learn that he comes from a lower social background than Verbytskys but is nonetheless tolerated by Ivetta as her son-in-law. This charming picture of a model family gradually unravels when old secrets come to the surface and begin to haunt the main protagonists. First, Stas has a myriad of male complexes and constantly tries to impress his wife, although in the end he comes across as a decent man. Second, Lida yields to a domineering mother, obeying her in all aspects, including taking care of her brother Platon. By putting his needs above her own she jeopardizes her health, losing her child through miscarriage. Then we learn through Anhelina, a devoted maid and nanny to the Verbytsky family, that Ivetta is not Lida's biological mother. Petro Hryhorovych unknowingly impregnated one of his nurse assistants and Ivetta convinced the woman to disappear after giving birth to baby girl Lida, but instead of caring for the baby herself she put her in an orphanage. When Ivetta finally got pregnant herself, quite possibly with one of her interns rather than with her own husband, she decided to reveal the truth to Petro Hryhorovych about his daughter and brought Lida back from the orphanage. She came up with a story for the little girl, telling her that her physician parents were forced to leave her in the orphanage because both were sent to Africa to take care of people there and could not possibly take an infant daughter with them.

Ivetta loves Platon more than anyone else and smoothing the puberty phase for her son, she brings female mannequins for him to fulfill his erotic needs. She eventually finds a more permanent solution by introducing him to a young girl Raia, whom she snatches from a large family somewhere on the outskirts of Kyiv, but does not manage to sterilize her in time before Platon impregnates her. Raia is supposed to have an abortion, but before being forced to go through the procedure she and Platon manage to escape into the countryside and simply disappear. Ivetta, stricken with pain eventually dies, never seeing Platon again. Lida returns to care for her sick mother but in the process undergoes a total transformation, morphing into a heartless woman who seemingly cares only about herself. She rejects caring for Platon's baby that Stas brought back to Kyiv, mercilessly dismisses Anhelina, and in the end is left all by herself. Stas divorces her and decides to care for Platon's baby on his own. Lida, believing that she is the only real Verbytska left, fully devotes herself to work, fulfilling her aspiration to become a well-renowned surgeon like her late father. At the end of the novel we see her in one of the hospitals in Berlin where she accepts residency, thriving professionally but being unhappy in her personal life.

Dashvar does not idealize her female characters; to the contrary, it seems that the more educated and culturally refined her character is, the more callous and calculating she turns out to be. Women of simpler origin, like Anhelina or Raia, are clearly so much more loving and caring than their masters. Lida, deprived of motherly love in her childhood, completely cedes to Ivetta's will in her adulthood, seeing in her the ultimate authority. But after learning the truth about her extraction she is in denial most of the time, becoming as selfish and self-centered as her adoptive mother. Ivetta, on the other hand, in pain after losing Platon, appears loving and generous, financially securing not only her son's immediate family but also Raia's many poor siblings.

Larysa Denysenko's fiction does not yield similarly strong female protagonists. She clearly prefers to dwell on low-key everyday life situations, in which male and female characters present their points of views with equal force. Her narratives often bear some characteristics of romance novels, as the author focuses primarily on relationships and romantic love between two people. Denysenko produces texts that are dynamic, intimate, lighthearted and frequently incorporating humor. Because of her focus on everyday life among social groups of predominantly the Ukrainian middle class, her fiction is very relatable and accessible. Educated as a lawyer and having opportunity to work for a number of government agencies and organizations, Denysenko occasionally betrays a penchant for satire or social critique of contemporary Ukrainian society but any serious issue she discusses is invariably linked to personal and intimate relationships of her protagonists.

Successful professional women populate popular novels by women authors in such a pronounced way that it must indicate urgent demand for such a new type of heroine. This trend no doubt also reflects enormous social transformations that have taken place in Ukraine since independence, though not all of them are mutually compatible. Reading these novels we admire women's acumen to be entrepreneurial, willing to take risks and/or to follow their creative urges, at the same time, we also witness their abuse, discrimination and constant undermining either by their partners or society at large, and then doubt if a true transformation has indeed taken root. Ukrainian popular fiction by female authors apparently has a two-pronged strategy: on the one hand, it promotes the idea of women's equal rights by underscoring their potential to be successful, on the other—it exposes cases of abuse, indicating their unattractiveness and self-defeating quality.

POPULAR GENRES AND NATIONAL IDENTITY CONSTRUCTION

In *Inventing Popular Culture*, John Storey rightly observes that "debates about popular culture are rarely if ever focused only on forms of entertainment: the idea of popular culture is always entangled with questions of social power, especially in terms of claims and counter-claims about, for example, class, gender, ethnicity, 'race,' generation, and sexuality."[26] And I would also add that in terms of claims about national identity. As I have already indicated, popular literature, thanks to its wide reach, plays an important role in the shaping of the public's opinion on the issue of national belonging. Popular historical novels, for example, bring to light events of the forgotten past, often reclaiming its interpretation and significance. What used to be considered treasonous by a colonizer, becomes heroic in the eyes of the colonized. But even genres that are popular and not necessarily relying on history, such as a detective story, psychological thriller, fantasy, romance and science fiction, can meaningfully advance the issue of national identity construction, should any given author desire to channel such ideas through his/her texts, either implicitly or explicitly. One thing is certain—it is possible to discern a conscious effort among Ukrainian writers of the late 1990s and early 2000s to produce a critical mass of works in lighter genres in order to compete with and stave off an overwhelming production of foreign pulp fiction flooding the domestic book market. No wonder, then, those popular novels that reached the Ukrainian audience at that time display a quality of being deliberately constructed.

Besides the three historical novels, analyzed at the outset of this chapter, the issue of national self-awareness comes across most forcefully in Vasyl Kozhelianko's popular fiction. He delights in hybridizing genres, combing historical and futuristic scenarios, all in an effort of delineating national differences. In his novel *A Parade in Moscow*,[27] for instance, Kozhelianko introduces the elements of science fiction, mainly to underscore the bravery of Ukrainians, as they defend, like nobody else, the planet Earth from threatening alien flying objects. It is perhaps best illustrated when the chief protagonist's great-grandson, also named Dmytro Levytsky, is sent to Mars on a secret mission to successfully destroy extraterrestrial enemies. There is quite a bit of subtle humor in Kozhelianko's narratives, so it is not easy to grasp whether or not he takes his version of nationalism seriously. But, regardless of what genre he employs—science fiction or historical novel, all his texts constitute signposts of sorts, showing how to help nurture a sense of national belonging. There is a canny manipulation going on there because, it seems, no matter which historical period (or what futuristic scenario) the author takes up, he always adheres to the same formula, wherein historical (or science fiction) events are twisted in such a way as to create alternative realities that point to the timeless gloriousness of the Ukrainian nation. In that sense Kozhelianko's novels consistently facilitate discussions on the significance of national identity and represent highly accessible commentaries on nationalism, nationhood, nation and state-building. His foregrounding of superior characteristics, supposedly inherent in the Ukrainian people, can be read in some way as a warning of sorts against any authoritarian and/or nationalistic (fascist) tendencies; on the other, it can also be perceived as a venue allowing Ukrainians to confront their deeply ingrained sense of inferiority, stemming from their colonial past. The fact that Kozhelianko incorporates many elements of pulp fiction in his novels would to some extent support the claim that there is a kind of mission on his part to popularize and bring to light a hidden nexus of colonial complexes and its consequences.

Fantasy genre is especially popular among Russophone Ukrainian authors, perhaps due to the fact that, in many ways—at least theoretically, this genre seems to transcend national identity issues. Among Ukrainian-speaking writers, fantasy is also incorporated, possibly most skillfully by Halyna Pahutiak,[28] whose award-winning novel *Servant from Dobromyl* combines history and fantasy in order to explicate rather than avoid the issues of national identity. In other words, the genre of fantasy can and does provide a platform to channel identity politics as readily as other popular genres. Thus it comes as no surprise that the Diachenkos and Lada Luzina, all three very popular and writing in Russian, create enough space in their fiction to allow for commentaries, however subtle or implicit, on the essence of cultural and national difference.[29]

Luzina exploits the popularity of witchcraft in her novels to present the multiplicity of cultural layers hidden in her hometown—the capital city of Kyiv, often situating them within the context of post-independence reality and, thus, necessarily admitting the importance of national/ethnic difference. Her cultural leanings might point in one direction but the reality on the ground, so to speak, might force her to accept Ukrainian national distinctiveness. Moreover, by foregrounding historical details about the Kyivan past, it may be that she inadvertently signifies its past and present glory, including its rejection of colonial rule.

In contrast to Luzina, the authors Maryna and Serhiy Diachenko situate their protagonists mostly in environments that are devoid of any geographic specificity, but engage other methods to underscore their link to things Ukrainian. As I have indicated in Chapter 4, their novel *Age of Witches*, for example, incorporates many folk elements and characters from the mythology preserved in the Hutsul tradition, that is, in the tradition of Ukrainian highlanders from the Carpathian Mountains. Despite the fact that this urban fantasy has no connection to any recognizable Ukrainian city, the utilization of Ukrainian folkloric material gives it an unmistakable Ukrainian flavor, even if the novel itself is written in Russian.

Romance novels find their niche too among contemporary Ukrainian writers, although one should not be surprised that there are many deviations from the prescribed form. For instance, Larysa Denysenko in her *The Sarabande of Sara's Band* (*Sarabanda bandy Sary*, 2008)[30] overwhelmingly dwells on relationships, romantic and non-romantic alike, examining, among other things, what makes people of the opposite sex attract each other, but she certainly does not follow the standard mold of a romance novel. Narrated in the first person, *The Sarabande of Sara's Band* relates the story from the perspective of an introverted professional man, whose first failed marriage leads to a new relationship with a woman from his college years—Sara, whom he immensely disliked during school days. Meeting Sara again after many years he is amazed how attractive she has become and it does not take him long to fall in love with her. The relationship ensues, but the novel, in a peculiar twist, focuses on it "in absentia" so to speak, as we observe how the main protagonist interacts with Sara's temporarily displaced relatives in her absence. Perhaps such an approach slightly diminishes the novel's romantic dimension, but Denysenko, with a considerable dose of humor, also shows that failed relationships do not always spell doom and gloom; to the contrary—they can occasionally lead to a more compatible and relatable union. The novel, so preoccupied with the nitty-gritty details of everyday life, is somewhat anticlimactic at the end but manages to preserve this overwhelming sense of emotional well-being among all concerned.

Iren Rozdobudko's award-winning *The Lost Button* (*Gudzyk*, 2008)[31] conforms more fittingly to the genre of psychological thriller than romance, even though at a heart of the novel lies the story of an unrequited love between Denys and an enigmatic woman whom he met while still a student back in the 1970s at a camp in the Carpathian Mountains. Liza Tenetska is a decade or so older than Denys and, at the time of their meeting, already an accomplished film director. The love-struck eighteen-year-old protagonist is unable to let go of his feelings for Liza, even though, being rejected, he makes all efforts to forego his directorial aspirations by leaving the film school and milieu in which encounters with her would be unavoidable. When after twenty years their paths cross again, this time in independent Ukraine, he resumes his pursuit of Liza through a young woman with whom he spotted her at a café. That young woman Lika turns to be Liza's daughter and Denys, now a successful advertising executive, decides to marry her, somehow smitten by her charms and artistic talent. By then he also realizes that Liza has not recognized him and treats him merely as her son-in-law. When Denys at last has an opportunity to reveal to Liza his feelings and is rejected by her again, he does not know that this heart-wrenching love story is also heard by his wife Lika, who instead of going to an artist colony, hides in a big wardrobe closet delivered to the apartment without Denys even noticing it. Lika thereafter disappears from his life forever and he is left alone to make sense with what to do with his conflicted emotions. In the end, he realizes that what he felt for Liza was illusory and what he had with Lika was real.

Finding real love is also thematized by Liuko Dashvar in her award-winning debut novel *A Village Is Not People*, although, unlike Rozdobudko, the author situates her protagonists in a small Ukrainian village Shanivka, where superstition, malice and ignorance lead to a series of tragedies for its inhabitants. Dashvar's love story in *A Village* is transgressive from the outset because it is between a thirteen-year-old girl Kateryna and a married man Roman, who nonetheless respects her and is willing to wait until she reaches adulthood. However, after his tragic death, when the village learns about their relationship, Kateryna is forced to flee and her parents' house is burned down in retaliation. Dashvar skillfully compares virtues and vices between different social strata, juxtaposing uneducated village people with Kyivan intelligentsia, and comes to the conclusion that betrayal, cruelty and vengeance transcend social status. When Kateryna seeks shelter in Kyiv, turning to a young aspiring archeologist Ihor Krupka who visited Shanivka earlier that year to excavate an old burial mound, she encounters indifference and outright exploitation. Rather than to help Kateryna, Ihor offers the thirteen-year-old girl to his parents as a housemaid. They then, instead of helping her, abuse her, especially as they learn the reason for her escape. Ihor's professor father demands sexual favors from her, and his Russian wife Tasia wants her out but not before Kateryna cleans her kitchen. What is especially ironic is that both converse in Russian between themselves and it is in Russian that they doubt the future of independent Ukraine, contemplating the country's widespread backwardness in its villages.

All three authors—Denysenko, Rozdobudko and Dashvar come from Russian-speaking environments. Denysenko, for example, learned Ukrainian as an adult when she started her legal career working for a governmental agency when proficiency in the official state language was required. Rozdobudko and Dashvar, both from the southeast provinces of Ukraine, grew up speaking Russian and one would think they would feel more comfortable in Russian cultural space. And yet, amazing as it may be, they express themselves artistically in Ukrainian rather than Russian. While Dashvar occasionally interjects Russian phrases into her narratives, mostly to underscore the novel's verisimilitude, Rozdobudko and Denysenko compose their work by and large in standard literary Ukrainian. And, even though their works do not explicitly underscore issues of national identity, the fact that these authors produce popular fiction in the Ukrainian language is in and of itself a significant development in Ukrainian belles-lettres.

Among all literary popular genres in post-independence Ukrainian literature, the detective novel has arguably a privileged position. As I have pointed out earlier, both Rozdobudko and Kononenko turned to the genre in the early 2000s. Their detective stories unfold in contemporary Kyiv, engaging either business or intellectual elites. Murders, while plentiful, are usually solved either by amateur investigators or by members of an official law enforcement agency, though, admittedly, the latter play a considerably less prominent role. In many ways, crime in these detective novels constitutes but a background that allows light to be shed on a variety of social, political and national issues. In Rozdobudko's writing, for instance, we see a subtle critique of the system in which many highly educated individuals are unable to earn a living in their chosen professions and are forced to seek employment in newly established businesses, even if that means getting involved in criminal activities or degrading tasks. Kononenko, on the other hand, provides another model of survival among intellectuals pointing to that slice of the Ukrainian society that is able to thrive thanks to its access to Western financing through grant money or outright employment by foreign firms. Again, while Rozdobudko and Kononenko do not necessarily explicitly consider identity issues, the mere fact that the protagonists of their highly popular and/or esteemed novels represent the Ukrainian upper classes that converse in Ukrainian is in and of itself quite significant. That gesture alone elevates the status of the Ukrainian language and widens its communicative reach beyond official capacities. The preference of these authors to focus on crime that occurs in the upper echelons of the business world and/or within the intellectual milieu does not mean that others, among them most prominently Andrii Kokotiukha (b. 1970), shy away from detective stories that prefer to deal with common folk instead.

Kokotiukha, a well-respected journalist and bilingual writer who published, among other things, a series of nonfiction works in Russian titled *Criminal Ukraine* (*Kriminal'naia Ukraina*, 2003–2005), is primarily known as an author of popular detective novels. He focuses on describing criminal acts mostly among lower- and middle-class Ukrainians—many a time in the provinces rather than in Kyiv, often motivating their delinquency by prevailing difficult social conditions and inadequate law enforcement methods of policing. In many ways, his approach somewhat reverberates the one taken by Oles Ulianenko, except that unlike the latter, Kokotiukha offers texts that are considerably more accessible and relatable. One reason for that could be that he creates contexts that are realistic and very much corresponding to the social reality on the ground. The author heavily relies on one type of protagonist—that of a disappointed former law enforcement official who quits his job (or is fired) in order to become a private investigator. Not surprisingly, his chief characters are mostly men, with women decisively playing a secondary role. In that respect, he appears to subtly nurture the cult of masculinity as a counterbalance to feminism, so strongly advocated in detective novels authored by female writers, with Rozdobudko and Kononenko leading the charts.

Kokotiukha delights in exposing the inner makings of fraudulent activities, so widespread in Ukraine of the 1990s, as well as in undermining the legitimacy of vast business enterprises that are inevitably criminal in nature and operating, for the most part, thanks to the connections with corrupt government officials, including those working for law enforcement agencies. This is perhaps best illustrated in the novel *The Return of a Sentimental Gangster* (*Povernennia sentymental'noho hanhstera*, 2001), in which Kokotiukha depicts mafia-like relations between various businesses and their boss, Petro Tkach, on the one hand, and, on the other, he also shows how an orphaned young man, Dmytro Maistrenko, evolves to become a dangerous gangster Merkurii. In many ways, *The Return of a Sentimental Gangster* offers a textbook description of successful money laundering schemes. Robberies, killings and pervasive corruption provide the overall background against which the story line unfolds in this rather grim novel, with one character concluding: "Everywhere there's such a mess—these rascals are not afraid of anything! My co-worker's son was stabbed right in downtown at noon."[32] When at last Merkurii is ready to leave the criminal world, he pays a heavy price for wanting his freedom back.

Slightly more upbeat is Kokotiukha's novel *Dark Waters* (*Temna voda*, 2006) in which the mysterious drowning of four fishermen near a quiet resort on the Desna River appear all to happen in a "cursed" place, according to local beliefs, until the mystery is solved by a private investigator, Vitalii Melnyk, who finds the perpetrator and proves that these are calculated murders rather than mystical happenings. Nowhere else the contrast between corrupted law enforcement officials and an honest private investigator is as stark as in this novel. Melnyk's professionalism in *Dark Waters* is juxtaposed against brutal methods used by local police officers to force the local delinquents to falsely confess to crimes they did not commit. In fact, Kokotiukha in great detail describes some of those methods that without any doubt amount to torture:

So Liuty and his gopniks confessed to what?
    They confessed to that what usually comes out when they handcuff you to the radiator and touch your penis with a naked electric wire. Or, when they put you

face down on the floor and thrust a rubber baton with a condom into your anus. Or, when they dress you in a gas mask and press its hose periodically, playing an "elephant." There is a whole bunch of recipes to obtain sincere confessions.[33]

In the end, it is not so much about legal consequences for those found guilty, as it is about solving the crime. And Melnyk, with the help of a local detective, exposes not only those guilty of murders but their motivations as well.

In Kokotiukha's yet another detective novel *The Crawling Snake* (*Povze zmiia*, 2005), we too see a positive hero in the character of private investigator Maks. A former law enforcement official, he is ready to defend a journalist Olena from a serial killer, Bohdan Bahlai, haunting her to take revenge. Again, Kokotiukha presents a critique of law enforcement agencies that are incapable of adequately securing streets and seem at a loss how to track the serial killer Bahlai after he manages to escape prison.

Detective novels reflect social ills in post-independence Ukrainian society perhaps most acutely; at the same time, by offering suspense, mystery, plenty of action and dynamic dialogues, they provide the public with popular easy-reads. While these kinds of books do not directly touch upon the issue of identity formation, the very fact of showing the viability of the Ukrainian language to convey convincing suspenseful stories constitutes in itself a serious paradigm shift. The language issue is an important one, and it occasionally surfaces as a reminder of the true state of affairs, as is the case in Kokotiukha's *The Crawling Snake*. Here the author provides the readers right at the outset with a note that he is aware that, to ring true, the language of communication for the majority of his main and secondary characters should be Russian or *surzhyk*.[34] And yet, he nonetheless deliberately offers novels in which protagonists speak a literary Ukrainian. And in that respect he is not the only one taking such an approach, as I already pointed out while discussing female popular authors. It is quite conceivable that by adopting popular genres in the 1990s Ukrainian writers en masse made a conscious effort to offset a considerable influx of mass culture products coming from Russia, including translations of popular works from the West. The situation began steadily improving in the early 2000s and the vacuum was filled by domestic production. Moreover, bestsellers from the West would now be translated directly into Ukrainian and published first in Ukraine instead of relying on Russian renditions. By the same token, Ukrainian popular literature has become sought after thanks to publishers ready to promote Ukrainian authors, especially those who have already developed a serious following. Clearly, Ukrainian popular literature goes well beyond merely being entertaining. It is possible to ascribe to it a mission of sorts—that of facilitating and consolidating a sense of national belonging.

NOTES

1. José Ortega y Gasset, *The Revolt of the Masses*, online, 8–10, accessed December 18, 2016, http://pinkmonkey.com/dl/library1/revolt.pdf.
2. Pierre Bourdieu, *Distinctions: A Social Critique of the Judgement of Taste*, trans. Richard Nice (Cambridge, MA: Harvard University Press, 1993), 5–6.
3. Ibid., 7.
4. John Storey, *Inventing Popular Culture: From Folklore to Globalization* (Maldan, MA: Blackwell Publishing, 2003), 46.
5. See his "Understanding Audience Segmentation: From elite and mass to omnivore and univore," *Poetics* 21 (1992): 243–58.
6. Storey, *Inventing Popular Culture*, 46.
7. Ibid., 78.
8. Of course, this is but just one such example. Other genres such as fantasy, romance and science fiction also figure as significant categories in the post-independence literary production. For my discussion of a few novels in the genre of fantasy, written in Russian, see Chapter 4.
9. It was published under this title first by Yaroslaviv Val in Kyiv and then almost simultaneously under the title *Zalyshenets'. Chornyi Voron (Banished. Black Raven)* by the Klub simeinoho dozvillia in Kharkiv.
10. The first edition of 10,000 copies went on sale on December 17, 2010 but quickly sold out, prompting the publisher to reissue the following month, in January 2011. The copy I have read has a 2011 imprint.
11. Lina Kostenko, one of the leading literary figures of the 1960s generation, known as *shistdesiatnyky*, is included in my examination of popular literature for her 2010 novel brought about a considerable reaction among literary circles, both positive and negative, as well as because its printing in 2011 was close to eighty thousand copies—a rare feat for Ukrainian books.
12. Also known as the Ukrainian People's Republic.
13. In fact, the Polish film director Jerzy Hoffman, who turned down an opportunity to adapt the novel for the screen, accused Shkliar of xenophobia and anti-Russian bias. Cf. http://glavred.info/archive/2011/10/24/183426–8.html, accessed December 20, 2016. Much was also made about Shkliar's prevalent use of derogatory names for ethnic Russians and/or for those who cooperated with the regime. However, as Liudmyla Tomilenko, pointed out, some of those designations (e.g., *katsap* or *katsapnia*) acquired notoriety long before Shkliar's incorporation of its usage. See her "Ekspresyvna leksyka na poznachennia nazv osib u romani Vasylia Shkliara *Zalyshenets'. Chornyi Voron*," *Kul'tura slova* 78 (2013): 77–78.
14. The book came out in 2009, long before a new war between Russia and Ukraine broke out in 2014, and no wonder that in the new political context this novel acquired new significance, with strong calls for movie adaptation coming from various quarters. Cf. http://www.ukrop.com.ua/uk/news/central/2666-nezabarom-rozpochnutsya-zyomki-khudozhnogo-filmu-za-romanom-vasilya-shklyara-chorniy-voron, accessed December 20, 2016. In one of his interviews, Shkliar also commented on the novel's popularity among those fighting on the frontlines in the Donbas. Cf. http://web.

archive.org/web/20160627172935/http://nv.ua/ukr/publications/zrosijshchena-ukra-jina-kvazirosija-nikomu-ne-tsikava-pismennik-vasil-shkljar-pro-te-v-jakih-mezhah-bude-ukrajina-145241.html, accessed December 20, 2016.

15. See his interview with Anastasiia Fedchenko: http://web.archive.org/web/20160627172935/http://nv.ua/ukr/publications/zrosijshchena-ukrajina-kvazirosija-nikomu-ne-tsikava-pismennik-vasil-shkljar-pro-te-v-jakih-mezhah-bude-ukrajina-145241.html, accessed December 20, 2016.

16. I am using both Russian and Ukrainian spellings of this well-known nineteenth-century author. It is worth mentioning that Kostenko is intertextually playing with the title of her novel, no doubt referring to Gogol's own short story "Diary of a Madman" (1835).

17. Lina Kostenko, *Zapysky ukrains'koho samashedshoho* (Kyiv: A-BA-BA-HA-LA-MA-HA, 2011), 22–23.

18. See the February 7, 2011 report on the ZIK site about the discussion, in which Ihor Kotyk, Viktor Neborak and Iurii Kucheriavy participated, accessed December 16, 2016, http://zik.ua/news/2011/02/07/zapysky_samashedshogo__tse_kostenko_v_mastsi_programista__triytsya_z_270856.

19. See Dmytro Drozdovs'kyi, "Informatsiine 'samashestviie:' perezavantazhennia," *Bukvoid*, August 5, 2011, accessed December 21, 2016, http://bukvoid.com.ua/digest/2011/08/05/110939.html.

20. Initially titled: *Pastka dlia zhar-ptytsi* (A Trap for the Firebird, 2000) and reprinted again under this title in 2007 by Folio Publishers in Kharkiv.

21. As the author observes, there are many well-off women who are often lonely: "Look around, open your eyes: every second woman is lonely, every fifth has her own business." Rozdobud'ko, *Eskort u smert'* (Lviv: Kal'variia, 2002), 22.

22. While such firms do exist in the West, in Ukraine, no doubt, that was a novel concept at the time of the novel's publication and, all the more, it is commendable that Rozdobudko challenges the patriarchal order and reverses the usual assumptions.

23. Published by Lviv's Kal'variia together with Kononenko's two other works "Bez muzhyka" and "Vtracheni stiny" under one title *Bez muzhyka* (2005) and then issued separately by the same publisher in 2013.

24. See, for example, Hundorova, *Pisliachornobyl's'ka biblioteka*, 257. Moreover, in *The Intellectual as Hero in 1990s Ukrainian Fiction*, Mark Andryczyk does not at all dwell on the detective component when he analyzes Kononenko's novel *Imitation*.

25. According to the Wikipedia entry on her, the total print run of her books is well over 300,000 copies.

26. Storey, *Inventing Popular Culture*, xii.

27. Discussed in detail in Chapter 2.

28. See Chapter 3 for more extensive discussion of her oeuvre.

29. For more information and analysis of their work see Chapter 4.

30. Glagoslav Publications issued the book-length translation of this novel in Michael M. Naydan and Svitlana Bednazh's rendition in 2013.

31. Translated by Michael M. Naydan and Olha Tytarenko and published by Glagoslav Publications in 2012.

32. Andrii Kokotiukha, *Povernennia sentymental'noho hanhstera* (Kyiv: Fakt, 2001), 12.

33. Kokotiukha, *Temna voda* (Kyiv: Nora-Druk, 2006), 236–37.

34. See his *Povze zmiia* (Kyiv: Nora-Druk, 2005), 4.

Conclusion

Toward a New National Literature

The political reality in Ukraine soon after independence exposed the legacy of Soviet colonial rule, yet at the same time promoted the rise of the plurality and hybridity of national and cultural identities. This indeterminacy, or hesitance, if you will, in the national consolidation project has found its reflection in literary texts, not just on the level of thematics alone, but also in the overall direction in which the literary process has moved since 1991. Plural identities, be they national, cultural or social, invariably bring about multiple literary canons. This in and of itself is neither positive nor negative, but as Sarah Corse rightly observes in her book *Nationalism and Literature*, "in order to proclaim cultural independence, a nation-state must produce and identify a literature that differentiates it from other states, particularly the most relevant others."[1] For Ukraine such a relevant Other is, of course, Russia. One would think that Ukraine, with its own national language, would have a relatively easy task in marketing its cultural difference, but the status of the Ukrainian language did not visibly improve in the first two decades of independence.[2] Therefore, the dichotomous standing of Ukrainian culture—that is, as one incorporating both colonial and postcolonial cultural consciousness—must be recognized, and that in turn has a direct bearing on the question of canon formation.[3]

In many ways the literary scene reflects the difficulties at large; that is, the question of how to consolidate a nation that seems to be fracturing along linguistic, ideological and regional lines concerns politicians as much as writers. To produce works of literature with an equal appeal in Lviv and Donetsk is a difficult task indeed. No wonder that one of the characteristic features of cultural trends in the post-Soviet period has been ever-increasing decentralization of literary production and distribution. Moreover, the topos of location, as I have previously indicated, has gained currency both among the writers of Western and Eastern Ukraine.[4]

Thus far there have been very few attempts to present a comprehensive account of contemporary Ukrainian literature from the perspective of identity construction. The most ambitious investigation to date is Ola Hnatiuk's Polish-language monograph *Farewell to Empire: Ukrainian Discussions on Identity* (*Pożegnanie z imperium: Ukraińskie dyskusje o tożsamości*), published in 2003,[5] but her account is more in the domain of intellectual rather than literary studies per se.[6] This study, on the other hand, focuses first and foremost on works of literature. It is deliberately limited to the most representative works of contemporary literature, produced by those who saw their debuts predominantly in the second half of the 1980s and then in the 1990s and 2000s, even though the post-Soviet period witnessed the continued activities of writers of the older generation.[7] The question I deemed important to consider is how various identities (national, ethnic, territorial, class and gender) are reflected in contemporary Ukrainian literature and whether or not literary texts exert any influence on forming these identities in post-independence reality.

One issue in the cultural politics of post-Soviet Ukraine that appears pervasive and sensitive, yet stubbornly eludes resolution, is the language question. Despite the official status of Ukrainian, the Russian language de facto represents the preferred means of communication for a large percentage of the country's population. The correlation between ethnic and linguistic identities is not always obvious; for example, in the case of some ethnic Ukrainians, Ukrainian is not necessarily the preferred language of communication.[8] Therefore, we might often face the situation in which the Russian ethnic minority (according to the official statistics) does not appear to be a minority when gauged by the language criterion. Of course, for writers wanting to express themselves specifically in Ukrainian this situation is problematical because it directly affects their pool of potential readers.[9] On the other hand, those writers who are Ukrainian citizens but write exclusively in Russian also might feel aggrieved for being pushed to the margins of the literary process. How then does one arrive at some kind of agreement as to what comprises the body of texts that can be considered a national literature: will it be literature written only in Ukrainian or literature written by Ukrainian citizens regardless of what language is being used? One thing is certain—there has been a noticeable evolution of views, from a strict understanding of national literature as the one written in a national language toward a more all-embracing one that considers any literary production on the Ukrainian territory as national regardless of what language is employed. Nevertheless, to shore up the expansion of the Ukrainian language usage, there has been a concerted effort to make available classics of world literature or Western popular literature in Ukrainian. One cannot underestimate the role of translations in this regard, especially when English-language bestsellers are rendered first into Ukrainian rather than into Russian. An important case in point is J.K. Rowling's Harry Potter series masterfully translated into Ukrainian by Viktor Morozov. He managed to publish the last three Harry Potter novels in Ukrainian well before they came out in Russian.[10]

Returning to the issue of language choice, in the early 2000s, there was an open disagreement about the status of Andrey Kurkov as a Ukrainian writer between his peers Vasyl Shkliar and Volodymyr Yavorivsky, the latter embracing Kurkov as part of Ukrainian letters and the former denying it.[11] Yavorivsky's passionate call to include Kurkov in the canon of Ukrainian literature corresponds to what Kurkov himself has stated on many occasions, namely, that he is a Ukrainian writer who just happens to write in Russian. After all, he does incorporate Ukrainian material and, as I have indicated before, hardly any other contemporary author in Ukraine seems to be writing about Kyiv and/or current Ukrainian affairs with such passion. I am foregrounding the language issue because it is indicative of potential disagreements but also paves the path toward approaches favoring building a consensus when it comes to establishing one authoritative literary canon—the body of texts that can act as a touchstone of taste and value.

To a large extent, the formation of canons is a measure of the strength or weakness of the institutions responsible for literary studies and artistic production. What this suggests is that those with cultural power—that is, those who publish, disseminate, purchase, preserve and quote—all contribute to the production and maintenance of literary value. Following the collapse of the Soviet Union, there was understandably a need to revisit old presuppositions as far as the literary canon was concerned.[12] In fact, this process began during the glasnost period. One of the most characteristic traits of those years was to restore the names of writers previously forbidden, as well as to introduce the output of Ukrainian émigré literary figures. Moreover, Ukraine's independence brought about the necessity to reevaluate the contributions and significance of those writers who had gained prominence under the Soviet regime. Judging by the *History of Ukrainian Literature in the 20th Century*, a collective work under the general editorship of Vitalii Donchyk published first in 1993 and reissued in 1998, more attention is devoted to Soviet Ukrainian writers than to those who made their debuts in the glasnost and post-independence periods.

Conservative academic canonical propositions no doubt have some bearing on what is being taught in schools; on the other hand, they are counterbalanced by the alternative propositions coming mostly from writers themselves.[13] The latter do not play a prominent role in establishing school curricula, but are active and known throughout the media. It is not inconceivable that we might also expect some propositions in the future from the literary quarters of

Russian-language writers who live and work in Ukraine, especially when it comes to their own perception of how their literary contributions fit into the fabric of overall Ukrainian culture.

One area that seems to draw universal consensus is the understanding that in the aftermath of the fall of the Soviet empire, there was a noticeable increase in political and cultural tensions surrounding the social role of a literary work and its creators. I am referring here to a radical paradigm shift that has occurred both on the level of production of literary texts and on the level of literary scholarship. This shift, which stems from the total collapse of communist ideology, is also a consequence of the new market dynamics in which a writer cannot solely rely on government subsidies to have his or her voice heard. For example, young people emerging in the literary milieu of the 1990s were soon aware of an entirely new relationship between readers and literary production. Their role was no longer limited to just coming up with interesting, imaginative writings, but often included fundraising, advertising and distribution responsibilities.[14] Also worth noting is that with the collapse of the Soviet Union literature itself seemed to have lost some of its pre-independence aura and significance. Ideologically constrained as the Soviet period was, there seemed to be considerably more appreciation for the printed word than is the case today. It is as if readers do not need literature to the same degree that they did in the pre-independence years. In this respect, the literary situation in present-day Ukraine resembles or is comparable to the one in the West, where serious literature must compete with many other cultural products, especially with those that are image-based, and often attracts but a relatively small numbers of readers.

On the level of literary scholarship, the transition from highly ideological interpretations and hackneyed methodologies to more innovative and theoretically interesting readings has been slow and not always reliable, primarily among conservative academic circles. There is an exception, though—a group of women literary scholars and critics who have introduced feminist theory and psychoanalysis as viable interpretative alternatives. Tamara Hundorova, Vira Aheieva, the late Solomiia Pavlychko and the late Nila Zborovska, to name just a few, have had a tremendous impact on rethinking and reinterpreting old canons. In fact, as I argued in Chapter 1, their propositions constitute the most interesting reading strategies in the post-independence period, especially when it comes to studying early Ukrainian modernism. Also worth mentioning is that, in addition to analyzing the Ukrainian classics, they focus attention on new literature, which scholars with a more conservative bent do not study as a rule.

It goes without saying that the post-Soviet period brought about many positive changes: first and foremost, freedom of expression, a general sense of freedom in creative undertakings, no censorship and no mandatory ideology.

On the negative side, publishing and distribution structures literally collapsed soon after independence, and there was no longer any government support for literary publications. In the first years after independence, to be published at all was quite an achievement. Literary magazines and journals struggled to publish regularly.[15] In the second half of the 1990s the situation with publishing and distribution somewhat improved, and by the late 2000s the book industry seemed to be functioning quite well, although distribution still was begging for considerable overhaul.

The past decades have seen a proliferation of new journals, almanacs and, most importantly, the establishment of new publishing houses willing to promote new talents and support new Ukrainian literature. And yet, what could have changed, but has not to a sufficient degree, is the role of the Ukrainian government in promoting a unique national culture through a variety of tax breaks and other subsidies. Instead, neither the executive nor the legislative branches of the government deemed it essential to introduce protective measures against the influx of cheap books coming from the Russian Federation.[16] Moreover, both have failed (unlike their Russian counterparts) to provide the Ukrainian publishing industry with necessary tax incentives.

For young Ukrainian writers entering the literary milieu in the second half of the 1980s and early 1990s the most important challenge was to assert their own independent voice. Rather than struggle to be heard individually, they often formed literary groups. More regional than aesthetic in nature, they helped aspiring writers to affirm their presence on the literary scene. Among the most notable groups were Bu-Ba-Bu (the name stands for the first syllables of *burlesk* [burlesque], *balagan* [mess/chaos] and *bufonada* [buffoonery]), Nova degeneratsiia (New Degeneration), Chervona fira (Red Wagon), Luhosad (referring to the first syllables of last names of its members—Luchuk, Honchar and Sadlovsky), and Propala hramota (The Lost Letter), to name the most significant ones. These various literary groups, not having easy access to official publishers, placed at first more importance on performance than printed word. Surfacing in cities other than the capital, they also signaled another shift in literary dynamics, namely the loss of a certain aura surrounding the center, Kyiv. In fact, a decentralization of the literary process in Ukraine has emerged as one of the chief characteristics of the post-Soviet period. The other two major trends, to which I have already alluded, are cultural hybridity and bilingualism, both on the levels of literary production and reception. With the literary process gaining some attributes of normalcy in the second half of the 1990s, the need for literary groups subsided in the following decade, although the trend toward regionalism and decentralization remained intact.

The process of canon and national identity formation is invariably a political activity, informed by historical thinking about ethnicity, empire, and linguistic and cultural difference. It is also a socially constructed undertaking promoted by concrete individuals in specifiable contexts.[17] Ever since the Ukrainian language emerged as a literary language, Ukrainian literature has carried the burden of responsibility for nurturing unique cultural identity. Literary production was not just tied to the issue of national identity but also to struggle for independence. Expectations were such that with the achievements of political sovereignty writers would at last be freed from such obligations. However, because of the ambiguous status of Ukrainian language, the post-independence literary generation has been thrust back into familiar dilemmas—namely, reflections on the social role of literature. No doubt its significance for the nation and state-building project has diminished in the post-Soviet era. There are now other political institutions and government structures to take over such functions. Of course, it is an entirely different matter how competent or incompetent they are in building a new democratic society, in which all its citizens would feel that their rights are protected, including ethnic, linguistic and cultural.[18]

The factors most influential (or potentially influential) in the formation of a national literature in post-independence Ukraine, including the construction of its literary canon, are language choice, ideology and the integrity of institutions responsible for literary production, its dissemination and evaluation. After more than two decades of independence, all three areas still display considerable weaknesses and uncertainties.[19] One consolation might be that as the new generation of literary scholars matures, the old Soviet ideology and practices will simply disappear. By the same token, the institutions that are contributing to the production and maintenance of literary value will also gradually shed the remnants of the ideologized past and entrenched traditions of Soviet ways as their associates begin to include younger individuals.

Among the most conspicuous trends in literary discourses in post-independence Ukraine is the emergence and assertion of powerful women's voices. As mentioned earlier, the most innovative approaches in literary scholarship have come from women critics. But in the area of belles-lettres this voice has also found its niche and can easily compete with male writings, whether prose or poetry. The politics of gender as reflected in post-independence literary texts created by women authors is notable because the construction of a new image for an independent female intellectual subject is often juxtaposed with the construction of a new vision for an independent Ukraine. This link, although not equally foregrounded in all creative writings, is especially pronounced in Oksana Zabuzhko's works, mainly in her novel *Fieldwork in Ukrainian Sex*, where the protagonist draws parallels between her personal failures and the failures of her nation. Yet, arguably, the novel ends on a positive note. The heroine overcomes her drama, although it remains open to interpretation whether the same awaits her country.

It is interesting to note, however, that younger female authors appear to thematize gender more than national identity aspects. Among those most vocal are Svitlana Pyrkalo, Marianna Kiianovska, Mariana Savka and Oksana Lutsyshyna. Besides Zabuzhko, among peers of her generation, there is also a strong cohort of talented female poets and writers, including Natalka Bilotserkivets, Liudmyla Taran, Yevheniia Kononenko and Halyna Pahutiak, who assert their presence on the literary scene as forcefully as their male counterparts.

To speak of territorial identity as reflected in literary texts is to speak about authors and works that originated by and large in Galicia, the westernmost part of Ukraine. Although, thanks in large measure to Serhiy Zhadan, called sometimes the bard of Eastern Ukraine,[20] the Donbas region of Ukraine also figures prominently in Ukrainian letters. But Galicia is the region that yields a substantial pool of Ukrainian-speaking readers inclined to follow what is happening in Ukrainian literature, and the region itself has produced some of the best-known and talented writers in present-day Ukraine. The most representative figure of this group is Yuri Andrukhovych who, at some point, especially in his essays, toyed with the idea of Galicia being an integral part of Central Europe, although without issuing outright calls for separation from the rest of Ukraine.[21] The connection between a strong territorial affinity to a particular region or city and issues of national identity can also be found in the writings of Yuri Vynnychuk who has written a series of works about his city Lviv, for example, *Legends of Lviv* and *Malva Landa*, Oleksandr Irvanets (especially his novel *Rivne/Rovno*), Taras Prokhasko (his novel *The UnSimple*) and to a lesser degree the works of Viktor Neborak.

In terms of ethnolinguistic identities, I contrast a group of writers whom I have dubbed "philologists" with those writers who express themselves exclusively in Russian. The former group is above all preoccupied with the Ukrainian language. Writers such as Yevhen Pashkovsky or Viacheslav Medvid cannot count on a wide readership, as their works are clearly intended for the select few. They do not explicitly advocate identity concerns, but do celebrate the richness of the language. If anything, for them the Ukrainian language becomes not just a medium of expression but an aim and center in its own right—indeed, a protagonist. Writers like Medvid and Pashkovsky have a strong sense of national identification in ethnic rather than political terms. This position is in stark contrast to Andrey Kurkov, whose work promotes a Ukrainian civic identity, one based on citizenship rather than blood.

Some authors such as Oles Ulianenko, Anatolii Dnistrovy, Liubko Deresh, and Svitlana Povaliaieva depict the dreary realities of Ukrainian everyday life, including the growing strata of the criminal world and many young people living on the margins of society. The issue of class distinction also comes to the forefront. Bohdan Zholdak, for example, often employs *surzhyk*, the street-language mixture of Ukrainian and Russian, in order to underscore the verisimilitude of the realities of his protagonists. There seems to be a tendency to ascribe *surzhyk* to protagonists that come from less affluent backgrounds and who are not that well educated, although this claim cannot be made with certainty. On many occasions *surzhyk* is employed for parody effects and contrast with those speaking standard Ukrainian. The question can be put whether such a portrayal of language distribution among various societal groups in works of literature might not implicitly suggest the higher standing of those speaking correct Ukrainian.

Exploring the connection between popular literature and national identity has also yielded interesting results. What has become quite obvious to a number of writers is that by turning to popular genres, such as detective stories, thrillers, romances or science fiction, they can count on having considerably more readers. They implicitly promote an all-Ukrainian identity since they are trying to appeal to an audience that is not necessarily keen on literature. One notable factor in the first years of post-independence period was the absence of popular works in Ukrainian. All literature written in Ukrainian appeared to be somehow too highbrow and too intellectual and thus inaccessible to ordinary citizens; and this, compounded with their reluctance to read in Ukrainian at all, was not conducive to gaining a wider readership. The Bu-Ba-Bu phenomenon is an exception in this regard. Employing so-called double-coding typical of postmodernism, the writers of this group appealed simultaneously to more sophisticated readers capable of deciphering many layers of intertextual allusions and to those whose tastes are satisfied merely by the carnivalesque and the performative.[22]

Notwithstanding independence, especially in the 1990s, there had been a considerable influx of mass culture products coming from Russia, including translations of popular works from the West. In the 2000s, however, the situation began steadily improving and the vacuum was filled, at least to some degree, by domestic production. Many publishing houses (most notably the Lviv-based publisher "Kal'variia" or Kharkiv's "Klub simeinoho dozvillia") have been eagerly issuing this kind of literature in the hope of selling their products. Thus, bestsellers from the West would be translated directly into Ukrainian and published first in Ukraine instead of relying on Russian renditions. By the same token, Ukrainian popular literature became sought after thanks to publishers ready to promote Ukrainian authors, especially those who have already developed a considerable following.[23]

Another interesting aspect of this category of writing is its seemingly constructed quality. It appears that some writers working in these lighter genres choose to write in such a manner either because they want their books to sell or because they believe it is necessary to promote things Ukrainian, including past national traumas, through popular culture. Perhaps, then, it would not be too far-fetched to ascribe to them a mission of sorts that goes well beyond merely being entertaining. And that directly affects the social role of literature, which, as mentioned earlier, has lost some of its past gravitas. For example, I was surprised to find references to two well-known poets whom I categorized as "philologists"—namely, Ihor Rymaruk[24] and Vasyl Herasymiuk[25]—in an otherwise very pulp detective story by Iren Rozdobudko. In her novel *Escort into Death* one of the protagonists recites lines from Herasymiuk's poetry, and a stanza from an Akhmatova poem is presented in Rymaruk's rendition (46, 49, respectively).

Contemporary Ukrainian literature amply reflects the nexus of complex identities present in post-indpendence Ukraine and, to some extent (but to a considerably smaller degree than was the case in the past), exerts influence on their construction. Plural identities—national, linguistic and cultural—invariably yield plural literary canons, and this may lead to disagreements in the future as to what a national literature should incorporate. Studying contemporary Ukrainian literary works through the prism of identities and cultural hybridity—might shed new insights into the intricacies of the literary process since independence.

NOTES

1. Sarah M. Corse, *Nationalism and Literature: The Politics of Culture in Canada and United States* (Cambridge: Cambridge University Press, 1997), 9.

2. Please refer to the statistics provided in Note 2, Chapter 4. According to more recent findings, the status of Ukrainian visibly deteriorated during the three-year span of the Yanukovych presidency, especially in the spheres of entertainment and media. See the study "Stanovyshche ukrains'koi movy v Ukraini v 2013 rotsi," published under the title "Ukrains'ka mova trymaie pozytsii v osviti i kinoprokati, ale vtrachaie u media i reklami," *texty.org.ua*, July 11, 2013, accessed July 3, 2017, http://texty.org.ua/pg/article/editorial/read/49503.

3. To date, the best study examining the postcolonial features in Ukrainian literature in the West is the monograph by Vitaly Chernetsky, *Mapping Postcommunist Cultures: Russia and Ukraine in the Context of Globalization* (Montreal: McGill-Queens University Press, 2007).

4. Territorial identities, as I have indicated in Chapter 2, figure strongly in the writings of Yuri Andrukhovych, Yuri Vynnychuk, Taras Prokhasko, Vasyl Kozhelianko, Andrey Kurkov and Serhiy Zhadan, to name just a few.

5. In 2005 this monograph was published in a Ukrainian translation: Olia Hnatiuk, *Proshchannia z imperiieiu: Ukrains'ki dyskusii pro identychnist'* (Kyiv: Krytyka, 2005).

6. Hnatiuk focuses on discursive aspects of identity formation in Ukraine shortly before and after independence, with special attention placed on juxtaposing it against two powerful supranational identities, European and Russian. Analysis of literary

works, with few exceptions, does not figure prominently in her text, and, as she writes in the introduction, that was not her intention.

7. One such writer is Valerii Shevchuk (b. 1939), who became very prolific especially in the 1980s and later in the post-independence period. For political reasons he could not publish in the 1970s but that did not stop him to write "to the drawer." Many novels he published in the 1980s were written then. He is best known for historical fiction and novels written in the magic realism genre. For more on Shevchuk see Vitaly Chernetsky, "Postcolonialism, Russia and Ukraine," *Ulbandus Review* 7 (2003): 48–53. See also his *Mapping Postcommunist Cultures*, chapter 6, 190–200.

8. For more insights on this issue see Stepanenko, "Identities and Language Politics," 114.

9. A number of Ukrainian writers boast of being widely popular also with Russian-speaking readers, as, for example, Oksana Zabuzhko. Another writer, also popular among Russian-speakers is Serhiy Zhadan from Kharkiv. However, the majority of writers writing in Ukrainian are by and large confined to the Ukrainian reading public, although it would be fair to say that their ambition is to reach the Russian-speaking audience in addition to the Ukrainian one.

10. Viktor Morozov, e-mail message to author, May 30, 2017.

11. I am referring to Shkliar's interview in *Knyzhnyk-Review* in 2003. (See Chapter 4 for more details.)

12. In his polemical article "Literaturne istoriopysannia ta ioho konteksty" George G. Grabowicz argues that not enough has been done in terms of reevaluating the past by such prominent institutions as the Academy of Sciences of Ukraine and its Institute of Literature. He also criticizes most literary scholars for failing to find new approaches to reading strategies, especially when presenting new authoritative histories of literary periods.

13. A good example of one such proposition is the literary encyclopedia "Mala ukrains'ka entsyklopediia aktual'noi literatury: Proekt Povernennia demiurhiv," edited by Yuri Andrukhovych and Volodymyr Yeshkiliev, and published as a special issue of *Pleroma* (Ivano-Frankivsk), no. 3 (1998).

14. Michael M. Naydan points out, for example, that a proliferation of homemade journals became the norm during the early 1990s. This is how the literary almanac *Chetver* began in Ivano-Frankivsk. See his "National Identity for the Ukrainian Writer: Writing into New Millennium," *Towards a New Ukraine II: Meeting the New Century. Proceedings of a Conference Held on October 2–3, 1998, at the University of Ottawa,* ed. Theofil Kis and Irena Makaryk with Roman Weretelnyk (Ottawa: Chair of Ukrainian Studies, University of Ottawa, 1999), 146.

15. Ibid., 144–45.

16. Of course, the situation in this respect has drastically changed since the start of the Russian aggression in 2014 following the Euromaidan tragic events.

17. Quite in line with the constructed or "imagined" nature of any nation, advocated by Benedict Anderson in his book *Imagined Communities: Reflections on the Origins and Spread of Nationalism*, Rev. ed. (London: Verso, 1991).

18. Judging by two revolutions that occurred since independence—the Orange Revolution in 2004 and Euromaidan in 2014–2015—the dissatisfaction with the

Ukrainian political elites, their corruption and disregard for the well-being of the nation and its citizens, had reached the breaking point levels.

19. For example, in one of his articles Mark Andryczyk states: "Centuries of censorship and provincialization of Ukrainian culture and the persecution of its most talented leaders have managed, in the minds of its citizens, to implant the idea that Ukrainian culture is an inferior culture. Even free access to ten years of vibrant and innovative cultural activity (such as what has been produced by the Lviv Bohema) is not yet enough to regenerate recognition of this presence. Ukrainian bookstores, which were once stocked with socialist-realist literature, today sell Russian-language translations of American romance novels and horror bestsellers. These outnumber books by contemporary Ukrainian writers, which continue to be circulated in small print runs among friends." See his "Four Bearings of West for the Lviv Bohema," in *Over the Wall/After the Fall: Post-Communist Cultures through an East-West Gaze*, ed. Sibelan Forrester, Magdalena J. Zaborowska and Elena Gapova (Bloomington: Indiana University Press, 2004), 248. That picture is more typical of the 1990s and the early 2000s. The new chain of bookstores "Ye," introduced first in Kyiv and then in other cities of Ukraine, has alleviated this deficiency to a considerable extent.

20. See Marci Shore, "The Bard of Eastern Ukraine, Where Things Are Falling Apart," *The New Yorker*, November 28, 2016, accessed November 30, 2016, http://www.newyorker.com/books/page-turner/the-bard-of-eastern-ukraine-where-things-are-falling-apart.

21. This view is especially advocated in Andrukhovych's essays, such as his *Dezoriientatsiia na mistsevosti*, but is also reflected in his novels.

22. See Michael M. Naydan, "Performative Text in the Narrative Design of Yuri Andrukhovych's Novel *Perverzion*," *Style and Translation* 1.2 (2015): 250–72; and Mark Andryczyk, "Bu-Ba-Bu: Poetry and Performance," *Journal of Ukrainian Studies* 27.1–2 (2002): 257–72.

23. Kal'variia, for example, has published all the novels of Vasyl Kozhelianko, whose first book *A Parade in Moscow* (Lviv, 2001) became a bestseller of sorts. By borrowing and incorporating many elements of popular genres such as science fiction, romance and suspense, Kozhelianko's novels represent highly accessible and readable commentaries on nationalism, nationhood, nation and state building. See my article "Alternative History, Science Fiction and Nationalism in Vasyl Kozhelianko's Novels," *Ukrainian Quarterly* 63 (2007): 70–78.

24. Ihor Rymaruk (1958–2008) is a Ukrainian poet belonging to the generation of the eighties and author of five books of poetry, known for his intellectualism, dense imagery and incorporation of many religious intertexts. He was Rozdobudko's husband at that time but their marriage eventually ended up in divorce.

25. For more details see Chapter 2.

Epilogue

Literature in a Time of War

Summing up the 2011 literary year in Ukraine, Iryna Slavinska, the well-known critic of contemporary Ukrainian literature, made a prediction that 2012 would witness an even more intense politicization of the literary process than in previous years, and that a majority of authors would not be able to shun away from the repercussions of the current political situation.¹ Little did the she know then that the following two years, 2013–2014, would bring the most dramatic paradigm shift in how people choose to identify themselves and what path forward they envisioned for their country. Facing the Russian aggression in the aftermath of the Revolution of Dignity, Ukrainian society seemingly no longer tolerates ambivalent identities. Ukrainians, especially those in the southeast, have been forced to choose whether they wanted to live under Ukrainian rule or under the separatists. Many chose to relocate to other regions of the country rather than stay behind and face a constant threat to their lives and identities. On the other end of the spectrum, those who continue volunteering and/or are drafted into the Ukrainian Army to fight on the front lines in the southeast know exactly who their enemy is. The Euromaidan Revolution, in which so many ordinary citizens participated with high hopes for more transparent governance and brighter future, and with a number among them paying the ultimate price, has left a perceivable imprint on the new literature since 2014. The ensuing and still unresolved conflict in the east of Ukraine also figures prominently in works of belles-lettres. One can easily argue that qualitatively it is a different kind of literature—a literary output with a different kind of aesthetic sensibility. At such important political and social junctures poets seemingly feel those changes more acutely than others and often reflect them in their works. Vasyl Lozynsky rightly observes that "Ever since Crimea's annexion in March 2014, and even earlier, during the Euromaidan, Ukraine has become a hostage of the global information war. Poets articulate emotions accompanying this social tragedy and the crisis of diplomatic relations more intensely, and offer the readers reflective and narrative poems, sometimes quite of documentary character."[2] The critic further elaborates that in an era when information is weaponized and we witness forces deliberately working to distort facts, genuine poetic voices matter because, being particularly sensitive to the spread of disinformation in social media, they are often the only independent and free of incitement channels.

How important the theme of ongoing war has become is evidenced by a recently published bilingual poetry anthology titled *Letters from Ukraine* (2016).[3] It includes an introduction written by Yuri Andrukhovych reminiscing about the Maidan days and the role poetry readings played then, at the same time underscoring the fact that freedom-loving artists, intellectuals and especially poets, were targets of the Yanukovych regime:

> Contemporary poetry was nearly absent from the Main Stage. However, it could be heard almost every night at the Artistic Barbican. This was a site in the middle of the Khreshchatyk, not far from the Kyiv City Hall. When Yanukovych fled, they found piles of secret papers at his estate. Among them was a detailed plan of the Maidan and its environs; on it Barbican was marked as "triangle 92." The plan was allegedly intended for snipers based on roofs along the Khreshchatyk. In case of necessity, Barbican could be shot at. The Yanukovych regime valued contemporary Ukrainian poetry very highly.[4]

While there are quite a few poems in the anthology alluding to the Revolution, the vast majority of them implicitly or explicitly refer to the war and its effects on the Ukrainian people. Kharkiv-based Russophone poet Anastasiia Afanas'eva asks, for example, if it is possible to write poetry after offensives and destructions that are taking place in a number of cities in Eastern Ukraine. Katia Babkina, in turn, pays homage to the memory of the Heavenly Hundred, Euromaidan protesters killed by snipers on February 20, 2014, and in another poem writes about a little girl who dreams about the end of the war. Mirek Bodnar invokes the city devastated by war in which even birds and stray dogs do not want to dwell. Andrii Bondar, who experimented earlier with writing poetry in the Latin script, in this anthology stoutly defends all thirty-three Cyrillic letters of the Ukrainian alphabet in the miniature poem titled "A Short Song About Love for the Native Tongue and National History." And then there are poets, such as Borys Humeniuk, who actually went to the front and defended the country. For Humeniuk, the poetically expressed "smell of gunpowder" or "smell of war" are not just constructs of his imagination but recollections that stem from his personal experience.

The images of war permeate Ukrainian poetry poignantly especially for those authors who come from the Donbas region and experienced displacement because of war. A Russophone poet from Donetsk, Volodymyr Rafeyenko, now residing in Kyiv, compares leaving his native region to a soul leaving the body, whereas for a Ukrainian-speaking poet from the Luhansk region, Liubov Yakymchuk, her hometown Pervomaisk disintegrated into *pervo* and *maisk*. She also declares that there is no more Luhansk for *lu* has been leveled into red asphalt. But, as Halyna Petrosaniak readily reminds us, one does not need to come from the war zone to experience conflict because "War seethed in the east of her country and the killed / often happened to be friends of friends or acquaintances."[5] In the same vein, for Hryhory Semenchuk, poet and compiler of the anthology, the horrors of war do not need be experienced, they can simply be dreamed. A Russophone poet Borys Khersonsky, on the other hand, imagines the end of the conflict but warns against retribution: "In the aftermath of victory—an era of postwar executions begins."[6] And Yuliia Musakovska reminds everyone about the need to prepare an "emergency suitcase" in times of high uncertainty.

No other poet has devoted so much attention to the Russian aggression in the Donbas as Serhiy Zhadan has: "Our city was built of stone and steel. / Now we are each left holding only one bag, / A suitcase filled with ashes, gathered under fire. / Now we smell the burning even in our dreams."[7] He seems to have personal stakes in the outcome of the conflict. The poet not only has written a number of poems about the war but also organized many actions to help people living in the conflict zone.[8] Zhadan's poetry refrains from judgment and many a time shows understanding for people on both sides of the barricades:

Well, I can only tell you about the losses.
Surely, a final reckoning awaits the guilty.
But it awaits the innocent and
Even those who had nothing to do with this.
[…]
I don't know anything about inevitable penance.
I don't know where and how you should live.
I can only speak of what's inside of us.
You must realize how unlucky we've all been.[9]

Equally significant is the poetry of Liubov Yakymchuk whose collection *Apricots of the Donbas* (*Abrykosy Donbasu*, 2015) brought the author considerable recognition. In July 2015 she was named as one of the top-100 most influential cultural figures in Ukraine by the magazine *Novoe vremia*.

Her poetry resonates because it captures the lives and experiences of people from the Donbas region before and after the armed conflict with the Russian-backed separatists began. Yakymchuk invents the character of Niam that first appears in the poem in order to apparently shield the lyrical heroine from disinformation by unplugging her TV and taking control of the remote. Niam assumes many roles—that of a trickster, witness, guardian angel, and even poet. But the most powerful cycle in the book, titled "Decomposition," comprises some of Yakymchuk's most powerful poems about the war, including the three that found their way into the anthology *Letters from Ukraine.*

While the ongoing war in the southeast of Ukraine captures the imagination of many contemporary Ukrainian authors, some among them prefer instead to immerse themselves in history to better understand the present. Tania Maliarchuk's novel *Oblivion* (*Zabuttia*, 2016), the winner of the 2016 BBC Prize for Ukrainian literature, foregrounds the story of Viacheslav Lypynsky (1882–1931), an ethnic Pole who devoted his entire life to fighting for Ukraine's independence. Currently residing in Vienna, Maliarchuk grapples with complex issues of identity by digging into the past of her own family and relatives, as well as into that of Lypynsky, the Ukrainian statesman of Polish descent. Historical events are also front and center in Yuri Vynnychuk's novel *Tango of Death* (*Tango smerti*, 2012), the 2012 winner of the BBC Prize for Ukrainian literature. Vynnychuk explores identity issues in the ethnically diverse Lviv before and during World War II by telling the story of four friends, each of different nationality—Jewish, German, Polish and Ukrainian. But in the typical Vynnychuk manner, the historical in his fiction is invariably interwoven with the contemporary, the factual with the mysterious, the inhumanity of atrocities witnessed by World War II with an engaging love story, all harmoniously layered in order to present an enticing picture of his beloved Lviv, with all its complexity and multicultural history. Yet another winner of the BBC Prize for Ukrainian Literature (2014), *Felix August* (*Feliks Avstriia*, 2014) by Sofiia Andrukhovych, also engages history and looks back nostalgically to the era of Austro-Hungarian Empire in her hometown Ivano-Frankivsk. The novel relates the stories of two strong female characters as they strive to make their lives meaningful in the late nineteenth and the early twentieth centuries. These three successful novels do not necessarily entail the beginning of a new trend but there can be no doubt that history, especially in its local ambience, inspires contemporary Ukrainian authors.

Whether it is the current conflict in the southeast, or historical ruminations about previous wars and epochs, Ukrainian writers, mindful of the national past, strive to reflect the complicated present in their works and, at the same time, make creative efforts to understand their own place on the map of Europe—Ukraine's chosen and preferable destination since 2014.

NOTES

1. See Chapter 1 for more details about the critic's arguments.

2. Vasyl' Lozyns'kyi, "Poetychna refleksiia u chas viiny i myru (teoriia Marshala Makliuena v ukrains'komu konteksti s'ohodennia)," *Krytyka* 20.11–12 (2016), 2.

3. The anthology presents both Ukrainian and Russophone poets. All original poems, whether in Ukrainian or Russian, have been then translated into English.

4. Yuri Andrukhovych, "An Emergency Bag with Letters," trans. by Vitaly Chernetsky, in *Letters from Ukraine: Poetry Anthology*, comp. Hryhory Semenchuk (Ternopil: Krok, 2016), 5.

5. *Letters from Ukraine*, 403. Translated by Ostap Kin and Ali Kinsella. Reprinted with permission.

6. Ibid., 476.

7. From the poem "Where are you coming from" translated by Virlana Tkacz and Wanda Phipps, included in the anthology *Letters from Ukraine*. Here, however, I refer to the latest version provided to author by the translators. Reprinted with permission.

8. In February 2017 he co-founded Serhiy Zhadan Charitable Foundation to provide humanitarian aid to front-line cities.

9. Ibid.

Bibliography

Acheraïou, Amar. *Questioning Hybridity, Postcolonialism and Globalization.* Houndmills: Palgrave Macmillan, 2011.

Aheieva, Vira, ed. *Don Zhuan u svitovomu konteksti.* Kyiv: Fakt, 2002.

———, ed. *Genderna perspektyva.* Kyiv: Fakt, 2004.

———, ed. *Im promovliaty dusha moia bude: "Lisova pisnia" Lesi Ukrainky ta ii interpretatsii.* Kyiv: Fakt, 2002.

———. "Intelektual'nyi portret." In *Feminizm,* by Solomiia Pavlychko, 5–16. Kyiv: Osnovy, 2002. Reprint of "Intelektual'na biohrafiia Solomii Pavlychko." *Dukh i litera* 7–8 (2001): 248–61.

———. "Khto boit'sia pryvydu matriarkhatu." *Krytyka* 3.5 (1999): 22–23.

———. "Na storozhi starozhytnostei." *Krytyka* 3.11 (1999): 28–29.

———. *Poetesa zlamu stolit': Tvorchist' Lesi Ukrainky v postmodernii interpretatsii.* Kyiv: Lybid', 1999.

———, ed. *Proza pro zhyttia inshykh: Iurii Kosach, teksty, interpretatsii, komentari.* Kyiv: Fakt, 2003.

———, ed. *Try doli: Marko Vovchok v ukrains'kii, rosiis'kii ta frantsuz'kii literaturi.* Kyiv: Fakt, 2002.

———. *Ukrains'ka impresionistychna proza.* Kyiv: Instytut literatury im. T. Shevchenka, 1994.

———. *Zhinochyi prostir: Feministychnyi dyskurs ukrains'koho modernizmu.* Kyiv: Fakt, 2003.

Aheieva, Vira, and Svitlana Oksamytna, eds. *Gender i kul'tura.* Kyiv: Fakt, 2001.

Ahmad, Aijaz. *In Theory: Classes, Nations, Literature.* London: Verso, 1992.

———. "The Politics of Literary Postcoloniality." In *Contemporary Postcolonial Theory: A Reader,* edited by Padmini Mongia, 276–93. London: Arnold, 1996.

Anderson, Benedict. *Imagined Communities: Reflections on the Origin and Spread of Nationalism.* London: Verso, 1983.

Andreichyk, Marko [Mark Andryczyk]. "Proza movnoi identychnosty." *Krytyka* 9.3 (2005): 23–24.

Andrukhovych, Iurii. *Dezoriientatsiia na mistsevosti*. Ivano-Frankivsk: Lileia-NV, 1999.

―――. *Dvanadtsiat' obruchiv*. Kyiv: Krytyka, 2003.

―――. *Dyiavol khovaiet'sia v syri*. 2nd ed. Kyiv: Krytyka, 2007.

―――. "An Emergency Bag with Letters." In *Letters from Ukraine: Poetry Anthology*, compiled by Hryhory Semenchuk and translated by Vitaly Chernetsky, 5–17. Ternopil: Krok, 2016.

―――. *Leksykon intymnykh mist: Dovil'nyi posibnyk z heopoetyky ta kosmopolityky*. Kyiv: Meridian Czernowitz, Maister Knyh, 2011.

―――. *The Moscoviad*. Translated by Vitaly Chernetsky. New York: Spuyten Duyvil, 2008.

―――. *Perverzion*. Translated by Michael M. Naydan. Evanston: Northwestern University Press, 2005.

―――. *Recreations*. Translated by Marko Pavlyshyn. Edmonton: Canadian Institute of Ukrainian Studies, 1998.

Andrukhovych, Iurii, and Andrzej Stasiuk. *Moja Europa: Dwa eseje o Europie zwanej środkową*. Wołowiec: Czarne, 2000.

Andrukhovych, Sofiia. *Feliks Avstriia*. Lviv: Vydavnytstvo Staroho Leva, 2014.

―――. *S'omha*. Kyiv: Nora-Druk, 2007.

―――. *Stari liudy*. Ivano-Frankivsk: Lileia-NV, 2008.

Andrusiv, Svitlana. "Suchasne ukrains'ke literaturoznavstvo." *Slovo i chas* 5 (2004): 48–53.

Andryczyk, Mark. "Bu-Ba-Bu: Poetry and Performance." *Journal of Ukrainian Studies* 27.1–2 (2002): 257–72.

―――. "Four Bearings of West for the Lviv Bohema." In *Over the Wall/After the Fall: Post-Communist Cultures through an East-West Gaze*, edited by Sibelan Forrester, Magdalena J. Zaborowska and Elena Gapova, 238–50. Bloomington: Indiana University Press, 2004.

―――. *The Intellectual as Hero in 1990s Ukrainian Fiction*. Toronto: University of Toronto Press, 2012.

Bakhtin, M.M. *The Dialogic Imagination: Four Essays*. Edited by Michael Holquist. Translated by Caryl Emerson and Holquist. Austin: University of Texas Press, 1981.

―――. *Rabelais and His World*. Translated by Helene Iswolsky. Cambridge, MA: MIT Press, 1968.

Baran, Ievhen. *Zoilovi treny*. Lviv: Lohos, 1998.

Barth, John. "The Literature of Exhaustion." *Atlantic* 220.2 (1967): 29–34.

Bauman, Zygmunt, and Leonidas Donskis. *Moral Blindness: The Loss of Sensitivity in Liquid Modernity*. Cambridge: Polity, 2013.

Berezovchuk, Larysa. "Pryshestia dyskursu." *Krytyka* 5.9 (2001): 24–29.

Berger, John. *The Look of Things: Essays*. New York: Viking, 1974.

Bhabha, Homi. *The Location of Culture*. With a new preface by the author. London: Routledge, 2004.

Bilaniuk, Laada. *Contested Tongues: Language Politics and Cultural Correction in Ukraine*. Ithaca: Cornell University Press, 2005.

Bilotserkivets', Natalka. *Hotel' Tsentral': vybrani virshi*. Lviv: Kal'variia, 2004.

"Bil'she polovyny hromadian Ukrainy hovoriat' ukrains'koiu u pobuti." *Ukrains'ka pravda*, August 23, 2011. Accessed August 24, 2011. http://www.pravda.com.ua/news/2011/08/23/6524063/.

Blacker, Uilleam. "Nation, Body, Home: Gender and National Identity in the Work of Oksana Zabuzhko." *Modern Language Review* 105.2 (2010): 487–501.

———. Review of *Pisliachornobyl's'ka biblioteka: ukrains'kyi literaturnyi postmodern*, by Tamara Hundorova. *Slavonic and East European Review* 86 (2008): 147–48.

Boehmer, Elleke. *Colonial and Postcolonial Literature: Migrant Metaphors*. Oxford: Oxford University Press, 1995.

Bohachevs'ka-Khomiak, Marta [Martha Bohachevsky-Chomiak]. *Bilym po bilomu: Zhinky v hromadians'komu zhytti Ukrainy, 1884–1939*. Kyiv: Lybid', 1995.

Bohachevsky-Chomiak, Martha. *Feminists Despite Themselves: Women in Ukrainian Community Life, 1884–1939*. Edmonton: Canadian Institute of Ukrainian Studies, 1988.

Bondar, Andrii. *Prymityvni formy vlasnosti*. Lviv: Piramida, 2004.

Bourdieu, Pierre. *Distinctions: A Social Critique of the Judgement of Taste*. Translated by Richard Nice. Cambridge, MA: Harvard University Press, 1984.

———. *The Field of Cultural Production: Essays on Art and Literature*. Edited by Randal Johnson. New York: Columbia University Press, 1993.

Brennan, Timothy. "Postcolonial Studies and Globalization Theory." In *The Postcolonial and the Global*, edited by Revathi Krishnaswamy and John C. Hawley, 37–53. Minneapolis: University of Minnesota Press, 2008.

Bulkina, Inna. "Zhinocha dohma." *Krytyka* 5.9 (2001): 24–29.

Canclini, Néstor García. *Hybrid Cultures: Strategies for Entering and Leaving Modernity*. Minneapolis: University of Minnesota Press, 1995.

Chaus, Oleksandra. "Halyna Pahutiak: Nasha literatura skhozha na khvoroho, shcho rozuchyvsia rukhatysia." Interview. Accessed October 10, 2013. http://sumno.com/article/galyna-pagutyak-nasha-literatura-shozha-na-hvorogo/.

———. "Vid redaktora." Forward to *Uriz'ka hotyka: roman*, by Halyna Pahutiak, 5–11. Kyiv: Duliby, 2009.

Chernetsky, Vitaly. "From Anarchy to Connectivity to Cognitive Mapping: Contemporary Ukrainian Writers of the Younger Generation Engage with Globalization." *Canadian American Slavic Studies* 44 (2010): 102–17.

———. *Mapping Postcommunist Cultures: Russia and Ukraine in the Context of Globalization*. Montreal: McGill-Queen's University Press, 2007.

———. "The New Ukrainian Literature: Between the Postmodern and the Postcolonial." *The Soviet and Post-Soviet Review* 28 (2001): 29–45.

———. "Postcolonialism, Russia and Ukraine." *Ulbandus Review* 7 (2003): 32–62.

———. "The Trope of Displacement and Identity Construction in Post-Colonial Ukrainian Fiction." *Journal of Ukrainian Studies* 27 (2002): 215–32.

———. "Ukrainian Literature." In "East-Central European Literatures Twenty Years After." *East European Politcs and Societies* 23 (2009): 578–80.

Corse, Sarah M. *Nationalism and Literature: The Politics of Culture in Canada and the United States*. Cambridge: Cambridge University Press, 1997.

Culler, Jonathan. *The Literary in Theory.* Stanford: Stanford University Press, 2007.

Dainotto, Roberto M. *Place in Literature: Regions, Cultures, Communities.* Ithaca: Cornell University Press, 2000.

Danylenko, Volodymyr. "Variatsii na temu kolonial'noi psykhoistorii." *Slovo i chas* 2 (2007): 79–84.

Dashvar, Liuko. *Maty vse.* Kharkiv: Klub simeinoho dozvillia, 2010.

———. *Selo ne liudy.* Kharkiv: Klub simeinoho dozvillia, 2007.

Deleuze, Gilles, and Felix Guattari. *Anti-Oedipus: Capitalism and Schizophrenia.* Minneapolis: University of Minnesota Press, 1983.

DeMause, Lloyd. *The Emotional Life of Nations.* New York: Karnac, 2002.

———. *Foundations of Psychohistory.* New York: Creative Roots, 1982.

Denysenko, Larysa. *Sarabanda bandy Sary.* Kyiv: Nora-Druk, 2008.

———. *The Sarabande of Sara's Band.* Translated by Michael M. Naydan and Svitlana Bednazh. London: Glagoslav Publications, 2013.

Deresh, Liubko. *Arkhe: monoloh, iakyi use shche tryvaie.* Kharkiv: Folio, 2009.

———. *Kul't.* Lviv: Kal'variia, 2002.

———. *Namir!* Kharkiv: Klub simeinoho dozvillia, 2009.

———. *Pokloninnia iashchirtsi: iak nyshchyty anheliv.* Lviv: Kal'variia, 2004.

———. *Trokhy pit'my, abo Na kraiu svitu.* Kharkiv: Klub simeinoho dozvillia, 2008.

Diachenko, Maryna and Serhii. *Vid'oms'ka doba.* Lviv: Kal'variia, 2000.

Dibrova, Volodymyr. *Vybhane.* Kyiv: Krytyka, 2002.

Dnistrovyi, Anatolii. *Drozofila nad tomom Kanta: roman.* Lviv: Piramida, 2010.

———. *Misto upovil'nenoi dii: roman.* Kyiv: Fakt, 2003.

———. *Patetychnyi blud.* Kharkiv: Folio, 2005.

Donchyk, Vitalii, ed. *Istoriia ukrains'koi literatury XX stolittia.* Kyiv: Lybid', 1993–95.

———. *Istoriia ukrains'koi literatury XX stolittia: u dvokh knyhakh.* Kyiv: Lybid', 1998.

———. "Pro 'Istoriiu literatury,' iakoi dosi ne bulo." *Akademichna "Istoriia ukrains'koi literatury" v 10 tomakh,* compiled by Ia. Tsymbal, 4–13. Kyiv: Feniks, 2005.

Donchyk, Vitalii, et al., eds. *Istoriia ukrains'koi literatury u dvanadtsiaty tomakh.* Kyiv: Naukova dumka, 2013-

Drozdovs'kyi, Dmytro. "Informatsiine 'samashestviie:' perezavantazhennia." *Bukvoid,* August 5, 2011. Accessed December 21, 2016. http://bukvoid.com.ua/digest/2011/08/05/110939.html.

Dubynians'ka, Iana. *Skhodovyi maidanchyk.* Kyiv: Fakt, 2005.

Dziuba, Ivan. *Spraha.* Kyiv: Ukrains'kyi svit, 2001.

———. *Z krynytsi lit.* 3 vols. Kyiv: Kyievo-Mohylians'ka akademiia, 2006–07.

Fanon, Frantz. *The Wretched of the Earth.* Translated by Constance Farrington. New York: Grove Press, 1963.

Fedchenko, Anastasiia. "Zrosiishchena Ukraina, kvazi Rosiia, nikomu ne tsikava. Pys'mennyk Vasyl' Shkliar—pro te, v iakykh mezhakh bude isnuvaty Ukraina." *Novoe vremia,* June 27, 2016. Accessed December 20, 2016. http://web.archive.org/web/20160627172935/http://nv.ua/ukr/publications/zrosijshchena-ukrajina-kvazirosija-nikomu-ne-tsikava-pismennik-vasil-shkljar-pro-te-v-jakih-mezhah-bude-ukrajina-145241.html.

Felski, Rita. *Beyond Feminist Aesthetics: Feminist Literature and Social Change.* Cambridge, MA: Harvard University Press, 1989.

Foucault, Michel. *Madness and Civilization: A History of Insanity in the Age of Reason.* Translated by Richard Howard. New York: Vintage Books, 1988.

———. *Power/Knowledge: Selected Interviews and Other Writings, 1972–1977.* New York: Pantheon Books, 1980.

Friedman, Jonathan. *Cultural Identity and Global Process.* London: Sage Publications, 1994.

Gillespie, Marie. *Television, Ethnicity and Cultural Change.* London: Routledge, 1995.

Halbwachs, Maurice. *The Collective Memory.* Translated by Francis J. Ditter, Jr. and Vida Yazdi Ditter. New York: Harper, 1980.

Hall, Stuart. "Cultural Identity and Diaspora." In *Identity: Community, Culture, Difference*, edited by Jonathan Rutherford, 222–37. London: Lawrence and Wishart, 1990.

Haraway, Donna. "A Manifesto for Cyborgs: Science, Technology, and Socialist Feminism in the 1980s." In *Feminisms*, edited by Sandra Kemp and Judith Squires, 474–82. Oxford: Oxford University Press, 1997.

Hassan, Ihab. "Queries for Postcolonial Studies." In *The Third Text Reader on Art, Culture and Theory*, edited by Rasheed Araeen, Sean Cubitt and Ziauddin Sardar, 232–43. London: Continuum, 2002.

Herasym'iuk, Vasyl'. *Dity trepety: Poezii.* Kyiv: Molod', 1991.

———. *Poet u povitri.* Lviv: Kal'variia, 2002.

Hnatiuk, Ola. "Nativists vs. Westernizers: Problems of Cultural Identity in Ukrainian Literature of the 1990s." *Slavic and East European Journal* 50 (2006): 434–51.

———. *Pożegnanie z imperium.* Lublin: Wyd. Uniwersytetu Marii Curie-Skłodowskiej, 2003.

Hrabovych, Hryhorii [Grabowicz, George G.]. "Pisliamova: Literaturne istoriopysannia ta ioho konteksty." In *Do istorii ukrains'koi literatury: Doslidzhennia, esei, polemika*, 591–607. Kyiv: Krytyka, 2003. Reprint of "Literaturne istoriopysannia ta ioho konteksty." *Krytyka* 5.12 (2001): 11–15.

Hrycak, Alexandra, and Maria G. Rewakowicz. "Feminism, intellectuals and the formation of micro-publics in postcommunist Ukraine." *Studies in East European Thought* 61 (2009): 309–33.

Hryn, Halyna. "A Conversation with Oksana Zabuzhko." *Agni* 53 (2001). Accessed September 28, 2013. http://www.bu.edu/agni/interviews/print/2001/zabuzhko-hryn.html.

Hundorova, Tamara. *Femina Melancholica: Stat' i kul'tura v gendernii utopii Ol'hy Kobylians'koi.* Kyiv: Krytyka, 2002.

———. *Franko—ne Kameniar.* Melbourne: Monash University Press, 1996.

———. *Franko ne Kameniar. Franko i Kameniar.* Kyiv: Krytyka, 2006.

———. *Kitch i literatura: Travestii.* Kyiv: Fakt, 2008.

———. "New Ukrainian Literature of the 1990s." *Journal of Ukrainian Studies* 26 (2001): 249–70.

———. *Pisliachornobyl's'ka biblioteka: Ukrains'kyi literaturnyi postmodern.* Kyiv: Krytyka, 2005.

————. *Proiavlennia slova: Dyskursiia rann'oho modernizmu.* Lviv: Litopys, 1997.

Hutcheon, Linda. *A Poetics of Postmodernism: History, Theory, Fiction.* New York: Routledge, 1988.

Iakymchuk, Liubov. *Abrykosy Donbasu: Poezii.* Lviv: Vydavnytstvo Staroho Leva, 2015.

Iavorivs'kyi, Volodymyr. "Kompleks tiazhiie nad ukrains'kym suspil'stvom." Interview. *Dzerkalo tyzhnia,* January 4, 2002. Accessed October 21, 2013. https://dt.ua/ SCIENCE/kompleks_tyazhie_nad_ukrayinskim_suspilstvom.html.

Irvanets', Oleksandr. *Rivne / Rovno.* Lviv: Kal'variia, 2002.

Izdryk. *Ostriv Krk ta inshi istorii.* Ivano-Frankivsk: Lileia-NV, 1998.

————. *Podviinyi Leon: istoriia khvoroby.* Ivano-Frankivsk: Lileia-NV, 2000.

————. *Votstsek &Votstsekurhiia.* Lviv: Kal'variia, 2002.

————. *Wozzeck.* Translated by Marko Pavlyshyn. Edmonton: Canadian Institute of Ukrainian Studies, 2006.

Jameson, Fredric. "Third World Literature in the Era of Multinational Capital." *Social Text* 15 (1986): 65–88.

Jameson, Fredric, and Masao Miyoshi, eds. *The Cultures of Globalization.* Durham: Duke University Press, 1998.

Jayawardena, Kumari. *Feminism and Nationalism in the Third World.* London: Zed Books, 1986.

Jordan, David, ed. *Regionalism Reconsidered: New Approaches to the Field.* New York: Garland, 1994.

Karpa, Irena. *50 khvylyn travy: koly pomre tvoia krasa.* Kharkiv: Folio, 2004.

————. *Bitches Get Everything.* Kharkiv: Klub simeinoho dozvillia, 2007.

————. *Froid by plakav.* Kharkiv: Folio, 2004.

————. *Supermarket samotnosti. Perlamutrove porno.* Kharkiv: Klub simeinoho dozvillia, 2008.

Kharchuk, R. B. "Khranytel'ka pisliachornobyl's'koi biblioteky." *Kur'ier Kryvbasu* 4 (2006): 181–86.

————. *Suchasna ukrains'ka proza: Postmodernyi period.* Kyiv: Akademiia, 2008.

Kiianovs'ka, Marianna. *Mifotvorennia: Poezii.* Kyiv: Smoloskyp, 2000.

————. *Zvychaina mova.* Kyiv: Fakt, 2005.

Kobets, Svitlana. "Review of *Pol'ovi doslidzhennia z ukrains'koho seksu,* by Oksana Zabuzhko." *Slavic and East European Journal* 41 (1997): 183–85.

Kokotiukha, Andrii. *Povernennia sentymental'noho hanhstera.* Kyiv: Fakt, 2001.

————. *Povze zmiia.* Kyiv: Nora-Druk, 2005.

————. *Temna voda.* Kyiv: Nora-Druk, 2006.

Kononenko, Ievheniia. *Bez muzhyka.* Lviv: Kal'variia, 2005.

————. *Heroini ta heroi.* Kyiv: Hrani-T, 2010.

————. *Imitatsiia.* Lviv: Kal'variia, 2001.

————. *Zrada.* Lviv: Kal'variia, 2002.

Kosovych, Leonid. "Postskrypt." In *Podviinyi Leon,* by Izdryk, 176–78. Ivano-Frankivsk: Lileia-NV, 2000.

Kostenko, Lina. *Zapysky ukrains'koho samashedshoho.* Kyiv: A-BA-BA-HA-LA-MA-HA, 2011.

Kostets'kyi, Ihor. "Stefan George: Osobystist', doba, spadshchyna. Peredmova." In *Vybranyi Stefan George*, edited by Ihor Kostets'kyi, Vol. 1, 29–206. Stuttgart: Na hori, 1968–71.

Kotsarev, Oleh. "Tania Maliarchuk: Literaturoiu maibutn'oho stanut' maliunky iedynorohiv na skeliakh." Accessed October 6, 2013. http://ukrlit.blog.net. ua/2007/05/22/tanya-malyarchuk-literaturoyu-majbutnoho-stanut-malyunky-je-dynorohiv-na-skelyah/.

Kozhelianko, Vasyl'. *Defiliada v Moskvi*. Lviv: Kal'variia, 2001.

———. *Sribnyi pavuk*. Lviv: Kal'variia, 2004.

Koznarsky, Taras. "Ukrainian Literary Scholarship in Ukraine Since Independence." *Canadian Slavonic Papers* 53 (2011): 433–60.

Koznars'kyi, Taras [Taras Koznarsky]. "Notatky na berehakh makabresok." *Krytyka* 2.5 (1998): 24–29.

Kraidy, Marwan M. *Hybridity, or the Cultural Logic of Globalization*. Philadelphia: Temple University Press, 2005.

Krishnaswamy, Revathi. "The Criticism of Culture and the Culture of Criticism: At the Intersection of Postcolonialism and Globalization Theory." *Diacritics* 32.2 (2002): 106–26.

Kruchyk, Ihor. "Dity radians'koi vdovy." *Krytyka* 16.5 (2012): 24–26.

Kruk, Halyna. *Oblychchia poza svitlynoiu*. Kyiv: Fakt, 2005.

———. [Selections of Poems]. *Poetry International Rotterdam*. Accessed September 30, 2013. http://www.poetryinternationalweb.net/pi/site/poet/item/5520/26/ Halyna-Krouk.

Kulyk, Volodymyr. "Language identity, linguistic diversity and political cleavages: evidence from Ukraine." *Nations and Nationalism* 17 (2011): 627–48.

Kurkov, Andrey. *The Case of the General's Thumb*. Translated by George Bird. London: Vintage, 2004.

———. *Death and the Penguin*. Translated by George Bird. London: Vintage, 2003.

———. *Dobryi angel smerti*. St. Petersburg: Amfora, 2006.

———. "Independent Ukraine as a Function of Soviet Inertia." J.B. Rudnyckyj Distinguished Lecture presented at the University of Manitoba, Winnipeg, February 23, 2006. Accessed September 11, 2008. http://umanitoba.ca/libraries/units/ archives/grants/rudnyckyj_lecture/lecture_13.html.

———. *A Matter of Death and Life*. Translated by George Bird. London: Vintage, 2006.

———. "Narodzhennia novoho bez stresu ne buvaie." *Den'*, November 26, 2004. Accessed September 11, 2008. http://www.day.kiev.ua/290619?idsource=128181 &mainlang=ukr.

———. *Nichnyi molochnyk*. Translated by Ostap Slyvyns'kyi. Kyiv: Nora-Druk, 2008.

———. *Ostannia liubov prezydenta*. Ternopil: Bohdan, 2005.

———. *Penguin Lost*. Translated by George Bird. London: Vintage, 2005.

Kyrylink, IE. P. ed., *Istoriia ukrains'koi literatury u vos'my tomakh*. Kyiv: Naukova dumka, 1967–71.

Larsen, Neil. "Imperialism, Colonialism, Postcolonialism." In *A Companion to Postcolonial Studies*, edited by Henry Schwarz and Sangeeta Ray, 23–54. Oxford: Blackwell, 2000.

Laundański, Paweł. "Wywiad z Mariną i Siergiejem Diaczenko." *Esensja*, February 9, 2005. Accessed November 10, 2013. http://esensja.stopklatka.pl/ksiazka/wzw/tekst. html?id=2008&strona=2#strony.

Lazutkin, Dmytro. *Paprika grez*. Moscow: Novoe literaturnoe obozrenie, 2006.

———. *Solodoshchi dlia plazuniv*. Kyiv: Fakt, 2005.

Lozyns'kyi, Vasyl'. "Poetychna refleksiia u chas viiny i myru (teoriia Marshala Makliuena v ukrains'komu konteksti s'ohodennia)." *Krytyka* 20.11–12 (2016): 2–8.

Lutsyshyna, Oksana. *Ia slukhaiu pisniu Ameryky*. Lviv: Vydavnytstvo Staroho Leva, 2010.

———. *Ne chervoniiuchy: novely*. Kyiv: Fakt, 2007.

———. *Sontse tak ridko zakhodyt': roman*. Kyiv: Fakt, 2007.

Lutwack, Leonard. *The Role of Place in Literature*. Syracuse: Syracuse University Press, 1984.

Luzina, Lada. *Kyivs'ki vid'my. Mech i khrest*. Kharkiv: Folio, 2012.

MacCabe, Colin. "An Interview with Stuart Hall, December 2007." *Critical Quarterly* 50 (2007): 12–42.

Makhno, Vasyl'. *Cornelia Street Café: Novi ta vybrani virshi, 1991–2006*. Kyiv: Fakt, 2007.

———. *Ia khochu buty dzhazom i rok-n-rolom: vybrani virshi pro Ternopil' i N'iu-Iork*. Ternopil: Krok, 2013.

———. *Kotylasia torba*. Kyiv: Krytyka, 2011.

———. *Park kul'tury ta vidpochynku imeni Gertrudy Stain*. Kyiv: Krytyka, 2006.

———. *38 virshiv pro N'iu-Iork i deshcho inshe*. Kyiv: Krytyka, 2004.

———. *Thread and Selected New York Poems*. Translated by Orest Popovych. New York: Meeting Eyes Bindery, 2009.

———. *Winter Letters*. Translated by Orest Popovych. New York: Meeting Eyes Bindery, 2011.

———. *Zymovi lysty*. Kyiv: Krytyka, 2011.

Mala ukrains'ka entsyklopediia aktual'noi literatury: Proekt Povernennia demiurhiv. Special issue of *Pleroma* 3 (1998).

Malkovych, Ivan. *Iz ianholom na plechi: virshi*. Kyiv: Poetychna ahentsiia "Kniazhiv," 1997.

Maliarchuk, Tania. *Hovoryty*. Kharkiv: Folio, 2007.

———. *Iak ia stala sviatoiu*. Kharkiv: Folio, 2008.

———. "Piznaiu vpovni prynady immihrantstva." Interview. *LitAktsent*, November 11, 2011. Accessed October 6, 2013. http://litakcent.com/2011/11/25/tanja-maljarchuk-piznaju-vpovni-prynady-immihrantstva/.

———. *Zabuttia: roman*. Lviv: Vydavnytstvo Staroho Leva, 2016.

———. *Zviroslov*. Kharkiv: Folio, 2009.

Matiiash, Bohdana. "Lazutkin as Luzutkin as Lazutkin—Traces Remain." *Poetry International Rotterdam*, April 1, 2007. Accessed November 18, 2013. http://www.poetryinternationalweb.net/pi/site/cou_article/item/8846/Lazutkin-as-Lazutkin-as-Lazutkin-traces-remain.

————. *Neproiavleni znimky: poezii.* Kyiv: Smoloskyp, 2005.

————. *Rozmovy z Bohom.* Lviv: Vydavnytstvo Staroho Leva, 2007.

————. "Serioznyi postmodern, abo 'literaturoznavstvo bez bromu'." *Znak* 10 (2005): 4.

Matiiash, Dzvinka. *Rekviiem dlia lystopadu.* 2nd rev. ed. Kyiv: Fakt, 2007.

————. *Roman pro bat'kivshchynu.* Kyiv: Fakt, 2006.

Matios, Mariia. *Solodka Darusia.* 4th ed. Lviv: Piramida, 2007.

McClintock, Anne. "No Longer in a Future Heaven: Nationalism, Gender and Race." In *Imperial Leather: Race, Gender and Sexuality in the Colonial Context*, 352–89. New York: Routledge, 1995.

McRobbie, Angela. "Post-Feminism and Popular Culture." *Feminist Media Studies* 4.3 (2004): 255–64.

Medvid', Viacheslav. *Krov po solomi.* Lviv: Kal'variia, 2001.

————. *Pro domo sua: shchodennyky, ese.* Kyiv: Ukrains'kyi pys'mennyk, 1999.

————. "Ukrains'ka liudyna dlia ukrains'koi literatury ie vse shche nerozhadanoiu materiieiu." *Knyzhnyk-Review* 6.63 (2003): 3.

Midianka, Petro. *Dyzhma.* Kyiv: Krytyka, 2003.

————. *Užhorodské kavárny.* Prague: Ukraijinská iniciativa v ČR, 2004.

Miller, Jim Wayne. "Anytime the Ground Is Uneven: The Outlook for Regional Studies and What to Look Out For." In *Geography and Literature: A Meeting of the Disciplines*, edited by William E. Mallory and Paul Simpson-Hously, 1–20. Syracuse: Syracuse University Press, 1987.

Moore-Gilbert, Bart. *Postcolonial Theory: Contexts, Practices, Politics.* London: Verso, 1997.

Moskalets', Kostiantyn. *Dosvid koronatsii: Vybrani tvory.* Lviv: Piramida, 2009.

Naydan, Michael M. "Emerging Ukrainian Women Prose Writers: Twenty Years After Independence." *WLT* (Nov.-Dec. 2011). Accessed October 27, 2011. http://www.ou.edu/worldlit/11_2011/essay-naydan.html.

————. "National Identity for the Ukrainian Writer: Writing into the New Millennium." In *Towards a New Ukraine II: Meeting the New Century. Proceedings of a Conference Held on October 2–3, 1998, at the University of Ottawa*, edited by Theofil Kis and Irena Makaryk with Roman Weretelnyk, 143–52. Ottawa: Chair of Ukrainian Studies, University of Ottawa, 1999.

————. "Performative Text in the Narrative Design of Yuri Andrukhovych's Novel *Perverzion.*" *Style and Translation* 1.2 (2015): 250–72.

————. "Ukrainian Avant-Garde Poetry Today: Bu-Ba-Bu and Others." *Slavic and East European Journal* 50 (2006): 452–68.

————. "Ukrainian Literary Identity Today: The Legacy of the Bu-Ba-Bu Generation after the Orange Revolution." *World Literature Today* 79.3–4 (2005): 24–27.

————. "Ukrainian Prose of the 1990s as It Reflects Contemporary Social Structures." *The Ukrainian Quarterly* 51.1 (1995): 44–61.

Neborak, Viktor. "Chytachi nad tomom Dnistrovoho." *Molodyi bukovynets'*, April 8, 2001. Accessed July 3, 2016. http://molbuk.ua/vnomer/kultura/36630-chitachi-nad-tomom-dnistrovogo.html.

————. *The Flying Head and Other Poems.* Translated by Michael M. Naydan and et al. Lviv: Sribne Slovo, 2005.

————. *Virshi z vulytsi Vyhovs'koho.* Lviv: Sribne Slovo, 2009.

Nederveen Pieterse, Jan. "Globalisation as Hybridisation." *International Sociology* 9 (1994): 161–84.

Nederveen Pieterse, Jan, and Bhikhu Parekh, eds. *The Decolonization of Imagination: Culture, Knowledge and Power.* London: Atlantic Highlands, 1995.

Nova istoriia ukrains'koi literatury: teoretyko-metodolohichni aspekty. Kyiv: Feniks, 2005.

"Oksana Zabuzhko pro Andrukhovycha: Iuryn psykholohichnyi vik—18 rokiv." *Ukrains'ka pravda,* August 9, 2011. Accessed June 15, 2017. http://life.pravda.com.ua/society/2011/08/9/83127/view_comments/.

Ortega y Gasset, José. *The Revolt of the Masses.* Online. Accessed December 18, 2016. http://pinkmonkey.com/dl/library1/revolt.pdf.

Pahutiak, Halyna. "Nasha literatura skhozha na khvoroho, shcho rozuchyvsia rukhatysia." Interview. *Sumno,* March 28, 2008. Accessed October 10, 2013. http://sumno.com/article/galyna-pagutyak-nasha-literatura-shozha-na-hvorogo/.

————. *Pysar Skhidnykh Vorit Prytulku.* Lviv: Piramida, 2003.

————. *Sluha z Dobromylia: roman.* Kyiv: Duliby, 2006.

————. *Uriz'ka hotyka: roman.* Kyiv: Duliby, 2009.

————. *Zakhid sontsia v Urozhi: roman, povisti, opovidannia ta novely.* 2nd rev. ed. Lviv: Piramida, 2007.

————. *Zapysky biloho ptashka: dva romany ta povist'.* Kyiv: Ukrains'kyi pys'mennyk, 1999.

Pan'o, Kateryna. "Knyzhkove zahostrennia: chomu vlada voiuie z pys'mennykamy." *Druh chytacha,* January 29, 2011. Accessed May 30, 2017. http://vsiknygy.net.ua/neformat/9026/.

Parry, Benita. "Signs of Our Times: A Discussion of Homi Bhabha's *The Location of Culture.*" In *The Third Text Reader on Art, Culture and Theory,* edited by Rasheed Araeen, Sean Cubitt, and Ziauddin Sardar, 243–55. London: Continuum, 2002.

Pashkovs'kyi, Ievhen. *Bezodnia: romany.* Lviv: Piramida, 2005.

————. *Shchodennyi zhezl: roman-ese.* Kyiv: Heneza, 1999.

————. *Vovcha zoria.* Kyiv: Molod', 1991.

Pavlychko, Solomiia. "Chy potribna ukrains'komu literaturoznavstvu feministychna shkola?" *Slovo i chas* 6 (1991): 10–15.

————. *Dyskurs modernizmu v ukrains'kii literaturi.* Kyiv: Lybid', 1997. 2nd rev. ed. 1999.

————. *Feminizm.* Kyiv: Osnovy, 2002.

————. "Feminizm iak mozhlyvyi pidkhid do analizu ukrains'koi kul'tury." In *Feminizm,* 29–36. Kyiv: Osnovy, 2002.

————. "Metodolohichna sytuatsiia v suchasnomu ukrains'komu literaturoznavstvi." In *Teoriia literatury,* 483–89. Kyiv: Osnovy, 2002.

————. *Natsionalizm, seksual'nist', oriientalizm: Skladnyi svit Ahatanhela Kryms'koho.* Kyiv: Osnovy, 2000.

————. "Progress on Hold: The Conservative Faces of Women in Ukraine." In *Post-Soviet Women: From the Baltic to Central Asia,* edited by Mary Buckley, 219–34. Cambridge: Cambridge University Press, 1997. Reprinted in *Feminizm,* by Solomiia Pavlychko, 101–16. Kyiv: Osnovy, 2002.

Pavlyshyn, Marko. "Andrukhovych's *Secret*: The return of colonial resignation." *Journal of Postcolonial Writing* 48 (2012): 188–99.

———. "Aspects of the Literary Process in the USSR: The Politics of Re-Canonisation in Ukraine After 1985." *Southern Review* 24 (1991): 12–25.

———. "Choosing a Europe: Andrukhovych, Izdryk, and the New Ukrainian Literature." In *Contemporary Ukraine on the Cultural Map of Europe*, edited by Larissa M.L. Zaleska Onyshkevych and Maria G. Rewakowicz, 249–63. Armonk, NY: M.E. Sharpe, 2009.

———. "Defending the Cultural Nation before and after 1991: Ivan Dziuba." *Canadian-American Slavic Studies* 44 (2010): 25–43.

———. "Demystifying High Culture? Young Ukrainian Poetry and Prose in the 1990s." In *Perspectives on Modern Central and East European Literature: Quests for Identity. Selected Papers from the Fifth World Congress of Central and East European Studies*, edited by Todd Patrick Armstrong, 10–24. Houndmills: Palgrave, 2001.

———. "Dva khudozhni tila suchasnoi prozy." *Svito-vyd* 3 (1997): 103–10.

———. *Kanon ta ikonostas*. Kyiv: Chas, 1997.

———. "Literary Canons and National Identities in Contemporary Ukraine." *Canadian American Slavic Studies* 40 (2006): 5–19.

———. "Literary Politics vs. Literature: Ukrainian Debates in the 1990s." *The Soviet and Post-Soviet Review* 28 (2001): 147–55.

———. "Post-colonial Features in Contemporary Ukrainian Culture." *Australian Slavonic and East European Studies* 6.2 (1992): 41–55.

———. "The Rhetoric of Geography in Ukrainian Literature, 1991–2005." In *Ukraine, the EU and Russia: History, Culture and International Relations*, edited by Stephen Velychenko, 89–107. Houndmills: Palgrave, 2007.

———. "Ukrainian Literature and the Erotics of Postcolonialism: Some Modest Propositions." *Harvard Ukrainian Studies* 12 (1993): 110–26.

Peterson, Richard A. "Understanding Audience Segmentation: From elite and mass to omnivore and univore." *Poetics* 21 (1992): 243–58.

Poderv'ians'kyi, Les'. *Heroi nashoho chasu*. Lviv: Kal'variia, 2000.

Povaliaieva, Svitlana. *Bardo Online*. Kharkiv: Folio, 2009.

———. *Ekshumatsiia mista*. Lviv: Kal'variia, 2003.

———. *Origami-bliuz*. Kharkiv: Folio, 2007.

———. *Simurg*. Kharkiv: Folio, 2006.

———. *Zamist' krovi*. Lviv: Kal'variia, 2003.

Prabhu, Anjali. *Hybridity: Limits, Transformations, Prospects*. Albany: SUNY Press, 2007.

Prokhas'ko, Taras. *FM "Halychyna."* Ivano-Frankivsk: Lileia-NV, 2001.

———. *NeprOsti*. Ivano-Frankivsk: Lileia-NV, 2002.

———. *Port Frankivs'k*. Ivano-Frankivsk: Lileia-NV, 2006.

———. *UnSimple*. Translated by Uilleam Blacker. *Ukrainian Literature: A Journal of Translations* 2–3 (2007–2011). Accessed June 15, 2012. http://sites.utoronto.ca/elul/Ukr_Lit/Vol02/03-Prokhasko-Unsimple1.pdf; http://sites.utoronto.ca/elul/Ukr_Lit/Vol03/06-ProkhaskoUnsimple-Part-2.pdf.

Puleri, Marco. "Ukrains'kyi, rosiis'komovnyi, rosiis'kyi [Ukrainian, Russian-speaking, Russian]: Self-identification in post-Soviet Ukrainian literature in Russian. *Ab imperio* 2 (2014): 367–97.

Pyrkalo, Svitlana. *Kukhnia ehoista.* Kyiv: Fakt, 2007.

———. *Ne dumai pro chervone: roman ne dlia molodshoho shkil'noho viku.* Kyiv: Fakt, 2004.

———. *Zelena Marharyta: povist'.* Kyiv: Smoloskyp, 2001.

Rewakowicz, Maria G. "Alternative History, Science Fiction and Nationalism in Vasyl Kozhelianko's Novels." *The Ukrainian Quarterly* 63 (2007): 70–78.

———. "Language Choice and the Notion of National Literature in Post-Soviet Ukraine: The Case of Andrey Kurkov." *Tilts/Mist/Tiltas* 1 (2007): 6–14.

Riabchuk, Mykola. *Dylemy ukrains'koho Fausta: hromadians'ke suspil'stvo i rozbudova derzhavy.* Kyiv: Krytyka, 2000.

———. "The Postcolonial Syndrome in Ukraine." Interview. *Euromaidan Press*, July 8, 2015. Accessed December 18, 2016. http://euromaidanpress.com/2015/08/07/the-postcolonial-syndrome-in-ukraine/#arvlbdata.

———. *Postkolonial'nyi syndrom. Sposterezhennia.* Kyiv: K.I.S., 2011.

Robertson, Roland. "Globalization or Glocalization." *Journal of International Communication* 1 (1994): 33–52.

Rodyk, Kostiantyn. "Halyna Pahutiak: perevantazhennia." *Ukraina moloda*, May 11, 2011. Accessed October 6, 2013. http://www.umoloda.kiev.ua/print/84/45/66727.

Romanets, Maryna. *Anamorphosic Texts and Reconfigured Visions: Improvised Traditions in Contemporary Ukrainian and Irish Literature.* Stuttgart: ibidem-Verlag, 2007.

Rozdobud'ko, Iren. *Eskort u smert'.* Lviv: Kal'variia, 2002.

———. *Gudzyk: psykholohichna drama.* Kharkiv: Folio, 2005.

———. *Mertsi.* Lviv: Kal'variia, 2001.

Rubchak, Bohdan. "Mandrivnyk, inodi ryba." Introduction. In *Cornelia Street Café*, by Vasyl' Makhno, 7–22. Kyiv: Fakt, 2007.

Rudnytzky, Leonid. "A Poetical Voice of the Ukrainian Diaspora: Random Notes on the Poetry of Vasyl Makhno." *The Ukrainian Quarterly* 67 (2011): 158–64.

Said, Edward. *Culture and Imperialism.* New York: Vintage Books, 1994.

———. *Orientalism.* New York: Vintage Books, 1979.

Savka, Mar'iana. *Hirka Mandrahora.* Lviv: Vydavnytstvo Staroho Leva, 2002.

———. *Kvity tsmynu.* Lviv: Vydavnytstvo Staroho Leva, 2006.

Semenchuk, Hryhory, comp. *Letters from Ukraine: Poetry Anthology.* Ternopil: Krok, 2016.

Shelukhin, Oleksandr. "Shche odyn oksiumoron. Chomu v Ukraini nebezpechno rozmovliaty ukrains'koiu?" *Ukrains'ka pravda*, March 12, 2012. Accessed March 13, 2012. http://www.pravda.com.ua/columns/2012/03/12/6960434/.

Shkandrij, Myroslav. *Russia and Ukraine: Literature and the Discourse of Empire from Napoleonic to Postcolonial Times.* Montreal: McGill-Queen's University Press, 2011.

Shkliar, Vasyl'. *Chornyi Voron.* Kyiv: Iaroslaviv Val, 2008.

———. "'Ia … 'poslav' legionera v Chechniu'." *Knyzhnyk-Review* 9.66 (2003): 4.

Shkorba, Mar'ian. "Genderni dity liberalizmu." *Krytyka* 5.9 (2001): 20–23.

Shohat, Ella. "Notes on the Post-colonial." *Social Text* 10.2–3 (1992): 99–113.

Shopin, Pavlo. "Voroshylovhrad Lost: Memory and Identity in a Novel by Serhiy Zhadan." *Slavic and East European Journal* 57 (2013): 372–87.

Shore, Marci. "The Bard of Eastern Ukraine, Where Things Are Falling Apart." *The New Yorker*, November 28, 2016. Accessed November 30, 2016. http://www.newyorker. com/books/page-turner/the-bard-of-eastern-ukraine-where-things-are-falling-apart.

Slavins'ka, Iryna. "2011: literaturni pidsumky." *Ukrains'ka pravda*, December 21, 2011. Accessed December 22, 2011. http://www.life.pravda.com.ua/culture/2011/ 12/21/91726/.

———. "Taras Prokhas'ko: Ukrains'ka ideia pov'iazana z lahidnym sydinniam." Interview. *Ukrains'ka pravda*, January 10, 2011. Accessed August 21, 2015. http:// life.pravda.com.ua/person/2011/01/10/69933/.

Smith, Anthony. *National Identity*. Reno: University of Nevada Press, 1991.

Sniadanko, Natalka. *Kolektsiia prystrastei, abo pryhody molodoi ukrainky*. Kharkiv: Folio, 2004.

Soja, Edward W. *Postmodern Geographies: The Reassertion of Space in Critical Social Theory*. London: Verso, 1989.

Sorokowski, Andrew. "The Status of Religion in Ukraine in Relation to European Standards." In *Contemporary Ukraine on the Cultural Map of Europe*, edited by Larissa M.L. Zaleska Onyshkevych and Maria G. Rewakowicz, 69–88. Armonk: M.E. Sharpe, 2009.

Spivak, Gayatri Chakravorty. *A Critique of Postcolonial Reason*. Cambridge, MA: Harvard University Press, 1999.

———. *Outside in the Teaching Machine*. New York: Routledge, 1993.

Stefanivs'ka, Lidiia [Lidia Stefanowska]. "Pisliamova." In *Votstsek & Votstsekurhiia*, by Izdryk, 187–94. Lviv: Kal'variia, 2002.

Stefanowska, Lidia. "Back to the Golden Age: The Discourse of Nostalgia in Galicia in the 1990s (Some Preliminary Remarks)." *Harvard Ukrainian Studies* 27 (2004–2005): 181–93.

Stepanenko, Viktor. "Identities and Language Politics in Ukraine: The Challenges of Nation-State Building." In *Nation-Building, Ethnicity and Language Politics in Transition Countries*, edited by Farimah Daftary and François Grin, 109–35. Budapest: Open Society Institute, 2003.

Storey, John. *Inventing Popular Culture: From Folklore to Globalization*. Maldan, MA: Blackwell Publishing, 2003.

Strikha, Maksym V. "Language and Language Policy in Ukraine." *Journal of Ukrainian Studies* 26 (2001): 239–48.

Taran, Liudmyla. "Buty samii sobi tsilliu: Do pytannia pro avtobiohrafizm suchasnoi zhinochoi prozy," *Suchasnist'* 3 (2006): 139–55.

———. *Kolektsiia kokhanok*. Lviv: Kal'variia, 2002.

———. *Liubovni mandrivky: novely, podorozhni notatky*. Kyiv: Fakt, 2007.

———. "Mizh namy, zhinkamy ... Rozmova Liudmyly Taran z Ievheniieiu Kononenko," *Kur'ier Kryvbasu* 2 (2006): 150–55.

———. "Obzhyty vnutrishnii prostir: Do problemy avtobiohrafizmu v suchasnii ukrains'kii prozi zhinok-avtoriv," *Kur'ier Kryvbasu* 6 (2005): 222–28.

————. "Pryvyd povstaloho zhinochoho dukhu." *Krytyka* 3.1–2 (1999): 18–21.

Tarnawsky, Maxim. "Images of Bonding and Social Decay in Contemporary Ukrainian Prose: Reading Serhii Zhadan and Anatolii Dnistrovy." In *Contemporary Ukraine on the Cultural Map of Europe*, edited by Larissa M.L. Zaleska Onyshkevych and Maria G. Rewakowicz, 264–74. Armonk, NY: M.E. Sharpe, 2009.

Tomilenko, Liudmyla. "Ekspresyvna leksyka na poznachennia nazv osib u romani Vasylia Shkliara *Zalyshenets'. Chornyi Voron*." *Kul'tura slova* 78 (2013): 77–81.

Tsiupyn, Bohdan. "Andrii Kurkov v hostiakh u Bi-Bi-Si." Interview. Accessed March 10, 2007. http://www.bbc.co.uk/ukrainian/forum/story/2005/11/051113_kurkov.shtml.

Tsymbal, Ia., comp. *Akademichna "Istoriia ukrains'koi literatury" v 10 tomakh.* Kyiv: Feniks, 2005.

Ul'ianenko, Oles'. *Serafyma: roman.* Kyiv: Nora-druk, 2007.

————. *Stalinka. Dofin Satany: romany.* Kharkiv: Folio, 2003.

————. *Syn tini: roman.* Ternopil: Dzhura, 2006.

Vil'chyns'kyi, Oleksandr. *Dereva na dakhakh.* Kharkiv: Folio, 2010.

Vol'vach, Pavlo. *Kliasa.* Kharkiv: Folio, 2010.

Vynnychuk, Iurii. *Mal'va Landa.* Lviv: Piramida, 2003.

————. *Tango smerti: roman.* Kharkiv: Folio, 2012.

Wachtel, Andrew. *Remaining Relevant After Communism: The Role of the Writer in Eastern Europe.* Chicago: University of Chicago Press, 2006.

Wanner, Catherine. *Communities of the Converted: Ukrainians and Global Evangelism.* Ithaca: Cornell University Press, 2007.

————. "Missionaries and Pluralism: How the Law Changed the Religious Landscape in Ukraine." In *Contemporary Ukraine on the Cultural Map of Europe*, edited by Larissa M.Z. Zaleska Onyshkevych and Maria G. Rewakowicz, 89–100. Armonk: M.E. Sharpe, 2009.

Yekelchyk, Serhy. "What Is Ukrainian about Ukraine's Pop Culture?: The Strange Case of Verka Serduchka." *Canadian American Slavic Studies* 44 (2010): 217–32.

Zabuzhko, Oksana. *Avtostop: poezii.* Kyiv: Ukrains'kyi pys'mennyk, 1994.

————. *Druha sproba: vybrane.* Kyiv: Fakt, 2005.

————. *Dyryhent ostann'oi svichky: poezii.* Kyiv: Radians'kyi pys'mennyk, 1990.

————. *Fieldwork in Ukrainian Sex.* Translated by Halyna Hryn. Las Vegas: Amazon Crossing, 2011.

————. *Filosofiia ukrains'koi idei ta ievropeis'kyi kontekst: Frankivs'kyi period.* Kyiv: Naukova dumka, 1992.

————. "I, Milena." In *Two Lands, New Visions: Stories from Canada and Ukraine*, edited by Janice Kulyk Keefer and Solomea Pavlychko, 125–61. Regina: Coteau Books, 1998.

————. *Inshyi format.* Ivano-Frankivsk: Lileia-NV, 2003.

————. *Khroniky vid Fortinbrasa: vybrana eseistyka 90-x.* Kyiv: Fakt, 2001.

————. *Kingdom of Fallen Statues: Poems and Essays.* Toronto: Wellspring, 1996.

————. *The Museum of Abandoned Secrets.* Translated by Nina Shevchuk-Murray. Las Vegas: Amazon Crossing, 2012.

————. *Muzei pokynutykh sekretiv.* Kyiv: Fakt, 2009.

————. *Notre Dame d'Ukraine: Ukrainka v konflikti mifolohii.* Kyiv: Fakt, 2007.

————. *Novyi zakon Arkhimeda.* Kharkiv: Akta, 2000.

————. *Pol'ovi doslidzhennia z ukrains'koho seksu.* 1996. Kyiv: Fakt, 1998.

————. *Shevchenkiv mif Ukrainy: Sproba filosofs'koho analizu.* Kyiv: Abrys, 1997.

————. *Travnevyi inii: poezii.* Kyiv: Molod', 1985.

Zborovs'ka, Nila. "Chomu v ukrains'kii literaturi nemaie liubovnykh romaniv." *Krytyka* 3.7–8 (1999): 27–31.

————. *Feministychni rozdumy na karnavali mertvykh potsilunkiv.* Lviv: Litopys, 1999.

————. "Feministychnyi tryptykh Ievhenii Kononenko v konteksti zahal'noukrains'koi tematyky," *Slovo i chas* 6 (2005): 57–73.

————. *Kod ukrains'koi literatury: Proekt psykhoistorii novitn'oi ukrains'koi literatury.* Kyiv: Akademvydav, 2006.

————. *Moia Lesia Ukrainka.* Ternopil: Dzhura, 2002.

————. "Pro romany Ievhena Pashkovs'koho." In *Feministychni rozdumy na karnavali mertvykh potsilunkiv,* 144–59. Lviv: Litopys, 1999.

————. "Shevchenko v 'zhinochykh obiimakh'." *Krytyka* 3.3 (1999): 25–28.

————. *Ukrains'ka Rekonkista: anty-roman.* Ternopil: Dzhura, 2003.

Zhadan, Serhii. *Anarchy in the UKR.* Kharkiv: Folio, 2005.

————. *Depesh Mod.* Kharkiv: Folio, 2004.

————., ed. *Hoteli Kharkova: Antolohiia novoi kharkivs'koi literatury.* Kharkiv: Folio, 2008.

————. *Kapital.* Kharkiv: Folio, 2009.

————. *Voroshilovgrad.* Translated by Isaac Stackhouse Wheeler and Reilly Costigan-Humes. Dallas: Deep Vellum Publishing, 2016.

————. *Voroshylovhrad.* Kharkiv: Folio, 2010.

Zherebkina, Irina. *Zhenskoe politicheskoe bessoznatel'noe: Problema gendera i zhenskoe dvizhenie v Ukraine.* Kharkiv: KhTsGI/F-Press, 1996.

Zholdak, Bohdan. *Antyklimaks.* Kyiv: Fakt, 2001.

Zhurzhenko, Tatiana. "(Anti)national Feminisms: Women's Voices of Transition and Nation Building in Ukraine." Paper presented at Munk Centre for International Studies, University of Toronto, March 18, 2002.

————. "Feminist (De)Constructions of Nationalism in the Post-Soviet Space." In *Mapping Difference: The Many Faces of Women in Contemporary Ukraine,* edited by Marian J. Rubchak, 173–91. New York: Berghahn Books, 2011.

Index

About the Author

Maria G. Rewakowicz teaches Ukrainian literature at Rutgers University—New Brunswick and is also affiliated with the Department of Slavic Languages and Literatures at the University of Washington. She is the author of *Literature, Exile, Alterity: The New York Group of Ukrainian Poets* (2014) and co-editor of *Contemporary Ukraine on the Cultural Map of Europe* (2009).

CPSIA information can be obtained
at www.ICGtesting.com
Printed in the USA
BVOW09*2224051017
496769BV00001B/2/P